VISUAL QUICKSTART GUIDE

APPLESCRIPT

FOR APPLICATIONS

Ethan Wilde

 Peachpit Press

Visual QuickStart Guide
AppleScript for Applications
Ethan Wilde

Peachpit Press

1249 Eighth Street
Berkeley, CA 94710
510/524-2178
800/283-9444
510/524-2221 (fax)
Find us on the World Wide Web at: http://www.peachpit.com
To report errors, send a note to errata@peachpit.com.
Peachpit Press is a division of Addison Wesley Longman

Copyright © 2002 by Ethan Wilde

Editor: Clifford Colby
Production Coordinator: Lisa Brazieal
Copyeditor: Kathy Simpson
Compositors: Christi Payne
Indexer: James Minkin
Cover Design: The Visual Group

Notice of rights

Notice of liability

Trademarks

ISBN 0-201-71613-5

9 8 7 6 5 4 3 2 1

Printed and bound in the United States of America

Dedication

This book is dedicated to my family: Rosalie, Ted, Maya, and Tania.

Acknowledgements

I'd like to thanks the following people who proved invaluable in the effort to create this book. Cliff Colby has been my editor, confidant, supporter and savior. The AppleScript team at Apple has always come through for me: Sal, Jason, Chris Nebel, and Chris Espinosa, and others as well. I have discovered that AppleScript attracts a wonderful collection of people with disparate interests. People such as Bill Cheeseman, Mark Alldritt, Cal Simone, Susan Dumont, and Andy Bachorski, have had big impacts on my understanding of AppleScript. I thank them. Developers supporting AppleScript in their products and those Scripting Addition creators who provide such useful tools deserve special thanks for helping to make the AppleScript environment thrive.

Bio

Ethan Wilde bought his first computer, an Apple II, in 1979 after taking a BASIC programming class at San Francisco's Exploratorium. The experience changed his life, and computers have been close to Ethan ever since. Now a principal at Mediatrope, an award-winning multimedia company in San Francisco, Ethan has many Macs to script, when he is not writing books and teaching about AppleScript.

TABLE OF CONTENTS

INTRODUCTION TO APPLESCRIPT

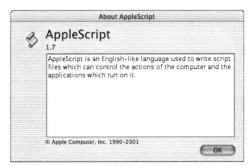

Figure i.1 The About AppleScript window for AppleScript 1.7 in Mac OS X 10.1.

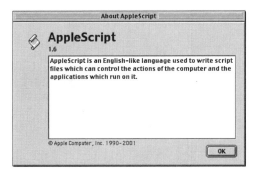

Figure i.2 The About AppleScript window for AppleScript 1.6 in Mac OS 9.2.1.

Welcome to the starting line. You're about to embark on a grand journey—I'll be your tour guide as we explore AppleScript, one of the greatest features ever to grace the Mac OS. In fact, AppleScript is unique: It's the most flexible and powerful scripting language ever seen on any OS, period. Once you begin to use AppleScript and understand its capabilities, it will change forever the way you use your Mac.

Our focus in these travels will be the use of AppleScript in conjunction with the applications you use everyday. These applications include many of the leading productivity, graphics, layout, and Internet programs. With the advent of Mac OS X, AppleScript has reached a new level of maturity—it *is* everywhere ... and it can help you.

On a personal note, my love of AppleScript began long before the Unix-flavored days of Mac OS X. In the early days of my relationship with AppleScript, I found a good many applications for its comparatively limited abilities. With each release of the Mac OS, AppleScript's abilities have grown, whether enabled by Apple or other dedicated individuals.

When our tour of the new modern AppleScript in Mac OS X 10.1 (**Figure i.1**) and Mac OS 9.2.1 (**Figure i.2**) is over, I hope you'll be as strong a believer in AppleScript as I am.

Become a Believer

Are you a believer? Perhaps you want to know more before taking the plunge? In simple terms, AppleScript lets you control applications and share data between programs. Now, what does this mean to you? As an AppleScripter, you gain the ability to use the millions of lines of C++ code contained in every commercial application for your own purposes!

To take advantage of the power of application scripting, you'll need to be familiar with the applications themselves. In fact, you probably already have enough applications to get started, because most of the mainstream productivity applications available today already support AppleScript.

BECOME A BELIEVER

Some Applications That Support AppleScript

◆ Adobe Illustrator

◆ Adobe Photoshop

◆ FileMaker Pro

◆ Microsoft Internet Explorer

◆ Microsoft Word

◆ Netscape Navigator

◆ Now Up-to-Date and Contact

◆ QuarkXPress

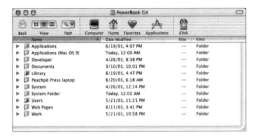

Figure i.3 The AppleScript command open startup disk opens the Finder window for my startup disk in Mac OS X.

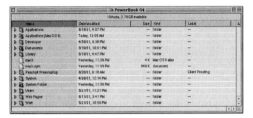

Figure i.4 The AppleScript command open startup disk also opens the Finder window for my startup disk in Mac OS 9.1.

How to Use This Book

In this book, we use several presentation styles meant to help you understand and work with AppleScript.

In the step-by-step instructions that accompany each script we present in the later chapters, a special typeface indicates actual AppleScript code. For example:

```
tell application "Finder"

    open startup disk

end tell
```

We show all AppleScript scripts in this book using the above typeface, with most commands in lowercase letters, making it easy to distinguish between the scripts and the rest of the text in the book (as well as giving my Shift-key finger a much-needed rest). Apple-Script itself is case-insensitive (that is, it doesn't distinguish between uppercase and lowercase letters) unless you tell it to behave otherwise.

For some scripts, we provide with the step-by-step instructions you'll have to do a little preparation, such as creating a FileMaker database. In these instances, I provide screenshots to help illustrate these preparations. Screenshots like **Figures i.3** and **i.4** also show information for some scripting exercises.

When a line of AppleScript code is too long to fit on a single line, I have broken it into multiple lines using AppleScript's built-in continuation character: ¬. To generate this character on your keyboard, type Option-Return in the Script Editor. Make sure your scripts include continuation characters to tie long lines of code together or you will encounter errors. For reference, here's a sample line with the continuation character in use:

```
delete word 1 of paragraph 2 ¬
of document "AS and the Internet"
```

Case Sensitivity and AppleScript

Sometimes, when you're manipulating text within your scripts, you may want to tell AppleScript to pay attention to the differences between uppercase and lowercase. See considering in Appendix 2 to learn how to make AppleScript consider case.

Figure i.5 The About This Mac window for the Mac OS X version used in this book: 10.1.

Which Mac OS Are You?

Things haven't been this exciting in the world of Macintosh for some time now. Mac OS X is a brand new operating system available from Apple that offers new power and complexity. AppleScript is a key part of the new Mac OS X, just as it has been in Mac OS 9 and earlier. In the current release of Mac OS X, version 10.1 (**Figure i.5**), the level of AppleScript often meets and sometimes exceeds that provided by Mac OS 9.

Mac OS X supports old Mac OS 9 and new Mac OS X applications. Mac OS X includes support for Mac OS 9 with the Classic environment, which uses Mac OS 9.2.1 or greater. AppleScript works in all applications that support it in Mac OS X, even Classic applications.

So what does this mean to you? Most scripts in this book will run in Mac OS X or Mac OS 9. If you script Mac OS 9 applications in Mac OS X, the Classic environment will be used.

All scripts in this book work in Mac OS X and Mac OS 9 unless noted. If a script only works in either native Mac OS 9 or Mac OS X, I will tell you about the reason why it does not work as well.

If you are using Mac OS 9 alone, you can use all of the scripts in this book not specifically noted as requiring Mac OS X.

✔ Tips

- If you upgraded to Mac OS X from a version of Mac OS 9, most of your familiar applications will run in the Classic environment in Mac OS X.

- When possible, be sure to get upgraded versions of applications redesigned for Mac OS X. Mac OS X applications run faster and better than Classic applications.

- Users of Mac OS X should read chapter 4 for many details about AppleScript in Mac OS X.

Save Your Fingers Some Walking

I provide all of the scripts I discuss at length in this book in their entirety. It doesn't hurt to type them yourself and try them out. Sometimes the act of hand-entering a script gives you time to digest it and gain a feel for how it really works. However, there is a time and place for this kind of learning. If you're in a hurry or have the grasp and just need *that* script *now,* I have just the Web site for you. As shown in **Figure i.6**, the companion Web site to this book lives at:

http://www.peachpit.com/vqs/applescript/

Figure i.6 The sample scripts in this book can be downloaded from the Peachpit Press Web site.

Time to Get Scripting

AppleScript is incredibly flexible and easy to use. The folks at Apple did everything they could to make it easy to write scripts just as you would write simple English sentences.

As we make progress in our travels, our scripts will often build on previous examples so that by the end, you'll be ready to tackle your own projects using AppleScript. Whether you find yourself needing to conquer such large tasks or you're just looking for quick solutions to specific problems, I think you'll find help here in *AppleScript for Applications: Visual QuickStart Guide.*

So let's get started by using some very simple scripts to do some surprisingly powerful things.

GETTING TO KNOW APPLESCRIPT

The concept of the user interface entered popular thinking with the Macintosh. Everything essential to what we think of as the user interface today—including the mouse, the Desktop, icons, and menus—originated for most of us with the Macintosh. All of these innovations made the Mac easier to use but harder to automate when compared with other operating systems' command-line interfaces.

It wasn't until AppleScript first publicly appeared with the release of System 7 Pro in 1993 that Apple released a script language, which embodied all of the important philosophies of the Mac OS.

Apple's early effort at automating the Mac OS, MacroMaker, let users record their mouse and keyboard actions for later playback. This technology disappeared after the first few versions of the Mac OS as system functions grew more complex.

With AppleScript came a host of unique features that make it the powerful and flexible language we use today:

◆ AppleScript can control many applications over an entire network, not to mention controlling other platforms over the Internet.

◆ In "recordable" applications, AppleScript can automatically create a script based on a recording of your real-time actions. Only a few applications are recordable, but those few are great demonstrations of the power of recording. We'll look at some of those, including Microsoft's Word 2001, to show the power of this feature.

◆ The AppleScript language is dynamically extensible: Each scriptable application has its own dictionary of supported commands, classes, and properties. However, you don't always need an entire application to add commands to AppleScript. There is another group of language extensions known as scripting additions. Scripting additions are small compiled libraries that also have dictionaries of commands, classes, and properties, which extend AppleScript's vocabulary and functionality. In a nutshell, scriptable applications and scripting additions both have dictionaries of additional commands that expand AppleScript.

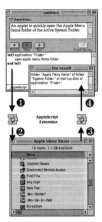

Figure 1.1 See steps 1 through 4 for a detailed discussion of the process.

How Does AppleScript Work?

At the heart of AppleScript is the AppleScript system extension. This extension is installed by default—along with Apple's editing application, Script Editor—in every Mac OS from System 7 through current versions of Mac OS 9 and X. **Figure 1.1** shows the sequence of events that occur when a simple script is run from the Script Editor.

When you write a series of AppleScript statements in an editor and run them, the AppleScript extension translates your script's statements into individual messages for different applications. These messages are called *Apple Events*. Here's how Apple Events work:

1. AppleScript statements are passed from the running script to the AppleScript extension.

2. The AppleScript extension sends Apple Events corresponding to the script statements to the application. Each of these events requests that the application perform a specific action.

3. The application returns Apple Events that contain results from the actions.

4. The AppleScript extension interprets the Apple Event results and sends them back to the script.

✔ Tip

■ AppleScript has just gone through a major revision for Mac OS X. In Mac OS X, AppleScript can be used to script new Mac OS X applications as well as older applications designed for Mac OS 9. AppleScript also works in Mac OS X's Classic environment, which uses Mac OS 9.2.1. This development means AppleScript is the first scripting language that can bridge two simultaneously running operating systems: Mac OS 9 and X.

What Can I Do with AppleScript?

Want to build an e-mail database? Automate the creation of sophisticated illustrations? Perform complex global search-and-replace routines on text files? Build an entire Web site from a database? Control another Mac or even a Windows machine from your Mac? People are using AppleScript to do all of these things right now. Because AppleScript is dynamically extensible, its functions are limited only by the range of scriptable applications that support it.

Historically, AppleScript has been most visible in automated publishing solutions, thanks to the complete AppleScript dictionary in QuarkXPress. More recently, Apple has made the Finder and many more system components scriptable. The Finder and Desktop are even recordable in Mac OS 9 and X. Anything you can do with your Desktop and files, you can easily automate. Renaming, copying, backing up, and modifying files are easy with AppleScript. And with conditional logic, you can make the Finder perform sophisticated tasks.

Coders use AppleScript extensively on the Internet to create CGIs on Mac-based Web servers. Now, with the arrival of Unix-based Mac OS X, AppleScript runs in Apple's new OS alongside the enterprise-class Web server Apache. This fully PowerPC-native, Unix-based AppleScript is perhaps the most powerful and easy-to-use CGI programming environment ever.

Conditional Logic: What Does It Mean?

Conditional logic refers to the concept of testing the state of a variable or property and responding to that state in your script. Examples of conditional logic include the ubiquitous if...then statements found in most computer languages:

```
if myVariable > 10 then display
dialog "Big number!"
```

CGI: Common Gateway Interface

"Common Gateway Interface" is the phrase that was coined to describe the manner in which local scripts on a server receive data from an Internet client and return results at the end of their execution. A group of standards describes the way CGIs communicate on each operating system. On the Mac, one natural avenue for CGIs is Apple Events, which makes AppleScript a natural choice for handling the passing of Web data.

Open Scripting Architecture

The system-level framework that underlies AppleScript is called *Open Scripting Architecture* (OSA). OSA allows the script language to be translated into the actual Apple Events that are sent to different applications. OSA uses Inter-Application Communication (IAC) to send Apple Events to scriptable applications and receive results.

The beauty of OSA is that many scripting languages and dialects can be implemented on top of it. A handful of OSA-compliant script languages are available for the Macintosh:

◆ JavaScript for OSA from Late Night Software is a port of the ubiquitous Web language, allowing anyone to write in JavaScript scripts that control their Mac and its applications in JavaScript—very cool!

◆ Frontier from UserLand is a complete scripting language that includes some powerful features not available in AppleScript. Frontier has a built-in database that can be used to store objects and data of all types.

◆ MacPerl is a port of the popular text-manipulation scripting language used throughout the Internet.

◆ MacTCL is a widely used scripting language brought over from the Unix world.

Aren't AppleScript and OSA amazing for their open architecture and ability to grow? Now let's get ready to write some elegant AppleScripts using this beautiful and democratic language.

✔ Tip

■ The scripts in this book are practical examples of ways that I have actually used AppleScript. As you will see, a little innovative AppleScript can go a long way toward producing creative solutions to many problems. The sky is the limit.

Learning the Basics

AppleScript makes it possible for you to control many applications on your Macintosh. To gain control, you need to write scripts. To write scripts, you need several things:

- You need to find out what commands each application supports and learn the syntax for those commands.

- You need a way to write scripts and test them.

- You need a way to save your scripts when you're done creating them.

The application you'll use for these functions throughout this book is Apple's free Script Editor. So to kick things off, this chapter first gives you a quick look at Script Editor. In Script Editor, you'll be able to look at scriptable applications and their dictionaries. You will also be able to check out scripting additions and their dictionaries and learn how to install scripting additions properly on your system.

Script Editor

When you write AppleScripts, you need an application that enables you to edit, compile, and save your scripts. For consistency and accessibility, all the scripts in this book were written with Script Editor. Every version of the Mac OS from System 7.1 through Mac OS X (including Mac OS 9.2.1) comes with AppleScript and Script Editor. **Figures 2.1** and **2.2** show you what Script Editor's application icon looks like in Mac OS X and 9.2.1, and **Figures 2.3** through **2.6** show the four windows of Script Editor:

Script. The Script window (**Figure 2.3**) is where you create your script by typing script statements or recording your actions in a recordable application. AppleScript compiles your script and tests for syntax errors whenever you click the Check Syntax button in the Script window. Then click the Run button to execute your script from Script Editor. The Script window also has a description field that you can use to describe your script. In Mac OS 9 and earlier, if you roll over your script's icon in the Finder with Balloon Help on, the script's description is displayed.

Event Log. Open the Event Log window (**Figure 2.4**) from the Controls menu. It displays all events and results generated by a running script, which makes it extremely useful for debugging your scripts.

Result. You can also open the Result window (**Figure 2.5**) from the Controls menu. It displays the results of the last event.

Script Editor

Figure 2.1 The Script Editor icon in Mac OS X.

Script Editor

Figure 2.2 The Script Editor icon in Mac OS 9.2.1.

Figure 2.3 The Script Editor's Script window.

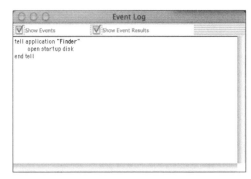

Figure 2.4 The Script Editor's Event Log window.

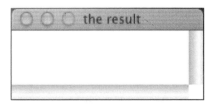

Figure 2.5 The Script Editor's Result window.

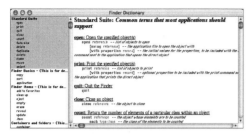

Figure 2.6 The Script Editor's Dictionary window for the Finder.

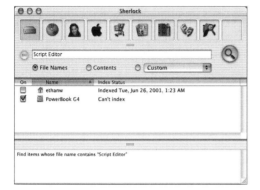

Figure 2.7 Finding the Script Editor using Sherlock.

Dictionary. You can open the dictionary of every application or scripting addition in Script Editor. Dictionaries can provide help with proper syntax and teach you an application's script statements, events, and objects (**Figure 2.6**).

In Mac OS 9 and earlier, you also can use two commercial, and more complete, editing applications: Scripter from Main Event Software and Script Debugger from Late Night Software. You can find out more about these products in Chapter 24. The Apple-Script application builder FaceSpan also includes a script-editing window. Chapter 23 covers FaceSpan.

Finding the Script Editor

Use Sherlock to locate the Script Editor application on your Mac (see **Figure 2.6**). In Mac OS X, the Script Editor can be found in the AppleScript folder inside of the Applications folder. In Mac OS 9.2.1, the Script Editor can usually be found inside of the Apple Extras folder. Once you've located the Script Editor, drag it onto your Dock in Mac OS X or make an alias of it on your Desktop in Mac OS 9.2.1 for easy access.

Scriptable Applications and Their Dictionaries

Any Macintosh application that supports AppleScript must have a dictionary. The dictionary defines the commands that the application will understand in AppleScript, from the most basic commands (such as Open) to commands that are unique to the application. Dictionaries also define all objects that you can reference with commands. Objects include things such as database records and fields, words and paragraphs in text documents, objects in drawing programs, and URLs in Web browsers. The dictionary defines what each object's properties are. Properties include file names, window positions, and window sizes.

You can learn all the supported AppleScript commands and objects for an application or scripting addition simply by opening the dictionary in Script Editor. **Figure 2.8** shows how to open a dictionary from Script Editor's File menu.

Figure 2.9 shows a sample entry from the Finder's dictionary.

Dictionaries are the only guaranteed way to discover a scriptable application's commands and syntax. With some practice, you will become adept at reading dictionaries in Script Editor (**Figure 2.10**).

✔ Tip

■ If you drop a scriptable application or scripting addition icon onto the Script Editor icon in the Finder, Script Editor opens the dictionary for that file.

Figure 2.8 Opening a dictionary from the Script Editor's File menu.

Figure 2.9 A sample entry from the Mac OS X Finder dictionary.

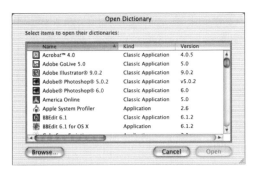

Figure 2.10 The Mac OS X Script Editor automatically locates many of the scriptable applications on your computer in its Open Dictionary window.

StandardAdditions.osax

StandardAdditions.osax

Figure 2.11 The Mac OS 9 and Mac OS X icons for a scripting addition.

ScriptingAdditions

Figure 2.12 Mac OS X's ScriptingAdditions folder icon.

Scripting Additions

Figure 2.13 Mac OS 9's Scripting Additions folder icon.

Where Scripting Additions Belong

In Mac OS X, there are multiple ScriptingAdditions folders. You can install additions accessible to all users inside /Library/ScriptingAdditions/. Each user can also have their own additions inside ~/Library/ScriptingAdditions/.

In Mac OS versions 8.0 through 9.2.1, the Scripting Additions folder is located directly inside of the System Folder (**Figure 2.13**).

In versions of the Mac OS prior to 8.0, the Scripting Additions folder is inside of the System Folder's Extensions folder.

Beware Scripting Additions

Many scripts in this book require special files that add commands to AppleScript. These files are known as *scripting additions;* acronym-toting geeks call them OSAX. (OSAX stands for Open Scripting Architecture eXtension, which is the official way of saying that AppleScript lets you add your own command libraries.)

Each scripting addition has its own dictionary of commands. These commands are added to AppleScript's set of commands when you put the addition in the Scripting Additions folder inside your System Folder. **Figure 2.11** shows the Mac OS 9 and Mac OS X icons for scripting additions, and **Figure 2.12** shows the ScriptingAdditions folder icon for Mac OS X. **Figure 2.13** shows the Scripting Additions folder icon for Mac OS 9.

Some scripting additions add powerful functions to AppleScript's basic command set, including text matching and replacement, control of system components such as control panels, and keyboard and mouse control.

Many of the scripts in this book use scripting additions. Wherever you need a scripting addition, I'll tell you where to get the addition on the Internet. Some scripting additions are available as freeware but many more are shareware. Be sure to support the Mac development community by purchasing any shareware scripting additions you end up using.

✔ Tip

■ Scripting additions must be rewritten to work with the Mac OS X version of AppleScript. It is possible to use Classic scripting additions from Mac OS X. See Chapter 4 for more details.

Interacting with Users

AppleScript is a model of simplicity and elegance in both its underlying structure and its scripting language. In this spirit of simplicity, AppleScript gives users just a few ways to interact directly with it. Using built-in commands, scripts can display dialog boxes and get user input via buttons and text entry. Most of our scripting examples use these simple methods to query users and get their input.

In Mac OS X 10.1, Apple brings AppleScript to a new level with AppleScript Studio. This Cocoa application-building development is due by the end of 2001 and may be shipping by the time you read this.

With FaceSpan from DTI, however, you get a fully scriptable application builder. FaceSpan is the secret weapon of AppleScripters. After you've developed a comfortable working relationship with AppleScript, FaceSpan offers a limitless opportunity to create standalone Mac applications written completely in AppleScript.

Every object in FaceSpan is attachable. This means you can attach an AppleScript to the object that responds to its events. **Figure 2.14** shows the range of objects that scripts in FaceSpan can create and control.

Figure 2.14 FaceSpan's object creation toolbar.

3

LET'S GET STARTED

Now that you're this far into your tour of AppleScript, you should have a fair idea of what it is and how it works. So you're ready to dive into the standard style (or syntax) of AppleScript and really learn how to script on the Mac.

In this chapter, you'll learn about variables and constants, two kinds of containers that hold values and information. You'll look at handling errors and making handlers. You'll also learn about control statements—commands that control when and how parts of scripts are run. You'll use the most common control statement, `tell`, to indicate the application or other object to which AppleScript should send commands.

Other control statements include conditional logic commands such as `if. . .then` and `repeat while`. These commands allow scripts to make intelligent decisions about what to do and how many times to do it.

Now, on to the syntax circus!

Making Statements

Every script you write will be made up of a series of statements. A *statement* is usually just that: a simple English-like sentence with a subject, predicate, and object in the form noun, verb, noun. **Figure 3.1** shows what happens after you run the following example from the Script Editor:

```
tell application "Finder" to ¬
open disk "PowerBook G4"
```

Statements are made up of commands and objects. The target of a statement should be a specific application program, such as the Finder in this example.

Commands are like verbs; they're words you use to request an action. The action usually points at an object. Objects generally are nouns: They're things you do stuff to.

In the preceding example statement, tell is directed at the Finder, which is an object. open is a command, or verb, and disk "PowerBook G4" is its object.

Each object can have parts, or elements. This means that objects such as disks can contain folders and files:

```
tell application "Finder" to ¬
open folder "Applications (Mac OS 9)" of ¬
disk "PowerBook G4"
```

In this example statement, the folder Applications is an element of the disk object PowerBook G4.

Figure 3.2 shows what happens when you run the preceding example from the Script Editor.

You may have intuitively understood what the example script did. That's AppleScript syntax at its best.

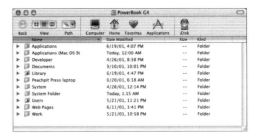

Figure 3.1 At our command, the Finder opens the hard disk window.

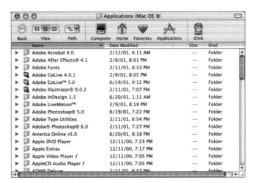

Figure 3.2 Now we've told the Finder to open one of the disk's folders.

More on Targets

In AppleScript, you need to specify the target of the commands in your script. You do this targeting with the tell command. Commands that appear outside tell blocks must be part of AppleScript's built-in set of commands instead of belonging to any specific application. You can think of the concept of using tell to target your commands as setting the context for your commands.

Fun with Variables

Variables are where you put values that you are using in your script:

```
set x to "me"
```

In this example, the command set tells AppleScript to set the variable x to the string value "me".

A *variable* is a kind of object that serves as a placeholder for any information you need to manipulate or share with other applications. Variable names in AppleScript follow a few rules:

◆ They must start with a letter.

◆ They can only contain letters, numbers, and underscores (_).

◆ They cannot be words that are reserved for commands or objects.

Different scripters have different attitudes about naming variables. Some type short, cryptic variable names in the interest of expedience. I suggest using descriptive variable names, even if it means a little extra typing.

✔ Tip

■ Variables come in many flavors, including strings, numbers, and Booleans. When you assign a value to a variable, you can tell AppleScript what kind of value it is. This is important, because commands often expect to receive values of particular types. You'll look at types in "A Family of Values" later in this chapter.

Properties Are Like Persistent Variables

Your script can define its own properties. A property behaves like a variable that keeps its value across executions. This means that the value in a property will be the same when it stops running as it will be when it runs again. You usually define properties in your script at the beginning of your script, like this:

```
property myUser: "me"
```

```
property myDelay: 15
```

Understanding Operators

AppleScript lets you perform many operations on values and variables. The type of operator you choose depends on what you are trying to accomplish and the kind of value that your variable holds.

You can combine strings by using the concatenation operator, &, as follows:

```
set x to "Hello" & "World"
```

Figure 3.3 shows the result of the script.

You can also add items to a list by using &:

```
set z to {"apple","pear"}& "banana"
```

Figure 3.4 shows the result of adding an item to a list.

You can use many operators on variables in AppleScript. **Table 3.1** lists numerical operators.

"Combining Comparisons" later in this chapter discusses logical, or Boolean, operators.

Figure 3.3 The result of concatenating two strings together.

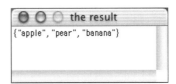

Figure 3.4 The result of adding an item to a list.

Table 3.1

Numerical Operators		
OPERATOR	MEANING	EXAMPLE
^	Raise to the power of	2^4=16
*	Multiply	1*3=3
+	Add	2+7=9
-	Subtract	5-2=3
/	Divide	8/2=4
div	Divide without remainder	11 div 2=5
mod	Divide, returning remainder	11 mod 2=1

A Family of Values

A value in AppleScript typically is a number, a string, a date, a list, or a record that you store inside a variable. Values in variables serve all kinds of purposes in your scripts. Values are manipulated by scripts and returned by applications as results of commands. You use values to exchange information—either between applications and AppleScript or between lines of code within your script. When you send commands to applications, you usually send values with them.

In most languages, values have types, such as integer, string, or array. Types are also called *classes* in some languages; I'll use both terms interchangeably in this book. AppleScript tries to set a value's type automatically unless it's explicitly defined. This automatic typing of values is almost always OK. Sometimes, however, you will concatenate strings or lists and need to tell AppleScript explicitly what type of value you want as a result. Or you may need to do other things, such as coerce a string value to be a reference to a file. In those cases, it's safest to set the types explicitly for your variables. The following sections discuss some value types and how you would set them in Script Editor.

Setting a string value

◆ `set x to 1 as string`

Strings are the most ubiquitous value types you'll see in this book. In this case, you specify that the value x will contain a 1, and you force, or coerce, the value to be a text string by specifying as `string`, even though 1 is a numerical digit. x will have the value 1 in it after this line of code. This coercion of a numerical value to a string is different from the other examples, because they only specify the value type that AppleScript would have chosen automatically anyway. **Figure 3.5** shows how this looks in the Script Editor.

◆ `set x to "me and you"`
`get the first word of x`

A string can be referenced by its elements: paragraphs, words, and characters. In this case, after you set x to a string, you ask AppleScript for the first word of that string by using the command `get`. **Figure 3.6** shows the result of this code in Script Editor.

◆ `set x to "you and I" as text`

Setting a value's type to text is the same as setting it to `string`.

Setting a numeric value

◆ `set k to 1+3.5 as number`

A *number* is either an integer or a real number. AppleScript tries to be as casual and carefree about value types as possible. Unless you insist on a type, AppleScript tries to pick one for you, based on the data stored in your variable.

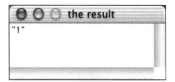

Figure 3.5 The result of coercing a number into a string.

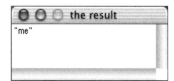

Figure 3.6 The result of getting the first word of a string.

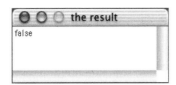

Figure 3.7 The result of setting a variable to a Boolean value.

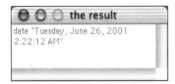

Figure 3.8 The result of setting a variable to the current date.

✔ **Tip**

■ Constants are values predefined by Apple-Script. You cannot change these terms, but you can use them in your code to make scripting easier. After all, `tab` is easier to remember than `ascii character 9`.

◆ `set j to -2 as integer`

An *integer* is a positive or negative number without decimals. You can use the standard addition function `round` to convert a `real` value (see the following paragraph) to an integer.

◆ `set q to 1.222 as real`

A *real* value is a positive or negative number including decimals.

Setting other values

◆ `set x to false as boolean`

A *Boolean* value can be only true or false. `if...then` statements always test a Boolean value, and Boolean variables are useful for storing the state of such tests. Think of them as being on/off or yes/no flags. **Figure 3.7** shows the result of this code in Script Editor.

◆ `set i to the current date`

Dates are their own value type; they specify a day of the week, month, year, and time. **Figure 3.8** shows the result of this code in Script Editor. You can coerce a date into a string by using `as string`.

◆ `set c to the class of {1,2,3}`

Classes are special value types that describe the value type of other values. If you get the class of a variable or literal value, AppleScript returns the value type. This command generates the result of `list`.

◆ `tell application "Finder"¬`
`to set d to the startup disk as alias`

A *reference* value holds a pointer to an object. In this case, an alias reference will be stored in variable d, which points to the startup disk.

Using unit types

AppleScript has included special value types since version 1.3.2 in Mac OS 8.5. There are value types for units of length, area, volume (liquid and solid), and temperature. You can coerce, or convert, values between these types by using the coercion operator, as. This means, for example, that you can convert between measurement systems:

```
set myEnglishLength to 10 as inches
set myMetricLength to myEnglishLength ¬
as centimeters
```

Setting the type for your value explicitly by using the coercion operator is necessary sometimes, because AppleScript can't always guess what value type you want. But some value types cannot be coerced to other value types. The following sample script generates an error in AppleScript, because a real value has to be numerical:

```
set x to "you" as real
```

More Value Types

AppleScript supports other value types, including Unicode text. The unicode text type has partially supported multilingual text in AppleScript since AppleScript 1.3.2 in Mac OS 8.5. In Mac OS X and Mac OS 9.2.1's AppleScript 1.6, unicode text is fully supported for string operations. AppleScript also supports the types international text, styled text, and script.

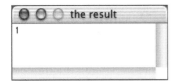

Figure 3.9 The result of requesting the third item from a list.

The Importance of Lists and Records

After you have defined variables for a script, you can manipulate those variables, store information in them, and reference them later. Variables typically hold a single value or complex values such as lists and records that hold a bunch of values together at one time (each of which can be of a different type, such as numbers, strings, and even other lists).

The advantage of storing your values in lists and records is that you can establish relationships between values easily and find values quickly. It also saves you a lot of typing time!

Defining a list

◆ set k to ¬
  {"apple","orange",1,2,3}
  get item 3 of k

   A *list* is an ordered (or linear) collection of values separated by commas. You can create your own lists by specifying each element of the list when you define the list value.

   Lists can be addressed as a whole or by individual comma-delimited values, also known as a list's *items*. **Figure 3.9** shows the result of this script in Script Editor.

◆ set k to ¬
  {"apple","orange",1,2,3}
  get items 2 thru 3 of k

   This line of code yields the list {"orange",1}.

◆ set k to ¬
  {"apple","orange",1,2,3}
  set k to k & "hey"

   You can add a new value to the end of a list by using the concatenation operator, &.

```
◆  set k to ¬
   {"apple","orange",1,"you"}
   set item 3 of k to "me"
   get k
```

You can also modify individual items within a list. If you want to change the value of a single item, just reference it by number. You can have numbers and strings intermixed as items in your lists. **Figure 3.10** shows the result of this script in Script Editor.

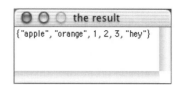

Figure 3.10 The result of modifying an item and adding a new item.

Defining a record

```
◆  set t to {name: "me",phone: ¬
   "111-222-3333"}
```

A *record* is a set of properties. More simply, records are lists in which each item is made up of a name-value pair. As you can see in this example, you define a record in the same way that you define a list, with items separated by commas. But in a record, each item has two parts: an item name and a value for that name.

```
◆  set t to {name: "me",phone: ¬
   "111-222-3333"}
   set q to name of t
```

In a record, you must address an item by name instead of by position, as you do in a list.

```
◆  set t to {name: "me",phone: ¬
   "111-222-3333"}
   set myProperties to length of t
```

The length property of a record tells you how many properties that record has. But you need to know the specific property names to access the values in records, unless you coerce them into being lists. This line of code returns the result 2.

```
◆  set t to {name: "me",phone: ¬
   "111-222-3333"}
   set myList to (t as list)
```

This line of code generates the list {"me","111-222-333"}.

✔ Tip

■ Just as you sometimes force AppleScript to recognize a variable as holding a particular kind of value—a string, a real number, or an integer—no matter what is stored in it, you can specify a type for individual items in lists and records. A record property or list item can hold a string value right next to an item that is a numeric value, for example.

THE IMPORTANCE OF LISTS AND RECORDS

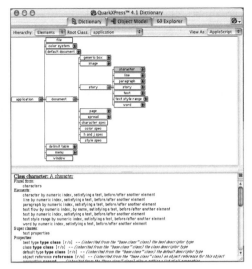

Figure 3.11 Script Debugger's Object Model pane of the Dictionary window visually displays the object containment hierarchy of Quark's [character] object.

Objects and References to Them

Objects are the things in applications, AppleScript, and Mac OS that respond to script commands. *Application objects* are objects stored in applications and their documents, such as text objects, database objects, and graphic objects. Objects can contain data in the form of values, properties, and elements that you can access or change from your scripts.

Each object belongs to an *object class*. Each object class is a category for objects that defines their properties and elements you can access from AppleScript. Object classes include applications, documents, windows, databases, fields, graphic elements, and characters. *Dictionaries* define object classes and indicate the object's properties and elements that can be set. *Properties* contain values, and *elements* are themselves objects that can be referenced separately from your script. **Figure 3.11** shows how Script Debugger lets you see the Object Model view of QuarkXPress's dictionary entry for the character object class in QuarkXPress.

You can store references to objects, such as character 2 of document 1, in variables, just like any other value. This way, you can simplify your code when you need to refer to an object many times in a script.

Object examples

◆
```
tell application "QuarkXPress"
    get character 2 of text box 1 ¬
of document 1
end tell
```
This code returns a single character as the result from QuarkXPress.

◆
```
tell application "Finder"
    set mySysFldr to alias ¬
"HD:System Folder:"
end tell
```
This code returns a reference to the System Folder on the volume named HD. The reference looks like this: alias "HD:System Folder:".

◆
```
tell application "Finder"
    set mySysFldr to alias ¬
"HD:System Folder:"
    open mySysFldr
end tell
```
This code makes the Finder open the file Test File on the volume HD because you stored this file reference in the variable mySysFldr. **Figure 3.12** shows the reference stored in mySysFldr displayed in Script Editor's Result window.

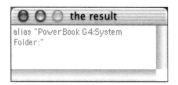

Figure 3.12 The reference stored in [mySysFldr] as displayed in the Script Editor's Result window.

✔ Tip

■ The best AppleScript dictionaries map the objects of the application in an obvious hierarchy made up of objects contained by other objects. This structure makes the relationship between objects and their properties especially easy to grasp and control via a script. This reliance on a well-related series of objects in an application's scripting implementation is called following the object model.

Comparisons and Control Statements

One of the most powerful features that AppleScript offers you is the ability to introduce logic along with automation. At its most basic, *logic* means making decisions based on comparisons between values. These values can be stored in variables or used literally.

To put these comparisons to good use, you need a command to use with them. The hands-down conditional command favorite is:

```
if. . .then. . .else. . .
```

The following examples show comparisons that can be used with the `if` command. You can use basic comparisons with numbers, strings, and Booleans to good purpose.

Comparing values

◆ `if 4 > 2 then beep`
`if 4 is greater than 2 then beep`

In these two examples, you are asking AppleScript to evaluate whether one value is greater than another. In the first example, AppleScript will beep if 4 is greater than 2, which of course it is. The second example is the same, except that the command is written in words rather than symbols. AppleScript lets you do this for added clarity.

◆ `if 1 < 8 then beep`
`if 1 is less than 8 then beep`

This example makes the same kind of comparison as the preceding example, but it asks AppleScript to tell you which of the values is less than the other.

- if 3 ≥ 1 then beep
  if 3 is greater than or equal to 1 ¬
  then beep

  In this comparison, AppleScript evaluates two values and tells you whether the first is either greater than or equal to the second. The statement evaluates to true if that is indeed the case, as it is here. You generate the ≥ character by pressing Option-. (period).

- if 1 ≤ 3 then beep
  if 1 is less than or equal to 3 ¬
  then beep

  This time, AppleScript determines whether 1 is less than or equal to 3. Because it is, you'll get a beep. You generate the ≤ character by pressing Option-, (comma).

- if 3 = 3 then beep
  if 3 is equal to 3 then beep

  Equality is the most typical comparison, and it works just the way it looks. Because 3 does still equal 3, your Mac will beep for this.

- if 1 ≠ 2 then beep
  if 1 is not equal to 2 then beep

  For every force there must be an opposing force. not equal is the dark side of equal. And because I do enjoy beeping, this example generates another beep. You generate the ≠ character by pressing Option-= (equal sign).

Figure 3.13 A dialog generated by our conditional [if... else... end if] test.

Using else Statements

Comparisons using if can also respond to failures when an else clause is included. **Figure 3.13** shows what happens when you run the following script:

```
set x to 10
if x = 1 then
    beep
else
    display dialog "I'm not 1."
end if
```

In this example, the initial if test fails, and the else clause is executed instead.

Advanced Comparisons for Strings, Lists, and Records

You can also use powerful character-matching comparisons such as `starts with`, `ends with`, and `contains` with strings, lists, and records. Using these comparisons, you can easily detect substrings inside larger strings.

Using starts with, ends with, and contains

◆ `if "Help me" starts with "Help" ¬`
  `then beep`

  In this example, you ask AppleScript to test where the string `Help` appears in the string `Help me`. If it appears at the start of the string, the expression is true, and AppleScript beeps.

◆ `considering case`
  `if "Help me" starts with "help" ¬`
  `then beep`
  `end considering`

  Usually, comparisons aren't case-sensitive. But when you invoke the `considering case` statement, Apple-Script considers case. This code does not generate a beep.

◆ `if "Take off" ends with "off"¬`
  `then beep`

  This time, you test whether the string `off` appears at the end of the first string. If `off` appears at the end of the string, the expression is true and you hear a beep.

Testing Lists

◆ `if "Red apple tree" contains ¬`
  `"apple" then beep`
  The least restrictive of these three comparisons is `contains`. In this example, if the string `apple` appears anywhere in the first string, the result is true and you hear a beep.

◆ `if {1,4,5} starts with 1 then beep`
  This test on a list generates a beep, because the list starts with 1.

◆ `if {"me", "you", "them"} contains ¬`
  `"you" then beep`
  This test yields a result of `true`, because the list contains an item that matches the test string.

Combining Comparisons

To add to the usefulness of comparisons, you can use three logical operators—and, or, and not—to create compound if...then statements. Using these command words, you can create much more elaborate comparisons that test many values at the same time. **Table 3.2** lists the logical operators and shows how they work.

Using logical operators

◆ if i contains "yes" and j > 5 ¬
then beep

Using the logical operator here lets you combine two if... then tests into one. Both conditions must be true for the overall test to return true and then beep. Here, the string i would have to contain "yes", and the number inside the variable j would have to be greater than 5 to return true. As in all comparisons, AppleScript goes on to the rest of the statement (and, in this case, beep) only if the comparisons return true.

◆ if i contains "no" or j = 1 then beep

With or, you can combine multiple if. . .then tests and return true for the overall test if one or more of the constituent tests is true. In this case, if the string i contains "no" or if the number inside the variable j equals 1, you hear a beep.

◆ if not (q contains "maybe") then beep

In this example, you tell AppleScript to check the value of q and see whether it contains the letters "maybe". If this test is true, the not reverses the result, generating a failure and bypassing the beep. The comparison is enclosed in parentheses to ensure that AppleScript sees it as a whole phrase to evaluate.

Table 3.2

Logical/Boolean Operators		
OPERATOR	MEANING	EXAMPLE
and	Returns true if both tests are successful.	x and y returns true only if x is true and y is true.
or	Returns true if either test succeeds.	x or y returns true as long as either x or y is true.
not	Returns true if test fails; returns false if test is successful.	not x returns false if x is true.

✔ Tip

■ The quoted text in the preceding examples is a string value. String values are enclosed in quotes in AppleScript.

Script 3.1 An infinite repeat loop.

```
                    script
set myList to {}
repeat
set myList to (myList & "me") as list
end repeat
```

Script 3.2 An infinite repeat loop with an exit.

```
                    script
set myList to {}
repeat
set myList to (myList & "me") as list
if the number of items in myList > 10 ¬
then exit repeat
end repeat
get myList
```

Repeat Loops

Now that you know AppleScript has the smarts provided by comparisons, let's look at the brute force added to AppleScript by repeat loops. A *repeat loop* makes a comparison continuously over a range of values until it gets a true result.

The repeat loop is one of AppleScript's essential features, because it lets you do many things over and over, saving work that would otherwise be done by your fingers. Repeat loops in their simplest form are infinite. The following script creates such a loop. It is displayed in its entirety in **Script 3.1.**

To run an infinite loop:

1. `set myList to {}`

   With this first line, you tell AppleScript to create an empty list variable `myList`.

2. `repeat`

   Now you start a repeat loop without any modifiers. This type of simple `repeat` will loops until an `exit repeat` command is encountered.

3. `set myList to (myList & "me") as list`

   You append the string "me" as a new item in the list `myList`. You tell AppleScript to set this variable as a list for clarity in your code. In this case, AppleScript would do so anyway.

4. `end repeat`

   Finally, you conclude the loop, sending the script execution back to the line immediately after repeat and starting the cycle all over again. If you run this script, the variable `myList` will fill with an infinite number of "me"s.

AppleScript gives you a way out of the infinite loop, however, as demonstrated in the following script, which is also shown in **Script 3.2.**

To exit an infinite loop:

1. `set myList to {}`

You begin this script just like the preceding one, by defining an empty list variable.

2. `repeat`

Again, you start an infinite repeat loop.

3. `set myList to (myList & "me") as list`

You append the string "me" as a new item in the variable `myList`.

4. `if the number of items in ¬`
`myList > 10 then exit repeat`

Here's the trick! This time, you test the number of items in the list. When that number exceeds 10, you exit the loop.

5. `end repeat`
`get myList`

Once out of the loop, we retrieve the value of the variable `myList`.

Figure 3.14 shows the result of this script.

Repeat loops can also count by using a variable. The next example (**Script 3.3**) calculates the factorial 10, using the variable i, by looping through the numbers 1 through 10 and multiplying the preceding result by the next number (1*2*3*4*5*6*7*8*9*10, for example).

To use a counting repeat loop:

1. `set x to 1`

You start by setting a variable outside the repeat loop to hold your factorial result.

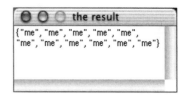

Figure 3.14 The result of adding items to a list in a repeat loop.

Script 3.3 A counting repeat loop that calculates factorials.

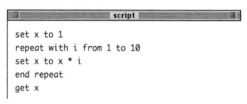

```
set x to 1
repeat with i from 1 to 10
set x to x * i
end repeat
get x
```

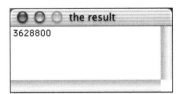

Figure 3.15 The result of looping from 1 through 10 and multiplying each successive number to get the factorial of 10.

Script 3.4 A conditional repeat loop.

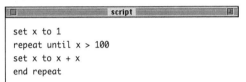

```
set x to 1
repeat until x > 100
set x to x + x
end repeat
```

2. `repeat with i from 1 to 10`

By defining a variable and a counting range with this repeat, you tell Apple-Script to execute the loop as many times as it takes to get from the starting value to the ending value (from 1 to 10, in this case). This technique allows you to limit the number of loops through the repeat when you start it, rather than inside the loop itself.

3. `set x to x * i`

Here, you set the value of x to equal its current value multiplied by the current counter value in the variable i.

4. `end repeat`
`get x`

Finally, you end the loop. Notice that you didn't need the conditional test you used in the preceding example to exit this repeat loop, as you took care of that in step 2.

Figure 3.15 shows the result of this calculation.

In their most exotic form, repeat loops are conditional, much like if commands. After each loop, the following script (**Script 3.4**) checks to see whether x is greater than 100.

To use a conditional repeat loop:

1. `set x to 1`

First, you initialize a variable to hold an increasing value.

2. `repeat until x > 100`

By defining a conditional test after the word until, you have told AppleScript that this loop should repeat until the condition returns a value of true. In this case, the loop repeats until the variable x holds a value larger than 100.

continues on next page

3. `set x to x + x`

Inside the repeat loop, you'll change the value of x by adding it to itself. The script keeps doubling x from 1 to 2 to 4 and so on until it hits 128, causing the loop to end. Each time the script adds x to itself, AppleScript checks the first line of the repeat loop again to see whether x is greater than 100.

4. `end repeat`

Now you end the loop.

✔ Tips

■ You can also skip numbers by using the by modifier. Here, you count from 2 to 50 by twos, skipping all odd numbers:

```
repeat with j from 2 to 50 by 2
    display dialog j
end repeat
```

■ You can use negative numbers in a by modifier to count down. Here, you go from 100 to 1 backward:

```
repeat with j from 100 to 1 by -1
    display dialog j
end repeat
```

■ AppleScript has a special repeat-loop construction that automates the process of moving through each item in a list. In this script, the values of the three items in myList are put individually into the variable myItem, one item for each cycle in the loop. You display the item's value in a dialog box.

```
set myList to {1,2,3}
repeat with myItem in myList
    display dialog myItem
end repeat
```

REPEAT LOOPS

Script 3.5 Handling an error with [try].

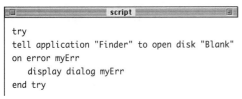

```
try
tell application "Finder" to open disk "Blank"
on error myErr
    display dialog myErr
end try
```

Script 3.6 Ignoring errors without the optional [on error] clause.

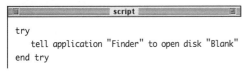

```
try
    tell application "Finder" to open disk "Blank"
end try
```

Finder got an error: Can't get disk "Blank".

Cancel   OK

Figure 3.16 Our script displays this dialog thanks to the [try... on error... end try] block in **Script 3.5**.

Ignoring Errors

You can use the try. . .end try statement to keep your script from failing by ignoring errors. You do this by omitting the on error block:

```
try
    –code goes here
end try
```

If anything goes wrong, the script silently fails and continues on its way.

Error Handling

As the scripts in this book get more robust and user-friendly, they will need to deal intelligently with errors. Errors happen. AppleScript gives you a way to intercept execution errors in your scripts with the try statement, as **Script 3.5** demonstrates. If you didn't use the try statement in this script, AppleScript would halt execution and display an error message.

To intercept errors with try:

1. try

You begin by invoking error handling with the try statement.

2. tell application "Finder" to open ¬ disk "Blank"

Next, you ask the Finder to open a disk named Blank. In this example, "Blank" doesn't exist, so an error will be created.

3. on error myErr
display dialog myErr
end try

Finally, you create a handler to let AppleScript know what to do if the actions in the script fail. A handler is a small piece of code that runs only if something asks it to. In this case, if the tell fails, the try statement generates an error, which makes this handler run. The handler then displays a dialog box with the error's name. To learn more about handlers, see "Handlers" later in this chapter.

Figure 3.16 shows what happens when the disk can't be opened. If everything goes well, execution of the script simply continues past the end try statement.

Using with timeout to Wait

Another failure-proofing command you'll want to know is with timeout, which is demonstrated in **Script 3.7**. Commands inside a with timeout statement execute for a specified duration; then the script generates a timeout error.

To control how long your script waits for results:

1. try

      with timeout of 50 seconds

You start with a try statement to prevent any timeout errors from stopping the execution of the script. Then you let AppleScript know that you want to restrict the time allowed for your script to run to 50 seconds.

2. tell application "Netscape 6" to ¬ OpenURL "http://www.apple.com/ applescript/"

You ask Netscape to open a window with the AppleScript Web site in it. Normally, the script would wait quite a while for Netscape 6 to finish. Inside the with timeout, however, the script continues executing after waiting 50 seconds. The same is true for all of the AppleScript statements you include inside the with timeout statement.

3. end timeout
end try

Finally, you let AppleScript know that you're done with the code for which you're defining the with timeout.

Script 3.7 Using [with timeout] to set an allowable duration for a script's execution.

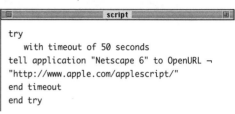

```
try
    with timeout of 50 seconds
tell application "Netscape 6" to OpenURL ¬
"http://www.apple.com/applescript/"
end timeout
end try
```

Script 3.7 Using [with timeout] to set an allowable duration for a script's execution.

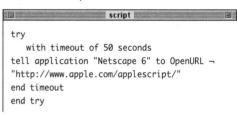

```
try
    with timeout of 50 seconds
tell application "Netscape 6" to OpenURL ¬
"http://www.apple.com/applescript/"
end timeout
end try
```

✔ Tip

■ Place your with timeout statement within a try. . .end try statement to prevent your script from stopping when a timeout occurs. Sometimes, you don't want your script to wait forever for something to happen.

Script 3.8 A simple script with a custom handler.

```
████  ██  ████ script ████  ██  █
on testValue(x)
if x > 100 then set x to 100
    if x < 1 then set x to 1
return x
end testValue
on run
    set z to testValue(200)
end run
```

Handlers

Handlers are important. A *handler* is simply a short modular script that performs one specialized task. If you have heard of a function or subroutine before, you will understand what a handler is. AppleScript lets you create handlers with input values and output values. Some of the scripts you'll create early in this book can be used in conjunction as independent handlers, or functions, that can be combined to make complex scripts.

Writing simple code based on handlers makes that code especially easy to reuse. As you become a regular AppleScripter, you'll find that many handlers you create for one purpose are useful over and over.

AppleScript makes it easy to define a snippet of code as a handler. You simply use the on statement and give your handler a name. **Script 3.8** shows a simple handler.

To define some AppleScript as a handler:

1. `on testValue(x)`

   By placing these comparisons within a handler, you create a snippet of code you can use whenever you want this comparison made, instead of having to type it every time. You define the handler by typing on, followed by the handler name. If you want to be able to pass data to the handler, you also need to define a variable in the first line of the handler to hold that data. This example uses x. Variables are always placed within parentheses in an on statement.

2. `if x > 100 then set x to 100`
   `if x < 1 then set x to 1`

   These two lines are the comparison that works inside the handler, setting the value of x, which is the data you passed to the handler when you called it.

continues on next page

Saving Script Libraries

You can save a separate compiled script filled with handlers as a library in a file. Any script can then easily access the handlers you save in the library. If you save the handler testValue in a file named mylib, you could do this:

```
set myLibrary to load script "HD:mylib"
tell myLibrary to set z to testValue(200)
```

A saved script library can have many handlers defined in it. The following example would work if both handlers were defined:

```
tell myLibrary to doHandler1()
tell myLibrary to doHandler2()
```

HANDLERS

35

3. `return x`

This important line tells AppleScript to return the value in x to the rest of the script.

4. `end testValue`

The end tells AppleScript the handler is over.

5. `on run`
```
    set z to testValue(200)
end run
```

This line calls the handler when the script is run.

This handler, named `testValue`, tests a value passed to it, ensuring that the value is within the range of 1 to 100 and then returning the adjusted value.

You can place each handler anywhere in your script outside other handlers.

Calling handlers is just as easy as defining them. You can pass a handler many values of any type, including strings, numbers, and lists. Separate multiple values with commas.

✔ Tips

■ If you want to define a handler that has multiple variables passed to it, you would create an on statement like this one:
```
on testMax(x,y)
    if x>y then
        return x
    else
        return y
    end if
end textMax
```

■ Handlers in AppleScript are based on the same programming concept as functions. AppleScript calls them handlers because they are routines called to handle something. Simple enough.

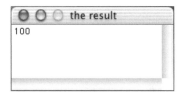

Figure 3.17 The result of a call to our sample handler.

Calling Handlers

`set z to testValue(200)`

In the preceding single line of code, you call the handler testValue, passing it the value 200. The handler returns its results into the variable z. **Figure 3.17** shows the result of this sample script.

After doing this for a bit, you will find yourself with a folder full of reusable handler-laden script libraries. Efficient use of handlers, like use of straightforward variable names, is an important part of good scripting.

HANDLERS

Figure 3.18 The two types of comments as displayed by the Script Editor.

Using Comments to Help Yourself

Good scripting techniques always seem to take longer at first but save time later. You've probably heard this before. In fact, I find that good scripting techniques help not only when you come back to your script later but also when you're in the process of creating it. Using clear variable names and handler-based scripts help keep your thinking clear and uncluttered.

Even more important than both of these techniques is the use of comments to annotate your scripts with additional information. **Figure 3.18** shows what comments look like in Script Editor. Comments are where you leave important notes for later visits to a script; they also help you clarify your thinking process while you're engaged in your scripting effort by letting you have some free space in which to outline your scripting approach.

AppleScript gives you two ways to enter comments in a script. The first syntax is for one-liners. You simply type two dashes to start a one-line comment:

```
--this is a quick one-line comment
```

AppleScript, always trying to be flexible, also gives the long-winded a chance to write many lines of comments quickly and easily. For a long comment, you start with an opening parenthesis and asterisk and close with another asterisk and a closing parenthesis:

```
(* this is a long rambling tale of my ¬
greatest hopes for this feeble script ¬
that it may one day be great *)
```

✔ Tip

■ Be generous with yourself as you think through your scripting. Take the time to write out what you're doing while you're doing it. You will not regret this effort later, and it's a good way to keep yourself organized.

Simple Interaction with the User

AppleScript gives you a few simple and elegant commands for getting input from the user while your script is running. You can get text data and button choices by using the `display dialog` command. The following script (**Script 3.9**) uses this basic interactive command. **Figure 3.19** shows what the dialog box looks like when the script runs.

To ask the user for information:

1. `display dialog "Please enter your ¬`
   `name" default answer "" buttons ¬`
   `{"First", "Last", "Cancel"} ¬`
   `default button "Cancel"`

   This code has AppleScript stop executing and display a dialog box asking the user to supply a name. **Figure 3.20** shows what happens if you enter Steve and click the button labeled First. In this example, you also define a `default answer`, which sets the initial string that appears in the dialog box's editable text field. In this case, you set it to an empty string. If you didn't include the `default answer`, AppleScript would not show a text field in the dialog box.

2. `set x to the button returned of ¬`
   `the result`

   Here, you access the results of `display dialog`. When this line is executed, the variable x will equal the string value `"First"`.

Script 3.9 Asking the user for input. Nothing happens until the user clicks one of the three buttons.

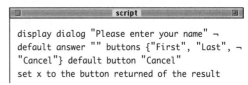

```
display dialog "Please enter your name" ¬
default answer "" buttons {"First", "Last", ¬
"Cancel"} default button "Cancel"
set x to the button returned of the result
```

Figure 3.19 A dialog generated by our `display dialog` command.

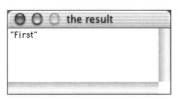

Figure 3.20 The result of the [button returned] from our `display dialog` command.

✔ Tips

- You can define up to three buttons in a `display dialog`.

- In the preceding example, you tell AppleScript to make the Cancel button the `default button`, which makes that button show up with a thick border and causes it to be triggered when the user presses the Return or Enter key.

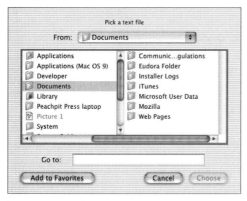

Figure 3.21 A file-selection dialog generated by a [choose file] command, limited to text files only.

Table 3.3

Some File Types to Use with choose file	
FILE TYPE	**DESCRIPTION**
EPSF	An EPS (encapsulated PostScript) image file
JPEG	A JPEG image file
PICT	A PICT image file
GIF	A GIF image file
PDF	An Adobe Acrobat file
APPL	An application file
osas	A compiled AppleScript script file

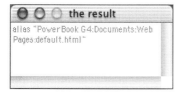

Figure 3.22 The result of a user selection from the [choose file] dialog.

Asking for a Choice

You can also interact with the user by asking him to pick and choose. AppleScript contains commands you can use to display standard Macintosh dialog boxes that let users select list items, files, folders, and applications.

To ask users to choose from a list:

◆ choose from list {"a","b","c"} ¬
  with prompt "Make a choice"

You ask the user to select a letter from a list of three choices. The result of choose from list is a list of the selected item or items or the Boolean value false if no item was selected. **Script 4.10** and **4.11** in Chapter 4 show how to use this command.

To ask users to pick a file:

1. choose file with prompt "Pick a text ¬
   file" of type {"TEXT"}

   With the choose file command, you ask the user to select a file via the standard file-selection dialog box (**Figure 3.21**). Note that only text files appear in it. If you want the user to be able to pick other kinds of files, substitute one of the values from **Table 3.3** for TEXT in the line above.

2. set myFile to the result

   This stores the reference to a file returned by choose file in the variable myFile.

   Figure 3.22 displays the result of the user's selection, which is an alias pointing to the selected file.

To ask users to pick a folder:

1. `choose folder with prompt "Select ¬ a folder"`

choose folder works in a similar way to choose file, except that the dialog box displays only folders.

2. `set myFolder to the result`

You store the reference to the folder chosen with choose folder in the variable myFolder.

To ask users to choose an application:

◆ `set myApp to (choose application ¬ with prompt "Select your favorite ¬ application")`

You can use choose application to have AppleScript ask the user to select a scriptable application from any running application on the local machine or other machines on the network. With this feature, you can allow the user to select the target for portions of a script. This time, you store the reference returned by choose application directly in the variable myApp. **Figures 3.23** and **3.24** show the dialog box generated by this command in Mac OS X and Mac OS 9.2.1.

✔ Tip

■ In Mac OS 8.5 or later, `display dialog` has an optional parameter called `giving up after` that allows you to specify how long (in seconds) the dialog box should appear before the script continues automatically. Following is an example:

`display dialog "Hello" giving up ¬ after 5`

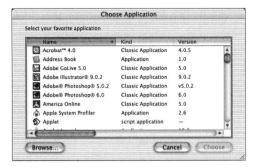

Figure 3.23 The application-selection dialog generated by a [choose application] command in Mac OS X.

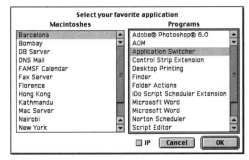

Figure 3.24 The application-selection dialog box from Mac OS 9.2.1's [choose application] command.

Script 3.10 A simple [on run] handler with one line of code in it.

```
on run
display dialog "hey!"
end run
```

Using on run and Saving Scripts as Applications

You've already seen how you tell AppleScript that you want to define a handler in a script by using the on. . .end statement in conjunction with a handler name.

You've also seen the special try. . .end try handler that AppleScript uses to deal with error handling during execution of a script. Well, AppleScript has set aside two other on. . .end handlers for special purposes. I'll cover one here and the other in the following section.

The most fundamental on. . .end handler is the on run. . .end run handler. This handler defines the main chunk of code that is executed when the script is run. **Script 3.10** shows a simple on run handler.

Every script you write starts with an implied on run and ends with an implied end run command if you don't type them. In scripts in which numerous handlers are defined, it is usually good practice to use on run. . .end run commands to make it clear where the main code exists in the script.

If no on run handler is explicitly defined, AppleScript runs the first line of code it finds. You can't have loose code and define an on run handler in one script.

To define a run handler:

1. on run

   You begin the script's main portion of code with on run to let AppleScript know that you want it to execute this code first whenever the script is run.

2. display dialog "hey!"

   In this example, the main code is this one line that shows the user a dialog box.

continues on next page

3. end run

> To let AppleScript know that the main code is over, you close the handler with an end run statement.

Saving your script as an application

When you save a script with an on run handler as an application, the main code within the handler executes when a user double-clicks your script's icon. **Figures 3.25** and **3.26** show the Save dialog box (for Mac OS X and Mac OS 9.2.1) that appears when you choose to save your script as a stand-alone application. This is the way you will save most of the scripts throughout this book.

Turning your script into an application makes it easy for a user to run the script. Double-click, and it is running.

✔ Tips

■ By selecting the option to never show the startup screen, you avoid AppleScript's default behavior of showing the script's description in a dialog box before every execution.

■ Almost every script in this book works optimally when saved as an application. AppleScript CGI applications should be saved as applications that stay open, to eliminate the launching time for the CGI script application.

■ Scripts saved as applications are often called *applets*.

Figure 3.25 The Mac OS X Script Editor's Save dialog, ready to save a script as a stand-alone Mac OS X applet.

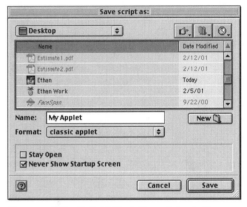

Figure 3.26 The Script Editor's Save dialog in Mac OS 9.2.1, ready to save a script as a stand-alone Classic applet.

Script 3.11 A simple [on open] handler.

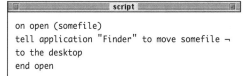

```
on open (somefile)
tell application "Finder" to move somefile ¬
to the desktop
end open
```

Making Drag-and-Drop Applications with on open

More interesting than the quite useful on run. . .end run handler is the on open. . .end open handler. This is a special handler, because when you save a script with an on open handler as a stand-alone application, it becomes a drag-and-drop-capable application. **Script 3.11** shows a simple on open handler.

Your script can have both on open and on run handlers defined in it. Each is executed according to how the script application is being run. If it is double-clicked, the on run code executes. If items are dropped onto its icon, the on open handler runs.

To define an on open handler:

1. on open (somefile)

A reference to any object that the user drags onto the script's application icon is passed to the script in the variable some-file, used as an argument for on open.

2. tell application "Finder" to move ¬ somefile to the desktop

With a reference to all the objects that you dropped onto the script stored in somefile, you have the Finder move them to the Desktop.

3. end open

You conclude the on open handler with the end open statement.

✔ Tips

■ The use of parentheses with the on open handler is optional in AppleScript.

■ Mac OS X supports the use of file suffixes on script files.

Making Droplets

Scripts with on open. . .end open handlers that are saved as applications are often called *droplets*.

Try entering the sample script in the preceding section and saving it as an application from Script Editor. Be sure to choose the Never Show Startup Screen option. **Figure 3.27** shows the standard icon for a drag-and-drop script application, or *droplet*.

Now try dragging a file or folder from anywhere other than your Desktop onto the application icon. The icon should become highlighted, and when you release the mouse button, the script launches. The script then moves the items you dropped onto it to the Desktop.

Sample Applet

My Applet

Figure 3.27 The standard icons for a drag-and-drop script application in Mac OS 9 (top) and Mac OS X (bottom).

Figure 3.28 The Mac OS X Script Editor's Open dialog.

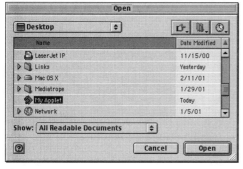

Figure 3.29 The Open dialog box from Mac OS 9.1's Script Editor.

Compiled Script

Compiled Script

Figure 3.30 The standard icons for a compiled script in Mac OS 9 (top) and Mac OS X (bottom).

Other Ways to Save Scripts

The only way to reopen scripts saved as applications in Script Editor is to drag and drop their icons onto the Script Editor icon or to choose the script explicitly in Script Editor's Open dialog box. **Figures 3.28** and **3.29** show this dialog box in Mac OS X and Mac OS 9.2.1 with a sample script application selected for reopening.

Script Editor allows you to save your scripts in other formats, such as compiled scripts. In this format, AppleScript checks the script's syntax as it is saved. When a script is compiled, AppleScript can execute it without recompiling it. You can open compiled scripts in Script Editor simply by double-clicking them in the Finder. This is often a good format for saving handlers that you expect to use as script libraries. **Figure 3.30** shows the standard icon for a compiled script.

✔ Tips

- You can also save your script as text-only. If you save your script as text-only, you can open it in any application that can edit text to perform modifications. You might want to reopen your script in a more sophisticated text editor, such as BBEdit, to perform cleaning operations such as global search-and-replaces of certain terms. Scripts saved as text do not have their syntax verified, so when they are reopened in Script Editor, this operation still needs to be performed. **Figure 3.31** shows the standard icon for a text-only script document.

- Scripts can be saved as run-only applications from Script Editor. After you've saved your script this way, you can never open it in Script Editor to change any of its code. This format is available so that you can distribute functional script applications to others without worrying about giving away your AppleScripting secrets! I avoid saving scripts this way, because most scripts continue to evolve. Always be certain to keep an editable copy of any script you choose to save as run-only; otherwise, you'll never see your precious code again!

Script Text

Script Text

Figure 3.31 The standard icons for a text-only script in Mac OS 9 (top) and Mac OS X (bottom).

AppleScript Evolution: Mac OS X 10.1

Mac OS X 10.1 is amazing, new, complicated, and from the Aqua user interface to the new System Preferences application, different from anything you already know about Mac OS 9. In the midst of this new terrain stands Apple-Script, your hero, working in harmony with Mac OS X.

Apple added many enhancements in version 10.1 of Mac OS X, including AppleScript 1.7.

AppleScript 1.7 works with Carbon and Cocoa applications developed just for Mac OS X, as well as with older Mac OS 9 applications running in the Classic environment of Mac OS X.

Yes, AppleScript is alive and thriving in Mac OS X. Version 10.1 offers the kind of functionality you need to get things done. Depending on your coding style, most of Mac OS 9 applications should work unchanged when run from Mac OS X 10.1. However, none of the scriptable Mac OS 9 system software components, such as control panels and extensions, exist in Mac OS X, which has no control panels or extensions.

With Mac OS X 10.1, AppleScript is a core part of both the new and old operating systems, and it is still maturing along with Mac OS X. When you move to Mac OS X, you will find that many fundamental things are different about this new operating system. The Finder in Mac OS X 10.1 does not support labels, for example, so accessing the label index of an item generates an error. Why? The Finder itself is changing in Mac OS X. In this new operating system, the Finder does not have responsibility for everything it used to control.

Mac OS X has changed things so dramatically, which you will come across regularly when you're scripting. This chapter covers the most notable aspects of using AppleScript in Mac OS X, beginning with an overview of what is the same and what has changed.

The first task when approaching AppleScript in Mac OS X is to locate the Script Editor. **Figure 4.1** shows the AppleScript folder inside the Applications folder, which is where Script Editor lives. I recommend that you drag the Script Editor icon onto your Dock for permanent easy access; you will use this tool often.

Figure 4.1 The AppleScript folder inside your Applications folder contains the Script Editor and Script Runner, as well as example scripts.

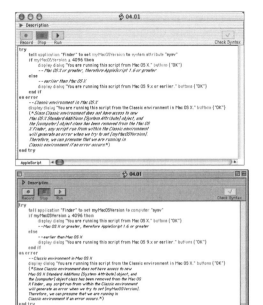

Figure 4.2 The same script in the Mac OS X Script Editor (top) and the Mac OS 9 Script Editor (bottom) shows that the only difference is the Aqua interface.

What Is the Same About AppleScript in Mac OS X?

The AppleScript engineering team at Apple has done an amazing job of making AppleScript consistent between Mac OS X and earlier versions of the Mac OS. Generally, any scripts you create should operate the same way whether you run them in Mac OS X, in Mac OS 9.2.1, or in the Classic environment of Mac OS X.

Apple worked to synchronize AppleScript in both Mac OS X 10.1 and Mac OS 9.2.1. This is not to say that the language in both operating systems is identical; many differences exist between the AppleScript language in Mac OS X 10.1 and Mac OS 9.2.1.

The following list discusses similarities between Mac OS X and Mac OS 9.2.1:

Script Editor. Apple has kept the functionality of the Mac OS X and Mac OS 9.2.1 versions of Script Editor identical. **Figure 4.2** compares the Classic and Mac OS X Script Editor windows, showing that the only difference is the Aqua interface.

Mac OS 9.2.1 Scripting Additions. You can still use older Mac OS 9.2.1-compatible Scripting Additions in Mac OS X. See "Scripting Additions in Mac OS X" later in this chapter for details on using old additions in your Mac OS X scripts.

Saved script file types. Script Editor in Mac OS X saves compiled scripts, text-only scripts, applets, and droplets with traditional Mac OS 9-compatible file types and icons. It also recognizes a new series of file extensions for each kind of script file to operate with Mac OS X's support for file extensions. See **Table 4.1** for a reference to the standard AppleScript file extensions.

Scriptable applications. In Mac OS X, AppleScript works with applications created for Mac OS X as well as with Classic applications. So you can write a single script in Mac OS X that controls applications running in Mac OS X and applications running in the Classic environment. Do note that the Mac OS X Finder, although similar to the Mac OS 9 version, has different capabilities and therefore has a different AppleScript dictionary.

File paths. In AppleScript 1.7 for both Mac OS X and Mac OS 9.2.1, file paths are delimited by colons (:). This delimiter remains the same for compatibility in Mac OS X, even though true file paths in Mac OS X are delimited by a forward slash (/).

Full Unicode support. AppleScript in both Mac OS X and Mac OS 9.2.1 supports all standard text operations with Unicode data, including comparisons and concatenation.

Bugs squashed. AppleScript in both versions of the Mac OS includes numerous bug fixes. These fixes include the prevention of a crash on `middle of {}`, proper error generation on accessing `item 0` of a list, and proper Keychain support in `mount volume`.

Program linking. Mac OS X 10.1 supports many forms of program linking, so your scripts can target applications on Mac OS 9, Mac OS X, and even other remote machines with its new Internet Services capabilities.

Scripted Internet connections. Connecting to the Internet can be scripted. The Internet-connection functions in Mac OS 9's Network Setup Scripting have been replaced by the Internet Connect application.

Flattened Script Files Supported in Mac OS X

Mac OS X supports the storage of compiled scripts in the data fork of a file, instead of relying on a resource fork. This feature is beneficial when you're transmitting a script over the Internet for execution locally. Now you can transmit a compiled script without encoding or BinHexing it.

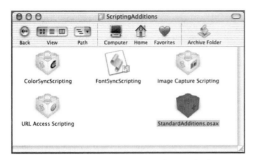

Figure 4.3 The system Scripting Additions folder (/System/Library/ScriptingAdditions/) contains Apple-installed Scripting Additions.

What Is Different About AppleScript in Mac OS X?

Now, for the strong of heart, the news about what has changed in AppleScript 1.7 for Mac OS X. Mac OS X is a new operating system with radically different underpinnings from those of Mac OS 9.2.1. Because of that, AppleScript needed to change in Mac OS X to accommodate the new OS's functionalities and requirements. With the differences between AppleScript in Mac OS X and Mac OS 9.2.1, you sometimes will need to include code in your own scripts to check the version of AppleScript. See "Detecting the Current Versions of AppleScript and Mac OS" later in this chapter for a useful version-detection script.

The following list describes the differences between Mac OS X and Mac OS 9.2.1:

Placement of Scripting Additions in the file system. Mac OS X has changed the way Scripting Additions are stored and accessed. Instead of using a single Scripting Additions folder, Mac OS X has multiple directories where you can place Scripting Additions for access. System-installed additions are placed in /System/Library/ScriptingAdditions/. You cannot add any files to this directory, which is reserved for Apple's use. Figure 4.3 shows all the system-installed Scripting Additions in Mac OS 10.1. See "Scripting Additions in Mac OS X" later in this chapter for more information.

Native Mac OS X Scripting Additions. Mac OS 9.2.1 Scripting Additions themselves must be rewritten to work natively in Mac OS X, although a Mac OS X script can access these additions through the Classic environment. See "Scripting Additions in Mac OS X" later in this chapter for more information.

Location of Scripts folder. In Mac OS X, each user can have a Scripts folder located at ~/Library/Scripts/ (~ is the home directory). The Script Runner application gives you access to compiled scripts saved in your Scripts folder. See "Advantages of Script Runner" for more information.

File extensions. Mac OS X supports the use of file extensions to indicate file type. One major impact of this change is that the info for command can now return a null value for the file type property of a file, because Mac OS 9 file types are optional in Mac OS X. Script Editor supports the file-extension convention along with Classic file types for script and Scripting Addition files. A set of standard file extensions is used for script files. Refer to **Table 4.1** for a complete list.

The Finder. Yes, Virginia, there is a Finder in Mac OS X 10.1. This Finder does many of the things that the Mac OS 9 Finder did—but not all of them. Scripts written for the Mac OS 9 Finder may need to be changed to work in Mac OS X. The computer class, for example, has been removed from the Finder's dictionary and replaced by the new System Attribute command in the Standard Additions OSAX. Some commands remain in the Finder dictionary in Mac OS X 10.1 but actually are carried out by other applications. **Figure 4.4** shows an example of some of the terminology in the new Mac OS X 10.1 Finder Legacy Suite.

Figure 4.4 The Finder's dictionary in Mac OS X 10.1 includes the Legacy suite.

Table 4.1

Standard AppleScript File Extensions in Mac OS X	
EXTENSION	**FILE DESCRIPTION**
.scpt	Compiled script
.applescript	Uncompiled text-only script
.app	Applets and droplets
.osax	Mac OS X Scripting Addition
.asdictionary	Mac OS X application dictionary file

Table 4.2

Scriptable Mac OS 9 System Components Not in Mac OS X

COMPONENT	COMMENT
AirPort Scripting	Available for Mac OS 9.2.1 in AirPort 1.3 upgrade
Apple Data Detectors	Not available in Mac OS X 10.1
Apple Menu Options	Not available in Mac OS X 10.1
Application Switcher	Not available in Mac OS X 10.1
ColorSync	Provided as ColorSync-Scripting application in Mac OS X 10.1
Desktop Printing Manager	Print Center has some scriptability in version 10.1 of Mac OS X
File Exchange	Not available in Mac OS X 10.1
File Sharing	Not available in Mac OS X 10.1
FileSharing Commands	File sharing can be started from the command line
Folder Actions	Not available in Mac OS X 10.1
FontSync Extension	Provided as the FontSync-Scripting application in Mac OS X 10.1
FontSync	Provided as the FontSync-Scripting application in Mac OS X 10.1
Keyboard Addition	No scripting access to these functions in Mac OS X 10.1
Keychain Scripting	No scripting access to these functions in Mac OS X 10.1
Location Manager	Not available in Mac OS X 10.1
Memory	Not available in Mac OS X 10.1
MonitorDepth	Use QuickTime Player for similar functionality
Mouse	Not available in Mac OS X 10.1
Network Setup Scripting	Some functions can be performed from Internet Connect or the command line
Sound Scripting	No sound support except for setvolume in Mac OS X 10.1
Speech Listener	Not available in Mac OS X 10.1
Startup Disk	Not available in Mac OS X 10.1

Scriptable operating-system components. Mac OS X has no control panels, extensions, or many other of the scriptable operating-system components you grew used to in Mac OS 9. The new System Preferences application is not scriptable. Network Setup Scripting is not available; neither is the scriptable Desktop Printing Manager. Expect to see more Mac OS X system components gain AppleScript support in coming releases. Until then, you'll need to find other ways of scripting the operating system.

Several Mac OS X Scripting Additions are already available that offer access to the Unix command line to execute shell commands. For now, these additions are your only recourse for scripting many OS settings. **Table 4.2** shows a partial list of scriptable Mac OS 9 system components that are no longer available in Mac OS X.

WHAT IS DIFFERENT?

Launching script applets at startup.
The Mac OS 9 Startup Items folder does not exist in Mac OS X. Use the Login pane of the System Preferences application to add your applet to the Login Items tab. **Figure 4.5** shows the Login Items tab.

Access to Unix from AppleScript (and vice versa). Mac OS X is based on Unix, which has a command line from which you can execute many powerful built-in system utility programs. Mac OS X provides a way for you to run scripts from the command line. Third-party developers have already released Mac OS X Scripting Additions that provide the means to access the Unix command line. See "Using a Scripting Addition or Terminal to Access Unix Commands" later in this chapter for more information.

Toolbar scripts instead of folder-action scripts. The Mac OS X 10.1 Finder does not support folder actions, although the Folder Action suite remains in the Standard Additions Scripting Addition. Instead, the Finder in Mac OS 10.1 lets you drag script applets and droplets into the toolbar.

Print Center. Desktop Printers are gone, but Print Center supports basic scripting. Existing printers and their jobs can be accessed via scripts, as well as the current printer.

Program linking SOAP and XML-RPC servers with Internet Services. The advanced capabilities of remote Web services are available to your AppleScripts for free in Mac OS X 10.1.

Figure 4.5 The Login System Preferences pane includes the Login Items tab. This tab is where you add and remove items that you want to open at startup, including scripts and applications.

TextEdit. SimpleText stays back in Mac OS 9.2.1, and Mac OS X 10.1 gets a scriptable text editor: TextEdit. Mac OS X comes with a very scriptable text editor that supports plain-text and Rich Text (RTF) formats.

AppleScript support in Cocoa. Cocoa applications have built-in AppleScript support. Because this support is standard, scripting behavior and limitations typically are the same across Cocoa applications. See Apple's notes on changes in AppleScript 1.7 for more details on Cocoa scripting issues at www.apple.com/applescript.

Changes in the item **class.** The Finder in Mac OS X 10.1 can access invisible Mac OS X system directories only with the item class, as follows:

```
tell application "Finder" to set ¬
myRef to item "etc" of the startup ¬
disk as alias
```

More Finder changes. The Finder in Mac OS X 10.1 behaves differently from the Mac OS 9 Finder. The following line will not work in Mac OS X but does in Mac OS 9:

```
tell application "Finder" to set ¬
myRef to move myAlias to Trash
```

See Apple's notes on changes in AppleScript 1.7 for more details on Cocoa scripting issues at www.apple.com/applescript.

Full-power development with AppleScript Studio. With the new AppleScript Studio, scripters can use AppleScript in Apple's complete development suite: Interface Builder and Project Builder.

Detecting the Current Versions of AppleScript and Mac OS

In the world of Mac OS X, your script may run in several environments:

◆ AppleScript in Mac OS X

◆ AppleScript in the Mac OS X Classic environment

◆ AppleScript in Mac OS 9.2.1 or earlier

Because the dictionaries of the Finder and many system components differ between Mac OS X and Mac OS 9.2.1, your script may need to know which environment it is running in. **Script 4.1** demonstrates a handler that determines whether it is running in Mac OS X, the Classic environment in Mac OS X, or Mac OS 9.2.1 or earlier.

Figures 4.6, 4.7, and **4.8** show the dialog box displayed by the script in each environment.

To determine whether a script is running in Mac OS X, Classic, or Mac OS 9.2.1:

1. `try`

   You start with a `try` statement to catch any errors. This statement is particularly useful in this script, because the next line will generate an error in the Classic environment.

2. `tell application "Finder" to set ¬ myMacOSVersion to computer "sysv"`

   Now you ask either Mac OS 9.2.1 or Mac OS X for the OS version.

3. `if myMacOSVersion ≥ 4096 then`

   If the value returned is greater than or equal to 4096, you are in Mac OS X. If the value is greater than or equal to 4112, you are in Mac OS X version 10.1 or later.

Script 4.1 This script determines whether it is running in Mac OS X, Mac OS 9, or the Classic environment

```
try
tell application "Finder" to set ¬
myMacOSVersion to computer "sysv"
if myMacOSVersion ≥ 4096 then
display dialog "You are running this script ¬
from Mac OS X." buttons {"OK"}
else
display dialog "You are running this script ¬
from Mac OS 9.x or earlier." buttons {"OK"}
    end if
on error
    display dialog "You are running this ¬
script from the Classic environment in Mac OS ¬
X." buttons {"OK"}
end try
```

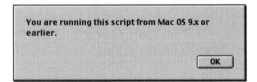

Figure 4.6 The script shows this dialog box when it detects that it is running in Mac OS X.

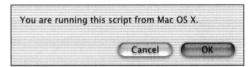

Figure 4.7 The script shows this dialog box when it detects that it is running in the Classic environment in Mac OS X.

Figure 4.8 The script shows this dialog box when it detects that it is running in Mac OS 9 or earlier.

4. `display dialog "You are running this ¬`
`script from Mac OS X." buttons {"OK"}`

You let the user know that the script is running in Mac OS X or later and therefore is using AppleScript 1.7 or later.

5. `else`

If the value is less than 4096, you're in Mac OS 9.x or earlier.

6. `display dialog "You are running this ¬`
`script from Mac OS 9.x or earlier." ¬`
`buttons {"OK"}`
`    end if`

A dialog box announces the OS used.

7. `on error`
`    display dialog "You are running ¬`
`this script from the Classic ¬`
`environment in Mac OS X." buttons {"OK"}`
`end try`

Because the Classic environment does not have access to the new Mac OS X Standard Additions System Attribute object, and because the computer object class has been removed from the Mac OS X Finder, any script run from within the Classic environment will generate an error when you try to set myMacOSVersion. Therefore, you can presume that you are running in Classic environment if an error occurs.

Scripting Additions in Mac OS X

You should know some basics about Scripting Additions in Mac OS X:

◆ Scripting Additions need to be designed to work natively with Mac OS X.

◆ Scripting Additions can be stored in several places on a Mac OS X machine, providing different user access levels.

◆ Older Scripting Additions will work only through the Classic environment. **Script 4.2** demonstrates how to use a Classic Scripting Addition from Mac OS X.

To add a Mac OS X Scripting Addition that all users can access on a machine:

1. Place Scripting Additions that you want to add for all users of a specific machine in /Library/ScriptingAdditions/.

2. Open the Library folder.

3. If a folder named ScriptingAdditions does not exist, create it.

4. Drag the new Mac OS X Scripting Addition into the ScriptingAdditions folder.

   Figure 4.9 shows the expanded folder with two additions.

Script 4.2 This handler contains a Classic Scripting Addition command within a `tell` statement targeting the Classic application Apple Guide. Write this script in the Classic Script Editor.

```
on oldReplaceOSAX(myfind, myreplace, mystring)
tell application "Apple Guide"
set mystring to ACME replace myfind with ¬
myreplace in mystring
Quit
    end tell
return mystring
end oldReplaceOSAX
```

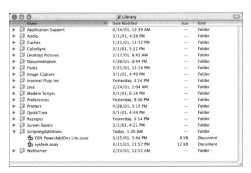

Figure 4.9 The local machine's ScriptingAdditions folder (/Library/ScriptingAdditions/) contains Scripting Additions that are available to all users.

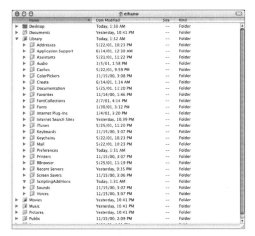

Figure 4.10 An individual user's ScriptingAdditions folder, shown here without any contents. The user's ScriptingAdditions folder resides inside the Library folder.

To add a Mac OS X Scripting Addition that a single user can access:

1. Place Scripting Additions that you want to add for a single user in that user's own Library folder (~/Library/ScriptingAdditions, in which ~ is the home directory inside of /Users/).

2. Open the user's home folder.

3. Open the Library folder inside the user's home folder.

4. If a folder named ScriptingAdditions does not exist, create it.

5. Drag one ore more Mac OS X Scripting Additions into the folder.

   Figure 4.10 shows the expanded folder with no Scripting Additions in it.

Script 4.3 in the following section demonstrates how to access the dictionaries of installed Classic scripting additions. To do so, you need to enclose the Classic Scripting Addition commands inside a `tell` block targeting a Classic application. You will also use the Classic Script Editor and the Mac OS X Script Editor to complete the scripting, as well as the ACME Script Widgets 2.5.2 Scripting Addition.

To use Classic Scripting Addition commands from a Mac OS X script:

1. `on oldReplaceOSAX(myfind, myreplace, ¬ mystring)`

   Start the handler in the Classic Script Editor while running Mac OS X or Mac OS 9 to get access to the Scripting Addition's dictionary terminology. If you omit this step, you'll have to write raw Apple Event codes (**Figure 4.11**), because the Mac OS X Script Editor does not have ready access to the terminology of Classic additions.

   This handler has three values passed to it. The handler receives a string to search for, a string to replace the search string with, and the full string to search and return modified.

2. `tell application "Apple Guide"`

   You need to put your Scripting Addition command inside a `tell` block that addresses a Classic application to get access the commands of any Classic Scripting Addition. I use Apple Guide because it is a faceless Classic application that launches quickly. Be sure to have the Classic environment launched before using any scripts that call Classic applications or additions.

3. `set mystring to ACME replace myfind ¬ with myreplace in mystring`

   Now the `mystring` variable is assigned to the result of the ACME Script Widgets Scripting Addition command `ACME replace`, which does the work for you.

4. `Quit`
   `    end tell`

Figure 4.11 The Classic Scripting Addition command, `ACME replace`, is displayed as Apple Event codes in the Mac OS X Script Editor because it cannot access the terminology of Classic additions.

Script 4.3 Uses handler written to call Classic Scripting Addition from Mac OS X. Add the main part of the script in the Mac OS X Script Editor and run it from there.

```
set myInput to text returned of (display ¬
dialog "Input string" default answer "A's ¬
become B's")
set myOutput to oldReplaceOSAX("A", "B", ¬
myInput)
display dialog myOutput
on oldReplaceOSAX(myfind, myreplace, mystring)
tell application "Apple Guide"
set mystring to ACME replace myfind with ¬
myreplace in mystring
Quit
    end tell
return mystring
end oldReplaceOSAX
```

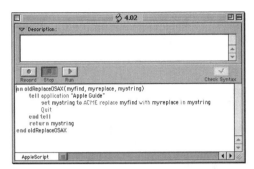

Figure 4.12 The handler shown in this window, written in the Classic Script Editor, calls a Classic Scripting Addition command, ACME replace.

Figure 4.13 The Mac OS X script prompts the user to enter a string to be modified by the Classic addition's string-replacement command.

Figure 4.14 The Mac OS X script shows the result of the ACME replace command from the Classic Scripting Addition ACME Script Widgets.

Using ACME Script Widgets

This script requires the Scripting Addition ACME Script Widgets. You must have ACME Script Widgets installed in your ScriptingAdditions folder for this script to work.

ACME Script Widgets is shareware. It costs $29 for a single-user license.

ACME Script Widgets is published by ACME Technologies (http://www.acmetech.com/).

You quit Apple Guide.

5. `return mystring`
`end oldReplaceOSAX`

The handler returns the updated string value in the mystring variable before ending.

When you are done, your script should look like the one in **Figure 4.12.** Save the script in the Classic Script Editor and close it before opening the Mac OS X Script Editor and continuing.

6. `set myInput to text returned of ¬`
`(display dialog "Input string" ¬`
`default answer "A's become B's")`

You add some code in the Mac OS X Script Editor. In this example, prompt the user for a string to be modified.

7. `set myOutput to oldReplaceOSAX("A", ¬`
`"B", myInput)`

Next, the handler that invokes the Classic Scripting Addition is called. The returned value is stored in the myOutput variable.

8. `display dialog myOutput`

A dialog box displays the updated text.

9. Run this script from the Mac OS X Script Editor to see screens like **Figures 4.13** and **4.14**.

Notice in the script window that the Mac OS X Script Editor displays the raw Apple Event codes for the Classic Scripting Addition command.

Life with File Suffixes and Path Delimiters

The file system itself has changed in Mac OS X to include the concept of domains. Domains relates to the file system and user permissions. The path to command has been updated to include a new from modifier that lets you request paths to special folders based on the domain. You can get file paths for special folders, such as the ScriptingAdditions folder for a user, for the whole machine, or for the system. **Figure 4.15** shows the dictionary entry for the Standard Additions path to command.

The new world of Mac OS X includes a different kind of file path from the one you've all grown used to: the Unix, or POSIX, file path with forward slash (/) delimiters (/System/Library). In AppleScript, however, the new file paths are not used; the traditional Macintosh file paths with colon (:) delimiters are still used for aliases and file specifications. **Script 4.4** shows how to get POSIX file paths for a file by using the system Scripting Addition for Mac OS X.

To get the POSIX file path for a file selected by the user:

1. `set myFile to choose file`

   Start by prompting the user to select a file, and store a reference to the file in the myFile variable.

2. `set myPosixFilepath to PosixPath ¬`
   `myFile`

   Next, use the system Scripting Addition command PosixPath to convert the alias reference stored in the myFile variable. You need to have installed the system.osax Scripting Addition file in ~/Library/ScriptingAdditions/ or /Library/ScriptingAdditions/ before starting.

Figure 4.15 The Mac OS X Standard Additions path to command's terminology includes a from modifier to allow you to access the paths of special folders in different user domains.

Script 4.4 Displays the POSIX and Mac file paths to a user-selected file. Requires the free third-party System Scripting Addition for Mac OS X.

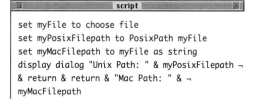

```
set myFile to choose file
set myPosixFilepath to PosixPath myFile
set myMacFilepath to myFile as string
display dialog "Unix Path: " & myPosixFilepath ¬
& return & return & "Mac Path: " & ¬
myMacFilepath
```

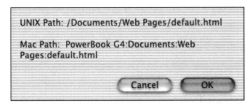

Figure 4.16 The script displays this dialog box, showing the POSIX file path and the Mac file path for the file chosen by the user.

Script 4.5

```
set myFile to choose file
tell application "Finder" to set myExtension ¬
to name extension of myFile
display dialog myExtension
```

3. `set myMacFilepath to myFile as string`

Now convert the file alias to a string.

4. `display dialog "Unix Path: " & ¬`
`myPosixFilepath & return & return & ¬`
`"Mac Path: " & myMacFilepath`

Finally, show both POSIX and Mac file paths to the same file in a dialog box. **Figure 4.16** shows a sample.

In Finder 10.1, you can access file extension attributes by using the `name extension` property of an item. **Script 4.5** demonstrates how easy it is to access the file extension of a file from the Finder.

✔ Tip

- When using the `info for` command, your scripts need to be ready to encounter missing file types, because Mac OS X doesn't require each file to have a creator and file type. File extensions such as .jpg and .txt are used in Mac OS X in place of file types and creator codes.

Using the System Scripting Addition

The System Scripting Addition was created by Hideaki Iimori. It is freeware. Visit `http://www.bekkoame.ne.jp/~iimori/` for more information.

Scripting Addition Global Context Supported in Mac OS X 10.1

In versions of Mac OS X before 10.1, terms that belonged to Scripting Additions were not handled within tell blocks as expected. In Mac OS X 10.1, terms that belong to Scripting Additions are once again handled by most applications inside tell blocks, so simple behaviors such as displaying a dialog box within a scriptable application will work in Mac OS X 10.1 as it does in Mac OS 9. Practically speaking, upgrade to Mac OS X 10.1.

Script 4.6 provides a simple demonstration of how user interaction dialog boxes are shown in the script's window layer, in versions of Mac OS X before 10.1.

Figure 4.17 shows the script running in the Script Editor behind GraphicConverter, waiting for the user to bring the script to the front for the display dialog command.

Run the following script on a Macintosh using a version of Mac OS X before 10.1.

To see how user-interaction commands show dialog boxes behind the frontmost application in versions of Mac OS X before 10.1:

◆
```
tell application "GraphicConverter"
    activate
    display dialog "Continue?"
end tell
```
This script launches an application and brings it to the front before invoking the display dialog command, which will show up behind the application's windows. Run this script from the Mac OS X Script Editor to see how the dialog box comes up in the Script Editor behind the GraphicConverter program.

Script 4.6 This simple script demonstrates how Scripting Addition commands are run in the context of the script itself and not in applications when run in Mac OS X versions before 10.1

```
tell application "GraphicConverter"
    activate
    display dialog "Continue?"
end tell
```

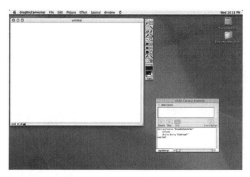

Figure 4.17 The script is running from Script Editor and waiting to be brought to the front by the user so that the dialog box can be shown.

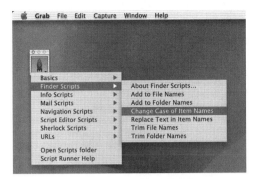

Figure 4.18 The Script Runner palette with a script selected from the menu.

Figure 4.19 A script launched from Script Runner runs in front of all applications.

ScriptMenu.menu

Figure 4.20 The brilliant new ScriptMenu menu extension from Apple can be dragged to your menu bar in Mac OS X 10.1 to add a system-level script menu to your Mac.

Using Script Runner and ScriptMenu

Mac OS X 10.1 provides two useful Apple-Script user interface enhancements: Script Runner and ScriptMenu. **Figure 4.18** shows the Script Runner palette opened by the user. Script Runner has permanent frontmost status in Mac OS X, so any script launched from Script Runner runs in front of whatever application is currently frontmost. **Figure 4.19** shows a script's dialog box floating on top of the GraphicConverter application, thanks to Script Runner.

In addition to Script Runner's palette, Mac OS X 10.1 gives you the ScriptMenu, which replaces the functionality provided in Mac OS 9 by Leonard Rosenthol's OSA Menu extension. To use ScriptMenu, download it from Apple's AppleScript site at http://www.apple.com/applescript. Installing ScriptMenu is easy; simply drag the ScriptMenu.menu file onto your menu bar in the Finder. The Script Menu icon will appear immediately. It shows all the scripts contained in both the Library/Scripts folder and the user's ~/Library/Scripts folder. ScriptMenu displays and runs AppleScript scripts, as well as Perl and shell scripts. Congratulations are due to Apple for providing this great AppleScript enhancement in Mac OS X 10.1.

Figure 4.20 shows the ScriptMenu.menu file that you drag onto your menu bar to enable ScriptMenu.

✔ Tip

■ Script Runner is located in the AppleScript folder inside your Applications folder.

Using a Scripting Addition or Terminal to Access Unix Commands

Several free and shareware Scripting Additions for Mac OS X give your scripts access to the Unix command line. In this section, you will explore the System Scripting Addition (system.osax) and some basic uses of the special system command that the Scripting Addition provides. This command provides interactive access to Unix command-line commands, with Unix-command-generated output returned to the script.

Script 4.7 uses the Unix uptime command to display interesting status information about the local machine.

To display system statistics from the Unix uptime command:

1. `set mySystemOnStats to system "uptime"`

   Start by assigning the output of the Unix uptime command to your AppleScript variable mySystemOnStats.

2. `say mySystemOnStats`

   Next, have the system speak the output text from uptime.

3. `display dialog mySystemOnStats`

   Finish by displaying the output in a dialog box. **Figure 4.21** shows an example.

Script 4.8 uses the Unix nslookup command to provide domain-name service information for machine host names, such as www.apple.com.

Script 4.7 Uses the System OSAX to get system statistics from the Unix uptime command, speak them, and display them to the user.

```
set mySystemOnStats to system "uptime"
say mySystemOnStats
display dialog mySystemOnStats
```

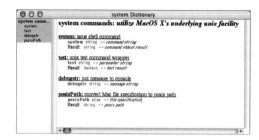

Figure 4.21 The result of the Unix uptime command.

Script 4.8 Uses the System OSAX to resolve host names with the Unix nslookup command.

```
set myHostname to text returned of (display ¬
dialog "Enter hostname to lookup:" default ¬
answer "www.apple.com")
if myHostname ≠ "" then
set myDNSResults to (system "nslookup " & ¬
myHostname)
display dialog paragraph 5 of myDNSResults & ¬
return & paragraph 6 of myDNSResults
end if
```

ACCESSING UNIX COMMANDS

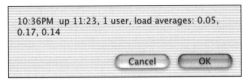

Figure 4.22 The result of the query to the Unix nslookup command displayed in a dialog box.

Using the System Scripting Addition

The System OSAX was created by Hideaki Iimori. It is freeware. Visit http://www.bekkoame.ne.jp/~iimori/ for more information.

Scripting the Terminal Application in Mac OS X 10.1

The Terminal application, located in your Utilities folder, supports basic scripting in version 10.1 of Mac OS X. Try this sample script:

```
tell application "Terminal" to do
script with command "date"
```

To resolve the IP address of a host name with the Unix nslookup command:

1. `set myHostname to text returned of ¬`
   `(display dialog "Enter hostname to ¬`
   `lookup:" default answer "www.apple.com")`

   Start by prompting the user to enter a host name to look up. A default value is shown.

2. `if myHostname ≠ "" then`

   If the user has entered anything, the script continues execution.

3. `set myDNSResults to (system ¬`
   `"nslookup " & myHostname)`

   Using the `system` command from the System Scripting Addition, you invoke the Unix `nslookup` command, passing it the host name entered by the user. The result of the command is returned in the `myDNSResults` variable.

4. `display dialog paragraph 5 of ¬`
   `myDNSResults & return & paragraph 6 ¬`
   `of myDNSResults`
   `end if`

   The IP address and host name of the response typically are in the fifth and sixth lines of the output returned from nslookup, so the script displays these two lines. **Figure 4.22** shows how the dialog box looks for a lookup on the default host, www.apple.com.

ACCESSING UNIX COMMANDS

Scheduling Scripts with cron and osascript

Now that you have the power of Unix inside your operating system, you can take advantage of it. Mac OS X features some basic, but useful, Unix command-line commands that provide access to AppleScript from Unix. The commands include:

> osascript. This command executes a compiled AppleScript file from the command line or cron. **Figure 4.23** shows the Unix man page for osascript.

> osacompile. This command lets you create compiled scripts from text.

> osalang. This command prints information about OSA languages.

You can run any of these commands from the Terminal application directly, or you can schedule the running of your own scripts by using the Unix cron utility and the osascript command.

To schedule a saved compiled script to run automatically with cron every hour:

1. Open the Terminal application (**Figure 4.24**).

   Terminal is located in the Utilities folder inside your Applications folder.

2. At the prompt in the open Terminal window, type:

   sudo pico /etc/crontab

   The system will prompt you to enter your password.

3. Enter the password, and press Return.

   Figure 4.25 shows what the password prompt should look like in the Terminal window.

Figure 4.23 The man-page entry for the Unix osascript command.

Figure 4.24 The Utilities folder, with the Terminal application selected.

Figure 4.25 The Terminal session showing the entry of the first command and the prompt for a password.

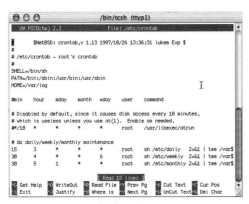

Figure 4.26 The pico editing session with the unedited /etc/crontab file displayed.

Figure 4.27 The pico editing session for /etc/crontab with your new line added.

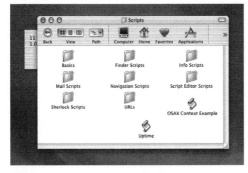

Figure 4.28 A dialog box displayed by a script run from cron and osascript is shown behind all other open windows.

After you enter the password, your Terminal window should look like **Figure 4.26.** The cron configuration file, /etc/crontab, is open.

4. Using the arrow keys, move the insertion point below the last line of the file.

5. Type the following to make your script run at 20 minutes past the hour, every hour:

   20 Tab * Tab * Tab * Tab * Tab root ¬
   Tab /usr/bin/osascript Tab

6. Enter the POSIX path to your compiled script file that you want to run.

   In the example in **Figure 4.27**, this path was /Users/ethanw/Library/Scripts/Uptime.

7. After you type your path, press Control-X to exit.

8. Type y to save the modified /etc/crontab file.

9. Quit the Terminal program.

✔ Tips

- Modifying Unix system files such as /etc/crontab is very serious business. Be careful that you don't delete any portion of the existing configuration file when you modify it.

- The osascript command doesn't allow all compiled scripts to run without flaw. Scripts with user-interaction commands have context problems, such as dialog boxes staying behind all other open windows (**Figure 4.28**).

- When you use the Terminal program, you can find out more about cron by typing man cron.

Adding Scripts to the Finder's Toolbar

The Finder in Mac OS X 10.1 supports an innovative new user-interface feature for accessing AppleScript applets and droplets. This feature is called Toolbar Scripts. The name sums it up. You can drag any applet or droplet onto your Finder's toolbar to place it there and remove it by Command-dragging it off the toolbar. I recommend that you keep all your Toolbar Scripts files in a common folder. I put mine in my Scripts folder. **Figure 4.29** shows the applet file in my Scripts folder and on my toolbar, ready to use. **Figure 4.30** shows what happens when the Finder can't find a Toolbar Script's original file.

The functionality of Toolbar Scripts helps make up for Mac OS X's lack of folder-action script support. **Script 4.9** shows a sample Toolbar Script that archives the frontmost Finder folder, adding the user name and date.

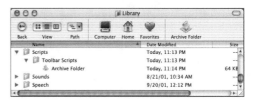

Figure 4.29 The Toolbar Scripts applet file Archive Folder appear current user's Scripts folder and toolbar, ready to use.

Figure 4.30 The Finder Toolbar shows a question-mark icon when a Toolbar Script's original file cannot be found.

Script 4.9 This script archives the frontmost Finder window in another folder.

```
                        script
on run
    set {myname, mypath} to frontWindowPath()
    if button returned of (display dialog ¬
    "Archive '" & myname & "'?") is "OK" then
    set myarchive to (choose folder with prompt ¬
    "Select folder to archive into")
    set myuser to characters 1 thru -2 of ¬
    (system "whoami") as string
    set mydate to year of (current date) & "-" & ¬
    getMonthNumber(current date) & "-" & day of ¬
    (current date) as string
    set mynewname to myname & "_" & mydate & "_" ¬
    & myuser
    tell application "Finder"
            set mynewarchive to duplicate alias ¬
    mypath to folder myarchive
            set name of mynewarchive to mynewname
        end tell
    end if
end run
on getMonthNumber(anydate)
    set mymonthnum to 0
    repeat with mymonth in {January, February, ¬
    March, April, May, June, July, August, ¬
    September, October, November, December}
        set mymonthnum to mymonthnum + 1
        if month of anydate is mymonth then ¬
    exit repeat
    end repeat
    return mymonthnum
end getMonthNumber
on frontWindowPath()
    tell application "Finder"
        set myfolderpath to target of front ¬
    Finder window as alias
        set myfoldername to name of myfolderpath
    end tell
    return {myfoldername, myfolderpath as ¬
    string}
end frontWindowPath
```

To archive the frontmost Finder window's folder:

1. `on run`

    `set {myname, mypath} to frontWindowPath()`

    The script starts by getting the name and path of the folder in the frontmost Finder window.

2. `if button returned of (display dialog ¬ "Archive '" & myname & "'?") is "OK" ¬ then`

    The user is prompted to decide whether to archive the folder. If the user clicks the OK button, the following steps are executed.

3. `set myarchive to (choose folder with ¬ prompt "Select folder to archive into")`

    Now the user chooses a folder in which to save the archived folder.

4. `set myuser to characters 1 thru -2 ¬ of (system "whoami") as string`

    The script uses the System Scripting Additions system command to issue a Unix whoami command and return the current short user name.

5. `set mydate to year of (current date) ¬ & "-" & getMonthNumber(current date) ¬ & "-" & day of (current date) as string`

    Now it is time to format a date string, using the getMonthNumber handler.

6. `set mynewname to myname & "_" & ¬ mydate & "_" & myuser`

    Next, a new file name is assembled in the mynewname variable.

continues on next page

7.
```
tell application "Finder"
   set mynewarchive to duplicate ¬
alias mypath to folder myarchive
   set name of mynewarchive to ¬
mynewname
end tell
```
It's time to talk to the Finder and have it duplicate the frontmost Finder folder in the archive folder and rename the new folder.

8.
```
end if
end run
```
The if statement is closed and the run handler ended.

9.
```
on getMonthNumber(anydate)
   set mymonthnum to 0
   repeat with mymonth in {January, ¬
February, March, April, May, June, ¬
July, August, September, October, ¬
November, December}
      set mymonthnum to mymonthnum + 1
      if month of anydate is mymonth ¬
then exit repeat
   end repeat
   return mymonthnum
end getMonthNumber
```
This handler receives a date value and returns an integer matching the month of the date (3 for March, for example).

10.
```
on frontWindowPath()
   tell application "Finder"
      set myfolderpath to target of ¬
front Finder window as alias
      set myfoldername to name of ¬
myfolderpath
   end tell
   return {myfoldername, myfolderpath ¬
as string}
end frontWindowPath
```
This handler gets the path to the frontmost Finder window's folder and returns the name and path of the folder in a list.

Script 4.10 This script lets the user choose a new default printer from a list of installed printers

```
tell application "Print Center"
    set myprinternames to name of every printer
set mydefaultprinter to current printer
set mydefaultprintername to name of ¬
mydefaultprinter
end tell
set myprinter to (choose from list ¬
myprinternames with prompt "Set new default ¬
printer" default items {mydefaultprintername}) ¬
as string
try
    tell application "Print Center"
        repeat with i from 1 to count of items ¬
in myprinternames
            if name of printer i = myprinter then
                set current printer to ¬
printer i
                exit repeat
            end if
        end repeat
        quit
    end tell
end try
```

Figure 4.31 The main Print List window of Print Center displays all installed printers.

Figure 4.32 The user is prompted to choose a new current printer.

Setting the Default Printer with Print Center

Mac OS X 10.1's Print Center provides access to all printers and jobs, including the default printer, known as `current printer` in Print Center's dictionary. **Script 4.10** lets the user choose a new default printer from a list of installed printers.

Figure 4.31 shows how Print Center's Print List window looks on the machine running the script. **Figure 4.32** shows the list displayed by **Script 4.10** when it prompts the user to select a new default printer.

To change the current printer with Print Center:

1. `tell application "Print Center"`
   `    set myprinternames to name of ¬`
   `every printer`

   The script starts by getting a list that contains the name of every printer installed in Print Center.

2. `set mydefaultprinter to current ¬`
   `printer`

   Next, the default printer object is stored in `mydefaultprinter` for later use.

3. `set mydefaultprintername to name of ¬`
   `mydefaultprinter`
   `end tell`

   The script retrieves the name of the default printer, using the printer object in `mydefaultprinter`.

4. `set myprinter to (choose from list ¬`
   `myprinternames with prompt "Set new ¬`
   `default printer" default items ¬`
   `{mydefaultprintername}) as string`

   Prompt the user with a list of available printer names. The script preselects the current printer name with `default items`.

continues on next page

5.
```
try
   tell application "Print Center"
      repeat with i from 1 to count ¬
of items in myprinternames
         if name of printer i = ¬
myprinter then
            set current printer to ¬
printer i
            exit repeat
         end if
      end repeat
      quit
   end tell
end try
```

The script loops through all available printer names until the name matching the user selection is found. When the desired name is found, that printer is made the current printer by an index reference. Print Center quits when everything else finishes.

Script 4.11 This script uses the simple XML-RPC protocol to call a publicly available spelling checker CGI that has a XML-RPC gateway

```
set myphrase to text returned of (display ¬
dialog "Spell check this phrase" default ¬
answer "Orangees and Aples")
set mycorrectphrase to ""
repeat with myword in every word of myphrase
set myfinalword to spelledright(myword)
if myfinalword = "" then
        set mycorrectphrase to mycorrectphrase ¬
& myword & " "
else
        set mycorrectphrase to mycorrectphrase ¬
& myfinalword & " "
    end if
end repeat
display dialog mycorrectphrase
on spelledright(anyword)
set myChoice to ""
tell application
"http://www.stuffeddog.com/speller/¬
speller-rpc.cgi"
        set mySpellCheckResults to call xmlrpc ¬
{method name:"speller.spellCheck", ¬
parameters:{anyword, {}}}
    end tell
if mySpellCheckResults ≠ "" then
        set myChoice to (choose from list ¬
(suggestions of item 1 of mySpellCheckResults) ¬
with prompt "Spelling for '" & anyword & "'")
        if class of myChoice is not list then ¬
set myChoice to ""
    end if
return myChoice
end spelledright
```

Access the World of Internet Services

Starting with AppleScript 1.7 in Mac OS X 10.1, scripts have access to the growing world of Web-based services on the Internet. Two new functions, call soap and call xmlrpc, give AppleScript scripts the capability to access Perl scripts and database CGIs that provide XML-RPC or SOAP gateways.

XML-RPC is a protocol that uses XML to make remote procedure HTTP calls over the Internet. SOAP (Simple Object Access Protocol) is a protocol designed for exchanging information in a distributed environment, in which a server may consist of a hierarchy of objects with methods and properties.

To begin using these new functions, you should be familiar with XML-RPC and SOAP. The XML-RPC specification is described at http://www.xmlrpc.com/spec. The SOAP specification is available at http://www.w3.org/TR.

Script 4.11 demonstrates the power of using these new protocols from your scripts.

Figures 4.33 and **4.34** show the dialog boxes displayed by the spelling checking of Script 4.11.

To check the spelling of a phrase with an Internet-based spelling CGI:

1. `set myphrase to text returned of ¬`
   `(display dialog "Spell check this ¬`
   `phrase" default answer "Orangees ¬`
   `and Aples")`

   First, the user is prompted to enter a phrase to spelling check.

2. `set mycorrectphrase to ""`

   A variable is initialized to hold the correctly spelled phrase.

3. `repeat with myword in every word of ¬`
   `myphrase`

   A loop is started to cycle through every word in the phrase to spelling check.

4. `set myfinalword to`
   `spelledright(myword)`

   The `spelledright` handler is called to get the correct spelling for the current word.

5. `if myfinalword = "" then`
   `    set mycorrectphrase to ¬`
   `mycorrectphrase & myword & " "`

   If a null string is returned, the word was spelled correctly, and `myword` is appended to the `mycorrectphrase` variable.

6. `else`
   `    set mycorrectphrase to ¬`
   `mycorrectphrase & myfinalword & " "`
   `end if`
   `end repeat`

   Otherwise, the word was spelled incorrectly, and `myfinalword` is appended to the `mycorrectphrase` variable.

7. `display dialog mycorrectphrase`

   The correctly spelled phrase is shown in a dialog box.

Figure 4.33 The script prompts the user to enter a phrase to spelling check.

Figure 4.34 The script offers a list of possible correct spellings provided by the spelling checking CGI.

8. `on spelledright(anyword)`

The `spelledright` handler takes one string argument.

9. `set myChoice to ""`

This handler returns the `myChoice` variable.

10. `tell application "http://www.stuffed¬dog.com/speller/speller-rpc.cgi"`
    `set mySpellCheckResults to call ¬`
`xmlrpc {method`
`name:"speller.spellCheck", ¬`
`parameters:{anyword, {}}}`
`end tell`

The spelling checker CGI is called at `http://www.stuffeddog.com`. A method and parameter are passed to the CGI with the `call xmlrpc` function. The parameter is the word to check.

11. `if mySpellCheckResults ≠ "" then`
    `set myChoice to (choose from list ¬`
`(suggestions of item 1 of ¬`
`mySpellCheckResults) with prompt ¬`
`"Spelling for '" & anyword & "'")`
    `if class of myChoice is not list ¬`
`then set myChoice to ""`
`end if`

If the result is a null string, the word was spelled correctly. Otherwise, the user is prompted to choose a word from a list of suggested words.

12. `return myChoice`
`end spelledright`

The handler returns the new spelling.

Figures 4.35 and **4.35** show the dialog boxes displayed by the English-to-Spanish translation of **Script 4.12**.

To translate an English phrase to Spanish using BabelFish via SOAP:

1. `property mySOAPmethod : "BabelFish"`
   `property mySOAPnamespace : ¬`
   `"urn:xmethodsBabelFish"`
   `property mySOAPaction : ¬`
   `"urn:xmethodsBabelFish#BabelFish"`
   `property myTranslationMode : "en_es"`

   This script starts by defining all the necessary SOAP values for proper operation of the BabelFish translation engine at `services.xmethods.net`.

2. `set myTranslationText to text ¬`
   `returned of (display dialog "English ¬`
   `to translate to Spanish" default ¬`
   `answer "")`

   The user is prompted for a English phrase to translate.

3. `set errFlag to false`

   An error flag variable is set up for later testing.

4. `try`
   `    tell application "http://services.¬`
   `xmethods.net:80/perl/soaplite.cgi"`
   `        set mySOAPresult to call soap ¬`
   `{method name:mySOAPmethod, method ¬`
   `namespace uri:mySOAPnamespace, ¬`
   `parameters:{translationmode:¬`
   `myTranslationMode, ¬`
   `sourcedata:myTranslationText}, ¬`
   `SOAPAction:mySOAPaction}`
   `    end tell`

   In a try block to intercept errors, the script talks to the remote Perl CGI at `services.xmethods.net` with the `call soap` function. The `call soap` function requires a `method name`, `method namespace uri`, parameters unique to each Web application, and a `SOAPaction`.

Figure 4.35 The script prompts the user to enter an English phrase for translation.

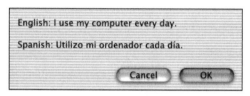

Figure 4.36 After getting results via SOAP from BabelFish, the script displays the phrase in both languages.

Script 4.12 This script uses the powerful SOAP protocol to call the BabelFish translation engine on the xMethods site.

```
                          script
property mySOAPmethod : "BabelFish"
property mySOAPnamespace : ¬
"urn:xmethodsBabelFish"
property mySOAPaction : ¬
"urn:xmethodsBabelFish#BabelFish"
property myTranslationMode : "en_es"
set myTranslationText to text returned of ¬
(display dialog "English to translate to ¬
Spanish" default answer "")
set errFlag to false
try
    tell application ¬
"http://services.xmethods.net:80/perl/soaplite.cgi"
        set mySOAPresult to call soap {method ¬
name:mySOAPmethod, method namespace ¬
uri:mySOAPnamespace, ¬
parameters:{translationmode:myTranslationMode, ¬
sourcedata:myTranslationText}, ¬
SOAPAction:mySOAPaction}
    end tell
on error errMessage number errNumber
    set errFlag to true
    if errNumber is -916 then display dialog ¬
"Could not connect to service."
end try

if not errFlag then display dialog "English: " ¬
& myTranslationText & return & return & ¬
"Spanish: " & my SOAPresult
```

Table 4.3

SITE	URL
Web Sites About XML-RPC and SOAP	
Apple's Internet Services Site	http://developer.apple.com/techpubs/macosx/Carbon/interapplicationcomm/soapXMLRPC/
Apache SOAP Site	http://xml.apache.org/soap/
IBM Web Services	http://xml.apache.org/soap/
UserLand's XML-RPC Site	http://www.xmlrpc.com/
W3C SOAP 1.1 Definition	http://www.w3.org/TR/SOAP/
WebServices.org	http://www.webservices.org/
XMethods SOAP Service List	http://www.xmethods.com/

5. ```
   on error errMessage number errNumber
       set errFlag to true
       if errNumber is -916 then display ¬
   dialog "Could not connect to service."
   end try
   ```

   If an error happens, the script checks the error number. If a connection error took place, the number matches -916, and a dialog box is displayed.

6. ```
   if not errFlag then display dialog ¬
   "English: " & myTranslationText & ¬
   return & return & "Spanish: " & ¬
   mySOAPresult
   ```

   If no error happened, a dialog box shows the phrase in both languages.

Connecting with Internet Connect

Although the Network Setup Scripting application of Mac OS 9 does not have a complete counterpart in Mac OS X 10.1, the Internet Connect application provides scriptable access to TCP/PPP and Remote Access connections. **Script 4.13** demonstrates how to use Internet Connect to make a dial-up connection to a phone number.

Figure 4.37 shows the dialog box that the script uses to prompt for a password.

To make a connection with Internet Connect:

1. `property mynumber : "415-555-1212"`
   `property myuser : "Ethan"`

   These properties set the phone number and user name to use in the dial-up connection attempt.

2. `set mypassword to text returned of ¬`
   `(display dialog "Password" default ¬`
   `answer "")`

   The script prompts the user for a password.

3. `tell application "Internet Connect"`
      `connect to telephone number ¬`
   `mynumber as user myuser with password ¬`
   `mypassword`
      `quit`
   `end tell`

   Finally, the connect command of Internet Connect makes a connection before the application quits.

Script 4.13 This script uses the Internet Connect application to make a dial-up connection.

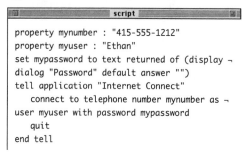

```
property mynumber : "415-555-1212"
property myuser : "Ethan"
set mypassword to text returned of (display ¬
dialog "Password" default answer "")
tell application "Internet Connect"
    connect to telephone number mynumber as ¬
user myuser with password mypassword
    quit
end tell
```

Figure 4.37 The script prompts the user for a password.

Script 4.14 This script uses the scriptable Cocoa application TextEdit to randomize the font size of each character in the current document.

```
script
tell application "TextEdit"
    if (count of documents) > 0 then
set mycharcount to count of every character ¬
of text of document 1
repeat with mycharnum from 1 to mycharcount
        set size of character mycharnum of ¬
text of document 1 to random number from 9 to 48
    end repeat
    end if
end tell
```

Figure 4.38 The current TextEdit window after Script 4.14 has run.

Scripting TextEdit for Fun

The Mac OS X application TextEdit demonstrates how Cocoa applications get AppleScript support built-in. The dictionary of TextEdit includes access to all documents and text in the application. **Script 4.14** modifies the font size of all text in the current document.

Figure 4.38 shows the TextEdit window after the script has run.

To randomize the font sizes of all characters in the current TextEdit document:

1. `tell application "TextEdit"`
   `    if (count of documents) > 0 then`

   The script tests to ensure that at least one document is open in TextEdit.

2. `set mycharcount to count of every ¬`
   `character of text of document 1`

   The number of characters in the current document is stored in `mycharcount`.

3. `repeat with mycharnum from 1 to ¬`
   `mycharcount`
   `    set size of character mycharnum of ¬`
   `text of document 1 to random number ¬`
   `from 9 to 48`
   `    end repeat`
   `    end if`
   `end tell`

   A `repeat` loop traverses the integers from 1 to `mycharcount`, setting the font size of each character at the index position `mycharnum` to a random number.

Full-Power Development with AppleScript Studio

The true power of AppleScript in Mac OS X 10.1 will be unleashed when Apple ships the new AppleScript Studio development environment. Based on Apple's sophisticated Project Builder and Interface Builder applications, AppleScript Studio integrates AppleScript development into these tools. AppleScript now becomes a development language on par with Java and Objective-C in Mac OS X.

Each AppleScript Studio project contains at least one compiled script in its bundle. All the AppleScript you could ever write can respond to a complete set of events for all the Cocoa interface elements, including menus, windows, and all window controls. Every compiled project from AppleScript Studio is a full Cocoa application.

Figure 4.39 shows the Interface Builder in AppleScript Studio with an open project named Watson. The palette in the lower-right show how easy it is to attach handlers in your AppleScripts to window object events—just choose a checkbox.

Figure 4.40 shows the Project Builder in AppleScript Studio, where you can create AppleScript scripts with sophisticated tools built into Project Builder. The handler pull-down menu in the figure shows how you can quickly jump to portions of your code. Notice some of the event-driven handlers like on clicked—these handlers will be hooked up to interface elements in Interface Builder.

Figure 4.41 shows the Project Builder's new dictionary view that lets you look up AppleScript dictionaries while you are writing your scripts inside of Project Builder.

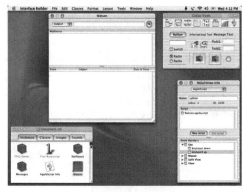

Figure 4.39 The Interface Builder portion of AppleScript Studio shows how easy it is assemble a complete Cocoa application built with AppleScript.

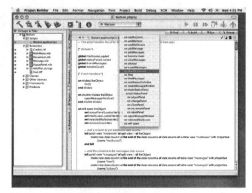

Figure 4.40 One of Interface Builder's palettes shows some of the AppleScript-enabled Cocoa user interface objects.

Figure 4.41 Another Project Builder feature in AppleScript Studio is the AppleScript dictionary viewer.

Script 4.15 This script has Sherlock find every file and folder with buddy in its name, returning its results in a window.

```
tell application "Finder"to set mydisk to ¬
home as alias
tell application "Sherlock"
    activate
search {mydisk} for "buddy" with display"
end tell
```

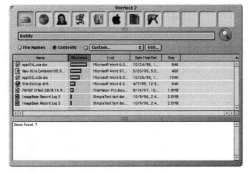

Figure 4.42 Sherlock with the results of our scripts' search.

Script 4.16 This script uses the Finder to find all files with buddy in their names in the System folder.

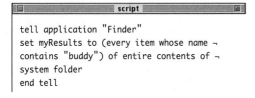

```
tell application "Finder"
set myResults to (every item whose name ¬
contains "buddy") of entire contents of ¬
system folder
end tell
```

Finding Files with Sherlock

Some of the capabilities of Sherlock are scriptable. **Script 4.15** shows you how to use Sherlock to search the content of files and folders. **Figure 4.43** shows the result of this script. **Script 4.16** shows you how to search just by file name using the Finder. Although the Finder is much slower than Sherlock, it allows you to use specific search criteria, such as file type, size, and modification date.

To search the contents of files and folders with Sherlock:

1. `tell application "Finder" to set mydisk to home as alias.`

   Get the path to the user's home directory. Change this to startup disk in Mac OS 9.

2. `tell application "Sherlock"`
   `activate`

   You begin by bringing Sherlock to the front.

3. `search {mydisk} for "buddy" with display`
   `end tell`

   Next, you have Sherlock search for files and folders with buddy in their content. By specifying with display, you have Sherlock return the results in its own window.

To search for files and folders with the Finder:

1. `tell application "Finder"`

   You begin by talking to the Finder.

2. `set myResults to (every item whose ¬`
   `name contains "buddy") of entire ¬`
   `contents of system folder`
   `end tell`

   You have the Finder return a list of every file or folder that has buddy in its name in the System folder of the startup disk. Using the Finder to search many files is slow compared with using Sherlock. It's really best to use the Finder to search only a folder or two at most. This script could take a long time to run if your startup disk has many files on it. Keep this in mind!

✔ Tip

- These scripts also work with the Mac OS 9 versions of Sherlock and the Finder.

FINDING FILES WITH SHERLOCK

Using summarize

You can employ the same cool search-indexing technology in Sherlock directly in AppleScript by using the command `summarize` to digest long strings of text into brief summaries. You can store a one-sentence summary of some text, for example, in the variable `myBlurb`:

```
set myBlurb to summarize "The long ¬
run-on sentence means nothing to me ¬
or to you or to anyone. Does it? Or ¬
does it?" in 1
```

Script 4.17 This script has Sherlock search the Web for the term buddy using its current search engine settings, returning a list of URLs to our script.

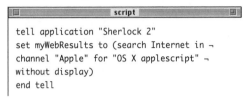

```
tell application "Sherlock 2"
set myWebResults to (search Internet in ¬
channel "Apple" for "OS X applescript" ¬
without display)
end tell
```

Figure 4.44 The Script Editor's Result window shows the list of URL strings returned from Sherlock on completion of our script's search request.

Figure 4.45 Sherlock displaying the results of our script's search of the Internet.

Searching the Internet with Sherlock

You can not only search your hard disk but also script some of the Internet capabilities of Sherlock. **Script 4.17** shows how to search the Web for a term by using Sherlock's Internet-searching capabilities.

To search the Internet with Sherlock:

1. `tell application "Sherlock"`

   First, you let AppleScript know that you want to talk to Sherlock.

2. `set myWebResults to (search Internet ¬ in channel "Apple" for "OS X ¬ applescript" without display)`

   You have Sherlock search the Internet for the term *buddy* by using its current search-engine settings. By specifying `without display`, you have Sherlock return the results to your script in the variable `myWebResults`, which will contain a list of matching URLs. **Figure 4.44** shows the result in Script Editor at this point in the script. **Figure 4.45** shows Sherlock's display if you use `with display` instead.

3. `end tell`

   Finally, you end the conversation with Sherlock.

✔ Tip

■ This script also works with the Mac OS 9 version of Sherlock.

SCRIPTING
MAC OS 9.2.1

The features of the Mac we all know and love by now are the tried-and-true traditional OS features from Mac OS 9.2.1. And in its mature state, Mac OS 9.2.1 is very scriptable. Many system features and components are accessible via AppleScript. In the arena of system customization, for example, some things can be done only via AppleScript.

Let's spend some time exploring the scriptability of the pieces of the Mac OS. I think you'll find something you'll appreciate.

Customizing the Application Switcher in Mac OS 9.2.1

The floating palette you can tear off from the Application menu is called the Application Switcher. When visible, it is a background application that is fully scriptable and highly customizable. **Script 5.1** lets the user customize the Application Switcher by choosing one of three preset styles, including the default settings for the palette. **Figure 5.1** shows the tiles preset style, while **Figure 5.2** shows the taskbar preset style.

To customize the Application Switcher:

1. `set myAnswer to button returned ¬ of (display dialog "Switch the ¬ switcher:" buttons {"tiles", "task ¬ bar", "default"})`

You begin by prompting the user to choose a new style for the Application Switcher. You store the button choice in myAnswer.

2. `tell application "Application Switcher"`
    `if myAnswer is "tiles" then`
        `set visible of palette to true`

Now you check to see whether myAnswer shows that the user chose the Tiles option. If so, you tell the Application Switcher to make the palette window visible. The other choices are handled by the code that appears after the else statement following step 9.

3. `set orientation of palette to vertical`

You set the palette to show the application tiles in a vertical column.

Script 5.1 This script lets the user customize the Application Switcher by choosing one of three preset styles, including the default settings for the palette.

```
                        script
set myAnswer to button returned of (display ¬
dialog "Switch the switcher:" buttons
{"tiles", "task bar", "default"})
tell application "Application Switcher""
    if myAnswer is "tiles" then
        set visible of palette to true
set orientation of palette to vertical
set button ordering of palette to launch order
set frame visible of palette to false
set icon size of palette to small
set names visible of palette to false
set position of palette to upper right
set anchor point of palette to upper left
```

Figure 5.1 The Application Switcher palette window after the script has been run and the Tiles setting has been selected.

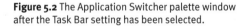

Figure 5.2 The Application Switcher palette window after the Task Bar setting has been selected.

4. `set button ordering of palette to ¬`
`launch order`

You set the sorting order of the application tiles to display in the order in which they were run.

5. `set frame visible of palette to false`

You make the palette window's frame invisible to make the palette smaller.

6. `set icon size of palette to small`

This code sets the size of the application icons in their tiles to small.

7. `set names visible of palette to false`

Here, you make the application names in the tiles invisible.

8. `set position of palette to upper right`

You set the palette's position to the top-right corner of the screen, right below the Application menu icon.

9. `set anchor point of palette to upper left`

Finally, you set the anchor point of the palette window to the top-left corner, so that as new applications are launched, the palette gets longer by extending down.

Customizing Appearance in Mac OS 9.2.1

The Appearance control panel in Mac OS 9.2.1 can be scripted to a great extent. **Script 5.2** demonstrates how you can change many of the standard system settings using AppleScript. This technique would prove highly useful for configuring a group of machines with identical custom Appearance settings. **Figure 5.3** shows the Appearance control panel with new settings from the following script.

To customize your system's Appearance control panel:

1. `tell application "Appearance"`

   You begin by letting AppleScript know that you want to talk to the Appearance control panel.

2. `set highlight color to {255, 255, 0}`

   You set the system's highlight color to maximum red, maximum green, and no blue. Color values range from 0 to 255 in the list in the following order: {red, green, blue}.

3. `set system font to "Charcoal"`

   You set the system font to Charcoal. You can use any active font name used here.

4. `set views font to "Helvetica"`

   You set the Finder's window and item font to Helvetica.

5. `set views font size to 10`

   You set the Finder's window and item font size to 10 points.

6. `set font smoothing to true`

   You turn on systemwide antialiasing for TrueType fonts.

7. `set minimum font smoothing size to 12`

   You set the minimum point size for antialiasing to 12.

Script 5.2 This script demonstrates how you can change many of the standard system settings from AppleScript.

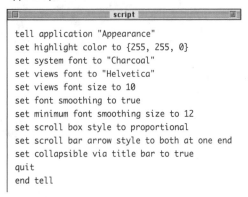

```
tell application "Appearance"
set highlight color to {255, 255, 0}
set system font to "Charcoal"
set views font to "Helvetica"
set views font size to 10
set font smoothing to true
set minimum font smoothing size to 12
set scroll box style to proportional
set scroll bar arrow style to both at one end
set collapsible via title bar to true
quit
end tell
```

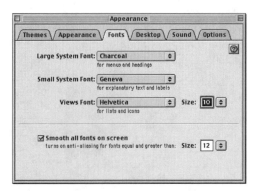

Figure 5.3 The Appearance control panel after our script has set many of the preferences shown here, including turning font smoothing on.

8. `set scroll box style to proportional`

You set all window scroll boxes system-wide to be sized proportionally.

9. `set scroll bar arrow style to both ¬`
`at one end`

You set both the scroll-bar arrows to appear at one end of the scroll bar systemwide.

10. `set collapsible via title bar to`
`true`

You turn on window collapsing system-wide. This feature is the same as the WindowShade settings from earlier versions of the system.

11. `quit`
`end tell`

Finally, you quit the Appearance control panel to make it go away.

✔ Tip

■ You can set both scroll arrows to appear at both ends of your windows' scroll bars by changing step 9 to read this way:

`set scroll bar arrow style to ¬`
`«constant ****dubl»`

Customizing File Exchange in Mac OS 9.2.1

Since Mac OS 8.5, File Exchange has been a nicely designed and scriptable control panel that provides PC-file and removable-media compatibility. **Script 5.3** demonstrates many of the properties that can be scripted in File Exchange. The code also shows you how to create a new PC Exchange extension mapping for aif2, associating the suffix with QuickTime Player. I just made up this extension, so you will want to replace the extension string with one that is useful to you.

Figure 5.4 shows the File Exchange control panel after the following script adds the new PC Exchange extension mapping aif2.

To customize File Exchange settings:

1. `tell application "File Exchange"`

   You start by getting File Exchange's attention.

2. `mount now`

   You have File Exchange mount all PC drives available.

3. `set mapping PC extensions to true`

   You turn on the mapping of PC file-name extensions to Macintosh file type and creator codes in the PC Exchange part of File Exchange.

4. `set mapping on opening files to true`

   You enable the opening of files without suitable Mac OS types and creators based on any file extension they might have

5. `set PC disks mount at startup to true`

   You enable the mounting of all available PC disks at startup.

6. `set automatic translation to true`

   You enable the automatic translation of documents when the application used to create the documents is not available.

Script 5.3 The File Exchange control panel after our script has added the new mapping for aif2.

```
tell application "File Exchange"
mount now
set mapping PC extensions to true
set mapping on opening files to true
set PC disks mount at startup to true
set automatic translation to true
set always shows choices to true
set dialog suppress if only one to true
set includes servers to false
set PC file system enabled to true
try
    get extension mapping "aif2"
on error
    make new extension mapping with properties ¬
{PC extension:"aif2", creator type:"TVOD", ¬
file type:"AIFF"}
    end try

    quit
end tell
```

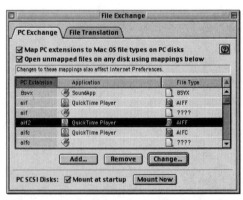

Figure 5.4 The File Exchange control panel after our script has added the new PC Exchange extension mapping for aif2.

7. `set always shows choices to true`

You make sure that the translation choices dialog box is always shown, even when a translation preference is already defined for a given file type.

8. `set dialog suppress if only one ¬`
`to true`

You enable the suppression of the translation choices dialog box when only one choice is available.

9. `set includes servers to false`

You disable the searching of applications on servers when searching for translation choices.

10. `set PC file system enabled to true`

You enable the PC file system so that the computer can read and write PC disks.

11. `try`

   `get extension mapping "aif2"`

Next, you try to get an extension mapping from File Exchange for the file extension aif2. If one is returned, you know that a extension mapping already exists for this extension.

12. `on error`

   `make new extension mapping with ¬`
`properties {PC extension:"aif2", ¬`
`creator type:"TVOD", file type:"AIFF"}`
`end try`
`quit`
`end tell`

✔ Tip

■ File Exchange generates an error if an extension mapping for the extension aif2 doesn't already exist. If the error occurs, you know that the mapping doesn't exist, so you create a new one. The creator type attribute defines the application that File Exchange will launch for aif2 files. TVOD is the creator type for Apple's QuickTime Player application. The file type attribute is passed to QuickTime Player when aif2 files are sent to it, so QuickTime Player knows what kind of file it's opening.

Switching, Starting, and Stopping Desktop Printers in Mac OS 9.2.1

With the Desktop Printing Manager background application, you get direct scripting control of any desktop printer. You can create new printers, change the current default printer, and start and stop an individual printer's print queues, among other things. **Script 5.4** lets the user stop the print queues of multiple printers selected from a list of current Desktop printers. The current default printer is selected automatically (**Figure 5.5**). If the user selects only one printer, the script makes it the default printer, in addition to stopping its queue.

To stop print queues:

1. `tell application "Desktop Printer ¬ Manager"`

   You begin by letting AppleScript know that you want to talk to the Desktop Printer Manager background application.

2. `set myPrinters to the name of every ¬ desktop printer`

   You retrieve a list of the names of all Desktop printers and store it in the variable `myPrinters`.

3. `set myCurrentPrinter to the name of ¬ the default printer`
   `end tell`

   Next, you get the name of the current default printer.

Script 5.4 This script lets the user stop the print queues of multiple printers selected from a list of current desktop printers.

```
                            script
tell application "Desktop Printer Manager"
set myPrinters to the name of every desktop ¬
printer
set myCurrentPrinter to the name of the ¬
default printer
end tell
set myNewPrinters to (choose from list ¬
myPrinters with prompt "Choose printers to ¬
stop:" default items myCurrentPrinter with ¬
multiple selections allowed)
if myNewPrinters is not false then
    tell application "Desktop Printer Manager"
if number of items in myNewPrinters = 1 then ¬
set the default printer to desktop printer ¬
(item 1 of myNewPrinters as string)
repeat with myNewPrinter in myNewPrinters
          set queue stopped of desktop printer ¬
(myNewPrinter as string) to true
        end repeat
    end tell
end if
```

Starting Print Queues

If you change the code in step 7 as follows, your script will start the print queues of the selected printers:

```
    repeat with myNewPrinter in ¬
myNewPrinters
        set queue stopped of desktop ¬
printer (myNewPrinter as string) to ¬
false
      end repeat
    end tell
end if
```

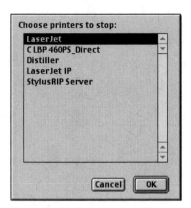

Figure 5.5 The dialog displayed by our script, with all current Desktop Printers shown.

4. `set myNewPrinters to (choose from`
`list myPrinters with prompt "Choose ¬`
`printers to stop:" default items ¬`
`myCurrentPrinter with multiple ¬`
`selections allowed)`

Now you prompt the user to choose printers from the list of those available. By specifying with `multiple selections allowed`, you let the user choose more than one printer. The list returned by this choice is stored in `myNewPrinters`.

5. `if myNewPrinters is not false then`
`    tell application "Desktop Printer ¬`
`Manager"`

You test the variable `myNewPrinters` to make sure that the user selected at least one printer. If so, you start talking to the Desktop Printer Manager again.

6. `if number of items in myNewPrinters ¬`
`= 1 then set the default printer ¬`
`to desktop printer (item 1 of ¬`
`myNewPrinters as string)`

You check whether the user selected only one printer. If so, you make that printer the default printer.

7. `repeat with myNewPrinter in ¬`
`myNewPrinters`
`    set queue stopped of desktop ¬`
`printer (myNewPrinter as string) ¬`
`to true`
`end repeat`
`    end tell`
`end if`

Finally, you loop through the list of printers the user chose and stop each printer's print queue.

Switching Location Manager Sets in Mac OS 9.2.1

In Mac OS 9.2.1, the Location Manager is scriptable. This means that after you create custom location sets of system settings, you can switch the current set from a script. The only drawback of the scripting implementation of the Location Manager is that it always shows a completion dialog box that requires user intervention when you have it switch sets.

Figure 5.6 shows the dialog box that the following script displays during execution. **Script 5.5** lets the user choose a Location Manager location set to make active from a list of available sets.

To change your current location set with the Location Manager:

1. `tell application "Location Manager"`
   `activate`

   You begin by letting AppleScript know that you want to talk to the Location Manager control panel and bringing it to the front.

2. `set myLocationRef to the current ¬`
   `location`
   `set myCurrentLocation to the name ¬`
   `of myLocationRef`

   You retrieve a reference to the current location set and store it in the variable myLocationRef. Using that reference, you get and store the name of the current location set in the variable myCurrentLocation.

3. `set myLocations to {}`

   You initialize a list variable, myLocations, to hold the names of all available location sets.

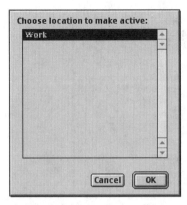

Figure 5.6 The dialog displayed by our script, with all current Location Manager sets shown.

Script 5.5 This script lets the user choose which of the available Location Manager sets to make active.

```
tell application "Location Manager"
    activate
set myLocationRef to the current location
    set myCurrentLocation to the name of ¬
myLocationRef
set myLocations to {}
repeat with i from 1 to count of every ¬
location
        set myLocations to myLocations & (name
of location i) as list
    end repeat
set myNewLocation to (choose from list ¬
myLocations with prompt "Choose location to ¬
make active:" default items myCurrentLocation ¬
without multiple selections allowed) as string
set the current location to location ¬
myNewLocation
quit
end tell
```

4. `repeat with i from 1 to count of ¬`
`every location`
   `set myLocations to myLocations & ¬`
`(name of location i) as list`
`end repeat`

Now you loop through each available location, appending each location name to the list variable `myLocations`.

5. `set myNewLocation to (choose from ¬`
`list myLocations with prompt ¬`
`"Choose location to make active:" ¬`
`default items myCurrentLocation ¬`
`without multiple selections allowed) ¬`
`as string`

You prompt the user to choose a location set from the list of available sets. By specifying `without multiple selections allowed`, you keep the user from choosing more than one set. The returned value is forced to be a string and is stored in `myNewLocation`.

6. `set the current location to location`
`myNewLocation`

You have Location Manager set the current location to the one chosen by the user. This command generates a dialog box in the Location Manager.

7. `quit`
`end tell`

Finally, you quit the Location Manager.

✔ Tip

■ If you want a simple way to change your TCP/IP configuration, use Network Setup Scripting to switch among configuration sets that you have created. For more control (and more-complicated code), see Chapter 22.

SCRIPTING THE FINDER

Figure 6.1 A new script window in the Mac OS 9.2.1 Script Editor, ready to record your actions.

Figure 6.2 A recorded script from the Mac OS 9.2.1 Finder shown in the Script Editor after recording.

✔ Tip

■ The Finder in Mac OS X version 10.1 is not recordable and has a partially implemented dictionary as discussed in Chapter 4. I let you know when a script in this chapter will not work in Mac OS X and why. But don't worry! Only a few scripts in the entire chapter do not work in Mac OS X 10.1.

If any one application is more powerful in combination with AppleScript than our 17-year-old friend the Finder, I'm at a loss to name it. We all know the Finder intimately, although we don't usually think of it as being an application in the normal sense. But the Finder is really just another application as far as the Mac is concerned. It is, in fact, an extremely scriptable application in its Mac OS 9.2.1 and Mac OS X forms. You can even record scripts with the Mac OS 9.2.1 Finder, which provides excellent opportunities for learning its scripting syntax.

If you are working in Mac OS 9.2.1 or earlier, try a quick recording session to get a feel for what the experience can be like. Open a new window in Script Editor, and click the Record button. **Figure 6.1** shows what your window should look like after you do this.

Now select a file in the Finder and drag it into the Trash. Switch back to Script Editor, and click the Stop button. Your recorded script should look similar to **Figure 6.2**. Although this amounts to a cheap thrill for now, imagine using this technique when you're desperately trying to figure out some particular syntax for scripting the Finder (or any other recordable application, for that matter).

Creating a File from Scratch

There are many, many reasons why you might want to create a file from within AppleScript. Although many scriptable applications let you create and save new documents, Apple-Script has its own means of creating text files and writing data to them: the `open for access`, `write`, and `close access` commands. You can use this ability to track the configuration of your system or the doings of your scripts. For analysis or logging, the ability to create text files on the fly is valuable, because a simple text-based log file can provide a wealth of information.

Script 6.1 builds a short text file that contains a list of all the Apple menu items on the current system. You can use this file to track the configuration of the Apple menu.

To create a text file from scratch:

1. `set myFilePath to choose file name ¬`
`default name "My Scripting Additions ¬`
`Snapshot.txt"`

First the script prompts the user to select a location and file name for a new file. The file specification returned from `choose file name` is stored in `myFilePath`.

Scripting the Finder

All of the scripts in this chapter were tested in the Mac OS 9.2.1 Finder and the Mac OS X 10.1 Finder.

The Finder is part of the Mac OS in all versions of the operating system. For more information about the Finder, visit `http://www.apple.com/`.

Script 6.1 This script gathers the names of all files in the ScriptingAdditions folder in the startup drive's Library folder and creates a new text file from scratch that lists each file name.

```
set myFilePath to choose file name default name "My Scripting Additions Snapshot.txt"
set myFolderContents to list folder (path to scripting additions folder from local domain) without ¬
invisibles
set myFileRef to (open for access myFilePath with write permission)
write "My Scripting Additions folder contains:" & return & return to myFileRef
repeat with x in myFolderContents
    write x & return as string to myFileRef
end repeat
close access myFileRef
```

2. `set myFolderContents to list folder ¬`
`(path to scripting additions folder ¬`
`from local domain) without invisibles`

You next use the `list folder` command to gather a list of all the file names (except invisible files) in the active scripting additions folder as fodder for the text file. We omit the Mac OS X optional term `from`, which specifies which domain's ScriptingAdditions folder path should be returned. In Mac OS X, the default will be the Mac alias form of the path `/System/Library/ScriptingAdditions` if it exists.

3. `set myFileRef to (open for access ¬`
`myFilePath with write permission)`

The next step is to open a new text file with write permission. If you didn't specify write permission, AppleScript would open this file as read-only. When AppleScript creates or opens a text file, it returns a reference number that all subsequent commands must use to refer to the now-open file. Because you didn't specify a complete path, this file will be created in the same folder as the current script. If you run this script from Script Editor, the file will be created in the same folder as Script Editor.

4. `write "My Scripting Additions folder ¬`
`contains:" & return & return to ¬`
`myFileRef`

You now have AppleScript write some static text to the new file. This text creates the beginning of the scripting addition item log.

continues on next page

5. `repeat with x in myFolderContents`
     `write x & return as string to ¬`
`myFileRef`
`end repeat`

This code puts AppleScript into a loop that repeats once for each item in the list `myFolderContents`, placing the current item in the variable `x`. Because `myFolderContents` is a list of all file names in the scripting additions folder, each instance of `x` is one of those file names. You then type that file name, followed by a return, to create a clean text file.

6. `close access myFileRef`

Finally, close the text file with a `close access` statement.

For a peek at your handiwork, drag and drop this new file onto your favorite browser icon to view it. **Figure 6.3** shows the text file created by this script, open in TextEdit.

✔ Tip

- The Standard Additions command `choose file name` lets a user pick a new file name and location that AppleScript returns to you as a file specification. This is a nice way to let the user specify a file that the script will create.

Figure 6.3 A sample text file created by our script when run in Mac OS X, shown in TextEdit.

Finding the End of a File (EOF)

AppleScript lets you determine the length of any open file by using the `get eof` command. This example stores the length of the file referenced by `myFileRef` in a variable:

`set myFileLength to get eof myFileRef`

CREATING A FILE FROM SCRATCH

Modifying File Attributes

Have you ever had a bunch of files that always open in the wrong program when you double-click them? Perhaps they're screen shots, which are tagged automatically as SimpleText files when they're created but you really want them to open in Photoshop. The Mac uses a file's creator type to decide which application owns the file and should open when the file is double-clicked. **Script 6.2** makes it quick and easy to change a file's creator type.

To change a file's creator type:

1. on run
       open {choose file}
   end run

   The run handler simply lets us test our script's open handler from the script editor without having to save the script first as a droplet application.

2. on open (myFileOrFolder)

   By using the on open handler, you create a drag-and-drop script application.

continues on next page

Script 6.2 Changing a file's creator type is easy in AppleScript. Note that file and creator types are optional in Mac OS X—not all files have them.

```
on open (myFileOrFolder)
    tell application "Finder"
        set myFileOrFolder to myFileOrFolder as alias
        try
            if kind of myFileOrFolder is not "folder" then display dialog (the creator type of ¬
myFileOrFolder) as string
        end try
    end tell
end open
```

3. `set x to button returned of ¬`
`(display dialog "Change to which ¬`
`application/creator?" buttons ¬`
`{"Photoshop", "Illustrator", ¬`
`"Cancel"} default button "Cancel")`

Now you prompt the user to choose one of two applications to be the new creator type for the file and store the selection in the variable x. **Figure 6.4** shows what the dialog box looks like. If the user clicks the Cancel button, AppleScript exits the script automatically.

4. `if x = "Photoshop" then`
`    set myCreator to "8BIM"`
`else`
`    set myCreator to "ART5"`
`end if`

At this point, you test to see which application the user selected and assign the appropriate creator type to the variable myCreator.

5. `tell application "Finder"`
`    set myFileOrFolder to ¬`
`myFileOrFolder as alias`
`    if kind of myFileOrFolder is not ¬`
`"folder" then set the creator type ¬`
`of myFileOrFolder to myCreator`
`end tell`
`end open`

Finally, you instruct the Finder to change the creator type to the new selection if the original object dropped onto the application is not a folder.

✔ Tip

■ Save **Script 6.3** as an application and drop any file or application onto it to display that file's creator type.

Script 6.3 A script that displays the creator type of any item dropped onto it when used as a droplet.

```
on open (myFileOrFolder)
    tell application "Finder"
        set myFileOrFolder to myFileOrFolder ¬
as alias
        try
            if kind of myFileOrFolder is not ¬
"folder" then display dialog (the creator ¬
type of myFileOrFolder) as string
        end try
    end tell
end open
```

Figure 6.4 The script displays a dialog with three button choices for the user.

Script 6.4 The short script lets us test for the existence of a particular scripting addition file before opening the Script Editor.

```
                    script
tell application "Finder"
set x to ((path to scripting additions folder ¬
from local domain) as text) & "system.osax"
if alias x exists then tell application ¬
"Script Editor" to run
end tell
```

✔ Tip

- If you have a script that moves files around, you might want to test for the existence of a same-named file in the destination folder before moving. Or you might test for the existence of the Scripting Additions folder itself in both the System Folder and the Extensions folder, to make sure that only one exists.

Testing for the Existence of a File or Folder

At times, all you want to do is make sure that something exists on your hard disk. A good example is when you want to confirm that a particular scripting addition is in the Scripting Additions folder before launching a script that depends on commands available only in that addition's dictionary. **Script 6.4** gives you the power to look around your Scripting Additions folder.

To verify the existence of a particular file in the Scripting Additions folder:

1. `tell application "Finder"`

   This statement lets AppleScript know that the following commands should be targeted to the Finder.

2. `set x to ((path to scripting ¬`
   `additions folder from local domain) ¬`
   `as text) & "system.osax"`

   Here, you assign a file path to the variable x. This path is made up of the full path to your active Scripting Additions folder, followed by the name of a particular scripting addition (System.osax, in this case).

3. `if alias x exists then tell ¬`
   `application "Script Editor" to run`
   `end tell`

   If the Finder confirms the existence of the needed addition, you invite it to launch the compiled script applet, named Widget User.

Renaming All the Files in a Folder

Imagine that you've just received a Zip disk with 10,000 JPEG images on it. Each of these images has been named with a nice, simple English file name—no file-format suffix such as .jpg to clutter things up. Now your boss wants you to get each one of these files ready for use on a Web site, where file suffixes are a way of life—in fact, a requirement. **Figure 6.5** shows two Finder windows for a before-and-after view of this script's handiwork.

Got your Return-key finger ready for 10,000 keystrokes as you furiously type an endless litany of dot-J-P-Gs? No need—**Script 6.5** saves you the trouble by adding the suffix automatically to every file in a folder.

Be sure to save this script as an application when you've typed it.

To rename all the files in a folder:

1. on run
    set x to choose folder
    tell me to open {x}
end run

The run handler simply calls the open handler and provides a convenient way to test the open handler without having to save the script as an application and drop items onto it.

2. on open (myFolder)

By using the on open handler, you create a drag-and-drop script application. Any folder dropped onto the application will be passed to the script in the variable myFolder.

3. set mySuffix to text returned of ¬
(display dialog "Suffix to add:" ¬
default answer ".jpg")

You prompt the user to enter a file suffix (or accept the default of .jpg), and store that value in the variable mySuffix.

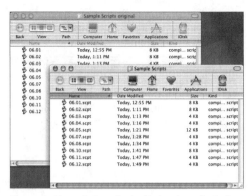

Figure 6.5 Two windows in the Finder show the before and after state of a folder of files processed by the file renaming script.

Script 6.5 The Finder is more than happy to do mundane file renaming for you using this script.

```
on run
    set x to choose folder
    tell me to open {x}
end run
on open (myFolder)
set mySuffix to text returned of (display ¬
dialog "Suffix to add:" default answer ".jpg")
AppendSuffix(item 1 of myFolder as alias, ¬
mySuffix)
end open
on AppendSuffix(myFolder, mySuffix)
tell application "Finder"
repeat with x in every file of myFolder
if name of x does not end with mySuffix then
try
            set name of x to (name of ¬
x & mySuffix)
        end try
    end if
  end repeat
if number of folders in myFolder > 0 then
repeat with y in every folder of myFolder
        AppendSuffix(y, mySuffix) of me
    end repeat
  end if
end tell
end AppendSuffix
```

4. `AppendSuffix(item 1 of myFolder as ¬`
`alias, mySuffix)`

Next, you call the function named
`AppendSuffix`; pass it two variables, getting the first item of the list `myFolder` as
a single alias; and gracefully end the on
open handler.

5. `end open`
`on AppendSuffix(myFolder, mySuffix)`

Here, you define the function
`AppendSuffix` and give it two arguments
to receive the main script's variables.

6. `tell application "Finder"`

You inform AppleScript that you want
to send subsequent statements to the
Finder.

7. `repeat with x in every file of ¬`
`myFolder`

You establish a repeat loop to cycle
through each file in the folder, storing the
current file reference in the variable x.
You get a list of file references from the
Finder with the phrase `every file`.

8. `if name of x does not end with ¬`
`mySuffix then`

This code determines whether the file's
name already ends with the desired suffix.

9. `try`
`    set name of x to (name of ¬`
`x & mySuffix)`
`end try`
`        end if`
`      end repeat`

You're ready to have the Finder set the
name of the file referred to by x by concatenating `mySuffix` with its current
name. You place this command inside a
`try`...`end try` handler to keep any errors
that might arise from halting the script's
execution.

continues on next page

RENAMING ALL THE FILES IN A FOLDER

10. `if number of folders in myFolder ¬`
`> 0 then`

You check to see whether myFolder contains any other folders.

11. `repeat with y in every folder of ¬`
`myFolder`
`  AppendSuffix(y, mySuffix) of me`
`end repeat`
`    end if`

If so, you loop through each folder once, sending a reference to the folder to the handler `AppendSuffix` to deal with nested folders.

12. `end tell`
`end AppendSuffix`

Finally, the script ends by closing the `tell` block and handler.

✔ Tips

■ Study the structure of this script, and you will be able to apply its capability to modify every file in a folder to any script you create. The key command is `repeat with x in every file in folder`. The `every file` reference gets the Finder to return a list of references for items in the specified folder. By implementing this loop in any of the preceding scripts, you could transform them into full-fledged batch processors.

■ You can also use the scripting addition command `list folder` to retrieve a list of all files and folders in a folder. This list differs from the list returned by the Finder for `every file` in that it is a list of file or folder names as strings, whereas the list returned by every file is a list of references to files. I will use both techniques in this book for batch-processing folders of files.

Moving a File or Folder

Have you ever wanted to rearrange a group of files into specific folders based on some attribute of the files? Perhaps you'd like to check the label status of files or folders and move them into different folders based on that status. This would be a quick way to file work that you've labeled as finished in an archive folder. **Script 6.6** shows how you can do this with AppleScript.

Before you run this script, create two folders on the Desktop and name them No Label and Label.

To move a file or folder based on its label status:

1. `on open (myFileOrFolder)`

   By using the `on open` handler, you create a drag-and-drop script application, as you saw in Chapter 3. Any folder that you drop onto this application will be passed in a list to the script in the variable `myFolder`.

2. `tell application "Finder"`

   You inform AppleScript that you want to target all the following statements to the Finder.

3. `if the label index of (myFileOrFolder ¬`
   `as alias) is equal to 0 then`

   You test the `label index` property of the object that was dropped onto the script application. If the `label index` is 0, no label is assigned.

4. `move myFileOrFolder to folder "No ¬`
   `Label"`

   If the object has no label, you have the Finder move it into the folder named `No Label`.

   continues on next page

5. else
```
    move myFileOrFolder to folder ¬
"Label"
end if
    end tell
end open
```

If the object's label index isn't 0, it must have a label assigned to it, so you tell the Finder to move it into the folder named Label.

Be sure to save this script as an application when you've typed it. Put the application icon on your Desktop. Now drag and drop some labeled and unlabeled objects onto it, and see what happens. **Figure 6.6** shows an example of what happens after a labeled folder is dropped onto this script application.

✔ Tip

■ **Script 6.6** does not operate properly in the Finder in Mac OS X 10.1 because labels are not yet supported.

Script 6.6 This droplet script sorts files in a folder dropped on it into two different subfolders based on each file's label settings.

```
script
```
```
on open (myFileOrFolder)
tell application "Finder"
if the label index of (myFileOrFolder as ¬
alias) is equal to 0 then
move myFileOrFolder to folder "No Label"
else
        move myFileOrFolder to folder "Label"
    end if
  end tell
end open
```

Figure 6.6 A view of the Label folder after a labeled folder is dropped onto the script application.

Script 6.7 Creating a new folder on your Desktop is a snap in AppleScript.

```
tell application "Finder"
make new folder at the desktop with ¬
properties {name:"holder"}
```

Script 6.8 This script creates a folder at a user-selected location on the hard drive.

```
set x to (choose folder with prompt "Choose ¬
a destination for new folder:")
tell application "Finder"
make new folder at x with properties ¬
{name:"holder"}
end tell
```

Making a Folder

Sometimes, in the course of a script, you'll want to create a folder to hold things. These things might be files and folders that your script is moving around or even new files spawned by the script itself. **Script 6.7** and **Script 6.8** demonstrate how you can instruct the Finder to make a new folder from scratch.

To create a new folder on the Desktop:

1. `tell application "Finder"`

   This code sends all following commands to the Finder.

2. `make new folder at the desktop with ¬`
   `properties {name:"holder"}`

   The make statement tells the Finder to create something—in this case, a new folder. The at clause describes the location for the new folder; the properties record defines the folder's name. You can define additional properties at this time.

✔ Tip

■ The scripting addition command mount volume lets your script log in automatically as a registered user with a password (or as a guest) to mount a network drive. To mount a disk named Shared on a Mac named My Mac as user John with password hey, you'd type:

```
mount volume "Shared" on server ¬
"My Mac" in AppleTalk zone "**"'as ¬
user name "john" with password "hey"
```

To create a new folder at a location chosen by the user:

1. `set x to (choose folder with prompt ¬`
`"Choose a destination for new ¬`
`folder:")`

The first order of business is to invite the user to choose where the new folder will be created. This location is saved in the variable x.

2. `tell application "Finder"`

With this `tell` statement, you instruct AppleScript to send all following commands to the Finder.

3. `make new folder at x with properties ¬`
`{name:"holder"}`
`end tell`

You create the folder in the location specified by x.

Figure 6.7 The Mac OS 9.2.1 Standard Additions dictionary entries for the Folder Actions Suite as shown in Script Editor.

Script 6.9 A Folder Action handler that makes a backup copy of every item added to the folder it is attached to.

```
on adding folder items to myFolder after ¬
receiving myNewFiles
tell application "Finder" to duplicate ¬
myNewFiles to folder "Backup" of myFolder
end adding folder items to
```

✔ Tips

- Folder actions can be launched only when a folder is open. Be aware that the Finder treats all spring-loaded folders as open folders.

- You can save folder-action scripts on any local disk. There is also a special place you can put them: the Folder Action Scripts folder inside the System Folder's Scripts folder.

- You can insert any code to manipulate the list of items in myNewFiles within this handler to make a script that automatically processes items added to the folder.

- **Script 6.9** does not operate properly in the Finder in Mac OS X 10.1 because Folder Actions are not yet supported.

Using Folder Actions in Mac OS 9.2.1

Folder actions allow you to attach scripts to open folders in Mac OS 9.2.1. You attach a folder-action script to a folder by selecting the folder in the Finder, Control-clicking, and then choosing Attach a Folder Action from the contextual menu.

There are five folder-action handlers: on opening folder, on closing folder window for, on moving folder window for, on adding folder items to, and on removing folder items from. Each handler statement is defined in **Figure 6.7,** which shows the dictionary entries. **Script 6.9** uses the on adding folder items to handler to make a backup copy of every item added to a folder.

To duplicate items added to a folder:

1. on adding folder items to myFolder ¬ after receiving myNewFiles

   You begin with an on adding folder items to handler, storing a reference to the folder modified in myFolder and a list of items added to the folder in myNewFiles.

2. tell application "Finder" to ¬ duplicate myNewFiles to folder ¬ "Backup" of myFolder

   You have the Finder copy any new files added to a folder named Backup in the same folder to which the files were added. The folder should exist already.

3. end adding folder items to

   You close the handler with an end statement.

Mounting iDisks via AppleScript

Apple gives every user of Mac OS 9 and Mac OS X access to a set of free services at www.mac.com. One of these services is access to a free 20-MB AppleShare IP volume of your very own, called an iDisk. When you complete the free registration process, you will have an account with a user name and password.

Script 6.10 gives you a simple script to mount your iDisk. **Figure 6.8** shows a typical iDisk open after the following script runs.

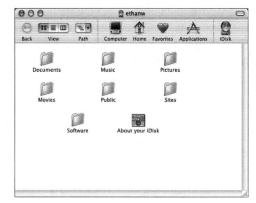

Figure 6.8 An open iDisk window in the Mac OS X Finder after running the iDisk mounting script.

To mount your iDisk:

1. `property myUsername : "`
   `property myPassword : ""`

   You start by initializing two properties to hold your iDisk account user and password information.

2. `set myErrorFlag to -1`
   `repeat while myErrorFlag is not 0`

   You set up a flag variable and start a repeat loop that will end when the flag variable equals 0.

Script 6.10 This script demonstrates how to mount any iDisk in Mac OS 9 or X.

```
property myUsername : ""
property myPassword : ""
set myErrorFlag to -1
repeat while myErrorFlag is not 0
set myUsername to text returned of (display dialog "mac.com User Name:" default answer myUsername)
    set myPassword to text returned of (display dialog "mac.com Password:" default answer myPassword)
try
        mount volume "afp://" & myUsername & ":" & myPassword & "@idisk.mac.com/" & myUsername & "/"
        set myErrorFlag to 0
on error
        set errdialog to display dialog "Unable to Authenticate " & "idisk.mac.com/" & myUsername ¬
            buttons {"Cancel", "Try Again"} default button "Try Again"
        if the button returned of errdialog is "Cancel" then set myErrorFlag to 0
    end try
end repeat
```

3.
```
set myUsername to text returned of ¬
(display dialog "mac.com User Name:" ¬
default answer myUsername)
set myPassword to text returned of ¬
(display dialog "mac.com Password:" ¬
default answer myPassword)
```

You prompt the user for user and password information and store this information in the properties.

4.
```
try
    mount volume "afp://" & myUsername ¬
& ":" & myPassword & ¬
"@idisk.mac.com/" & myUsername & "/"
    set myErrorFlag to 0
```

You try to mount the AppleShare IP volume that is your iDisk. If you succeed, the next line executes, setting the flag variable to 0 and ending the repeat loop.

5.
```
on error
    set errdialog to display dialog ¬
"Unable to Authenticate " & ¬
"idisk.mac.com/" & myUsername ¬
        buttons {"Cancel", "Try Again"} ¬
default button "Try Again"
    if the button returned of ¬
errdialog is "Cancel"" then set ¬
myErrorFlag to 0
end try
end repeat
```

If you encounter an error, you ask the user whether he wants to try again. If so, the repeat loop executes again. Otherwise, the flag variable is set to 0, ending the repeat loop.

✔ Tip

- Apple iDisks mount using the AppleShare IP TCP/IP protocol. The URL form `afp://user:password@idisk.mac.com` provides access to a user's iDisk.

Customizing the Finder in Mac OS 9.2.1

The Finder has been customizable from AppleScript for some time now, but these scripts take advantage of the current Finder in Mac OS 9.2.1 **Figure 6.9** shows the complete set of properties for Finder preferences that you can set from a script. **Script 6.11** changes some of the settings available from AppleScript. **Script 6.12** shows how you can also change your Apple Menu Options control-panel settings from AppleScript in Mac OS 9.2.1.

To customize some Finder preferences:

1. `tell application "Finder"`

   You begin by letting AppleScript know that you want to talk to the Finder.

2. `set mydisk to startup disk`
   `add to favorites (mydisk)`

   You set the variable myDisk to be a reference to your startup disk. Then you tell the Finder to add the startup disk to the Favorites folder inside the System Folder.

3. `set the calculates folder sizes of ¬`
   `Finder preferences to true`

   Tell the Finder to turn on folder size calculations for the standard item view settings.

4. `set the shows label of Finder ¬`
   `preferences to true`

   You have the Finder show labels for items in the standard item view settings.

5. `set the name of label 1 of Finder ¬`
   `preferences to "Label 1"`

   You change the name of the first of the Finder's item labels.

6. `set the uses wide grid of Finder ¬`
   `preferences to false`

   Finally, you have the Finder use tight grid spacing on the Desktop.

Figure 6.9 The Mac OS 9.2.1 Finder's dictionary entry for the preferences class.

Script 6.11 This script sets some of the properties of the Finder's preference that can be accessed from AppleScript.

```
tell application "Finder"
set mydisk to startup disk
    add to favorites (mydisk)
set the calculates folder sizes of Finder ¬
preferences to true
set the shows label of Finder preferences to ¬
true
set the name of label 1 of Finder preferences ¬
to "Label 1"
set the uses wide grid of Finder preferences ¬
to false
```

Script 6.12 This script sets the properties of the Apple Menu Options control panel that are scriptable in Mac OS 9.

```
tell application "Apple Menu Options"
set submenus enabled to true
set recent items enabled to true
set maximum recent applications to 5
set maximum recent documents to 10
set maximum recent servers to 3
end tell
```

To customize the Apple Menu Options control panel:

1. `tell application "Apple Menu Options"`

   You begin by letting AppleScript know that you want to talk to the Apple Menu Options control panel.

2. `set submenus enabled to true`

   This line turns on the submenus in the Apple menu.

3. `set recent items enabled to true`

   You turn on the display of recent items in the Apple menu.

4. `set maximum recent applications to 5`

   Here, you set the number of recent applications to remember to 5.

5. `set maximum recent documents to 10`

   You set the number of recent documents to remember to 10.

6. `set maximum recent servers to 3`
   `end tell`

   Finally, you set the number of recent servers to remember to 3.

✔ Tips

- **Script 6.11** does not operate properly in the Finder in Mac OS X 10.1 because labels are not yet supported.

- **Script 6.12** works in the Classic environment of Mac OS X.

CUSTOMIZING THE FINDER IN MAC OS 9.1

MICROSOFT OFFICE 2001

Microsoft Office is one of the most ubiquitous application suites around. Most everyone uses it and has an opinion about it. In Office 2001, Microsoft includes three applications that support AppleScript extensively: Word; Excel; and a newcomer to the suite, Entourage. With Entourage, Microsoft adds a completely scriptable personal information manager (PIM) with a contact database, scheduling, tasks, and an e-mail client.

As you experiment in AppleScript with Word, Excel, and Entourage, you'll discover that each has a different approach to supporting AppleScript. Word and Excel, for example, are fully recordable applications, so you can create scripts simply by recording your actions. Word uses Visual Basic for Applications (VBA) to implement many of the functions available from AppleScript. Entourage appears to be recordable, but in fact it records only very basic actions, such as closing windows.

In this chapter, you will work with the scripting recordability of Word to investigate how to control Word with AppleScript. Have a trick in Word you'd like to script? First, perform the operations manually in Word while recording, and you'll get executable AppleScript with embedded Visual Basic. Word supports Visual Basic commands embedded in your scripts with the do Visual Basic command.

Scripting Office 2001

All the scripts in this chapter were designed and tested for the Microsoft Office 2001 suite of applications.

Microsoft Office 2001 is developed by Microsoft Corporation, which can be reached at http://www.microsoft.com/.

Recording a Script in Word to Modify Type Styles

You'll begin your AppleScripting of Word by recording your actions in the application, using Script Editor's record mode. While doing this, you'll create a script that finds all bold text and makes it bold and italic, as shown in **Script 7.1**.

Before you begin, it's a good idea to familiarize yourself with the following steps, because any mistakes you make while recording will be recorded as well.

To record a script in Microsoft Word:

1. In Microsoft Word, create a new window; and then type some text and style a few words as bold.

   Figure 7.1 shows a sample document.

2. Switch to Script Editor, make a new script, and click the Record button in your new script's window.

3. Switch back to Word, and choose Edit > Replace.

   The Find and Replace dialog box opens.

4. Click the More button, and choose Any Character from the Special pull-down menu.

5. Choose Font from the Format pull-down menu, and choose Bold from the Font Style list.

6. Tab to the Replace With box, and choose Find What Text from the Special pull-down menu.

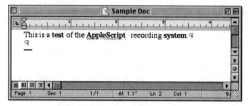

Figure 7.1 Our sample Word document will have some text in it after we get done typing.

Script 7.1 Your recorded script for formatting text.

```
tell application "Microsoft Word"
    activate
    do Visual Basic " ¬
Selection.Find.ClearFormatting"
    do Visual Basic "¬
Selection.Find.Font.Bold = True"
    do Visual Basic "¬
Selection.Find.Replacement.ClearFormatting"
    do Visual Basic "¬
Selection.Find.Replacement.Font.Italic = True"
    do Visual Basic " With Selection.Find
        .Text = \"^?\"
        .Replacement.Text = \"^&\"
        .Forward = True
        .Wrap = wdFindContinue
        .Format = True
        .MatchCase = False
        .MatchWholeWord = False
        .MatchWildcards = False
        .MatchSoundsLike = False
        .MatchAllWordForms = False
    End With"
    do Visual Basic "¬
Selection.Find.Execute Replace:=wdReplaceAll"
end tell
```

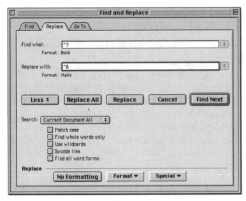

Figure 7.2 Word's Find and Replace window should be filled out to match this screen.

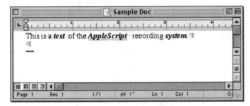

Figure 7.3 After the global find and replace is complete, your sample document will look something like this.

Figure 7.4 The Object Browser window of Microsoft's Visual Basic Editor works in much the same fashion as a Script Editor dictionary window.

7. Choose Font from the Format pull-down menu, and choose Italic from the Font Style list.

When you're done, the Find and Replace dialog box should look like **Figure 7.2**. Whew!

8. Click the Replace All button.

Your document should look like **Figure 7.3**.

9. Switch back to Script Editor, and click the Stop button.

You should see some magical code appear in your window, with lots of do Visual Basic statements in it.

10. Save your new script, and thank your Mac for speaking AppleScript most of the time instead of VBA.

✔ Tip

■ Finding out all the details about the Visual Basic that Word supports is not as hard as you might think. Simply open the Visual Basic Editor by choosing Tools > Macro > Visual Basic Editor. When the editor environment opens, the menu bar will change. Choose View > Object Browser to open what is essentially the dictionary of Visual Basic supported by Word (**Figure 7.4**).

RECORDING A SCRIPT IN WORD

Modifying a Recorded Script for Batching Word Files

In the preceding section, you performed the simple and elegant act of recording a script in Script Editor and were rewarded with the awful-looking syntax of Visual Basic for Applications, thanks to the double-edged sword of Word.

Now you'll modify this script to create an AppleScript that will batch-process folders of Word documents and change styles as requested by the user (**Script 7.2**).

To modify a recorded script for batch processing:

1. **on open myFolder**

   Begin by defining an on open handler to receive a reference in the myFolder variable to the folder dropped onto your script application from the Finder.

2. **set findStyle to the button returned ¬ of (display dialog "Select a style ¬ to find" buttons {"Bold", "Italic", ¬ "Cancel"} default button "Cancel") set replaceStyle to the button ¬ returned of (display dialog "Select ¬ a style to add" buttons {"Bold", ¬ "Italic", "Cancel"} default button ¬ "Cancel")**

   Next, you use a dialog box to prompt the user for a style to find (either bold or italic) and store the choice in the findStyle variable. Then you prompt the user for a style to replace the original with and store it in the replaceStyle variable.

Script 7.2 Batch-process a folder of Word documents, changing the font styles in each based on user selection.

```
script

on open myFolder
set findStyle to the button returned of (display ¬
dialog "Select a style to find" buttons {"Bold", ¬
"Italic", "Cancel"} default button "Cancel")
    set replaceStyle to the button returned ¬
of (display dialog "Select a style to add" ¬
buttons {"Bold", "Italic", "Cancel"} default ¬
button "Cancel")
tell application "Finder"
        set myFolderContents to list folder ¬
myFolder without invisibles
        repeat with i in myFolderContents
            if kind of alias (myFolder & i as ¬
text) is not "folder" then
                goReplace((myFolder & i as text), ¬
findStyle, replaceStyle) of me
            end if
        end repeat
    end tell
end open
on goReplace(myFile, findStyle, replaceStyle)
set myFile to alias myFile
    tell application "Microsoft Word"
        activate
        open myFile
do Visual Basic
"Selection.Find.ClearFormatting"
do Visual Basic "Selection.Find.Font." & ¬
findStyle & " = True"
do Visual Basic
"Selection.Find.Replacement.ClearFormatting"
do Visual Basic
"Selection.Find.Replacement.Font." & ¬
replaceStyle & " = True"
do Visual Basic "  With Selection.Find
        .Text = \"^?\"
        .Replacement.Text = \"^&\"
        .Forward = True
        .Wrap = wdFindContinue
        .Format = True
        .MatchCase = False
        .MatchWholeWord = False
        .MatchWildcards = False
        .MatchSoundsLike = False
        .MatchAllWordForms = False
    End With"
        do Visual Basic "Selection.Find.Execute ¬
Replace:=wdReplaceAll"
close front window saving yes saving in myFile
    end tell
end goReplace
```

3.
```
tell application "Finder"
    set myFolderContents to list ¬
folder myFolder without invisibles
        repeat with i in myFolderContents
            if kind of alias (myFolder & i ¬
as text) is not "folder" then
                goReplace((myFolder & i ¬
as text), findStyle, replaceStyle) of me
            end if
        end repeat
    end tell
end open
```

Now you're ready to get the list of items in the folder from the Finder; store the list in myFolderContents; and loop through the items, calling the goReplace function for each item.

4.
```
on goReplace(myFile, findStyle, ¬
replaceStyle)
```

Here, you define the goReplace function and tell AppleScript that it takes three arguments.

5.
```
set myFile to alias myFile
tell application "Microsoft Word"
    activate
    open myFile
```

You let AppleScript know that you want to talk to Word, and you tell Word to come to the front and open the file referred to by myFile.

6.
```
do Visual Basic ¬
"Selection.Find.ClearFormatting"
```

You send instructions to Word with the do Visual Basic statement, followed by a Visual Basic command contained in quotes. In this case, you clear all formatting for the find string in the Find and Replace dialog box.

continues on next page

7. do Visual Basic ¬
"Selection.Find.Font." & findStyle ¬
& " = True"

Although it is not elegant-looking, this statement demonstrates how you can customize the VBA command sent by inserting variables into the string passed. In this case, you pass the string from the findStyle variable as the style to be found.

8. do Visual Basic "Selection.Find.¬
Replacement.ClearFormatting"

Now you tell Word, via VBA, to clear all formatting for the replace string.

9 do Visual Basic
"Selection.Find.Replacement.Font." ¬
& replaceStyle & " = True"

Again, you use a variable, replaceStyle, to customize the VBA command to Word, this time setting the style for the replace string.

10. do Visual Basic " With Selection.Find
.Text = \"^?\"
.Replacement.Text = \"^&\"
.Forward = True
.Wrap = wdFindContinue
.Format = True
.MatchCase = False
.MatchWholeWord = False
.MatchWildcards = False
.MatchSoundsLike = False
.MatchAllWordForms = False
  End With"
do Visual Basic
"Selection.Find.Execute ¬
Replace:=wdReplaceAll"

```
tell application "Microsoft Word"
    activate
    do Visual Basic "    Selection.Find.ClearFormatting"
    do Visual Basic "    Selection.Find.Font.Bold = True"
    do Visual Basic "    Selection.Find.Replacement.ClearFormatting"
    do Visual Basic "    Selection.Find.Replacement.Font.Italic = True"
    do Visual Basic "    With Selection.Find"
        .Text = \"^?\"
        .Replacement.Text = \"^&\"
        .Forward = True
        .Wrap = wdFindContinue
        .Format = True
        .MatchCase = False
        .MatchWholeWord = False
        .MatchWildcards = False
        .MatchSoundsLike = False
        .MatchAllWordForms = False
    End With"
    do Visual Basic "    Selection.Find.Execute Replace:=wdReplaceAll"
end tell
```

Figure 7.5 Our recorded script as shown in the Script Editor.

These two lines pass VBA commands to Word, telling it to find any character and replace it with the same character, styled differently, and also setting all other parameters for the find-and-replace operation. The first line is abbreviated in this example but shown in full in the script listing. Without the magic of AppleScript recording, figuring out the syntax of this operation would be difficult, to say the least.

11. `close front window saving yes saving ¬`
    `in myFile`
    `  end tell`
    `end goReplace`

    Ask Word to close the document window and save it over the existing file referred to by `myFile`.

✔ Tip

- Make sure that you followed the instructions in "Recording a Script in Word to Modify Type Styles" earlier in this chapter to record the majority of this script, which should look like **Figure 7.5**. When your script looks correct in Script Editor, save it as an application.

MODIFYING A RECORDED SCRIPT

Creating Excel Charts from Spreadsheets

Many people use Excel to process and analyze numbers of all kinds. Excel is such a ubiquitous format that you may regularly encounter Excel files full of numbers that you want to analyze in a chart. Perhaps you download a weekly stock-market spreadsheet or a quarterly company financial report. Wouldn't it be nice to create one script that you run to chart the data every time you get an updated spreadsheet from headquarters?

Script 7.3 demonstrates how to create a script that parses a spreadsheet, looking for a series of columns of data, and then makes a formatted 3-D bar chart from that data.

To create a chart from a found set of columns in a spreadsheet:

1. ```
   property myfirstcolumn : "Stock Symbol"
   property mylastcolumn : "52 Week High"
   ```

   You start by setting up two variables to hold the column titles for the chart. In the sample document shown in **Figure 7.6**, the first column is titled Stock Symbol and the second column is titled 52 Week High.

2. ```
   tell application "Microsoft Excel"
       Activate
       Select Cell "R1C1"
   ```

   You immediately select the top-left cell of the active sheet of the current workbook so that the search will start from the top.

3. ```
   set mystartcell to Address of ¬
       (Find every Cell What myfirstcolumn ¬
           after ActiveCell LookIn xlFormulas
           LookAt xlPart SearchBy xlByColumns
           direction xlNext with handler ¬
           without MatchCase)
   ```

Script 7.3 Create a 3-D bar chart from a found set of columns in an Excel spreadsheet.

```
property myfirstcolumn : "Stock Symbol"
property mylastcolumn : "52 Week High"
tell application "Microsoft Excel"
    Activate
    Select Cell "R1C1"
set mystartcell to Address of ¬
        (Find every Cell What myfirstcolumn ¬
            after ActiveCell LookIn xlFormulas ¬
            LookAt xlPart SearchBy xlByColumns ¬
            direction xlNext with handler without ¬
MatchCase)
set myendtopcell to Address of (Find every ¬
Cell What mylastcolumn after ActiveCell LookIn ¬
xlFormulas LookAt xlPart SearchBy xlByColumns ¬
direction xlNext with handler without ¬
MatchCase)
    set myendcell to Address of (LastCell Range ¬
myendtopcell Direction xlDown)
    Select Range (mystartcell & ":" & myendcell)
set mynewchart to Create New Chart
    set Type of mynewchart to xl3DColumn
    set HasTitle of ActiveChart to true
    set text of Characters of ChartTitle of ¬
ActiveChart to "Stock Review"
    set HasTitle of Axis 2 of AxisGroup 1 of ¬
ActiveChart to true
    set text of Characters of AxisTitle of ¬
Axis 2 of AxisGroup 1 of ActiveChart to "$"
    set HasTitle of Axis 1 of AxisGroup 1 of ¬
ActiveChart to false
end tell
```

Figure 7.6 The chart window in our sample document.
```

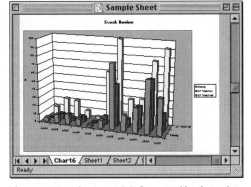

Figure 7.7 The range of cells in our sample spreadsheet once they are selected.

Figure 7.8 Our chart once it is formatted by the script.

✔ Tip

■ Excel is fully recordable, like its Office partner Word. You can perform few operations in either Word or Excel that you cannot record in AppleScript. With a little experimentation, you can find a way to script these surprisingly scriptable apps.

Next, you get the address of the cell that contains the first data column's title, in preparation for selecting the range of cells that contain data in the desired series of columns.

4.
```
set myendtopcell to Address of (Find ¬
every Cell What mylastcolumn after ¬
ActiveCell LookIn xlFormulas LookAt ¬
xlPart SearchBy xlByColumns direction¬
xlNext with handler without MatchCase)
set myendcell to Address of (LastCell¬
Range myendtopcell Direction xlDown)
Select Range (mystartcell & ":" & ¬
myendcell)
```

In final preparation for selecting the range, you get the cell address for the last column's title and the bottom cell in that column containing any data. Finally, you select the range of cells containing the desired data (**Figure 7.7**).

5.
```
set mynewchart to Create New Chart
set Type of mynewchart to xl3DColumn
```

With the selection active, you make a new chart and set its type to be a three-dimensional column chart. Excel automatically assigns the data series for the chart based on the selected columns.

6.
```
set HasTitle of ActiveChart to true
set text of Characters of ChartTitle ¬
of ActiveChart to "Stock Review"
set HasTitle of Axis 2 of AxisGroup 1 ¬
of ActiveChart to true
set text of Characters of AxisTitle ¬
of Axis 2 of AxisGroup 1 of ¬
ActiveChart to "$"
set HasTitle of Axis 1 of AxisGroup 1 ¬
of ActiveChart to false
end tell
```

You format the chart with a title and axis label, as shown in **Figure 7.8**. You can use AppleScript to set many more attributes of the chart.

Sharing Excel's Advanced Functions with FileMaker Pro

At times, you might want to use one of Excel's advanced financial or mathematical functions in a script or other application. This section describes a scenario for using an advanced financial function: the double-declining-balance method of depreciation. This function calculates one of the depreciation methods used to deduct business purchases from income taxes.

You'll need a basic inventory database, shown in browse and field-definition views, so that you can follow along (**Figures 7.9** and **7.10**).

When we have an inventory record with purchase date, amount, and depreciation years in place, you can run the sample script. This script uses Excel to plot the depreciation values for each year and return them to the repeating fields in the FileMaker database. The result is a complete inventory record with tax information included (**Figure 7.11**).

To calculate depreciation by using Excel for inclusion in a FileMaker database:

1. ```
tell application "Microsoft Excel"
    set myworkbook to Create New ¬
Workbook
        set Formula of Range "R1C1" to "year"
        set Formula of Range "R1C2" to ¬
"amount"
        set NumberFormat of Range ¬
"R2C1:R11C2" to "###0.00"
end tell
```

   Begin by making a new workbook in Excel, entering some column name in the first row and setting up the number formatting for the range of cells in which you'll enter data.

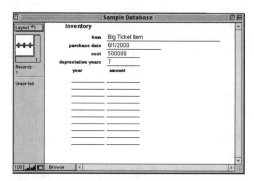

**Figure 7.9** Our sample FileMaker database shown in browse mode with sample data.

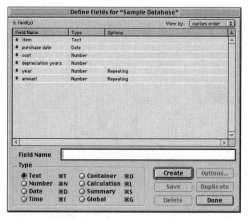

**Figure 7.10** Remember to define at least the fields shown for your sample FileMaker database.

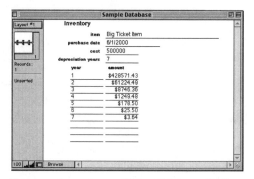

**Figure 7.11** A sample record in our database after the script has run. Notice that the repeating fields now contain tax depreciation information!
```

2.
```
tell application "FileMaker Pro"
    set mydepyears to cell "depreciation¬
years" of current record
    set mycost to cell "cost" of ¬
current record
    set mydate to cell "purchase date" ¬
of current record
end tell
```

Next, you get the relevant data for the current item displayed in the FileMaker inventory database. This data includes the number of years to depreciate the item, as well as its cost and purchase date.

3.
```
repeat with myrow from 2 to ¬
mydepyears + 1
    set mydepformula to "=DDB(" & ¬
mycost & ",," & mydepyears & "," & ¬
(myrow - 1) & ", " & word 1 of ¬
mydate & ")"
    tell application "Microsoft Excel"
        set Formula of Range ("R" & ¬
myrow & "C1:R" & myrow & "C1") to ¬
myrow - 1
        set Formula of Range ("R" & ¬
myrow & "C2:R" & myrow & "C2") to ¬
mydepformula
    end tell
end repeat
```

Now you are ready to loop and build a range of cells in Excel with a formula that includes the double-declining-balance function for each of the years you can depreciate the item. You put the month in the first column and the formula from the mydepformula variable in the second column.

4.
```
tell application "Microsoft Excel"
    set myyears to (Value of every ¬
Cell of Range ("R2C1:R" & (mydepyears ¬
+ 1) & "C1"))
    set myamounts to (Value of every ¬
Cell of Range ("R2C2:R" & (mydepyears ¬
+ 1) & "C2"))
end tell
```

continues on next page

After the loop is done, you get a list of the years and a list of the corresponding depreciation amounts for each year.

5. ```
tell application "FileMaker Pro"
    set cell "year" of current record ¬
to myyears
    set cell "amount" of current ¬
record to myamounts
end tell
```

Because you got the Excel data all at once in two lists, you already have the data in a form you can use directly to set the repeating fields in the FileMaker Pro database. You set each repeating field with one of the lists stored in the myyears and myamounts variables.

```
tell application "Microsoft Excel"
    Close myworkbook saving No
end tell
```

Finally, you tidy up by closing the temporary Excel workbook you used to create your scratch calculations for permanent storage in the FileMaker Pro record.

Script 7.4 Calculate depreciation by using Excel to include values in a FileMaker database.

```
script

tell application "Microsoft Excel"
    set myworkbook to Create New Workbook
    set Formula of Range "R1C1" to "year"
    set Formula of Range "R1C2" to "amount"
    set NumberFormat of Range "R2C1:R11C2" to ¬
"###0.00"
end tell
tell application "FileMaker Pro"
    set mydepyears to cell "depreciation years"¬
 of current record
    set mycost to cell "cost" of current record
    set mydate to cell "purchase date" of ¬
current record
end tell
repeat with myrow from 2 to mydepyears + 1
    set mydepformula to "=DDB(" & mycost & ",," ¬
& mydepyears & "," & (myrow - 1) & ", " & word ¬
1 of mydate & ")"
    tell application "Microsoft Excel"
        set Formula of Range ("R" & myrow & ¬
"C1:R" & myrow & "C1") to myrow - 1
        set Formula of Range ("R" & myrow & ¬
"C2:R" & myrow & "C2") to mydepformula
    end tell
end repeat
tell application "Microsoft Excel"
    set myyears to (Value of every Cell of ¬
Range ("R2C1:R" & (mydepyears + 1) & "C1"))
    set myamounts to (Value of every Cell of ¬
Range ("R2C2:R" & (mydepyears + 1) & "C2"))
end tell
tell application "FileMaker Pro"
    set cell "year" of current record to ¬
myyears
    set cell "amount" of current record to ¬
myamounts
end tell
tell application "Microsoft Excel"
    Close myworkbook saving No
end tell
```
```

Script 7.5 Duplicate an existing calendar event.

```
tell application "Microsoft Entourage"
   activate
   set myeventnames to name of every event
set myeventname to (choose from list ¬
myeventnames with prompt "Event to duplicate:")
if class of myeventname is not boolean then
set myproperties to properties of event (my ¬
getOffsetInList(myeventnames, myeventname)) ¬
--(offset in list myeventnames of myeventname)
      make new event with properties ¬
myproperties
   end if
end tell
on getOffsetInList(mylist, mysearchitem)
   set myoffset to 0
   repeat with i from 1 to count of items in ¬
mylist
      if item i of mylist contains ¬
mysearchitem then
         set myoffset to i
         exit repeat
      end if
   end repeat
   return myoffset
end getOffsetInList
```

Figure 7.12 The script is prompting the user to select an existing event by name.

Duplicating Calendar Events in Entourage

Microsoft Entourage has a fairly complete AppleScript library with only a few unscriptable holes. This exercise explores a way to implement functionality in a script that Entourage doesn't quite build in for you. In this case, you'll make a script to duplicate an existing calendar event. Entourage's AppleScript dictionary supports the standard `duplicate` command but not on the event object. The script in **Script 7.5** shows you a way around.

To duplicate an existing calendar event in Entourage:

1. `tell application "Microsoft Entourage"`
   `activate`
     `set myeventnames to name of every ¬`
   `event`

   The script starts by bringing Entourage to the front and getting the name of every event in the calendar.

2. `set myeventname to (choose from list ¬`
   `myeventnames with prompt "Event to ¬`
   `duplicate:")`

   You prompt the user to choose an event to duplicate. Figure 7.12 shows what this dialog box looks like.

3. `if class of myeventname is not ¬`
   `boolean then`

   Finally, you test to make sure a selection was made. If the user canceled or selected nothing, `choose list` returns the Boolean value `false`.

   continues on next page

4. set myproperties to properties of ¬
event (my getOffsetInList(myeventnames, ¬
myeventname)) --(offset in list ¬
myeventnames of myeventname)
make new event with properties ¬
myproperties
   end if
end tell

If the user made a selection, you figure out the position of that event's name in the overall list of event names. Then you use the position to reference the existing event so you can get its properties and store them in myproperties. At last, you make a new event and set its properties to match the existing one. Note that not all properties for an event can be accessed from AppleScript. Try running the script and see what doesn't carry over to the new event. **Figure 7.13** shows the new event's window.

Figure 7.13 The newly duplicated event's window shows that it picked up almost all of the properties of the original event.

5. on getOffsetInList(mylist, ¬
mysearchitem)
   set myoffset to 0
   repeat with i from 1 to count of ¬
items in mylist
     if item i of mylist contains ¬
mysearchitem then
       set myoffset to i
       exit repeat
     end if
   end repeat
   return myoffset
end getOffsetInList

This handler looks up the first position in a list that contains a matching value.

Sending E-Mail and Linking Contacts to Events

With the power of AppleScript built into Entourage, it could easily become a script-enabled personal-productivity hub. Are you managing tons of contact names and meetings through e-mail? With AppleScript and Entourage's Scripts menu, you can make the whole experience a simple point-and-click operation. Think about it: A script can let you choose an existing event and all the people to invite and link. **Script 7.6** works through this idea with a simple, user-friendly script that can be run on its own as an applet or placed in Entourage's Scripts menu and called inside the application.

To send e-mail announcements and link selected contacts to a chosen event:

1.
```
tell application "Microsoft Entourage"
    activate
    set mymeetingnames to {}
    repeat with mymeeting in every event
        if the category of mymeeting ¬
contains {category "Work"} then
            set mymeetingnames to ¬
mymeetingnames & (name of mymeeting) ¬
as list
        end if
    end repeat
    set mymeetingname to (choose from ¬
list mymeetingnames with prompt ¬
"Meeting to announce:")
```

Begin by creating a list of the names of all meetings that are in the category Work. First, you initialize an empty list variable, mymeetingnames, and then check for category matches on each event in a loop. Then you prompt the user to choose an event to announce and store the event's name in mymeetingname.

continues on next page

2. set myallcontactnames to name of
every contact
set mycontactnames to (choose from
list myallcontactnames ¬
    with prompt "Contacts for meeting:"
with multiple selections allowed)

Now you get the user to choose one or
more contacts to link to the chosen event
and to send e-mail announcements.

3. if class of mycontactnames is not
boolean and class of mymeetingname is
not boolean then
    set mymeetingname to item 1 of
mymeetingname
    set myallmeetingnames to name of
every event

Script 7.6 Send e-mail announcements and link selected contacts to a user-selected event.

```
tell application "Microsoft Entourage"
    activate
    set mymeetingnames to {}
    repeat with mymeeting in every event
        if the category of mymeeting contains {category "Work"} then
            set mymeetingnames to mymeetingnames & (name of mymeeting) as list
        end if
    end repeat
    set mymeetingname to (choose from list mymeetingnames with prompt "Meeting to announce:")
set myallcontactnames to name of every contact
    set mycontactnames to (choose from list myallcontactnames ¬
        with prompt "Contacts for meeting:" with multiple selections allowed)
if class of mycontactnames is not boolean and class of mymeetingname is not boolean then
        set mymeetingname to item 1 of mymeetingname
        set myallmeetingnames to name of every event
set mymeetingindex to offset in list myallmeetingnames of mymeetingname
        set mymeetingdate to start time of event mymeetingindex as string
repeat with mycontactname in mycontactnames
            set mycontactindex to offset in list myallcontactnames of mycontactname
link contact mycontactindex to event mymeetingindex
set mycontactemail to address of contact mycontactindex
            set mymessage to make new outgoing message with properties {subject:"Meeting: " & ¬
mymeetingname, content:"Please come to our meeting on " & mymeetingdate ¬
                , recipient:{{recipient type:to recipient, address:{display name:¬
                mycontactname, address:mycontactemail}}}}
        end repeat
    end if
end tell
```

Before you start working away at links, contacts, and sending e-mail, make sure that the user selected an event and at least one contact. If the user made those selections, you do several preparatory things. You store the meeting's name in `mymeetingname` and set aside a list of every event name in the `myallmeetingnames` variable to use later.

4.
```
set mymeetingindex to offset in list ¬
myallmeetingnames of mymeetingname
set mymeetingdate to start time of ¬
event mymeetingindex as string
```

You look up the index positions of the contact and event to construct a valid reference for the link. Notice that this simple script will not work properly if events or contacts in Entourage have identical names.

5.
```
repeat with mycontactname in ¬
mycontactnames
    set mycontactindex to offset in ¬
list myallcontactnames of ¬
mycontactname
```

You're ready to loop through all the selected contact names.

6.
```
link contact mycontactindex to event ¬
mymeetingindex
```

Now you link the contact to the event.

continues on next page

7. set mycontactemail to address of ¬
contact mycontactindex
set mymessage to make new outgoing ¬
message with properties
{subject:"Meeting: " & mymeetingname ¬
, content:"Please come to our ¬
meeting on " & mymeetingdate ¬
, recipient:{{recipient type:to ¬
recipient, address:{display name:¬
mycontactname, ¬
address:mycontactemail}}}}
     end repeat
   end if
end tell

You create an outgoing e-mail message
and attach a recipient. **Figure 7.14**
shows a new outgoing message created
by this script.

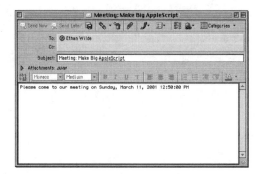

Figure 7.14 An outgoing email message created from
AppleScript.

FileMaker Pro 5.5

Figure 8.1 The dictionary entry for FileMaker Pro 5.5's get remote URL command.

FileMaker Pro was one of the first scriptable applications and is still one of the most useful. Its complete dictionary obeys the object model for syntax quite well, making FileMaker Pro powerful and easy to script.

AppleScript not only is useful for scripting FileMaker Pro as a data repository in conjunction with other applications but also can enhance FileMaker databases greatly by incorporating embedded AppleScripts into your databases, as you'll see in this chapter. To start, you'll explore the concept of creating a database with a simple event-calendar example.

✔ Tip

■ For http delivery of data, FileMaker's built-in server, Tango for FileMaker from Pervasive Software, or Lasso from Blue World Communications are faster Web connections to your FileMaker Pro database than an AppleScript CGI. FileMaker also supports direct TCP/IP connections with FileMaker client applications as well as XML delivery of data via http.

Big News: Remote Database Access via AppleScript in FileMaker Pro 5.5

FileMaker, Inc. has heard the requests of the scripting community. In version 5.5, the new command get remote URL lets you open remote databases from a script. **Figure 8.1** shows the dictionary entry for FileMaker Pro 5.5's get remote URL command.

Scripting FileMaker Pro

All the scripts in this chapter that use FileMaker refer to a single simple database, Test Database, which you will create in the following exercise. This database is a simple event-calendar database.

To get ready for AppleScripting FileMaker:

1. Launch FileMaker Pro.

2. Choose File > New to open the New Database dialog box.

3. Click the radio button labeled Create a New Empty File; then click the OK button.

4. When you are prompted to do so, name and save your new database.

   The Define Fields dialog box opens.

5. Define fields for the database as shown in **Figure 8.2**.

   For this exercise, define the fields event title, event description, event location, and event date. Be sure to create event date as a field of type Date.

6. Click the Done button.

7. Populate the database with at least a couple of records.

   Figure 8.3 shows two records that contain sample data. The scripts that follow assume that these records exist in the sample database.

Now you're ready to proceed with your scripts.

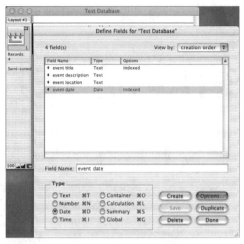

Figure 8.2 The Define Fields window of our sample database is shown with all fields required.

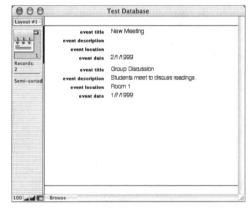

Figure 8.3 Two records containing sample data—the scripts here assume that these records exist in the database.

Scripting FileMaker Pro

All the scripts in this chapter were designed and tested for FileMaker Pro version 5.5. Most of these scripts should also work with versions of FileMaker as early as 4.0.

FileMaker Pro is developed by FileMaker Inc. FileMaker may be reached at http://www.filemaker.com/.

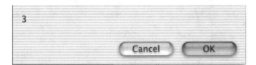

Figure 8.4 The dialog showing the number of records in the database.

Script 8.1

```
                    script
tell application "FileMaker Pro" activate
    show (every record of database "Test ¬
Database" whose cell "event date" > "1/1/01")
    display dialog (count of records in ¬
document "Test Database")
end tell
```

Finding Records in a Content Database

What's more natural to do with a database than trying to find something contained within it? A script gives you powerful options for finding things. You can search for values stored in variables and conduct custom searches conditionally, depending on different settings and states that AppleScript can read, such as the current date.

The first script, **Script 8.1,** finds records in the database that have values in the event date field greater than January 1, 2001, or 1/1/01. You can run this script directly from Script Editor window. You might open the Event Log window to see what goes on behind the scenes between AppleScript and FileMaker while the script is running. **Figure 8.4** shows the dialog created by the script displaying the number of records in the database.

To find some records in a database:

1. `tell application "FileMaker ¬`
   `Pro"activate`

   First, you need to let AppleScript know which application you want to address.

2. `show (every record of database ¬`
   `"Test Database" whose cell "event ¬`
   `date""01/01/01")`

   Now you tell FileMaker to find, or show, all the records in the database that have values greater than January 1, 2001, in the event date field.

3. `display dialog (count of ¬`
   `records in document "Test Database")`
   `end tell`

   You generate a dialog box that displays the number of records FileMaker found.

Syntax Issue: Dealing with the Found Set of Records Versus All Records

One peculiarity of FileMaker Pro that deserves special attention: You need to specify whether you want to address only records in the current found set or all the records in the database. Use the object database when you want to deal with all records. Use the object document when you want to deal only with the records in the current found set.

Try changing document in line 3 of **Script 8.1** to database to see the difference.

Sorting the Records in a Content Database

You may want to sort your database for many reasons, especially if your script is going to manipulate data from the database. Perhaps you'll want to take existing data and order it alphabetically or by date so that you can write an HTML file with everything in proper order.

Sometimes, you may want to sort your data by more than one field. You can do this easily with FileMaker by using nested sort commands. FileMaker also makes it easy for you to reverse the order of your sort by using the modifier in order descending.

Script 8.2 sorts the database in descending order by date. You might try adding an acti-vate command right after tell so that you can watch FileMaker in action as the script is running. **Figure 8.5** shows the database in FileMaker, nicely sorted.

To sort the records in a content database:

1. tell application "FileMaker Pro" ¬ activate

   First, tell AppleScript which application you want to address.

2. show every record in database ¬ "Test Database

   Next, ask FileMaker to find all records in the database so that the sort will apply to every record.

3. sort database "Test Database" ¬ by field "event date" in order ¬ descending
   end tell

   Finally, get down to the matter at hand and sort the database's records. If you omit the in order descending modifier, FileMaker defaults to sorting in ascend-ing order.

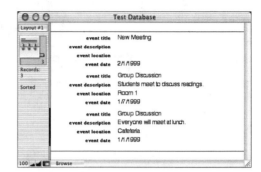

Figure 8.5 The sorted records in the database after the script has run.

Script 8.2

```
tell application "FileMaker Pro" activate
    show every record in database "Test Database"
    sort database "Test Database" by field ¬
"event date" in order descending
end tell
```

Different Tricks for Different Scripts

You can use another method to get data from FileMaker besides requesting one field or cell at a time, which can be a slow process.

If asked, FileMaker will return an entire record's data as a list:

```
set myList to record 1 of database ¬
"Test Database"
```

You need a way of knowing which field is first and so on. Check the order of the fields in FileMaker's Define Fields window so this situation isn't a problem.

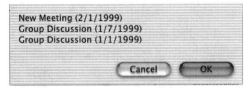

New Meeting (2/1/1999)
Group Discussion (1/7/1999)
Group Discussion (1/1/1999)

Cancel   OK

Figure 8.6 This dialog contains the text of the sorted records' fields.

Script 8.3

```
script

tell application "FileMaker Pro"

    show every record in database "Test Database"

    sort database "Test Database" by field ¬
"event date" in order descending

    set myInfo to ""

    repeat with i from 1 to count of records ¬
in database "Test Database"

        set myInfo to myInfo & cell "event ¬
title" of record i of database "Test Database"

        set myInfo to myInfo & " (" & cell ¬
"event date" of record i of database "Test ¬
Database" & ")" & return

    end repeat

    display dialog myInfo

end tell
```

Getting Data from a Record in a Database

Manipulating databases is fine and dandy, but don't you really just want to get some data out of them to play with? Well, getting data out is just as easy as finding and sorting, thanks to FileMaker's exquisite implementation of AppleScript.

You've seen how to find with show and sort with sort. Any guesses about a command to retrieve data? How about get?

The script in **Script 8.3** expands on the sort script by including a repeat loop to traverse all records in the database in sort order and then extract some data from their fields to display in a dialog box. More exciting things, such as creating folders full of files, are not such a big step away (see "Merging Data with Text Templates to Create Files" later in this chapter).

Figure 8.6 shows the product of Script 8.3: a lovely dialog box populated with bits of sorted data.

To get data from a record in a content database:

1. `set myInfo to ""`

   After you get and sort the data as described in the preceding section, you need to create a string variable to hold the data that you'll request from FileMaker and eventually display. First, you initialize the myInfo variable by setting it to a null string.

2. `repeat with i from 1 to count ¬`
   `of records in database "Test Database"`

   The script begins its repeat loop here, filling the variable i with the next record incrementally from 1 to the number of records in the database.

continues on next page

3. `set myInfo to myInfo & cell ¬`
`"event title" of record i of database ¬`
`"Test Database"`

Hidden in this line of code is the first
request to get data from FileMaker. The
set command tells FileMaker to return
the value of the cell from record i.

4. `set myInfo to myInfo & "(" & ¬`
`cell "event date" of record i ¬`
`database "Test Database" & ")" & ¬`
`return`

Again, you retrieve another field of data
from record i and add it to the myInfo
variable.

5. `end repeat`

This statement closes the repeat loop and
lets AppleScript know that it should
increment the variable i. If i is still less
than or equal to the number of records,
AppleScript can move its execution back
up to the line after repeat.

6. `display dialog myInfo`
`end tell`

You're ready to have AppleScript display
the result of the loop by showing you the
value stored in the myInfo variable.

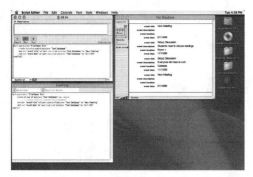

Figure 8.7 The script and Event Log windows in Script Editor are visible after the script has been run—in addition to the FileMaker database.

Script 8.4

```
                    script
tell application "FileMaker Pro"

    create record at end of database "Test ¬
Database"

    set cell "event title" of last record of ¬
database "Test Database" to "New Meeting"

    set cell "event date" of last record of ¬
database "Test Database" to "2/1/99"

end tell
```

✔ Tips

■ If you know that you created the fields in Test Database in the order listed at the beginning of this chapter (event title first and event date fourth), you can replace steps 2 and 3 with this code to make your script faster:

```
create new record with data {"New ¬
Meeting", "", "", "2/1/01"}
end tell
```

■ FileMaker Pro processes the single event of creating a new record much faster than it processes the multiple events of creating a record and responding to a series of separate set commands.

Creating a New Record in a Content Database

Now that you're a master at commanding FileMaker to find, sort, and display existing data in a database, you'll want to teach it to add records to a database and populate them with fresh data (**Script 8.4**). Then your palette of basic FileMaker Pro tricks will be complete.

Figure 8.7 shows the script and Event Log windows in Script Editor after the script has been run—as well as the newly modified FileMaker database in the background.

To create a new record in a database:

1. `tell application "FileMaker Pro"`

   As always, you need to let AppleScript know which application you want to address.

2. `create record at end of ¬`
   `database "Test Database"`

   You ask FileMaker to create a new record at the end of the database.

3. `set cell "event title" of last ¬`
   `record of database "Test Database" ¬`
   `to "New Meeting"`
   `set cell "event date" of last record ¬`
   `of database "Test Database" to "2/1/01"`
   `end tell`

   Next, you set the values in two of the fields of the new record, which you know is the last record in the database, because you asked FileMaker to create it at the end of the database.

143

Merging Data with Text Templates to Create Files

Perhaps one of the most powerful uses for FileMaker is creating files by combining FileMaker data with template files. **Script 8.5** gracefully works with any FileMaker database that is currently open. It searches a template text file for database field names enclosed by number signs (#) and replaces them with the actual data from that field.

Figure 8.8 shows the template HTML file viewed in Netscape, with database field-name placeholder tags enclosed in number signs.

Figure 8.8 The template HTML file viewed in Netscape.

To merge data with templates to create HTML files:

1. ```
   set myTemplateFile to (choose file with
   prompt "Select HTML template:")
   if (myTemplateFile as string) ends ¬
   with ".html" then
   ```
   Begin by prompting the user to select a template HTML file. Test the file name to make sure that it ends in .html before proceeding.

2. ```
   set myFileRef to (open for ¬
   access myTemplateFile)
   set myTemplate to read myFileRef
   close access myFileRef
   ```
   Next, you load the contents of the template file into the myTemplate variable.

3. ```
   tell application "FileMaker Pro"
        set myFields to name of every ¬
   cell of layout 0
        set myRecordNumber to number ¬
   of records
     end tell
   ```
   You retrieve a list of the field names for the current database from FileMaker as well as the number of records in the database.

Scripting with Acme Widgets

This script requires the scripting addition Acme Scripting Widgets. You must have Acme Script Widgets installed in your Scripting Additions folder for this script to work.

Acme Script Widgets adds the offset in list statement, which finds matches in lists, and the acme replace statement, a useful string find-and-replace command.

Acme Script Widgets is shareware; it costs $29 for a single-user license. You can reach Acme Technologies at http://www.acmetech.com/.
   ```

Figure 8.9 One of the HTML files produced by the script, with field-name tags replaced by actual data.

Making an HTML Template File

You can make a template file in any text editor: SimpleText, BBEdit, Word, or any other program that is capable of saving a text-only file.

You can also create one in a visual HTML editor even more quickly than you can in a text editor. Follow these steps:

1. In the text editor of your choosing, make a new file.

2. Create a set of minimal HTML tags, with a database-field placeholder:

   ```
   <HTML><HEAD>
   <TITLE>Page Name</TITLE>
   </HEAD>
   <BODY>
   <P><B>#event title#</B>
   <P><I>#event date#</I>
   <P>#event description#
   </BODY></HTML>
   ```

3. Save the template file with the .html extension.

Figure 8.9 shows one of the HTML files produced by the script, with field-name tags replaced by actual data.

4. ```
   repeat with x from 1 to ¬
   myRecordNumber
        set myHTML to myTemplate tell ¬
   application "FileMaker Pro"
            set myCells to cellValue ¬
   every cell of record x of layout 0
        end tell
   ```

   Here, you begin a loop through each record of the database, initializing a variable to hold this record's HTML by loading the template contents into it. Next, you retrieve a list of all values for the fields of the current record.

5. ```
   repeat with myField in myFields
            set mySearch to ("#" & ¬
   myField & "#") as string
   ```

   You loop through each field name in the list of fields. You set the mySearch variable to be the search string by adding number signs to the field name.

6. ```
   set myCell to item (offset in ¬
   list myFields of myField) of myCells
   ```

   You retrieve the value from the database's field by looking for the position of the field name in the list of field names, called myFields. You use the same offset position to look up the value of the field in the list of field values in myCells. These two lists match up, creating a name–value pair scheme across two lists.

7. ```
   set myHTML to (ACME replace ¬
   mySearch in myHTML witmyCell)
            end repeat
   ```

   You use ACME Script Widgets' ACME replace statement to substitute the value of the current field for the placeholder text.

continues on next page

MERGING DATA WITH TEXT TEMPLATES

8. set myHTMLFile to (ACME replace ¬
".html" in (myTemplateFile astring) ¬
with (x & ".html" as string))
  set myFileRef to (open for ¬
access file myHTMLFile with write ¬
permission)
  write myHTML to myFileRef close ¬
access myFileRef
 end repeat
end if

After you complete the loop through each field in the current record, you build the new HTML file name by adding the record number before the .html suffix.

✔ Tip

■ This script relies on a Mac OS 9 scripting addition, Acme Script Widgets. Therefore, it must be run in Mac OS 9 or the Classic environment of Mac OS X.

Script 8.5

```
set myTemplateFile to (choose file with prompt "Select HTML template:")
if (myTemplateFile as string) ends with ".html" then
    set myFileRef to (open for access myTemplateFile)
    set myTemplate to read myFileRef
    close access myFileRef
    tell application "FileMaker Pro"
        set myFields to name of every cell of layout 0
        set myRecordNumber to number of records
    end tell
    repeat with x from 1 to myRecordNumber
        set myHTML to myTemplate
        tell application "FileMaker Pro"
            set myCells to cellValue of every cell of record x of layout 0
        end tell
        repeat with myField in myFields
            set mySearch to ("#" & myField & "#") as string
            set myCell to item (offset in list myFields of myField) of myCells
            set myHTML to (ACME replace mySearch in myHTML with myCell)
        end repeat
        set myHTMLFile to (ACME replace ".html" in (myTemplateFile as string) with (x & ".html" as string))
        set myFileRef to (open for access file myHTMLFile with write permission)
        write myHTML to myFileRef
        close access myFileRef
    end repeat
end if
```

MERGING DATA WITH TEXT TEMPLATES

Figure 8.10 The script in ScriptMaker's Specify AppleScript window.

Script 8.6 Prompt the user to choose a file; then store the file's path and type a text field in the current record of a FileMaker database.

```
script

set myfilepath to (choose file "Select file")
as string
set myfiletype to file type of (info for alias
myfilepath)
tell application "FileMaker Pro"
    set cell "path" of current record to
myfilepath
    set cell "type" of current record to
myfiletype
end tell
```

Capturing Data in ScriptMaker by Using AppleScript

At the beginning of the chapter, we mentioned how powerful AppleScript can be when it is used to embed AppleScripts inside FileMaker. You can do this by adding a Perform AppleScript command to your ScriptMaker script in FileMaker Pro. The capability to use AppleScript inside FileMaker has been especially powerful since version 4.0 of FileMaker, when the application began supporting extensive control of itself from embedded AppleScripts. As a result, you can write AppleScripts to manipulate FileMaker and your database and embed them in the database.

Script 8.6 prompts the user to choose a file and then store the file's path and type in a text field in the database. **Figure 8.10** shows the script in ScriptMaker's Specify AppleScript window—the database layout can be seen behind.

To capture a user-selected file's path as a string and store it in a FileMaker field:

1. Create the sample database shown in Figure 8.10. The database includes two text fields named path and type.

2. In FileMaker Pro, create a new Script-Maker script that contains a single Perform AppleScript step (**Figure 8.10**).

3. In ScriptMaker, select the Perform AppleScript step in ScriptMaker; then click the Specify button.

   You enter the script in the following steps.

   continues on next page

4. `set myfilepath to (choose file ¬ "Select file") as string`

First, the script prompts the user to select a file. You store the alias path as a string in the `myfilepath` variable.

5. `set myfiletype to file type of ¬ (info for alias myfilepath)`

Next, you get the file type of the file and store it in the `myfiletype` variable.

6. `tell application "FileMaker Pro"`
`    set cell """"path" of current ¬`
`record to myfilepath`
`    set cell "type" of current record ¬`
`to myfiletype`
`end tell`

Finally, you set the two cells in the current record of the database with the values stored in the `myfilepath` and `myfiletype` variables. The current record will be the same one that is displayed when the user runs the ScriptMaker script in FileMaker.

Embedding AppleScripts in FileMaker Pro Databases

FileMaker is one of the few programs that let you store AppleScripts inside its own documents—in this case, databases. To do so, you add `Perform AppleScript` steps to your ScriptMaker scripts inside FileMaker.

You should consider using embedded AppleScripts for two significant reasons:

Speed. AppleScripts embedded in FileMaker that operate on FileMaker run significantly faster than scripts that access FileMaker externally.

Power. With AppleScripts that operate on your database, you can do things you have never been able to do before with the functionality built into FileMaker. Now you can duplicate a record and all its related records or perform live finds and sorts based on user-entered or database-generated strings.

Figure 8.11 The sample fax database includes three text fields named name, fax, and message.

Script 8.7 The first part of a two-part fax-on-demand script to be used as an embedded script in a FileMaker ScriptMaker script that includes a print step between this script and Script 8.8.

```
script
tell application "FileMaker Pro"
    set mynote to cell "message" of current ¬
record
    set myname to cell "name" of current record
    set myfax to cell "fax" of current record
end tell
set myfirstname to word 1 of myname
set mylastname to last word of myname
set myareacode to word 1 of myfax
set myphone to word 2 of myfax & "-" & word 3 ¬
of myfax
init fax note mynote
set myoldprinter to set printer "faxPrint"
set mydestination to create destination area ¬
code myareacode number myphone
recipient info index mydestination first ¬
myfirstname last mylastname
set the clipboard to myoldprinter
```

Sending a Fax with FAXstf 6 from ScriptMaker

AppleScript can extend the power of FileMaker Pro on the Macintosh to tremendous levels with little effort. One such area for extending FileMaker is printing. FileMaker allows you to create ScriptMaker scripts that print but gives you no way to switch printers or settings via script. AppleScript can solve this problem with some help from a scripting addition: FAXstf Commands, available from Smith Micro, the maker of FAXstf. This addition includes a command, set printer, that switches your current Chooser setting to any available printer, whether or not it is a desktop printer. The addition also allows you to send faxes via FAXstf software to the recipients of your choice, all under script control.

In **Script 8.7** and **Script 8.8,** you create an embedded AppleScript inside a FileMaker database that can send faxes to the contacts contained in the database's records.

To send a fax based on data in the current record in a database:

1. Create the sample database shown in **Figure 8.11**. The database includes three text fields named name, fax, and message.

2. In FileMaker Pro, create a new ScriptMaker script that contains a single Perform AppleScript step.

3. In ScriptMaker, select the Perform AppleScript and then click the Specify button.

   You enter the script in the following steps.

continues on next page

4. `tell application "FileMaker Pro"`
    `set mynote to cell "message" of ¬`
`current record`
    `set myname to cell "name" of ¬`
`current record`
    `set myfax to cell "fax" of ¬`
`current record`
`end tell`
`set myfirstname to word 1 of myname`
`set mylastname to last word of myname`
`set myareacode to word 1 of myfax`
`set myphone to word 2 of myfax & "-" ¬`
`& word 3 of myfax`

You start the first scriptlet by getting the message, first name, last name, and fax number for the recipient and storing them in variables to use later.

5. `init fax note mynote`
`set myoldprinter to set printer ¬`
`"faxPrint"`

Next, you start a new fax with the scripting addition's `init fax` command. You also switch the Chooser printer settings with the scripting addition's `set printer` command.

6. `set mydestination to create ¬`
`destination area code myareacode ¬`
`number myphone`
`recipient info index mydestination ¬`
`first myfirstname last mylastname`

You add a destination, with area code and number, and you add some basic recipient information with `recipient info`. Now you are ready to print. In this case, you will use a `print` command in the ScriptMaker script in which you are embedding this AppleScript and Script 8.8.

Script 8.8 The second part of a two-part fax-on-demand script to be used as an embedded script in a FileMaker ScriptMaker script that includes a print step before this script and after Script 8.7.

```
script
set myoldprinter to the clipboard
set printer myoldprinter
```

7. `set the clipboard to ¬`
`myoldprinter`

Before you end this first script and start printing in a ScriptMaker step, you store the name of the original printer in the Clipboard for retrieval by the second scriptlet after the printing is done.

8. Switch the current printer to FaxPrint in the Chooser, and try printing a test fax.

FileMaker needs to have FaxPrint selected when you create the next script in ScriptMaker.

9. After the first step of the ScriptMaker script, insert a `print` step that does not display a dialog box.

10. Create another `Perform AppleScript` step.

11. In ScriptMaker, select the step and then click the Specify button.

In the following step, you enter **Script 8.8.**

12. `set myoldprinter to the ¬`
`clipboard`
`set printer myoldprinter`

In the second embedded scriptlet, you switch the Chooser printer settings back to the original printer you saved in `myoldprinter` at the beginning of the script.

✔ Tip

■ These scripts rely on a Mac OS 9 scripting addition, FAXstf Commands. Therefore, they must be run in Mac OS 9 or the Classic environment of Mac OS X.

Scripting with FAXstf Commands

This script requires the scripting addition FAXstf Commands. You must have FAXstf Commands installed in your Scripting Additions folder for this script to work. FAXstf Commands adds a series of commands that support automated faxing and fax processing.

You can find FAXstf at ftp://ftp.stfinc.com/.

Creating a Record Containing All Field Names in a Database

Sometimes when you are working in FileMaker Pro, you need to perform administrative functions such as changing the database, making a new layout, or writing that great new script. AppleScript can help you gain knowledge about the databases you are working with and speed that administrative process right along.

This script, **Script 8.9,** demonstrates how a short script can be useful. It creates a single new record in the database of your choice that contains the field names for every field. It has proved itself invaluable in times of scripting when you want to know the position of each field in the list returned by a `get data` request. **Figure 8.12** shows the database selection dialog the script displays.

To create a record that contains every field name in the database:

1. `set mydbs to {}`

You start by initializing a list variable, `mydbs`, that you'll use to hold a list of the names of every database open in FileMaker.

2. `tell application "FileMaker Pro"`

You start talking to FileMaker.

3. `repeat with i from 1 to count of ¬`
`databases`

You begin a loop through all available databases.

4. `set mydbs to mydbs & name of database ¬`
`i as list`
`    end repeat`
`end tell`

You append the name of the current database in your loop to the list of databases, `mydbs` before ending the loop.

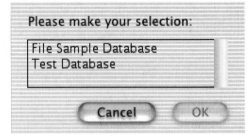

Figure 8.12 The script prompts the user to choose one of the open databases.

Script 8.9 A simple script to create a new record in a database.

```
set mydbs to {}
tell application "FileMaker Pro"
    repeat with i from 1 to count of databases
        set mydbs to mydbs & name of database ¬
i as list
    end repeat
end tell
set mydb to (choose from list mydbs) as string
tell application "FileMaker Pro"
    set mynames to name of every field of ¬
database mydb
set myrec to create new record at database ¬
mydb
    repeat with myName in mynames
        try
            set cell (myName as string) of ¬
myrec to (myName as string)
        end try
        end repeat
end tell
```

Figure 8.13 A newly created record in which each field is populated with its field name.

5. `set mydb to (choose from list mydbs) ¬`
`as string`

Now you can prompt the user to choose a database name from the list of available databases.

6. `tell application "FileMaker Pro"`

You begin your conversation with FileMaker once again.

7. `set mynames to name of every field ¬`
`of database mydb`

You get the list of every field name in the current database in your loop and store the list in the variable mynames.

8. `set myrec to create new record at ¬`
`database mydb`

Now you make a new record in the current database, storing a reference to the newly created record in the variable myrec.

9. `repeat with myName in mynames`

You start a repeat loop through each field name in the list mynames.

10. `try`
`    set cell (myName as string) of ¬`
`myrec to (myName as string)`
`end try`

Now you try to set the cell value in the new record with its corresponding field you name. If we cannot set the current cell, the error generated by FileMaker is caught by our try statement.

11. `end repeat`
`end tell`

You conclude your loop and conversation with FileMaker now. **Figure 8.13** shows what the new record looks like in the database that was selected.

Now Up-to-Date and Contact 4

Now Up-to-Date and Now Contact have survived for many years. They continue to be the most popular commercial scheduling and contact-management software on the Mac. Why? The two programs are simple, work reliably and quickly, take little memory, can be networked, and are scriptable. Without scripting support, the two programs would be good and useful. With the level of robust scripting incorporated into the latest versions, these programs deserve special attention.

Most of the common tasks that you conduct in Now Up-to-Date and Now Contact can now be controlled from AppleScript. With the inclusion of a Scripts menu in version 4, Power On Software has opened the door for you to make these programs the hub of your script-enabled daily life. You can change contact records systematically, import and export contact data across applications, create events, and manage contact and calendar data with much more control.

Scripting Now Up-to-Date and Now Contact 4

The scripts in this chapter were tested with version 4 of Now Up-to-Date and Now Contact.

Now Up-to-Date and Now Contact 4 are developed by Power On Software (http://www.poweronsw.com/).

Now Contact's AppleScript dictionary includes the rarely seen Table Suite of commands and objects. This suite lets you write scripts that can filter and sort the contact entries quickly as though they were columns and rows in a spreadsheetlike object. **Figure 9.1** shows Now Contact's dictionary window in Script Editor.

Now Up-to-Date's AppleScript dictionary includes the only remaining implementation of the Schedule Suite of commands and objects. This suite includes objects for events and people. **Figure 9.2** shows the Schedule Suite entries from the dictionary of Now Up-to-Date 4.

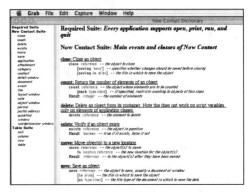

Figure 9.1 Now Contact's dictionary window in Script Editor including the Tables Suite.

Figure 9.2 The Schedule Suite entries from the dictionary of Now Up-to-Date 4.

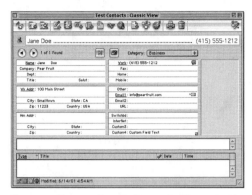

Figure 9.3 The sample contact record with new text in the Custom4 field after the script has run.

Script 9.1 This script assigns a constant value to the Custom4 field of all contacts in the current list view.

```
tell application "Now Contact"
    tell document 1
        set myPeopleIDs to unique id of every ¬
row of table 1
        if class of myPeopleIDs is not list ¬
then set myPeopleIDs to {myPeopleIDs}
        repeat with myPersonID in myPeopleIDs
            set (custom 4 of person id ¬
myPersonID) to "Custom Field Text"
        end repeat
    end tell
end tell
```

Adding Information to Every Contact in a List View

AppleScript introduces some powerful administrative and housekeeping capabilities to Now Contact. Managing a large contact file—especially a shared file from a contact server—can involve lots of work if you do everything by hand. Simply being able to add a value to a field in all visible contacts in a list can be a powerful capability. Consider using the script in **Script 9.1** to flag groups of records by assigning values to one or more custom fields.

Figure 9.3 shows the sample contact record after the script has run. Notice the string in the Custom4 field entered by the script.

To add information to a field in every contact in a list view:

1. `tell application "Now Contact"`

Start the conversation with Now Contact.

2. `tell document 1`

To access the frontmost contact file, address `document 1`.

3. `set myPeopleIDs to unique id of ¬`
`every row of table 1`

You store a list containing the ID of each person shown in the current list view, always known as `table 1`.

4. `if class of myPeopleIDs is not list ¬`
`then set myPeopleIDs to {myPeopleIDs}`

If only one person is in the list view, you need to coerce the variable to be a list, because Now will return just the ID as an integer.

5. `repeat with myPersonID in myPeopleIDs`

Now you can start a repeat loop that runs once for each person in the current list view of the frontmost contact file.

continues on next page

ADDING INFORMATION TO EVERY CONTACT

6. `set (custom 4 of person id ¬`
   `myPersonID) to "Custom Field Text"`

In the loop, you can set the value of the Custom4 field in the current person's contact record to anything you want.

7. `end repeat`
   `   end tell`
   `end tell`

You conclude the loop and the nested tell blocks.

✔ Tip

- Power On Software appears to be committed to expanding its support for AppleScript. The product CD-ROM includes well-written example scripts and notes.

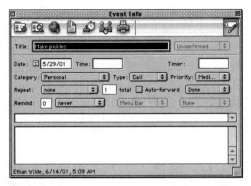

Figure 9.4 A sample event window with the Done flag set by the script.

Marking Events As Done

The most important use of scripting is to make you feel that you are getting things finished. What better way to check off all those old nagging to-do items from your Now Up-to-Date calendar than to run a script?

This section illustrates how easily you can access events and manipulate them. It also introduces a special aspect of Now Up-to-Date calendar events that are normally hidden from the user of the application: time blocks.

Think of time blocks as being a series of entries denoting the days an event takes place on. Any repeating, or *banner*, event uses multiple time blocks to store this multiple-day information. In AppleScript, each time block is an element of the event to which it belongs (**Script 9.2**).

Figure 9.4 shows a sample event window with the Done flag set by the script.

To mark all events with starting dates before today as done:

1. `set mydate to current date`

   Start the script by storing the current date in the `mydate` variable.

2. `tell application "Now Up-to-Date"`

   Now you can start talking to Now Up-to-Date.

3. `set myCalendars to name of every ¬`
   `calendar of document 1`

   Store the list of names of all calendar categories in the `myCalendars` variable.

4. `repeat with myCalendar in myCalendars`

   Now you can loop through each category in the open calendar document. If you wanted to make changes in only some categories, you could add an `if...then` to test the name of the current category, stored in `myCalendar`.

continues on next page

5. `set myeventcount to count of (every ¬`
`event of calendar (myCalendar as ¬`
`string) of document 1)`

Now you get the total number of events in the current category.

6. `repeat with myeventnum from 1 to ¬`
`myeventcount`

You loop through each event in the current category so that you can check the event's time blocks and mark any old events as done.

7. `set mytimeblocknum to count of (every ¬`
`timeblock of (event myeventnum of ¬`
`calendar (myCalendar as string) of ¬`
`document 1))`

By now, this code should look familiar. You need to get the number of time blocks in the current event. Each time block is essentially one day in a multiple-day repeating event. Typically, only banner events have multiple time blocks.

Script 9.2 This script marks all events with starting dates before today as done.

```
                              script
set mydate to current date
tell application "Now Up-to-Date"
    set myCalendars to name of every calendar of document 1
    repeat with myCalendar in myCalendars
set myeventcount to count of (every event of calendar (myCalendar as string) of document 1)
        repeat with myeventnum from 1 to myeventcount
            set mytimeblocknum to count of (every timeblock of (event myeventnum of calendar (myCalendar ¬
as string) of document 1))
            repeat with myblocknum from 1 to mytimeblocknum
                set myStart to startdatetime of timeblock 1 of event 1 of calendar (myCalendar as string) ¬
of document 1
                    if myStart < mydate then
                    set completed of (timeblock myblocknum of (event myeventnum of calendar (myCalendar ¬
as string) of document 1)) to true
                else
                    set completed of (timeblock myblocknum of (event myeventnum of calendar (myCalendar ¬
as string) of document 1)) to false
                    end if
end repeat
        end repeat
    end repeat
end tell
```

8. `repeat with myblocknum from 1 to ¬`
`mytimeblocknum`

Now you can loop through each time block.

9. `set myStart to startdatetime of ¬`
`timeblock 1 of event 1 of calendar ¬`
`(myCalendar as string) of document 1`

To make things simpler, store the starting date of the time block in myStart.

10. `if myStart < mydate then`
`  set completed of (timeblock ¬`
`myblocknum of (event myeventnum of ¬`
`calendar (myCalendar as string) of ¬`
`document 1)) to true`
`else`
`  set completed of (timeblock ¬`
`myblocknum of (event myeventnum of ¬`
`calendar (myCalendar as string) of ¬`
`document 1)) to false`
`end if`

You check the start date of the current time block. If that date is older than today, set the completed flag for the time block so the event will appear as completed.

11. `end repeat`
`      end repeat`
`    end repeat`
`end tell`

You end the nested loops and tell block.

Moving Calendar Events Between Categories

A Now Up-to-Date calendar can get filled up with thousands of events over time. A calendar can include many categories, especially when it is shared in a group. With all this event data floating around the office, who is going to keep it tidy and straighten things up once in a while? Well, if you're that person, you will like this script.

Script 9.3 shows some real power for the calendar administrator. This script lets you copy events from one category to another quickly, preserving almost every detail from the original event. This process is invaluable if you want to perform any category housekeeping in Up-to-Date.

Figures 9.5 and **9.6** show the List view with two events and their categories, before and after the script has been run.

To move calendar events from one category to another:

1. `tell application "Now Up-to-Date"`

   You start sending commands to Now Up-to-Date.

2. `set myfromcategories to {}`
   `set mytocategories to {}`

   You initialize two list variables to hold the lists of available calendar categories among which to move events.

3. `repeat with myCalendarNum from 1 to ¬`
   `count of (every calendar of document 1)`

   This loop repeats once for each calendar category in the frontmost calendar file so that can build up your lists of categories in `myfromcategories` and `mytocategories`.

   continues on next page

Figure 9.5 List view with two events and their categories before the script has been run.

Figure 9.6 List view with two events and their categories after the script has been run.

Script 9.3 This script moves calendar events from one category to another.

```
tell application "Now Up-to-Date"
set myfromcategories to {}
   set mytocategories to {}
repeat with myCalendarNum from 1 to count of ¬
(every calendar of document 1)
if (count of (every event of calendar ¬
myCalendarNum of document 1)) > 0 then set ¬
myfromcategories to myfromcategories & (name ¬
of calendar myCalendarNum of document 1) as list
set mytocategories to mytocategories & (name ¬
of calendar myCalendarNum of document 1) as list
   end repeat
end tell
set mysource to (choose from list ¬
myfromcategories with prompt "Select category ¬
to merge (moves all events)") as string
set mydestination to (choose from list ¬
mytocategories with prompt "Select category ¬
to merge into") as string
if mysource is not "false" and mydestination ¬
is not "false" then
tell application "Now Up-to-Date"
set myevents to every event of calendar named ¬
mysource of document 1
set mynumberofevents to count of (every event ¬
of calendar named mysource of document 1)
if mynumberofevents > 0 thenrepeat with
myeventnum from mynumberofevents ¬
to 1 by -1
```

(script continues on next page)

Script 9.3 *continued*

```
                                                    script

try
set myevent to (a reference to event myeventnum of calendar named mysource of document 1)
set mystartdates to {}
                set mystarttimes to {}
                set myendtimes to {}
                set mydurations to {}
                set mycompleteds to {}
repeat with mytimeblocknum from 1 to count of (every timeblock of myevent)
                set mystartdates to mystartdates & (startdate of timeblock mytimeblocknum of ¬
myevent) as list
                set mystarttimes to mystarttimes & (starttime of timeblock mytimeblocknum of ¬
myevent) as list
                set myendtimes to myendtimes & (endtime of timeblock mytimeblocknum of myevent) ¬
as list
                set mydurations to mydurations & (duration of timeblock mytimeblocknum of myevent) ¬
as list
                set mycompleteds to mycompleteds & (completed of timeblock mytimeblocknum of ¬
myevent) as list
                end repeat
set myfirstnames to {}
                set mylastnames to {}
                set myphones to {}
                set myphtitles to {}
                set mycompanynames to {}
                set mycontactlinks to {}
repeat with myEntityNum from 1 to count of (every person of myevent)
                set myfirstnames to myfirstnames & (firstname of person myEntityNum of myevent) ¬
as list
                set mylastnames to mylastnames & (lastname of person myEntityNum of myevent) as list
                set myphones to myphones & (phone of person myEntityNum of myevent) as list
                set myphtitles to myphtitles & (phonetitle of person myEntityNum of myevent) as list
                set mycompanynames to mycompanynames & (companyname of person myEntityNum of ¬
myevent) as list
                set mycontactlinks to mycontactlinks & (contactlink of person myEntityNum of ¬
myevent) as list
                end repeat
set myname to name of myevent
                set mydescription to description of myevent
                set myowner to owner of myevent
                set mypriority to priority of myevent
                set myremindermethod to remindermethod of myevent
                set myremindbefore to remindbefore of myevent
                set myeventtype to eventtype of myevent
                set mycarryforward to carry forward of myevent
                set mystartdate to startdate of myevent
                set mystarttime to starttime of myevent
                set myendtime to endtime of myevent
                set myduration to duration of myevent
set mynewevent to make new event at calendar named mydestination of document 1 with properties ¬
{name:myname, description:mydescription, owner:myowner, priority:mypriority, ¬
```

(script continues on next page)

MOVING EVENTS BETWEEN CATEGORIES

4. if (count of (every event of calendar ¬
myCalendarNum of document 1)) > 0 ¬
then set myfromcategories to ¬
myfromcategories & (name of calendar ¬
myCalendarNum of document 1) as list

Here is a trick. You only want categories
that have events in them appearing in the
list of categories available to the user to
choose to move events from, so you
check whether the category has any
events in it before adding the category
name to the myfromcategories list.

Script 9.3 *continued*

```
                                        script
remindermethod:myremindermethod, remindbefore:myremindbefore, eventtype:myeventtype, carry ¬
forward:mycarryforward, startdate:mystartdate, starttime:mystarttime, endtime:myendtime, ¬
duration:myduration}
repeat with mytimeblocknum from 1 to count of (every timeblock of myevent)
            set mystartdateitem to item mytimeblocknum of (mystartdates as list)
            set mystarttimeitem to item mytimeblocknum of (mystarttimes as list)
            set myendtimeitem to item mytimeblocknum of (myendtimes as list)
            set mydurationitem to item mytimeblocknum of (mydurations as list)
            set mycompleteditem to item mytimeblocknum of (mycompleteds as list)
            make new timeblock at mynewevent with properties {startdate:mystartdateitem ¬
                , starttime:mystarttimeitem, endtime:myendtimeitem, duration:mydurationitem ¬
                , completed:mycompleteditem}
            end repeat
repeat with myEntityNum from 1 to count of (every person of myevent)
            set myfirstnameitem to item myEntityNum of (myfirstnames as list)
            set mylastnameitem to item myEntityNum of (mylastnames as list)
            set myphoneitem to item myEntityNum of (myphones as list)
            set myphtitleitem to item myEntityNum of (myphtitles as list)
            set mycompanynameitem to item myEntityNum of (mycompanynames as list)
            set mycontactlinkitem to item myEntityNum of (mycontactlinks as list)
            make new person at mynewevent with properties {firstname:myfirstnameitem ¬
                , lastname:mylastnameitem, phone:myphoneitem, phonetitle:myphtitleitem ¬
                , companyname:mycompanynameitem, contactlink:mycontactlinkitem}
            end repeat
set myDeleteFlag to true
on error
            set myDeleteFlag to false
        end try
if myDeleteFlag then delete (event myeventnum of calendar named mysource of document 1)
end repeat
        end if
    end tell
end if
```

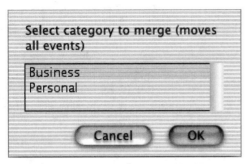

Figure 9.7 The list dialog box displayed by the choose from list command.

5. set mytocategories to mytocategories ¬
& (name of calendar myCalendarNum of ¬
document 1) as list
  end repeat
end tell

All categories in the calendar should be available as a destination for the events to move, so you append each category name to the mytocategories list before ending the loop.

6. set mysource to (choose from list ¬
myfromcategories with prompt "Select ¬
category to merge (moves all ¬
events)") as string

Now you ask the user to choose a category from which to move events. **Figure 9.7** shows the list dialog box that is displayed by the choose from list command.

7. set mydestination to (choose from ¬
list mytocategories with prompt ¬
"Select category to merge into") as ¬
string

Next, you ask for the category into which to move events.

8. if mysource is not "false" and ¬
mydestination is not "false" then

This code makes sure that the user did not click the Cancel button in either of the Choose List dialog boxes.

9. tell application "Now Up-to-Date"

You chat with Up-to-Date again as you prepare to move events around.

10. set myevents to every event of ¬
calendar named mysource of document 1

You gather a list of references to every event in the original category.

continues on next page

MOVING EVENTS BETWEEN CATEGORIES

11. `set mynumberofevents to count of ¬`
`(every event of calendar named`
`mysource of document 1)`

You also store the number of events in the list in a variable for easy use later.

12. `if mynumberofevents > 0 then`

Before proceeding, you check to make sure that you have some events to move.

13. `repeat with myeventnum from ¬`
`mynumberofevents to 1 by -1`

Now you can loop through each event in the category from which you are moving events.

14. `try`

A try block will help you avoid any execution-stopping errors.

15. `set myevent to (a reference to event`
`myeventnum of calendar named`
`mysource of document 1)`

You store an object reference to the current event in the myevent variable to make things simpler later in the code.

16. `set mystartdates to {}`
`set mystarttimes to {}`
`set myendtimes to {}`
`set mydurations to {}`
`set mycompleteds to {}`

These list variables are initialized so that you can fill them with the useful properties of the time blocks for the current event. You do this because you will be making a new event in the destination category that matches the original one as closely as possible. To create this new event, you need to collect all the details about the existing one first. You are not actually moving the events in this script; the process is more like copying them.

17.
```
repeat with mytimeblocknum from 1 to ¬
count of (every timeblock of
myevent)
  set mystartdates to mystartdates & ¬
(startdate of timeblock ¬
mytimeblocknum of myevent) as list
  set mystarttimes to mystarttimes ¬
& (starttime of timeblock ¬
mytimeblocknum of myevent) as list
  set myendtimes to myendtimes & ¬
(endtime of timeblock mytimeblocknum ¬
of myevent) as list
  set mydurations to mydurations & ¬
(duration of timeblock mytimeblocknum ¬
of myevent) as list
  set mycompleteds to mycompleteds ¬
& (completed of timeblock ¬
mytimeblocknum of myevent) as list
end repeat
```

This loop builds the lists of properties for each time block in the variables for later use.

18.
```
set myfirstnames to {}
set mylastnames to {}
set myphones to {}
set myphtitles to {}
set mycompanynames to {}
set mycontactlinks to {}
```

In addition to time blocks, you want to gather all you can about any contacts linked to the event. These variables will hold the relevant properties for any people attached for use in creating the new event later.

continues on next page

MOVING EVENTS BETWEEN CATEGORIES

19.
```
repeat with myEntityNum from 1 to ¬
count of (every person of myevent)
  set myfirstnames to myfirstnames & ¬
(firstname of person myEntityNum of ¬
myevent) as list
  set mylastnames to mylastnames & ¬
(lastname of person myEntityNum of ¬
myevent) as list
  set myphones to myphones & (phone ¬
of person myEntityNum of myevent) as ¬
list
  set myphtitles to myphtitles & ¬
(phonetitle of person myEntityNum of ¬
myevent) as list
  set mycompanynames to ¬
mycompanynames & (companyname of ¬
person myEntityNum of myevent) as list
  set mycontactlinks to ¬
mycontactlinks & (contactlink of ¬
person myEntityNum of myevent) as list
end repeat
```
This loop populates the lists of properties for each contact linked to the event you're copying.

20.
```
set myname to name of myevent
set mydescription to description of ¬
myevent
set myowner to owner of myevent
set mypriority to priority of myevent
set myremindermethod to ¬
remindermethod of myevent
set myremindbefore to remindbefore ¬
of myevent
set myeventtype to eventtype of ¬
myevent
set mycarryforward to carry forward ¬
of myevent
set mystartdate to startdate of ¬
myevent
set mystarttime to starttime of ¬
myevent
set myendtime to endtime of myevent
set myduration to duration of myevent
```
Now you collect the useful individual properties from the event itself.

21.
```
set mynewevent to make new event at ¬
calendar named mydestination of ¬
document 1 with properties {name:¬
myname, description:mydescription, ¬
owner:myowner, priority:mypriority, ¬
remindermethod:myremindermethod, ¬
remindbefore:myremindbefore, ¬
eventtype:myeventtype, carry ¬
forward:mycarryforward, ¬
startdate:mystartdate, starttime:¬
mystarttime, endtime:myendtime, ¬
duration:myduration}
```

Finally, you are ready to make the new event in the destination category with all the old event's properties stored in variables.

22.
```
repeat with mytimeblocknum from 1 to ¬
count of (every timeblock of myevent)
   set mystartdateitem to item ¬
mytimeblocknum of (mystartdates as list)
   set mystarttimeitem to item ¬
mytimeblocknum of (mystarttimes as list)
   set myendtimeitem to item ¬
mytimeblocknum of (myendtimes as list)
   set mydurationitem to item ¬
mytimeblocknum of (mydurations as list)
   set mycompleteditem to item ¬
mytimeblocknum of (mycompleteds as list)
   make new timeblock at mynewevent ¬
with properties {startdate:¬
mystartdateitem ¬
   , starttime:mystarttimeitem, ¬
endtime:myendtimeitem, duration:¬
mydurationitem ¬
   , completed:mycompleteditem}
end repeat
```

With the new event in place, you loop and add time blocks to the new event to match the old event.

continues on next page

MOVING EVENTS BETWEEN CATEGORIES

23.
```
repeat with myEntityNum from 1 to ¬
count of (every person of myevent)
   set myfirstnameitem to item ¬
myEntityNum of (myfirstnames as list)
   set mylastnameitem to item ¬
myEntityNum of (mylastnames as list)
   set myphoneitem to item myEntityNum ¬
of (myphones as list)
   set myphtitleitem to item ¬
myEntityNum of (myphtitles as list)
   set mycompanynameitem to item ¬
myEntityNum of (mycompanynames as list)
   set mycontactlinkitem to item ¬
myEntityNum of (mycontactlinks as list)
  make new person at mynewevent with ¬
properties {firstname:myfirstnameitem ¬
     , lastname:mylastnameitem, ¬
phone:myphoneitem, phonetitle:¬
myphtitleitem ¬
     , companyname:mycompanynameitem, ¬
contactlink:mycontactlinkitem}
end repeat
```
Last but not least, you create contact links to the new event in a loop to match any links from the old event.

24.
```
set myDeleteFlag to true
```
Remember that you have been executing inside a try block. If any errors happen before this line, AppleScript jumps immediately to the on error portion of the try block. Therefore, if this line is processed, you can be sure that you've successfully made a new event and attached everything you needed to attach. So you store this information in a simple variable, myDeleteFlag, for later use.

25.
```
on error
  set myDeleteFlag to false
end try
```
If an error occurs while trying to make a new event to match the old one, you set the flag variable myDeleteFlag to false so that the code doesn't delete the original event.

26. `if myDeleteFlag then delete (event ¬`
`myeventnum of calendar named mysource ¬`
`of document 1)`

When the work is over, you can decide whether to delete the original event. Delete it only if you're sure that the new event was created successfully.

27. `end repeat`
`      end if`
`   end tell`
`end if`

You conclude the loop, conditionals, and `tell` block.

Creating a Multiple-Day Banner Event

The scope of this script's efforts is clear: make a banner in the active Now Up-to-Date calendar. This process probably sounds simple to you. But this seemingly simple exercise will teach you about the relationship between calendar events and time blocks. If you are a longtime user of Now Up-to-Date, you possibly haven't come face to face with a time block yet. Time blocks track multiple-day events, such as repeating events or banners.

To help you learn how to make multiple-day events, **Script 9.4** creates a banner event. This functionality could be easily tied to a FileMaker database, for example, to let you map project phases to a calendar.

Figure 9.8 shows the script-created banner event in the Month view of Now Up-to-Date.

Figure 9.8 The script-created banner event in the Month view of Now Up-to-Date.

To create a multiple-day banner event in the active calendar file:

1. ```
   set mycategory to "Personal"
   set mystartdate to current date
   set myduration to 10
   ```
   Before you make the banner event, set up the calendar category, start date, and length (in days) for the event in some variables.

2. ```
   tell application "Now Up-to-Date"
       set myevent to make event at ¬
   calendar mycategory of document 1 ¬
   with properties {name:"My Event", ¬
   description:"A great time", ¬
   eventtype:banner, remindermethod:¬
   remindnone, startdate:mystartdate}
   end tell
   ```
   You chat with Now Up-to-Date, telling it to create a new banner event.

Script 9.4 This script creates a multiday banner event in the active calendar file.

```
script

set mycategory to "Personal"
set mystartdate to current date
set myduration to 10
tell application "Now Up-to-Date"
    set myevent to make event at calendar ¬
mycategory of document 1 with properties ¬
{name:"My Event", description:"A great time", ¬
eventtype:banner, remindermethod:remindnone, ¬
startdate:mystartdate}
end tell
repeat with myTimeBlocks from 1 to myduration
tell application "Now Up-to-Date"
        make new timeblock at myevent with ¬
properties {startdate:mystartdate}
    end tell
set mystartdate to mystartdate + days * 1
end repeat
```

3. `repeat with myTimeBlocks from 1 to ¬`
`myduration`

You need to loop to create a time block for each day in the banner.

4. `tell application "Now Up-to-Date"`
`    make new timeblock at myevent with ¬`
`properties {startdate:mystartdate}`
`end tell`

Here, you ask Now Up-to-Date to add time block to the event you created with the date stored in mystartdate.

5. `set mystartdate to mystartdate + days * 1`
`end repeat`

Before ending the loop, add a day to the date value mystartdate.

CREATING A MULTIPLE-DAY BANNER EVENT

Exporting Contact Data to FileMaker Pro

When you start scripting Now Up-to-Date and Now Contact, it becomes apparent that they are basically database applications. A calendar filled with events and an address book filled with contacts can be databases filled with records. Scripting lets you share the data from Now with other databases easily, without user intervention. Why would you want to do such a thing? Perhaps you manage your office projects in FileMaker and want to use contact information from Now Contact in the project records. Why should you type that information twice or put up with tedious exports and imports of data that might change regularly? Use a script to sync your data from Now, and you will spend less time typing.

Script 9.5 demonstrates how to move the names and work phone numbers of the contacts in the current list view into an empty FileMaker Pro database. You need to have a database open in FileMaker, with fields named name and work phone, before running this script.

Figure 9.9 shows the records created in the FileMaker Pro database by the script.

To export contact data to FileMaker Pro:

1. `tell application "Now Contact"`

   You start by letting AppleScript know that you want to talk to Now Contact.

2. `try`

   You use a `try` block here in case no contacts are visible in the current list, in which case Now Contact generates an error normally.

Figure 9.9 Records created in the FileMaker Pro database by the script.

Script 9.5 This script exports contact data to FileMaker Pro.

```
                    script
tell application "Now Contact"
try
set myPeopleInfo to {name, work phone} of ¬
every row of table 1 of document 1
        set myPeopleCount to count of every ¬
row of table 1 of document 1
on error
        set myPeopleInfo to {}
end try
end tell
if myPeopleInfo is not {} then
tell application "FileMaker Pro"
delete every record of database 1
repeat with myPeople from 1 to myPeopleCount
        create new record at database 1
        end repeat
set field "name" of database 1 to (item 1 of ¬
myPeopleInfo)
        set field "work phone" of database 1 ¬
to (item 2 of myPeopleInfo)
end tell
end if
```

3. `set myPeopleInfo to {name, work ¬`
`phone} of every row of table 1 of ¬`
`document 1`
`set myPeopleCount to count of every ¬`
`row of table 1 of document 1`

You ask Now Contact to give you a list of the names and work phone numbers of the visible contacts in the current list view. A standard convention of Now Contact is to call the current list view `table 1`. When you talk about the contacts list view as a `table`, each contact is considered to be a `row` of the `table`.

4. `on error`
`    set myPeopleInfo to {}`

If an error occurs, set the information variable to an empty list as a flag to the code later.

5. `end try`
`end tell`

You conclude the `try` block and finish talking to Now Contact.

6. `if myPeopleInfo is not {} then`

It's good to make sure that you have some data in `myPeopleInfo` before proceeding, because without data, you have nothing else to do.

7. `tell application "FileMaker Pro"`

With some data, you start talking to FileMaker.

8. `delete every record of database 1`

You clear out the database so that it will contain only the new records.

9. `repeat with myPeople from 1 to ¬`
`myPeopleCount`
`    create new record at database 1`
`end repeat`

You loop to create a new record for each person displayed in Now's list view.

continues on next page

10. `set field "name" of database 1 to ¬`
`(item 1 of myPeopleInfo)`
`set field "work phone" of database 1 ¬`
`to (item 2 of myPeopleInfo)`

With only the new records in the database, now you can set the data for each record. Set the data for the name and work phone cells in every record at the same time by putting the lists you got from Now Contact into the `field` object. A `field` is a list that contains the data for a single cell across every record.

11. `end tell`
`end if`

You conclude your conversation with FileMaker and the `if...then` test.

✔ Tip

- When you need to find out whether a contact exists, and use a whose or where clause to filter, be aware of the way Now Contact behaves with whose and where clauses. Now Contact always says that something exists when asked about it in such a clause. The code `every person whose first name starts with "A" exists`, for example, always returns `true` from Now Contact, so to find out about the existence of an object, test to see whether you have more than zero of them. The code `(count of every person whose first name starts with "A")>0` returns the correct result: `true` or `false`.

ADOBE
INDESIGN 1.5

Scripting Adobe InDesign 1.5

The scripts in this chapter were tested with Adobe InDesign 1.5.

Adobe InDesign is developed by Adobe Systems Inc. (http://www.adobe.com/).

Adobe Systems has established a solid track record of bringing AppleScript support to its product line, starting with InDesign 1.0 and Illustrator 9.0. The Scripting Guide documentation that comes with InDesign provides exhaustive coverage of every detail of AppleScript in InDesign. Visit the Adobe InDesign Web site for access to online scripting resources, including a monitored user forum. **Figure 10.1** shows the extensive AppleScript dictionary included with InDesign.

Figure 10.1 InDesign's extensive AppleScript dictionary.

When Adobe decided to build its own page-layout superapplication, its designers may have looked at the benchmark QuarkXPress set in this application space. Perhaps that helps explain why such a complete and robust scripting implementation is incorporated into InDesign.

Whether you're a changeover from Quark or a new page-layout user who's used only InDesign, you are bound to appreciate the help AppleScript can give you in your day-to-day work. With InDesign, almost every aspect of document creation and manipulation can be controlled from a script. In this chapter, you'll explore some of these aspects as you modify page elements selectively, create an index page based on tagged document text, and change styles in a text selection.

Modifying Graphic Shapes and Text in a Spread

Often, when you have a multiple-page document filled with text and art, you want to apply uniform settings to objects in the document.

The script in **Script 10.1** performs selective changes on objects in the current spread based on what kinds of objects they are. Graphic shapes are stroked with a 2-point line, and any text wrap is removed from them. All text objects are changed so they have a fill color of none or transparent.

Figure 10.2 shows a sample document that includes 1-point lines and a filled rectangle with a runaround setting. **Figure 10.3** shows the same document after the script runs. Note the transparency and lack of any runaround for the rectangle, as well as the heavier weight of the lines.

To modify graphic shapes and text in the active spread:

1. `tell application "InDesign 1.5"`

You start by letting AppleScript know you are ready to talk to InDesign.

2. `activate`

Next, you bring the application to the foreground.

3. `set mySpread to active spread of ¬`
`active window`

Now you store a reference to the active spread of the frontmost document in the mySpread variable for later use.

4. `repeat with myItemNum from 1 to ¬`
`(number of page items of mySpread)`

You begin a loop with an instance for each item in the current spread.

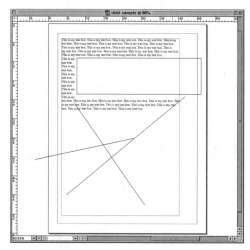

Figure 10.2 Sample document that includes 1-point lines and a filled rectangle with runaround.

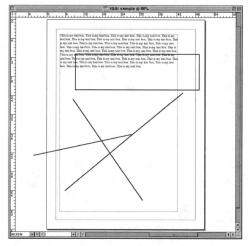

Figure 10.3 The document in Figure 10.2 after the script runs.

Script 10.1 This script performs selective changes to objects in the current spread based on what kind of object they are.

```
                    script
tell application "InDesign 1.5"
activate
set mySpread to active spread of active window
repeat with myItemNum from 1 to (number of ¬
page items of mySpread)
set myPageItem to page item myItemNum of ¬
mySpread
if class of myPageItem is rectangle or class ¬
of myPageItem is oval or class of myPageItem ¬
is polygon or class of myPageItem is graphic ¬
line then
set the text wrap of myPageItem to none
set the stroke weight of myPageItem to 2
else if class of myPageItem is text frame then
set the fill color of myPageItem to swatch ¬
"None" of active document
end if
    end repeat
end tell
```

5. `set myPageItem to page item ¬`
`myItemNum of mySpread`

You store a reference to the current page item of the loop in the `myPageItem` variable.

6. `if class of myPageItem is rectangle ¬`
`or class of myPageItem is oval or ¬`
`class of myPageItem is polygon or ¬`
`class of myPageItem is graphic ¬`
`line then`

Now you can test the page item to see whether it is a graphic shape. If so, you will modify its attributes.

7. `set the text wrap of myPageItem ¬`
`to none`

You set the text wrap to off for the page item.

8. `set the stroke weight of myPageItem ¬`
`to 2`

Set the stroke weight to 2 points.

9. `else if class of myPageItem is text ¬`
`frame then`

If the page item is a text object, you will modify it in a different way from the way you modify the shapes.

10. `set the fill color of myPageItem to ¬`
`swatch "None" of active document`

Set the fill color of the text object to transparent.

11. `end if`
`  end repeat`
`end tell`

Finally, you end the loop and `tell` block.

Creating an Index Page of Specially Styled Text

Creating long cross-referenced documents is a normal operation in InDesign. It would be nice to have some script tools to help manage a large document that needs an index or table of contents.

The script in **Script 10.2** gives you a big break by creating an index page that contains all specially styled words and the page numbers where they occur.

Figure 10.4 shows the result of the script: a new page displaying all styled words found and the pages on which they occur.

To create an index page of all specially styled words:

1. `property myTagStyle : "Index"`

   You start by defining a property to contain the name of the character style you are searching for in the script.

2. `set myIndexEntries to {}`

   You also must initialize a variable, `myIndexEntries`, to contain the list of index-styled words and page numbers as you progress.

3. `tell application "InDesign 1.5"`

   Now you are ready to talk to InDesign.

4. `tell active document`
   `   set myTag to character style ¬`
   `myTagStyle`

   You really want to talk to the frontmost document.

5. `set myDocStories to object reference ¬`
   `of stories`

   You ask the frontmost document for a reference to every story it contains. You store this result in `myDocStories`.

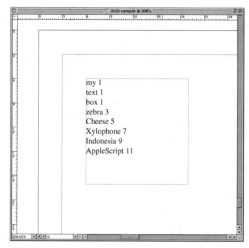

Figure 10.4 A new page displaying all styled words found and the pages on which they occur.

Script 10.2 This script creates an index page that contains all specially styled words and the page numbers where they occur.

```
script
property myTagStyle : "Index"
set myIndexEntries to {}
tell application "InDesign 1.5"
tell active document
    set myTag to character style myTagStyle
set myDocStories to object reference of ¬
stories
repeat with myDocStoryNum from 1 to count ¬
items of myDocStories
set myDocStory to object reference of item ¬
myDocStoryNum of myDocStories
repeat with myWordNum from 1 to count (words ¬
of myDocStory)
set myWord to object reference of word ¬
myWordNum of myDocStory
tell myWord
set myAppStyle to applied character style
        if myAppStyle ≠ none then
            if myAppStyle = myTag then
set myPage to parent
                set myPage to parent ¬
of myPage
set myPageNum to name of myPage
set myText to myWord & " " & myPageNum & return
set myIndexEntries to myIndexEntries & myText
end if
        end if
      end tell
    end repeat
  end repeat
  end tell
if myIndexEntries ≠ {} then
set myIndexPage to make new page at end of ¬
active document
tell myIndexPage
set myTextFrame to make text frame with ¬
properties {geometric bounds:{"6p", "6p", ¬
"19p", "19p"}}
set text of myTextFrame to (myIndexEntries ¬
as string)
end tell
  end if
end tell
```

6. `repeat with myDocStoryNum from 1 ¬`
`to count items of myDocStories`

You start a loop to traverse every story in the document.

7. `set myDocStory to object reference ¬`
`of item myDocStoryNum of myDocStories`

Next, you store a reference to the current story of the loop in the myDocStory variable.

8. `repeat with myWordNum from 1 to ¬`
`count (words of myDocStory)`

When you have the story, you loop through each word in the story.

9. `set myWord to object reference of ¬`
`word myWordNum of myDocStory`

In the loop through each word, you store a reference to the current word of the loop in the myWord variable.

10. `tell myWord`

You stored the referenced word so you can talk to the word. Yes, that's right. You want to get information about the word, so you target it directly.

11. `set myAppStyle to applied character ¬`
`style`
`if myAppStyle ≠ none then`
`  if myAppStyle = myTag then`

Here, because you are talking to the word, you get the character style that is applied to the word itself and compare it with the character style for which you are looking.

continues on next page

CREATING AN INDEX PAGE OF TEXT

181

12. `set myPage to parent`
`set myPage to parent of myPage`

Now you want to get the page reference that contains the word that is styled the way you want. To do so, you ask for the parent of the parent of the word. The parent of the word is a text frame, and the parent of the text frame is the page on which the word appears.

13. `set myPageNum to name of myPage`

It turns out that the name of any InDesign page is its page number, so you get the name of the page to retrieve its page number for the index entry.

14. `set myText to myWord & " " & ¬`
`myPageNum & return`

Now you are ready to create a string for the index entry by combining the word found and the number of the page on which it was found.

15. `set myIndexEntries to myIndexEntries ¬`
`& myText`

Last, you append the new index entry to the list of entries for later use.

16. `end if`
`            end if`
`         end tell`
`      end repeat`
`   end repeat`
` end tell`

You close all the conditionals, `tell` blocks, and loops.

17. `if myIndexEntries ≠ {} then`

When you are done looking through the document, you can test to see whether any entries were put in the `myIndexEntries` variable. If the variable is not empty, you have entries.

18. `set myIndexPage to make new page at ¬`
`end of active document`

To create the index, first make a new page and store a reference to it in the myIndexPage variable.

19. `tell myIndexPage`

Now you talk directly to the new page.

20. `set myTextFrame to make text frame ¬`
`with properties {geometric ¬`
`bounds:{"6p", "6p", "19p", "19p"}}`

You create a new text frame on the page and store a reference to it in the myTextFrame variable.

21. `set text of myTextFrame to ¬`
`(myIndexEntries as string)`

You set the text of the new frame to contain the index entries you have been collecting.

22. `end tell`
`  end if`
`end tell`

To conclude, close the tell blocks and conditional statement.

Modifying Matching Words in the Current Selection

InDesign is a master of text in many forms and fashions, but it is not capable of making intelligent changes in text based on its content. That task has been your ongoing responsibility. Now, with a little AppleScript, you can put some intelligence into the way InDesign formats text. A good example of smart formatting is the need to style certain words with special attributes.

In the script in **Script 10.3,** you look at all the text in the current selection and underline the words that match your choice. You easily could extend this script to operate on an entire document, if you want.

Figure 10.5 shows the dialog box that prompts the user for a word to search for in the current selection. **Figure 10.6** shows the InDesign document after the script has underlined the matching words.

To modify matching words in the current selection with underlines:

1. `set myWordMatch to text returned of ¬`
   `(display dialog "Word to find?" ¬`
   `default answer "AppleScript")`

   First, you set up the word you want to find in the selected text.

2. `tell application "InDesign 1.5"`

   Next, you begin talking to InDesign.

3. `set mySelection to selection`

   You assign the current selection to the mySelection variable.

4. `if class of mySelection = text then`

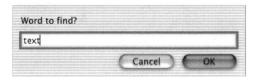

Figure 10.5 The dialog box that prompts the user for a word to search for in the current selection.

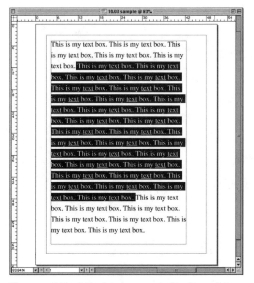

Figure 10.6 The InDesign document after the script has underlined the matching words.

Script 10.3 This script changes the attributes of the words that match the user's choice.

```
                    script
set myWordMatch to text returned of (display ¬
dialog "Word to find?" default answer ¬
"AppleScript")
tell application "InDesign 1.5"
set mySelection to selection
if class of mySelection = text then
set myTargetWords to (object reference of ¬
(every word of mySelection whose contents = ¬
myWordMatch))
repeat with myTargetWord in myTargetWords
        set underline of myTargetWord to ¬
true
      end repeat
end if
end tell
```

You test to see whether the selection contains text by testing its class. If some objects are selected in a document instead of text, the class of the selection is list.

5. `set myTargetWords to (object ¬`
   `reference of (every word of ¬`
   `mySelection whose contents = ¬`
   `myWordMatch))`

   Now you ask InDesign to give you a list of references to every word that matches your search work stored in myWordMatch. To do so, you use the powerful AppleScript filtering clause whose, which performs a search and return only the elements that match your criteria.

6. `repeat with myTargetWord in ¬`
   `myTargetWords`
   `    set the underline of myTargetWord ¬`
   `to true`
   `end repeat`

   Now you repeat through every reference to every word in the list of matching words, underlining each word.

7. `end if`
   `end tell`

   Finally, you end the conditional statement and tell block.

Counting Words in the Current Selection

Sure, you can make lots of long, complicated scripts to solve the detailed problems you encounter along the way. But what about those short and sweet scripts that truly satisfy? This section shows you just such a project: a short script that tells you how many words are in the current selection. This script is infinitely useful, yet brief and simple.

Script 10.4 counts all the words in the current selection in InDesign and displays a dialog box showing the word count.

Figure 10.7 shows the dialog box that displays the current word count.

To count all words in the current selection:

1. `tell application "InDesign 1.5"`

   You begin talking to InDesign.

2. `set mySelection to selection`

   You assign the current selection to the `mySelection` variable.

3. `if class of mySelection = text then`

   Now you test to see whether the selection contains text by testing its class. If some objects are selected in a document instead of text, the class of the selection is `list`.

4. `set myWordCount to count words of ¬ mySelection`

   Because you have text selected, you can ask InDesign to count the words in the selection by using its count command.

5. `end if`
   `end tell`
   `display dialog myWordCount & " words ¬ found in selection." as string`

   You end the conditional statement and tell block and display the number of words found in a dialog box

Figure 10.7 The script displays a dialog box that shows the word count of the current selection in InDesign.

Script 10.4 This script displays a dialog to the user with the word count for the current selection.

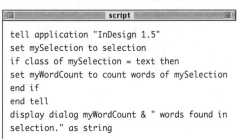

```
tell application "InDesign 1.5"
set mySelection to selection
if class of mySelection = text then
set myWordCount to count words of mySelection
end if
end tell
display dialog myWordCount & " words found in
selection." as string
```

ADOBE PHOTOSHOP 5 AND PHOTOSCRIPTER

Figure 11.1 PhotoScripter's dictionary entries for its Photoshop Basics Suite.

Before Photoshop 5.0, it was difficult to get impressive results with scripts for Photoshop. Armed only with the do script command to trigger actions I had to create manually, I was not having dazzling success with my Photoshop scripting efforts. Then, a new plug-in for Photoshop called PhotoScripter appeared.

PhotoScripter makes the world's most popular and powerful image-editing software, Adobe Photoshop 5, fully AppleScript-aware. And thanks to PhotoScripter, the AppleScript it speaks is clear and coherent, relying on an elegant and intuitive object model.

Figure 11.1 shows PhotoScripter's dictionary entries for file formats.

✔ Tips

- PhotoScripter is one of the few third-party implementations that support unit types such as pixels and inches. PhotoScripter lets you specify unit types by using the coercion operator as:
  ```
  set selection to {0 as pixels, 0 as
  pixels, 100 as pixels, 100 as pixels}
  ```

- Because of changes Adobe made to Photoshop 6.0, PhotoScripter works only with versions 5.0 and 5.5. If you want to use PhotoScripter, you need to stick with Photoshop 5.0 and 5.5

Creating and Exporting Graphical Text

Now that you've got scriptable Photoshop, what are you going to do with it?

Good question.

Many people use Photoshop to produce graphical text. This script automates that task.

This script in **Script 11.1** creates a yellow oval and draws blue text on top of it before exporting the image as an interlaced GIF. Simply set the list variable myMastheads to the list of strings you want to produce as graphics, and the script creates a series of interlaced GIF images, using a minimal color palette. **Figure 11.2** shows the document in Photoshop after the first item of text has been drawn and the image has been flattened in the conversion process. You can draw any shapes you want besides filled ellipses by using the draw command.

To create and export graphics and text:

1. set myFolder to (choose folder) as text

   You prompt the user to select a folder. You save a reference to the folder in the myFolder variable.

2. tell application "Adobe® Photoshop® ¬ 5.0.2"

   Next, you bring Photoshop to the front.

3. set mymastheads to {"Hello ¬ Earthlings!", "What's Up?"}

   You define the list of strings to rasterize on top of the drawing layer in myMastheads.

4. set myfont to "Helvetica"

   You use this variable, myFont, to define the font to use with the graphical text.

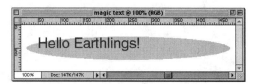

Figure 11.2 Our document in Photoshop after the first item of text has been drawn and the image has been flattened and converted.

Scripting Photoshop with PhotoScripter

All the scripts in this chapter were designed and tested for Adobe Photoshop 5.x and Main Event PhotoScripter 1.0.1.

When this book was published (in the fall of 2001), PhotoScripter did not support Photoshop 6.

Photoshop is developed by Adobe Systems Inc., which you can reach at http://www.adobe.com. PhotoScripter is published by Main Event Software, which you can reach at http://www.mainevent.com.

5. `set mysize to 30.5`

This variable, `mySize`, sets the point size of the graphical text.

6. `set mytextcolor to RGB color ¬`
`{red:0.0, green:0.0, blue:204.0}`

`myTextColor` defines the color (blue) that you'll use for the text. RGB colors are defined by a record with the properties `red`, `green`, and `blue`. Values for each property range from 0 to 255.

7. `set myobjectcolor to RGB color ¬`
`{red:255.0, green:204.0, blue:0.0}`

`myObjectColor` defines the color that you'll use for the filled oval—in this case, yellow, because 100% red plus 80% green yields a nice, rich, yellow RGB color.

8. `set myfileinfo to {caption:"Copyright ¬`
`2001 Ethan"}`

Here, you do something sly: set the variable `myFileInfo` as a caption field for the image with a copyright statement in a string. This information will be saved with the GIF image and will stay attached to it when it is transmitted over the Web.

9. `activate`
`set mynewdoc to make new document ¬`
`with properties {name:"magic text", ¬`
`color space:RGB mode, width:500 as ¬`
`pixels, height:100 as pixels, ¬`
`resolution:72 as density, fill ¬`
`contents:white}`

You create a new Photoshop RGB document named `magic text` that is 500 pixels wide by 100 pixels tall. You start with the document filled with white and set to a resolution of 72 dpi. The `make` command returns a reference to the new document, which you store in the `myNewDoc` variable.

continues on next page

10. `set the file info of mynewdoc to ¬`
`myfileinfo`

Now you set the `file info` property of the new document to the `myFileInfo` variable, where you saved the caption information.

11. `set the current foreground color to ¬`
`mytextcolor`
`repeat with i from 1 to number of ¬`
`items in mymastheads`

You begin a loop through each of the text strings stored in the list variable `myMastheads`.

12. `set mymasthead to item i of ¬`
`mymastheads`

Here, you store the current item from the list in `mymasthead`.

13. `make new layer`

You have Photoshop create a new layer.

14. `set selection to ellipse {25, 25, ¬`
`475, 75}`

You set the current selection to an ellipse defined by the list `{left,top,right,bottom}`.

15. `set the current foreground color ¬`
`to myobjectcolor`

Set Photoshop's foreground color to the object color you stored in `myObjectColor`.

16. `fill selection filling with ¬`
`foreground color with antialiasing`

Fill the current selection with the foreground color, antialiasing the edge of the selection.

17. `set the current foreground color ¬`
`to mytextcolor`

Now you set Photoshop's foreground color to the text color you stored in `myTextColor`.

18. `make new text layer with properties ¬`
`{text:mymasthead, position:{10 as ¬`
`pixels, 50 as pixels}, font:myfont, ¬`
`size:mysize, alignment:left justify, ¬`
`leading:mysize, tracking:0.0, auto ¬`
`kerning:true, antialiasing:true, ¬`
`rotating edges:true, orientation:¬`
`horizontally, is vertical:false, ¬`
`writing system:0}`

You create a new text layer, using variables to define the text to draw, its font, and its point size. You set the text to start appearing at 10 pixels from the left and 50 pixels from the top of the current document. You set the alignment on the text to left, set the leading to the same as the point size, turn on antialiasing, and draw the text horizontally.

19. `delete layer "Background" of ¬`
`current document`

You delete the old, useless Background layer.

20. `convert current document to indexed ¬`
`color mode {palette:web, dither ¬`
`method:diffusion, color matching ¬`
`quality:better, preserving exact ¬`
`colors:true} with flattening layers`

You convert the image to the Web palette, flattening any layers in the process.

21. `convert current document to RGB mode`

You convert back to RGB for a moment to perform a little trick.

22. `convert current document to indexed ¬`
`color mode {palette:exact, color ¬`
`matching quality:better, preserving ¬`
`exact colors:true} with flattening ¬`
`layers`

This step is the trick. You convert back to an indexed palette, using the same method to create a palette includes only the Web colors the image actually uses. This procedure can make files significantly smaller.

23. `save current document in file ¬`
`(myFolder & i & ".gif" as ¬`
`international text) as Compuserve ¬`
`GIF {interlacing:true}`

Save the interlaced GIF image under a new file name, using the .gif extension.

24. `convert current document to RGB mode`
`    end repeat`
`end tell`

You convert back to RGB mode for the next cycle of the loop.

Script 11.1 This script creates a yellow oval and draws blue text on top of it before exporting the whole thing as an interlaced GIF with the smallest possible color palette.

```
                                  script

set myFolder to (choose folder) as text"
tell application "Adobe® Photoshop® 5.0.2"
set mymastheads to {"Hello Earthlings!", "What's Up?"}
set myfont to "Helvetica"
set mysize to 30.5
set mytextcolor to RGB color {red:0.0, green:0.0, blue:204.0}
set myobjectcolor to RGB color {red:255.0, green:204.0, blue:0.0}
set myfileinfo to {caption:"Copyright 2001 Ethan"}
activate
    set mynewdoc to make new document with properties {name:"magic text", color space:RGB mode, ¬
width:500 as pixels, height:100 as pixels, resolution:72 as density, fill contents:white}
set the file info of mynewdoc to myfileinfo
set the current foreground color to mytextcolor
    repeat with i from 1 to number of items in mymastheads
set mymasthead to item i of mymastheads
make new layer
set selection to ellipse {25, 25, 475, 75}
set the current foreground color to myobjectcolor
fill selection filling with foreground color with antialiasing
set the current foreground color to mytextcolor
make new text layer with properties {text:mymasthead, position:{10 as pixels, 50 as pixels}, ¬
font:myfont, size:mysize, alignment:left justify, leading:mysize, tracking:0.0, auto kerning:true, ¬
antialiasing:true, rotating edges:true, orientation:horizontal, is vertical:false, writing system:0}
delete layer "Background" of current document
convert current document to indexed color mode {palette:web, dither method:diffusion, color matching ¬
quality:better, preserving exact colors:true} with flattening layers
convert current document to RGB mode
convert current document to indexed color mode {palette:exact, color matching quality:better, ¬
preserving exact colors:true} with flattening layers
save current document in file (myFolder & i & ".gif" as international text) as Compuserve GIF ¬
{interlacing:true}
convert current document to RGB mode
    end repeat
end tell
```

Figure 11.3
Photoshop's Layers palette looks like this as the script runs, cycling through the layers as it saves them to separate PICT files.

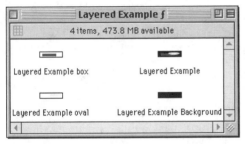

Figure 11.4 The new files in the folder, showing a file was created for each layer in the Photoshop document.

Exporting Each Layer of a Document As a Separate File

Have you ever had a huge Photoshop file filled with layers that were really wonderful—so wonderful that you wanted to make each layer its own file, to start the creative process with a cleaner slate? This script will do the trick. Just drop your many-layered Photoshop file onto the script-application icon after you save **Script 11.2** as an application.

Figure 11.3 shows Photoshop's Layers palette as it looks when the script is running, cycling through the layers as it saves them to separate PICT files. **Figure 11.4** shows the new files in the folder's Finder window, with a new file for each layer of the original file.

To export each layer of the current document as a separate file:

1. `on open (myfile)`

    The on open handler stores the file reference passed to it in the myFile variable.

2. `set mynewfile to (item 1 of myfile) ¬`
   `as string`

    Next, you save the path to the file as a string in the myNewFile variable.

3. `tell application "Adobe® Photoshop® ¬`
   `5.0.2"`
   `    activate`

    You bring Photoshop to the front.

4. `open myfile`

    You have Photoshop open the file referenced by the myFile variable.

5. `repeat with i from 1 to number of ¬`
   `layers in current document`

    You start looping through each layer in the document you've opened.

continues on next page

6. `select layer i of current document`

You make the layer with index number i in the loop the active layer.

7. `show layer i of current document ¬`
`with hiding others`

You show the layer with index number i, turning others off.

8. `set myfinalfile to (mynewfile & " " ¬`
`& (name of layer i of current ¬`
`document)) as international text`

You create a new file name made up of the original file name and the layer's name. You store this new name in the myFinalFile variable.

9. `save document 1 as PICT file ¬`
`{resolution:pixel depth 32, JPEG ¬`
`quality:maximum} in file myfinalfile ¬`
`with making copy without appending ¬`
`file extension`
`     end repeat`

Now you save the visible layer as a PICT file with the new file name.

10. `close document 1 saving no`
`   end tell`
`end open`

Finally, when the loop is finished, you close the original document without saving your changes.

Script 11.2 This script saves each layer as a separate PICT file for any Photoshop document you drop on it.

```
on open (myfile)
set mynewfile to (item 1 of myfile) as string
tell application "Adobe® Photoshop® 5.0.2"
        activate
open myfile
repeat with i from 1 to number of layers in ¬
current document
select layer i of current document
show layer i of current document with hiding ¬
others
set myfinalfile to (mynewfile & " " & (name of ¬
layer i of current document)) as international ¬
text
save document 1 as PICT file {resolution:pixel ¬
depth 32, JPEG quality:maximum} in file ¬
myfinalfile with making copy without ¬
appending file extension
        end repeat
close document 1 saving no
   end tell
end open
```

Figure 11.5
Photoshop's Layers palette as it appears while the script runs.

Importing a Folder of Files into a Document As Layers

Sometimes, you want to do the opposite of what you did in the preceding script—turn a bunch of flattened image files into layers in a single file. **Script 11.3** lets the user drop a folder of image files onto a script-application icon to make one new file in Photoshop. The script cycles through each file in the folder, flattening it and making it a new layer with the same name as the original file. **Figure 11.5** shows Photoshop's Layers palette as it looks while the script runs.

To import a folder of files into a new document as layers:

1. `on open (myFolder)`

   The `on open` handler stores the reference to the folder dropped on it in the `myFolder` variable.

2. `set myfiles to list folder myFolder ¬`
   `without invisibles`

   Next, you store the list of items in the folder `myFolder` in the `myFiles` variable. You use `without invisibles` to ignore invisible files.

3. `set myfirstfile to ((myFolder as ¬`
   `string) & item 1 of myfiles) as ¬`
   `string`

   You get the name of the first file in the list `myFiles`. You'll start with this file in the layer-building process

4. `set myFolder to myFolder as string`

   Make sure that `myFolder` holds the path to the folder as a string.

continues on next page

5. `tell application "Finder" to set ¬`
`mynewfile to (duplicate alias ¬`
`myfirstfile)`

Here, you have the Finder duplicate the file for which you stored a path in `myfirstfile`. You store the reference that the Finder returns in `mynewfile`. This reference points to the new duplicated file, which you'll have Photoshop open first.

6. `tell application "Adobe® Photoshop® ¬`
`5.0.2"`
`  activate`

Bring Photoshop to the front.

7. `open mynewfile`

You have Photoshop open the new duplicated file for which stored a reference in the `mynewfile` variable.

8. `flatten current document`

Have Photoshop flatten the document you just opened.

9. `repeat with i from 2 to number of ¬`
`items in myfiles`

Now you loop through all the other files that follow the first one in the list of files you stored in `myFiles`.

10. `set myfile to (myFolder & item i of ¬`
`myfiles) as international text`

In `myFile`, store the path to the file from the current item in the loop.

11. `open alias myfile`

You have Photoshop open the current file in the loop, which you've stored in `myFile`.

12. `flatten current document`

Photoshop flattens the document.

13. `set the selection to all pixels`

Select the entire document.

14. `copy`

Copy the entire document.

15. `close current document saving no`

You close the document without saving any changes.

16. `paste`

The current document is the one you started with, so paste in the copy of the document you just opened as a new layer.

17. `set the name of current layer to ¬`
`(item i of myfiles as international ¬`
`text)`
     `end repeat`
   `end tell`
`end open`

You set the name of the new layer you just created to the same name as the file that was the source for its image.

Script 11.3 This script create a single multilayered document from a series of flattened image files.

```
on open (myFolder)
set myfiles to list folder myFolder without invisibles
set myfirstfile to ((myFolder as string) & item 1 of myfiles) as string
set myFolder to myFolder as string
tell application "Finder" to set mynewfile to (duplicate alias myfirstfile)
tell application "Adobe® Photoshop® 5.0.2"
      activate
open mynewfile
flatten current document
repeat with i from 2 to number of items in myfiles
set myfile to (myFolder & item i of myfiles) as international text
open alias myfile
flatten current document
set the selection to all pixels
copy
close current document saving no
paste
set the name of current layer to (item i of myfiles as international text)
      end repeat
   end tell
end open
```

Adding Transparency to Grayscale Images

One wonderful feature of Photoshop is its capability to use an alpha channel so that layers can have levels of transparency. But when you scan something from a scanner, you get a fully opaque image without any transparency in it.

Script 11.4 batch-processes a folder of grayscale image files (such as line-art scans), eliminating the backgrounds so that the shapes float on a transparent layer. **Figures 11.6** and **11.7** show before-and-after views of an image containing shapes that need to be filled with white and then placed on a transparent layer.

To add transparency to a folder of grayscale images:

1. `property whiteX : 10`
   `property whiteY : 10`

   These properties define where the script will use the magic wand to click a white pixel.

2. `on run`
   `    tell me to open {(choose file)}`
   `end run`

   The run handler lets us test our open handler within Script Editor.

3. `on open (myFolder)`

   The on open handler stores the folder reference it receives in myFolder.

4. `set myfiles to list folder myFolder ¬`
   `as alias without invisibles`

   You store the list of items in the folder myFolder in myFiles.

5. `repeat with myfile in myfiles`

   Begin a loop through each item in myFiles, placing the current item in myFile.

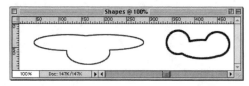

Figure 11.6 An opaque grayscale image ready to be converted to a transparent masked image.

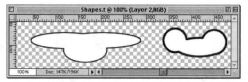

Figure 11.7 The same image made transparent with all closed shapes masked in white.

Script 11.4 This script converts opaque grayscale images, such as those created by scanning line art, to transparent masked images.

```
                         script
property whiteX : 10
property whiteY : 10
on run
    tell me to open {(choose file)}
end run
on open (myFolder)
set myfiles to list folder myFolder as alias¬
without invisibles
repeat with myfile in myfiles
set mycurrentfile to ((myFolder as string) & ¬
(myfile as string)) as string
tell application "Finder" to set mykind to ¬
kind of alias mycurrentfile
if mykind ≠ "folder" then
        maketransparent(mycurrentfile)
else
        tell me to open (mycurrentfile as ¬
alias)
    end if
  end repeat
end open
on maketransparent(myfile)
tell application "Adobe® Photoshop® 5.0.2"
        activate
open alias myfile
convert document 1 to grayscale mode without ¬
flattening layers
set the selection to all pixels
        copy
        paste
invert channel 1 of document 1
set the selection to channel 1 of document 1
set mylayer to (make new layer at document 1)
        fill the selection filling with black ¬
color
delete layer 1 of document 1
        delete layer "Background" of document 1
set the selection to the magic point {whiteX ¬
as pixels, whiteY as pixels}
expand by 1 as pixels
modify the selection using the inverse ¬
selection
set mylayer to (make new layer at document 1 ¬
with properties {blending mode:multiply mode})
fill the selection filling with white
merge layers document 1
set mynewfile to myfile as international text
        set mynewfile to mynewfile & ".t" as ¬
international text
```

(script continues on next page)

6. `set mycurrentfile to ((myFolder as ¬`
`string) & (myfile as string)) as ¬`
`string`

Now construct the path to the current file in the loop as a string and store it in the `myCurrentFile` variable.

7. `tell application "Finder" to set ¬`
`mykind to kind of alias mycurrentfile`

You have the Finder return in `myKind` the property of `mycurrentfile`.

8. `if mykind ≠ "folder" then`
`    maketransparent(mycurrentfile)`

If the item isn't a folder, it's a file, so you call the handler `makeTransparent` to convert the image.

9. `else`
`    tell me to open (mycurrentfile as ¬`
`alias)`
`end if`
`  end repeat`
`end open`

If the item is a folder, call your own open handler with a reference to the folder.

10. `on maketransparent(myfile)`

The `makeTransparent` handler receives a reference to the file it should try to convert in the `myFile` variable.

11. `tell application "Adobe® Photoshop® ¬`
`5.0.2"`
`    activate`

You bring Photoshop to the front.

12. `open alias myfile`

Open the current file referenced by `myFile`.

13. `convert document 1 to grayscale mode ¬`
`without flattening layers`

Have Photoshop convert the image to grayscale without flattening its layers.

continues on next page

14. `set the selection to all pixels`
`copy`
`paste`

You select the entire document, copy it, and paste it to create a new layer that is the same as the flattened image.

15. `invert channel 1 of document 1`

Then invert the color channel of the image.

16. `set the selection to channel 1 of ¬`
`document 1`

You select all the white pixels in the inverted image completely and select the gray ones with some transparency.

17. `set mylayer to (make new layer at ¬`
`document 1)`
`fill the selection filling with ¬`
`black color`

Create a new layer and fill the selection from the step above with black.

18. `delete layer 1 of document 1`
`delete layer "Background" of ¬`
`document 1`

Now you can delete the two layers you created in the process.

19. `set the selection to the magic point ¬`
`{whiteX as pixels, whiteY as pixels}`

You magic-wand the new transparent image, expecting to click a completely transparent pixel. This step begins the process of filling any closed shapes with white as a mask that you can use to color shapes later. You may need to change the values in `whiteX` and `whiteY`, depending on your image.

20. `expand by 1 as pixels`

Expand the magic wand's selection by 1 pixel to eat into the black lines.

Script 11.4 *continued*

```
save document 1 in file mynewfile
close document 1 saving no
    end tell
tell application "Finder" to set the label ¬
index of alias mynewfile to 1
end maketransparent
```

21. `modify the selection using the ¬`
`inverse selection`

You invert the selection so that you have selected the interiors of any closed shapes in the document.

22. `set mylayer to (make new layer at ¬`
`document 1 with properties {blending ¬`
`mode:multiply mode})`

You create a new layer with its blending mode set to `multiply`.

23. `fill the selection filling with white`

Fill the selection made earlier with white.

24. `merge layers document 1`

You merge the white layer and black layer of the document to create a transparent layer with filled, closed shapes.

25. `set mynewfile to myfile as ¬`
`international text`
`set mynewfile to mynewfile & ".t" ¬`
`as international text`

Here, you set `mynewfile` to a new file name by adding the `.t` extension to the original file name.

26. `save document 1 in file mynewfile`

You save the new document with the new file name.

27. `close document 1 saving no`
`  end tell`

You close the document without saving changes over the original.

28. `tell application "Finder" to set the ¬`
`label index of alias mynewfile to 1`
`end maketransparent`

Finally, have the Finder set the label of the new file.

Creating Animations

One of the most interesting features of PhotoScripter is the capability to script filters and lighting effects. The script in **Script 11.5** takes an image, duplicates it to a new layer, applies a filter to it, and then repeats the process five times. **Figures 11.8** and **11.9** show a document before and after being processed by this script.

To create an animation in a series of layers by repeated filtering:

1. `tell application "Adobe® Photoshop® ¬`
   `5.0.2"`
   　`activate`

   First, bring Photoshop to the front.

2. `set the selection to all pixels`
   `copy`
   `paste`

   You select the entire current document, copy it, and paste it to create a new layer with a copy of the original image.

3. `repeat with i from 1 to 5`

   Now you start a loop that you'll cycle through five times.

4. `paste`

   Paste the current image on the Clipboard into a new layer.

5. `set the selection to all pixels`

   Now you select that entire image.

6. `filter current document applying ¬`
   `twirl {angle:20}`

   Apply the twirl filter to the current selection, using a twirl angle of 20 degrees.

7. `copy`
   　`end repeat`
   `end tell`

   Finally, you copy the processed image to the Clipboard before continuing the loop.

Figure 11.8 Our original image file with some red graphical text in it.

Figure 11.9 The final layer of our document after the script has run, creating six layers, each progressively more filtered.

Script 11.5 This script creates a series of layers for use as animation frames.

```
tell application "Adobe® Photoshop® 5.0.2"
    activate
set the selection to all pixels
    copy
    paste
repeat with i from 1 to 5
paste
set the selection to all pixels
filter current document applying twirl ¬
{angle:20}
copy
    end repeat
end tell
```

✔ Tip

- You could combine this script with the following two scripts to preview and create animated GIFs directly in Photoshop.

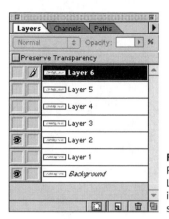

Figure 11.10
Photoshop's
Layers palette as
it looks while the
script is running.

Script 11.6 This script previews an animation created as
multiple layers by turning each layer on in sequence.

```
on run
    tell application "Adobe® Photoshop® 5.0.2"
        activate
hide every layer of document 1
set mylayers to number of layers in document 1
repeat with i from 1 to mylayers by 1
show layer i of document 1
if i > 1 then hide layer (i - 1) of document 1
        end repeat
    end tell
end run
```

Previewing an Animation Created As Separate Layers

When you've composed an animated scene in Photoshop in which each frame is a separate layer in your document, the script in **Script 11.6** will preview your animation in Photoshop by displaying the layers of the document one at a time. If you have a Background layer, this script ignores it. **Figure 11.10** shows what Photoshop's Layers palette looks like as the script runs.

To preview an animation created as separate layers:

1. `on run`
   `    tell application "Adobe® Photoshop®¬`
   `    5.0.2"`
   `        activate`
   Start by bringing Photoshop to the front.

2. `hide every layer of document 1`
   You hide every layer of the current document. In the current version of PhotoScripter, the hide command does not affect the Background layer. To modify this script to deal with the Background layer of a document, refer to it by name as `layer "Background"`.

3. `set mylayers to number of layers in ¬`
   `document 1`
   In the `myLayers` variable, you store the number of layers in the current document.

4. `repeat with i from 1 to mylayers by 1`
   Begin a loop through each layer in the document. If your animation goes in reverse order, change this line to read `repeat with i from myLayers to 1 by -1`.

continues on next page

5. `show layer i of document 1`

Have Photoshop make the current layer in the loop visible.

6. `if i > 1 then hide layer (i - 1) of ¬`
`document 1`
`        end repeat`
`    end tell`
`end run`

Here, you check to see whether you're in a layer after the first layer. If so, you turn off the layer before the current one before closing the loop and ending the run handler.

PREVIEWING AN ANIMATION

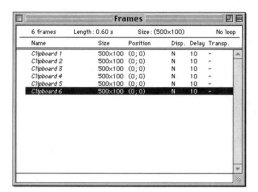

Figure 11.11 The Frames window in GifBuilder after our script has run, creating a six-frame GIF animation from the current layered Photoshop document.

Script 11.7 This script makes a multiframe GIF animation in GifBuilder from the current layered Photoshop document.

```
on run
    tell application "GifBuilder"
        activate
        new
    end tell
    tell application "Adobe® Photoshop® 5.0.2"
        activate
        show every layer of document 1
        set mylayers to number of layers in document 1
    end tell
    repeat with i from mylayers to 1 by -1
        tell application "Adobe® Photoshop® 5.0.2"
            activate
            select layer i of document 1
            set the selection to all pixels
            copy
        end tell
        tell application "GifBuilder"
            activate
            paste
        end tell
    end repeat
end run
```

Exporting a Layered Document As an Animated GIF with GifBuilder

If you've created a cool frame-based animation as a layered Photoshop document, this script is for you. **Script 11.7** works with GifBuilder to make an animated GIF from the current open document in Photoshop. **Figure 11.11** shows the Frames window in GifBuilder with a six-frame GIF animation created from a six-layer Photoshop file.

To export a layered Photoshop document as an animated GIF with GifBuilder:

1. `on run`
    `tell application "GifBuilder"`
        `activate`
        `new`
    `end tell`

Start by having GifBuilder come to the front and clearing its animation frames for a new animation.

2. `tell application "Adobe® Photoshop® ¬`
`5.0.2"`
    `activate`

Next, you have Photoshop come to the front.

3. `show every layer of document 1`

Then you have Photoshop make every layer in the current document visible.

4. `set mylayers to number of layers in ¬`
`document 1`
    `end tell`

In the `myLayers` variable, you store the number of layers in the current document.

continues on next page

EXPORTING A DOCUMENT WITH GIFBUILDER

5. `repeat with i from mylayers to 1 by -1`

Begin a loop through the layers, starting with the last one and going backward to the first layer.

6. `tell application "Adobe® Photoshop® ¬`
`5.0.2"`
   `activate`

You bring Photoshop to the front again.

7. `select layer i of document 1`

Make the current layer in the loop the active layer in Photoshop.

8. `set the selection to all pixels`
`copy`
     `end tell`

You select the entire image in the active layer and copy it to the Clipboard. Note that only nontransparent (opaque) pixels will be copied.

9. `tell application "GifBuilder"`
   `activate`
   `paste`
`end tell`
   `end repeat`
`end run`

Now bring GifBuilder to the front and paste the image from the Clipboard to a new frame in the current animation before closing the loop.

Scripting GifBuilder

This script uses GifBuilder 1.0. GifBuilder is freeware.

GifBuilder 1.0 is developed by Yves Piguet, who can be reached at http://homepage. mac.com/piguet/gif.html.

QUARKXPRESS 4.1

The fact that QuarkXPress is Apple-Scriptable and has a complete and useful dictionary may be one of the biggest reasons that AppleScript has remained so popular and indispensable. Numerous publishing professionals have developed truly amazing AppleScripts that make Quark sit up, roll over, and beg.

In this chapter, you'll swim through the desktop publishing depths of Quark scripting. You'll use Quark to create nicely formatted pages of HTML source code, which is useful for documenting a Web site. You'll also batch-export pages as EPS images, which is helpful for rasterization in Photoshop. Finally, you'll batch-export all text in a document for repurposing.

Scripting QuarkXPress

Quark's AppleScript dictionary is one of the most complete available for any application. You can create entire documents from scratch via scripting.

Your Quark scripts will operate on the front-most open document. Before you begin scripting with QuarkXPress, you'll need to create a new document and set it up to work with your first script.

Figure 12.1 Creating a new document in Quark 4.1.

To get ready for the following AppleScript for XPress:

1. Launch Quark, and create a new document by choosing New from the File menu (**Figure 12.1**).

   Quark displays the New Document dialog box, which allows you to set the attributes of your new document (**Figure 12.2**).

2. Make sure that the Automatic Text Box checkbox is checked; then click the OK button.

3. Save your new empty document, and be sure to leave it open.

Now you're ready to script Quark.

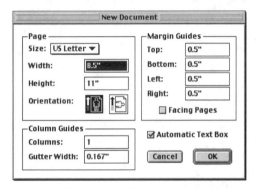

Figure 12.2 Setting the attributes of your new Quark document.

Scripting QuarkXPress 4.1

All the scripts in this chapter were designed and tested for QuarkXPress 4.1.

QuarkXPress is developed by Quark Inc. (http://www.quark.com/).

Script 12.1 This script checks all linked images in a document, suppressing the printout of all missing linked images and opening all available linked images in Photoshop.

```
                          script
tell application "QuarkXPress™ 4.1"
if document 1 exists then
repeat with myImageNum from 1 to count of ¬
every image of document 1
if missing of image myImageNum of document 1 ¬
then
set suppress printing of image myImageNum ¬
of document 1 to true
else
set myFilePath to file path of image ¬
myImageNum of document 1
if myFilePath ≠ null then
tell application "Adobe® Photoshop® 5.0.2" ¬
to open myFilePath
            end if
end if
      end repeat
   end if
end tell
tell application "Adobe® Photoshop® 5.0.2" ¬
to activate
```

Working with Linked Images

Any good Quark document ends up being filled with linked images. Managing these images and their respective source files can be a daunting challenge. Let AppleScript help.

Script 12.1 moves through every image in the open Quark document and suppresses the printing of any linked image that is missing its source file. The script also opens any linked image file available in Photoshop. The script ends by switching Photoshop to the front so that you can look at all your linked images.

You could easily modify this script to make uniform visual changes in each image, such as changing contrast, rotation, scale, skew or offset.

To suppress printing of all missing linked images and open all available linked images:

1. `tell application "QuarkXPress™ 4.1"`
   You start by talking to Quark.

2. `if document 1 exists then`
   Your first task is to ensure that an active document exists. To do so, you check for the existence of document 1, which is always the frontmost document.

3. `repeat with myImageNum from 1 to ¬`
   `count of every image of document 1`
   Because a document exists, you can begin your loop starting at 1 and ending at the number of images in the document. You're creating this loop to inspect each image in the document.

4. `if missing of image myImageNum of ¬`
   `document 1 then`
   Your first test of the current image in your loop makes sure that the source file is not missing.

continues on next page

continues on next page

WORKING WITH LINKED IMAGES

5. `set suppress printing of image ¬`
`   myImageNum of document 1 to true`

If your source file is missing, you set the `suppress printing` property of the image to keep it from printing anymore.

6. `else`

If your source file is not missing, you will open it in Photoshop.

7. `set myFilePath to file path of image ¬`
`   myImageNum of document 1`

To get ready to open the image in Photoshop, you get the path to the file from Quark and save it in a variable named `myFilePath`.

8. `if myFilePath ≠ null then`

You need to make sure that a link exists for this image, so you can paste raw image data from the Clipboard into a box in Quark.

9. `tell application "Adobe® Photoshop® ¬`
`   5.0.2" to open myFilePath`
`                end if`

Because you found a path, you tell Photoshop to open the image.

10. `end if`
`      end repeat`
`   end if`
`end tell`

You continue your loop through every image in the document before concluding your conversation with Quark.

11. `tell application "Adobe® Photoshop® ¬`
`   5.0.2" to activate`

Finally, you tell Photoshop to come to the front so that you can see all the images that are open in it.

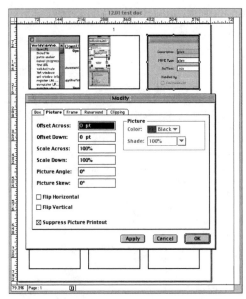

Figure 12.3 The Modify window of the selected picture box shows that the printout of this picture has been suppressed by the script.

Figure 12.4 The folder of new EPS files created by the script shown in the Finder.

Script 12.2 This script exports each page of the frontmost document as a separate EPS file.

```
script
set myFolder to (choose folder with prompt ¬
"Select a folder to save EPS files in:")
tell application "QuarkXPress™ 4.1"
    activate
repeat with i from 1 to count of pages in ¬
document 1
save page i of document 1 ¬
in file (myFolder & i as ¬
text) EPS format Mac Color ¬
EPS data binary EPS
end repeat
end tell
```

Exporting All Pages of a Document as EPS Files

At times, you face a seemingly insurmountable task, such as creating EPS files from a 100-plus-page Quark document for later conversion to print or Web graphics. You'll take on just such a task in this section.

You'll start to chip away at this waste of your good time with **Script 12.2**, which exports every page in the open Quark document as an EPS file to a folder of the user's choosing. Then these EPS files can be batch-processed in a program such as Adobe Photoshop or Macromedia FreeHand.

Figure 12.4 shows a Finder window with the fruits of your script's processing: a small (three-page) Quark document.

To export all pages of a document as EPS files:

1. `set myFolder to (choose folder with ¬ prompt "Select a folder to save EPS ¬ files in:")`

   You begin by prompting your user for a folder destination for the EPS files produced by the script.

2. `tell application "QuarkXPress™ 4.1" activate`

   Now you're ready to speak with Quark and bring it to the front.

3. `repeat with i from 1 to count of ¬ pages in document 1`

   You'll loop through each page in the current document with this repeat.

   continues on next page

4. `save page i of document 1 ¬`
`in file (myFolder & i as ¬`
`text) EPS format Mac Color ¬`
`EPS data binary EPS`

For each page of the current document, you tell Quark to save the page as a binary Macintosh color EPS file. To help identify the files, you name each file with the current page number i.

5. `end repeat`
`end tell`

You close your loop and end your conversation with Quark.

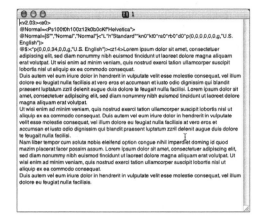

Figure 12.5 A sample story exported by the script, including XPress Tags, shown in TextEdit.

Script 12.3 This script saves all text in the current document as plain text with or without XPress Tags.

```
set myFolder to (choose folder with prompt
"Select a folder to save text into:")
tell application "QuarkXPress™ 4.1"
    activate
repeat with i from 1 to count of stories of ¬
document 1
        save story i of document 1 in (myFolder ¬
& i as text)
end repeat
end tell
```

✔ Tip

■ A more elaborate script might manipulate the exported text with XPress Tags in BBEdit to produce formatted HTML from these text files.

Exporting All Text from a Document

The script in this section exports each story in the current Quark document to a new text file in a user-selected folder. **Script 12.3** saves each story as plain text, with or without XPress Tags. See the following exercise for details on how to change the output settings.

Figure 12.5 shows a sample story exported with XPress Tags. See the following exercise to learn how to change the script's export properties.

To export all text from a document:

1. `set myFolder to (choose folder with ¬`
   `prompt "Select a folder to save text ¬`
   `into:")`

   You begin by prompting the user to select a destination folder for the text files.

2. `tell application "QuarkXPress™ 4.1"`
   `activate`

   Next, you tell Quark to come to the front.

3. `repeat with i from 1 to count of ¬`
   `stories of document 1`
   `save story i of document 1 in ¬`
   `(myFolder & i as text)`

   Now you begin your repeat loop, continuing through each story in the current document and saving each in the destination folder as text only, without XPress Tags. To include XPress Tags, change the save command to `save story i of document 1 in (myFolder & i as text)` as `"TEXT"`.

4. `end repeat`
   `end tell`

   You end your loop and conversation with Quark.

Replacing Styles Throughout a Story or Document

The script in this section prompts a user to choose a style sheet from the current document to find. The script also asks the user to select the style sheet with which to replace the found style. When your script knows what two style sheets to work with, it asks the user one more important question: whether to change the styles in the whole document or just the currently selected story.

Script 12.4 demonstrates the tremendous power of AppleScript's whose clause to filter and select objects within an application and modify them, all in one command.

Figure 12.6 shows the dialog box displayed by the script, which lets the user choose the scope of changes.

To replace all styles in a story or document:

1. `tell application "QuarkXPress™ 4.1"`
   You start by talking to Quark.

2. `activate`
   Next, you tell Quark to come to the front.

3. `if document 1 exists then`
   Your first task is to ensure that an active document exists. To do so, you check for the existence of document 1, which is always the frontmost document.

4. `tell document 1`
   Now you can start talking to the frontmost document.

5. `set myStyleSheets to the name of ¬`
   `every paragraph spec`

Figure 12.6 The dialog box displayed by the script, letting the user choose the scope of changes.

Script 12.4 This script replaces the paragraph style for all text in the current document with another paragraph style.

```
tell application "QuarkXpress™ 4.1"
activate
if document 1 exists then
tell document 1
set myStyleSheets to the name of every ¬
paragraph spec
if the class of myStyleSheets is list then
set myFindSheet to (choose from list ¬
myStyleSheets with prompt "Select style to ¬
find") as string
set myReplaceSheet to (choose from list ¬
myStyleSheets with prompt "Select style to ¬
replace") as string
set myStoryOnly to button returned of (display ¬
dialog "Change styles globally or in current ¬
story only?" buttons {""Global", "Current ¬
Story", "Cancel"})
try
if myStoryOnly is "Current Story" then
tell (every paragraph of story 1 of the ¬
current box whose name of paragraph style is ¬
myFindSheet)
                    set paragraph style to ¬
myReplaceSheet
                end tell
else
tell (every paragraph of every story whose ¬
name of paragraph style is myFindSheet)
                    set paragraph style to ¬
myReplaceSheet
                end tell
end if
        end try
    end if
    end tell
  end if
end tell
```

To let the user choose which style sheets to find and replace, you first must collect the names of all the style sheets by putting them in a variable named myStyleSheets. Note that the AppleScript dictionary entry for a style sheet is paragraph spec.

6. `if the class of myStyleSheets is ¬`
`list then`

A quick check of the variable's class shows whether only one style sheet exists. If only one exists, Quark will return just the name of the style sheet, as a string, not in a list. If the variable's class is list, you should proceed, because you have at least two style sheets to work with when a list is returned.

7. `set myFindSheet to (choose from list ¬`
`myStyleSheets with prompt "Select ¬`
`style to find") as string`

Now you can ask the user to choose which style sheet to find for replacement.

8. `set myReplaceSheet to (choose from ¬`
`list myStyleSheets with prompt ¬`
`"Select style to replace") as string`

Next, you ask for the style sheet that will replace the one found.

9. `set myStoryOnly to button returned ¬`
`of (display dialog "Change styles ¬`
`globally or in current story only?" ¬`
`buttons {"Global", "Current Story", ¬`
`"Cancel"})`

The last question for the user is whether to change all style sheets globally or only those in the currently selected text box.

10. `try`

With your questions answered, you can attempt to change style sheets. You'll perform this task inside a try block to catch any errors.

continues on next page

11. `if myStoryOnly is "Current Story" ¬`
`then`

Your `myStoryOnly` variable contains the name of the button that the user selected earlier. You check to see whether the user wants to change styles in the current story.

12. `tell (every paragraph of story 1 ¬`
`of the current box whose name of ¬`
`paragraph style is myFindSheet)`
`  set paragraph style to myReplaceSheet`
`end tell`

Now you can switch styles. To do so, you tell Quark that you want to talk to every paragraph in the current story that has its style set to the style name contained by `myFindSheet`. You tell these paragraphs to set their own paragraph styles to the new style name contained by `myReplaceSheet`. This code is a simple, powerful demonstration of AppleScript's whose clause at work.

13. `else`

This `else` clause executes if the user selected the Global button.

14. `tell (every paragraph of every story ¬`
`whose name of paragraph style is ¬`
`myFindSheet)`
`  set paragraph style to myReplaceSheet`
`end tell`

Now you can switch styles globally.

15. `end if`
`        end try`
`      end if`
`    end tell`
`  end if`
`end tell`

You end your try block, conditional statements, and conversation with the frontmost document and Quark. Whew!

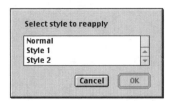

Figure 12.7 The script prompts the user to select the style to reapply from the available styles in the document.

Reapplying a Style Throughout a Document

After working too long with your Quark document, don't you sometimes get suspicious about the integrity of the individual styling of characters within paragraphs? Perhaps someone made a mess of things for you, and all you want to do is clean everything up with the least amount of hassle. The easiest way to clean up styled text mistakes in Quark is to reapply a style to a paragraph. This procedure removes any individual character-level changes in the text, ensuring that each paragraph has consistent font settings. But this process is tedious to perform by hand, so why not script it? **Script 12.5** does just that.

To reapply a style throughout a document:

1. `tell application "QuarkXPress™ 4.1"`
   You start by talking to Quark.

2. `activate`
   Next, you tell Quark to come to the front.

3. `if document 1 exists then`
   Your first task is to ensure that an active document exists. To do so, you check for the existence of document 1, which is always the frontmost document.

4. `tell document 1`
   Now you can start talking to the frontmost document.

5. `set myStyleSheets to the name of ¬ every paragraph spec`
   To let the user choose which style sheet to reapply, you first must collect the names of all the style sheets by putting them in a variable named myStyleSheets. Note that the AppleScript dictionary entry for a style sheet is paragraph spec.

continues on next page

6. `if the class of myStyleSheets is ¬`
`list then`

A quick check of the variable's class shows whether only one style sheet exists. If so, Quark returns just the name of the style sheet as a string, not in a list. If the variable's class is a list, you should proceed, because you have at least two style sheets with which to work.

7. `set mySheet to (choose from list ¬`
`myStyleSheets with prompt "Select ¬`
`style to reapply") as string`

Now you can ask the user to choose the style sheet to find for replacement.

8. `try`

With your questions answered, you can attempt to reapply the style sheet. You'll perform this task inside a `try` block to catch any errors.

Script 12.5 This script reapplies a selected paragraph style throughout a document, thereby removing any character-level formatting.

```
tell application "QuarkXPress™ 4.1"
activate
if document 1 exists then
tell document 1
set myStyleSheets to the name of every paragraph spec
if the class of myStyleSheets is list then
set mySheet to (choose from list myStyleSheets with prompt "Select style to reapply")
as string
try
set myParagraphs to the object reference of every paragraph of selection whose name ¬
of paragraph style is mySheet
if the class of myParagraphs is not list then set myParagraphs to {myParagraphs}
repeat with i from (count of items in myParagraphs) to 1 by -1
set paragraph style of paragraph 1 of (item i of myParagraphs) to null
set paragraph style of paragraph 1 of (item i of myParagraphs) to mySheet
end repeat
                        end try
                end if
        end tell
    end if
end tell
```

9. `set myParagraphs to the object ¬`
`reference of every paragraph of ¬`
`selection whose name of paragraph ¬`
`style is mySheet`

You set the `myParagraphs` variable to a reference to all the paragraphs that have the style sheet named in `mySheet` applied to them.

10. `if the class of myParagraphs is ¬`
`not list then set myParagraphs to ¬`
`{myParagraphs}`

If you have fewer than two paragraphs, you won't get a list in `myParagraphs`, so you coerce the variable to be a list no matter what. Now you can loop through the items in the list next.

11. `repeat with i from (count of items ¬`
`in myParagraphs) to 1 by -1`

You loop through the paragraphs in the list that have matching style sheets.

12. `set paragraph style of paragraph 1 ¬`
`of (item i of myParagraphs) to null`

You set the style sheet of the current paragraph to `null` to reset it.

13. `set paragraph style of paragraph 1 of ¬`
`(item i of myParagraphs) to mySheet`

You set the style sheet of the current paragraph to the style sheet named in `mySheet`.

14. `end repeat`
`        end try`
`      end if`
`    end tell`
`  end if`
`end tell`

You end your loop, your try block, conditional statements, conversation with the frontmost document and Quark.

Placing an Image on Every Page of a Document

Quark documents are often long, complex creatures with a long lifespan and many iterations. How many times have you wished you could add a special watermark or other indicator to the current version of a document? **Script 12.6** adds an image of your choosing to every page of the current document.

Figures 12.8 and **12.9** show a document before and after this script runs.

To place an image on every page of a document:

1. `property myPageGraphic : ""`

   You start by defining a property, `myPageGraphic`, that will hold a reference to the image file you select.

2. `if myPageGraphic = "" then set ¬`
   `myPageGraphic to (choose file)`

   You check the property to see whether it contains its default value. If so, you prompt the user to select a file. When the user selects the image file one time, the script remembers it and doesn't ask again.

3. `tell application "QuarkXPress™ 4.1"`
   `   activate`

   Now you're ready to speak with Quark and bring it to the front.

4. `if document 1 exists then`

   Your first task is to ensure that an active document exists. To do so, you check for the existence of `document 1`, which is always the frontmost document.

5. `tell document 1`

   Now you can start talking to the front-most document.

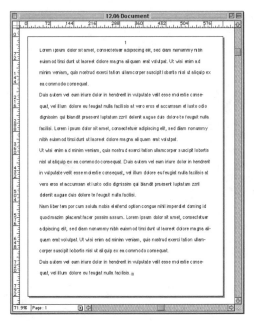

Figure 12.8 The first page of a sample document before running the script to add a user-selected image to every page.

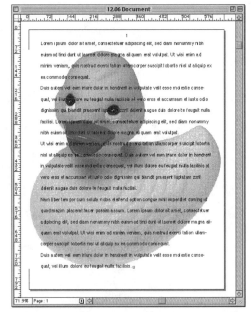

Figure 12.9 The first page of a sample document after running the script that adds an image to every page.

Script 12.6 This script adds an image on every page in a document behind all other elements.

```
property myPageGraphic : ""
if myPageGraphic = "" then set myPageGraphic ¬
to (choose file)
tell application "QuarkXPress™ 4.1"
    activate
if document 1 exists then
tell document 1
set color of every generic box to "None"
repeat with myPageNum from 1 to count of pages
make new picture box at beginning of page ¬
myPageNum
set bounds of picture box 1 of page myPageNum ¬
to {"0", ""0", page height, page width}
set color of picture box 1 of page myPageNum ¬
to "None"
tell picture box 1 of page myPageNum
if runaround is not none runaround then set ¬
runaround to none runaround
set image 1 to myPageGraphic
set bounds of image 1 to proportional fit
                end tell
move picture box 1 of page myPageNum to end ¬
of page myPageNum
            end repeat
        end tell
    end if
end tell
```

6. `set color of every generic box to ¬ "None"`

You make all pictures and text boxes in the document transparent so that you will be able to see the image you place behind them.

7. `repeat with myPageNum from 1 to ¬ count of pages`

You start a loop through each page number in the document.

8. `make new picture box at beginning ¬ of page myPageNum`

You make a new picture box on top of all other items on the page.

9. `set bounds of picture box 1 of page ¬ myPageNum to {"0", "0", page height, ¬ page width}`

Next, you set the size of the picture box to fill the entire page.

10. `set color of picture box 1 of page ¬ myPageNum to "None"`

Now you set the color of the picture box to transparent.

11. `tell picture box 1 of page myPageNum`

Now you can talk to the image inside the picture box to set its attributes.

12. `if runaround is not none runaround ¬ then set runaround to none runaround`

You also set the runaround of the box to none so that it doesn't interfere with the page layout.

13. `set image 1 to myPageGraphic`

You assign the image file to this image, thereby linking the image to the image box.

continues on next page

PLACING AN IMAGE ON EVERY PAGE

14. `set bounds of image 1 to ¬`
`proportional fit`
`        end tell`

You scale the placed image to fit the full size of the picture box without distorting it.

15. `move picture box 1 of page myPageNum ¬`
`to end of page myPageNum`
`      end repeat`
`   end tell`
` end if`
`end tell`

Last, you move the image behind all other items on the current page before continuing your loop.

STONE CREATE FOR MAC OS X

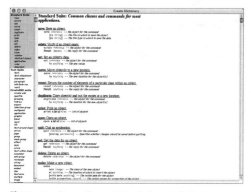

Figure 13.1 Stone Create's AppleScript dictionary entries includes the Standard Suite and then some.

Stone Create is a full-fledged illustration program with many advanced features. This program is not a version 1.0 product, because its life started back in the days of NeXT. But don't be discouraged by its association with the past; Stone Create takes full advantage of the Mac OS X platform with complete AppleScript support.

Stone Create offers some unique scripting-enabled features. The most notable Apple-Script feature of Create is its capability to save any document as an AppleScript. The script will re-create the entire document from scratch, essentially containing a history of the document. By modifying and extending the automatic scripts created by Stone Create, you can build batch-processing routines with great sophistication.

✔ Tip

■ Many people hope Stone Create will help set the standard for Cocoa applications that support AppleScript. **Figure 13.1** shows the Create AppleScript dictionary, which includes commands and objects that conform to the standards established by Mac OS 9 programs.

Scripting Stone Create

Stone Create is developed by Stone Software (http://www.stone.com/).

Saving a Document As an AppleScript

Stone Create can do something that no other application I have encountered can do. Sure, the best AppleScript-enabled applications allow script recording of your actions. But no other application lets you preserve an existing document by saving an AppleScript that can re-create the entire thing.

In this section, you experiment with this capability and take the first step in making a batch-processing script to create a form letter. **Script 13.1** shows the script that Stone Create saved when you asked it to save the document you created as an AppleScript. In the following exercise, you create a similar document and save it as a script.

To save a document you've created as an AppleScript:

1. Launch Stone Create.

   A new document window appears. You'll create a form letter in this new document.

2. Click the rectangle tool in Create's pop-out toolbar, and draw a tall rectangle like the one on the left in **Figure 13.2**.

3. To set a fill, click the Effects tab and set the fill.

4. Next, click the text-area tool in the toolbar, and draw a text area for an address block like the one in Figure 13.2.

5. Type the text shown in the figure.

6. Create another text area, and type a short message.

7. Draw a circle, and fill it with a nice blue.

8. To see the fruits of your labors as an AppleScript, choose Save Other As AppleScript from the File menu.

Figure 13.2 The sample document you can create manually to save as a script.

9. Open the saved script in Script Editor to view it.

The script should look something like **Script 13.1.** The actual values used for the objects will vary.

Script 13.1 This script is the result of saving the document created manually as an AppleScript.

```
                              script

tell application "Create"
 make new document at before front document
 tell the front document
   tell page 1
make new rectangle at before graphic 1 with properties {x position:51, y position:40, width:88, ¬
height:592, rotation:0.000000, scale x:1.000000, scale y:1.000000, shear x:0.000000, shear y:1.000000, ¬
flip horizontal:0, flip vertical:0}
tell rectangle 1
         make new stroke at before effect 1 with properties {linewidth:1.00, number:10, use neon:0, ¬
neon width:5.00, closepath:0, linejoin:0, linecap:0, miter limit:10.00, flatness:1.00, ¬
interpolation:0, antialias:1, color fall off:0, apply:0}
          set the stroke color to "0.000000 0.000000 0.000000"
          make new fill at before effect 1 with properties {linewidth:2.00, number:100, filltype:0, ¬
fill with lines:0, apply:0}
          set the fill color to "1.000000 0.000000 0.000000"
      end tell
make new text area at before graphic 1 with properties {x position:154, y position:43, width:419, ¬
height:116, rotation:0.000000, scale x:1.000000, scale y:1.000000, shear x:0.000000, shear y:1.000000, ¬
flip horizontal:0, flip vertical:0, antialias:0, text contents:"Name

Address

City, State Zip"}
          set the font of the text contents of text area 1 to "Helvetica"
          set the size of the text contents of text area 1 to 12
          set the color of the text contents of text area 1 to "0.000000 0.000000 0.000000"
          tell text area 1
          end tell
make new text area at before graphic 1 with properties {x position:159, y position:175, width:424, ¬
height:434, rotation:0.000000, scale x:1.000000, scale y:1.000000, shear x:0.000000, shear y:1.000000, ¬
flip horizontal:0, flip vertical:0, antialias:0, text contents:"Dear Name,


   Welcome to the new world of AppleScript and OS X."}
          set the font of the text contents of text area 1 to "Helvetica"
          set the size of the text contents of text area 1 to 12
          set the color of the text contents of text area 1 to "0.000000 0.000000 0.000000"
          set the size of characters 14 through 62 of the text contents of text area 1 to 48.00
          tell text area 1
          end tell
make new circle at before graphic 1 with properties {x position:299, y position:454, width:58, ¬
height:58, rotation:0.000000, scale x:1.000000, scale y:1.000000, shear x:0.000000, shear y:1.000000, ¬
flip horizontal:0, flip vertical:0}
tell circle 1
```

(script continues on next page)

To understand your document saved as an AppleScript:

1. `tell application "Create"`

Your document saved as a script always starts with a `tell` block to let AppleScript know that this script controls Create.

2. `make new document at before front ¬ document`
  `tell the front document`
    `tell page 1`

Create adds a `make new document` command automatically as well as `tell` blocks targeting the new frontmost document and first page at the beginning of its saved scripts.

3. `make new rectangle at before graphic ¬ 1 with properties {x position:51, y ¬ position:40, width:88, height:592, ¬ rotation:0.000000, scale x:1.000000, ¬ scale y:1.000000, shear x:0.000000, ¬ shear y:1.000000, flip horizontal:0, ¬ flip vertical:0}`

Here's the first rectangle that you created.

Script 13.1 *continued*

```
                                script

        make new stroke at before effect 1 with properties {linewidth:1.00, number:10, use neon:0,
neon width:5.00, closepath:0, linejoin:0, linecap:1, miter limit:10.00, flatness:1.00,
interpolation:0, antialias:1, color fall off:0, apply:0}
        set the stroke color to "0.000000 0.000000 0.000000"
        make new fill at before effect 1 with properties {linewidth:2.00, number:100, filltype:0,
fill with lines:0, apply:0}
        set the fill color to "0.003199 0.244264 1.000000"
      end tell
redraw
end tell
    end tell
end tell
```

4.
```
tell rectangle 1
    make new stroke at before effect 1 ¬
with properties {linewidth:1.00, ¬
number:10, use neon:0, neon ¬
width:5.00, closepath:0, linejoin:0, ¬
linecap:0, miter limit:10.00, ¬
flatness:1.00, interpolation:0, ¬
antialias:1, color fall off:0, ¬
apply:0}
    set the stroke color to "0.000000 ¬
0.000000 0.000000"
    make new fill at before effect 1 ¬
with properties {linewidth:2.00, ¬
number:100, filltype:0, fill with ¬
lines:0, apply:0}
    set the fill color to "1.000000 ¬
0.000000 0.000000"
end tell
```

Here is where you set the effect on the new rectangle to apply a stroke and fill.

```
make new text area at before graphic ¬
1 with properties {x position:154, y ¬
position:43, width:419, height:116, ¬
rotation:0.000000, scale x:1.000000, ¬
scale y:1.000000, shear x:0.000000, ¬
shear y:1.000000, flip horizontal:0, ¬
flip vertical:0, antialias:0, text ¬
contents:"Name
Address
```

5.
```
City, State Zip"}
    set the font of the text contents of ¬
text area 1 to "Helvetica"
    set the size of the text contents of ¬
text area 1 to 12
    set the color of the text contents ¬
of text area 1 to "0.000000 0.000000 ¬
0.000000"
    tell text area 1
end tell
```

continues on next page

SAVING A DOCUMENT AS AN APPLESCRIPT

Next, you made a text-area object. Create saved this action as several operations, including the making of the object and setting the object's properties to the defaults when you made the object. It's not clear why Create includes the extra empty tell block.

```
make new text area at before graphic ¬
1 with properties {x position:159, y ¬
position:175, width:424, height:434, ¬
rotation:0.000000, scale x:1.000000, ¬
scale y:1.000000, shear x:0.000000, ¬
shear y:1.000000, flip horizontal:0, ¬
flip vertical:0, antialias:0, text ¬
contents:"Dear Name,
```

6. ```
   Welcome to the new world of ¬
   AppleScript and OS X."}
   set the font of the text contents of ¬
   text area 1 to "Helvetica"
   set the size of the text contents of ¬
   text area 1 to 12
   set the color of the text contents of ¬
   text area 1 to "0.000000 0.000000 ¬
   0.000000"
   set the size of characters 14 through ¬
   62 of the text contents of text area ¬
   1 to 48.00
   tell text area 1
   end tell
   ```

Here, you made a second text-area object. Create saved this action as a series of operations. You again see the extra empty tell block.

7. ```
   make new circle at before graphic 1 ¬
   with properties {x position:299, y ¬
   position:454, width:58, height:58, ¬
   rotation:0.000000, scale x:1.000000, ¬
   scale y:1.000000, shear x:0.000000, ¬
   shear y:1.000000, flip horizontal:0, ¬
   flip vertical:0}
   ```

As your last flourish, you made a circle. This code is the script command for this operation.

8.
```
tell circle 1
  make new stroke at before effect 1 ¬
with properties {linewidth:1.00, ¬
number:10, use neon:0, neon ¬
width:5.00, closepath:0, linejoin:0, ¬
linecap:1, miter limit:10.00, ¬
flatness:1.00, interpolation:0, ¬
antialias:1, color fall off:0, ¬
apply:0}
    set the stroke color to "0.000000 ¬
0.000000 0.000000"
    make new fill at before effect 1 ¬
with properties {linewidth:2.00, ¬
number:100, filltype:0, fill with ¬
lines:0, apply:0}
set the fill color to "0.003199 ¬
0.244264 1.000000"
end tell
```

You also set the color of the circle to deep blue. Notice the unique color-reference values that Create uses in AppleScript: a series of three real values represented inside a string, separated by spaces. The three positions represent the red, green, and blue channels of the color.

9.
```
redraw
```

Create includes a `redraw` command in its saved script to refresh the screen after it draws everything.

10.
```
end tell
  end tell
end tell
```

All the nested `tell` blocks get closed before the script ends. Nice scripting, Create!

SAVING A DOCUMENT AS AN APPLESCRIPT

Modifying a Saved Script for Batch Processing

In the preceding section, you explored Create's unique capability to save any document as a series of AppleScript statements that re-create the document from scratch. In this section, you use the saved script as the basis for a batch-processing script that makes multiple personalized form letters.

The best way to write **Script 13.2** is to follow the steps in the preceding section to create a document and save it as a script. Using this saved script as a starting point, follow the steps in this section to make the script create multiple unique documents.

Figure 13.3 shows a series of new document windows created by the script.

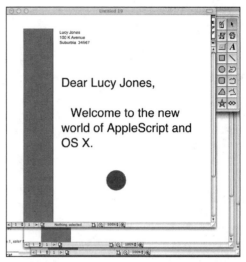

Figure 13.3 A series of new document windows created by the script, with the front one showing the customized text set by the script.

To modify the saved script for batch processing of form letters:

1.  ```
    set myNames to {"John Doe", "Fred ¬
    Smith", "Lucy Jones"}
    set myAddresses to {"10 Main Street", ¬
    "20 Broadway", "100 K Avenue"}
    set myCities to {"Metropolis", ¬
    "Smalltown", "Suburbia"}
    set myZips to {"12345", "23456", ¬
    "34567"}
    ```

    You start your modifications by initializing your list variables to hold the data for your batch process. In this case, you set up three address blocks' worth of data.

2.  ```
    repeat with myNum from 1 to the ¬
    number of items in myNames
    ```

    Your big change to make the original script work as a batch processor is adding a `repeat` loop containing the steps that create the form-letter document.

3.
```
set myName to item myNum of myNames ¬
as string
set myAddressBlock to myName & return ¬
& (item myNum of myAddresses) & ¬
return & (item myNum of myCities) & " ¬
" & (item myNum of myZips) as string
```

Within the loop, you store the current name and address block in a couple of variables.

4.
```
tell application "Create"
 make new document at before front ¬
document
  tell the front document
   tell page 1
     make new rectangle at before ¬
graphic 1 with properties {x ¬
position:51, y position:40, width:88, ¬
height:592, rotation:0.000000, scale ¬
x:1.000000, scale y:1.000000, shear ¬
x:0.000000, shear y:1.000000, flip ¬
horizontal:0, flip vertical:0}
      tell rectangle 1
        make new stroke at before ¬
effect 1 with properties {linewidth:¬
1.00, number:10, use neon:0, neon ¬
width:5.00, closepath:0, linejoin:0, ¬
linecap:0, miter limit:10.00, ¬
flatness:1.00, interpolation:0, ¬
antialias:1, color fall off:0, ¬
apply:0}
        set the stroke color to ¬
"0.000000 0.000000 0.000000"
        make new fill at before ¬
effect 1 with properties {linewidth:¬
2.00, number:100, filltype:0, fill ¬
with lines:0, apply:0}
        set the fill color to ¬
"1.000000 0.000000 0.000000"
      end tell
```

So far, the script remains the same as the original one saved by Create.

continues on next page

Script 13.2 This script is created by starting with a document saved as an AppleScript and then modified in Script Editor to turn it into a batch-processing script.

```
set myNames to {"John Doe", "Fred Smith", "Lucy Jones"}
set myAddresses to {"10 Main Street", "20 Broadway", "100 K Avenue"}
set myCities to {"Metropolis", "Smalltown", "Suburbia"}
set myZips to {"12345", "23456", "34567"}
repeat with myNum from 1 to the number of items in myNames
set myName to item myNum of myNames as string
    set myAddressBlock to myName & return & (item myNum of myAddresses) & return & ¬
(item myNum of myCities) & " " & (item myNum of myZips) as string
tell application "Create"
 make new document at before front document
 tell the front document
    tell page 1
        make new rectangle at before graphic 1 with properties {x position:51, y ¬
position:40, width:88, height:592, rotation:0.000000, scale x:1.000000, scale ¬
y:1.000000, shear x:0.000000, shear y:1.000000, flip horizontal:0, flip vertical:0}
        tell rectangle 1
            make new stroke at before effect 1 with properties {linewidth:1.00, ¬
number:10, use neon:0, neon width:5.00, closepath:0, linejoin:0, linecap:0, miter ¬
limit:10.00, flatness:1.00, interpolation:0, antialias:1, color fall off:0, apply:0}
            set the stroke color to "0.000000 0.000000 0.000000"
            make new fill at before effect 1 with properties {linewidth:2.00, ¬
number:100, filltype:0, fill with lines:0, apply:0}
            set the fill color to "1.000000 0.000000 0.000000"
        end tell
make new text area at before graphic 1 with properties {x position:154, y ¬
position:43, width:419, height:116, rotation:0.000000, scale x:1.000000, scale ¬
y:1.000000, shear x:0.000000, shear y:1.000000, flip horizontal:0, flip vertical:0, ¬
antialias:0, text contents:myAddressBlock}
set the font of the text contents of text area 1 to "Helvetica"
        set the size of the text contents of text area 1 to 12
        set the color of the text contents of text area 1 to "0.000000 0.000000 ¬
0.000000"
        tell text area 1
        end tell
make new text area at before graphic 1 with properties {x position:159, y ¬
position:175, width:424, height:434, rotation:0.000000, scale x:1.000000, scale ¬
y:1.000000, shear x:0.000000, shear y:1.000000, flip horizontal:0, flip vertical:0, ¬
antialias:0, text contents:"Dear Name,
```

(script continues on next page)

5. make new text area at before graphic ¬
   1 with properties {x position:154, y ¬
   position:43, width:419, height:116, ¬
   rotation:0.000000, scale x:1.000000, ¬
   scale y:1.000000, shear x:0.000000, ¬
   shear y:1.000000, flip horizontal:0, ¬
   flip vertical:0, antialias:0, text ¬
   contents:myAddressBlock}

Here, you make your first modification to the existing code by replacing the literal text that was used to set the contents of the text area to the myAddressBlock variable. You have genericized the functionality of the script.

continues on next page

Script 13.2 *continued*

```
     Welcome to the new world of AppleScript and OS X."}
        set the font of the text contents of text area 1 to "Helvetica"
        set the size of the text contents of text area 1 to 12
        set the color of the text contents of text area 1 to "0.000000 0.000000 ¬
0.000000"
        set the size of every character of the text contents of text area 1 to 36.00
tell text area 1
        end tell
        make new circle at before graphic 1 with properties {x position:299, y ¬
position:454, width:58, height:58, rotation:0.000000, scale x:1.000000, scale ¬
y:1.000000, shear x:0.000000, shear y:1.000000, flip horizontal:0, flip vertical:0}
            tell circle 1
                make new stroke at before effect 1 with properties {linewidth:1.00, ¬
number:10, use neon:0, neon width:5.00, closepath:0, linejoin:0, linecap:1, miter ¬
limit:10.00, flatness:1.00, interpolation:0, antialias:1, color fall off:0, apply:0}
                set the stroke color to "0.000000 0.000000 0.000000"
                make new fill at before effect 1 with properties {linewidth:2.00, ¬
number:100, filltype:0, fill with lines:0, apply:0}
                set the fill color to "0.003199 0.244264 1.000000"
            end tell
            redraw
        end tell
    end tell
end tell
end repeat
```

6. set the font of the text contents of ¬
text area 1 to "Helvetica"
set the size of the text contents of ¬
text area 1 to 12
set the color of the text contents ¬
of text area 1 to "0.000000 0.000000 ¬
0.000000"
tell text area 1
end tell

Again, all this code is untouched from
Script 13.1.

make new text area at before graphic ¬
1 with properties {x position:159, y ¬
position:175, width:424, height:434, ¬
rotation:0.000000, scale x:1.000000, ¬
scale y:1.000000, shear x:0.000000, ¬
shear y:1.000000, flip horizontal:0, ¬
flip vertical:0, antialias:0, text ¬
contents:"Dear Name,

7. Welcome to the new world of ¬
AppleScript and OS X."}
set the font of the text contents of ¬
text area 1 to "Helvetica"
set the size of the text contents of ¬
text area 1 to 12
set the color of the text contents ¬
of text area 1 to "0.000000 0.000000 ¬
0.000000"
set the size of every character of ¬
the text contents of text area 1 to ¬
36.00

Here, you change the contents of the new
text area to include the person's name
(from myName). You also set the font size to
a uniform 36 points to keep things simple.

8.
```
tell text area 1
end tell
make new circle at before graphic 1 ¬
with properties {x position:299, y ¬
position:454, width:58, height:58, ¬
rotation:0.000000, scale x:1.000000, ¬
scale y:1.000000, shear x:0.000000, ¬
shear y:1.000000, flip horizontal:0, ¬
flip vertical:0}
tell circle 1
    make new stroke at before effect 1 ¬
with properties {linewidth:1.00, ¬
number:10, use neon:0, neon width:¬
5.00, closepath:0, linejoin:0, ¬
linecap:1, miter limit:10.00, ¬
flatness:1.00, interpolation:0, ¬
antialias:1, color fall off:0, ¬
apply:0}
    set the stroke color to "0.000000 ¬
0.000000 0.000000"
    make new fill at before effect 1 ¬
with properties {linewidth:2.00, ¬
number:100, filltype:0, fill with ¬
lines:0, apply:0}
    set the fill color to "0.003199 ¬
0.244264 1.000000"
end tell
redraw
    end tell
  end tell
end tell
```

These lines are identical to those in Script 13.1.

9.
```
end repeat
```

You close your new repeat loop and complete your changes in the script. You now have a batch-processing script.

Creating Animations with AppleScript

Stone Create allows you to create complex shapes with many attributes from AppleScript. Draw an object, save it as a script, and you can do anything. After you've drawn some art, a great application of scripting is to animate the still art for exportation.

Script 13.3 is a simple script that shows how easily you can animate art in a document. In this case, you rotate a filled rectangle around its center by 10-degree increments through the full 360 degrees of motion.

Figure 13.4 shows the document window while the script is running.

To create animation for export:

1. `tell application "Create"`

   You start by letting AppleScript know you want to talk to Create.

2. `activate`

   You bring Create to the front.

3. `make new document at before front ¬`
   `document`

   Now you can have Create make a new document.

4. `tell the front document`
   `    tell page 1`

   All your remaining operations will take place on the first page of the new document, so you use two nested `tell` blocks to let AppleScript know that all commands are to be applied to the first page.

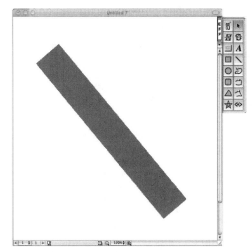

Figure 13.4 The document window while the script is running, showing the script-controlled rectangle in the middle of its rotation.

Script 13.3 This script shows how to create animations with AppleScript and Stone Create.

```
script

tell application "Create"
activate
make new document at before front document
tell the front document
        tell page 1
make new rectangle at before graphic 1 with ¬
properties {x position:250, y position:40, ¬
width:88, height:592, rotation:0.0, scale ¬
x:1.0, scale y:1.0, shear x:0.0, shear y:1.0, ¬
flip horizontal:0, flip vertical:0}
tell rectangle 1
            make new fill at before effect 1 ¬
with properties {linewidth:2.0, number:100, ¬
filltype:0, fill with lines:0, apply:0}
                set the fill color to "1.000000 ¬
0.000000 0.000000"
repeat with myRotation from 0.0 to 360.0 by ¬
10.0
set rotation to myRotation
redraw
                end repeat
end tell
        end tell
    end tell
end tell
```

5. `make new rectangle at before graphic` ¬
   `1 with properties {x position:250,` ¬
   `y position:40, width:88, height:592,` ¬
   `rotation:0.0, scale x:1.0, scale` ¬
   `y:1.0, shear x:0.0, shear y:1.0,` ¬
   `flip horizontal:0, flip vertical:0}`

   You make a simple tall rectangle.

6. `tell rectangle 1`
   `  make new fill at before effect 1` ¬
   `with properties {linewidth:2.0,` ¬
   `number:100, filltype:0, fill with` ¬
   `lines:0, apply:0}`
   `    set the fill color to "1.000000` ¬
   `0.000000 0.000000"`

   Now you fill the rectangle with pure red.

7. `repeat with myRotation from 0.0 to` ¬
   `360.0 by 10.0`

   You start your loop through 360 degrees by steps of 10 degrees at a time.

8. `set rotation to myRotation`

   You tell Create to change the rotation of the rectangle, because you issue this **set** command inside a **tell** block for the rectangle itself.

9. `redraw`
   `        end repeat`

   Next, you have Create update the screen so that you can see what's happened before ending the loop.

10. `end tell`
    `    end tell`
    `  end tell`
    `end tell`

    You must close all your nested **tell** blocks before ending.

ADOBE
ILLUSTRATOR 9

Figure 14.1 Adobe Illustrator has an extensive and well-formed AppleScript dictionary.

Anyone who has ever used Adobe Illustrator will tell you that it is a world unto itself. With each new version, Adobe adds new things to answer users' requests for features and functionality. Read any upgrade offer for Illustrator 9, and you will see a plethora of features—but no mention of scripting support.

Did you know Illustrator 9 is almost completely scriptable in AppleScript? Well, it's about time everyone realized this. The scripting support for Illustrator 9 does not get installed unless you install it yourself from the SDK provided on the product CD-ROM. Illustrator not only becomes incredibly scriptable when you install the plug-in that supports scripting but also has extremely detailed documentation for scripting, including hundreds of sample scripts and a 500-page electronic manual. **Figure 14.1** shows a portion of Illustrator's extensive AppleScript dictionary.

Now that you know the surprising truth about how scriptable Illustrator is, you're ready to dive in and look at what you can do by scripting the popular vector art program.

Scripting Illustrator 9

The scripts in this chapter were designed and tested on Adobe Illustrator 9.0.2.

Adobe Illustrator is developed by Adobe Systems Inc. (http://www.adobe.com/).

Moving Every Object onto Its Own Layer

As your Illustrator document becomes more and more complex, sometimes all you want to do is sort out the mess on one of the layers. A simple and effective way to make clarity out of chaos is to use **Script 14.1** to clear the fog from your page. This script operates on the selected layer in the frontmost document by sifting through each object in the layer, moving each one to a new layer.

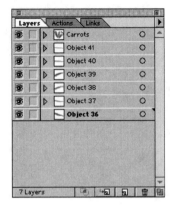

Figure 14.2 The Layers palette after the script has run, showing each new layer created. Layer names match the objects they contain.

Figure 14.2 shows Illustrator's Layers palette after the script has run. Notice the new layers are named after the objects they contain.

To move every object on the current layer to its own new layer:

1. `tell application "Adobe Illustrator® ¬ 9.0.2"`

   You start by letting AppleScript know that you want to talk to Illustrator.

2. `activate`

   Next, you bring Illustrator to the front so that you can watch the activity of your script.

3. `set mylayer to current layer of ¬ current document`

   Now you store a reference to the current layer in the frontmost document in a variable, `mylayer`, to use later when you want to find objects in that layer.

4. `repeat with j from (number of page ¬ items in mylayer) to 1 by -1`

   Your loop goes backward, starting with the maximum number of objects in your layer and going down to 1. You do this because Illustrator constructs its own object references by using the index numbers of an object, so the first path on a layer might be called `path item 1 of`

Script 14.1 This script moves each object found in the current layer to its own new layer.

```
                    script
tell application "Adobe Illustrator® 9.0.2"
activate
set mylayer to current layer of current ¬
document
repeat with j from (number of page items in ¬
mylayer) to 1 by -1
set myName to ""
        try
            set myName to name of page item j of ¬
mylayer
        end try
if myName = "" then set myName to "Object " ¬
& j as string
make new layer at end of current document ¬
with properties {name:myName}
move page item j of mylayer to beginning of ¬
layer myName of current document
    end repeat
end tell
```

layer 1 of document 1. This arrangement is fine as a reference until you add a new path item on top of the first. The object reference does not update itself and point to path item 2 of layer 1 of document 1; it now points the new first path in the layer. You work around this problem by going backward.

5. `set myName to ""`
   `try`
      `set myName to name of page item j ¬`
   `of mylayer`
   `end try`

   You try to get the name of the object, if it is named or can be named. If the object has no name property, any error will be caught by your try statement.

6. `if myName = "" then set myName to ¬`
   `"Object " & j as string`

   If the name is empty, you set your myName variable to contain a calculated string.

7. `make new layer at end of current ¬`
   `document with properties`
   `{name:myName}`

   Now you can make a named layer at the end of the document so you don't disturb the index numbering of the existing layers. Remember that if the layer index numbers get changed, all references to objects become invalid.

8. `move page item j of mylayer to ¬`
   `beginning of layer myName of current ¬`
   `document`
      `end repeat`
   `end tell`

   Finally, you move the page object to the new layer.

Exporting Folders of Files in EPS Format

The most basic scripting tasks involve batch processing of files. Batch processing is handy when you have to convert many Illustrator files to other formats or modify them in a common way.

Script 14.2 provides the basic shell of a batch processing script for your use. The whole script is written modularly so that you can reuse portions of it. The only specific functionality in the whole script that needs changing is the doExport handler at the end. This handler is where you put the good stuff: the code that actually does something with each file passed to it from the batch-processing code. You'll reuse the batch handler processFilesOrFolders in your next script.

Figure 14.3 shows a folder of EPS files created by the script.

To export folders of files in EPS format:

1. ```
   property myOutputFolder : ""
   property mysuffix : ".eps"
   ```
   You start this script by defining two properties. myOutputFolder is a reference to the folder in which you want to save exported files. You initialize this reference in your property as a null string so that you can check later to see whether it has been set. The mysuffix variable contains the file extension your script will add to the exported files' names.

2. ```
   on open (myfilesorfolders)
   ```
   You have an open handler here so that files and folders dropped on the script (saved as a droplet) can be processed. AppleScript will pass to the myfilesorfolders variable any references to items dropped on your script.

Figure 14.3 A folder of exported EPS files shown in the Finder.

Script 14.2 This script exports folders of Illustrator files as EPS files.

```
property myOutputFolder : ""
property mysuffix : ".eps"
on open (myfilesorfolders)
if myOutputFolder = "" then
set myOutputFolder to choose folder with ¬
prompt "Select folder to save " & mysuffix & ¬
"'s into:"
    end if
processFilesAndFolders(myfilesorfolders)
end open
on run
set myOutputFolder to ""
set myFolder to choose folder with prompt ¬
"Select folder containing Illustrator files ¬
to export as " & mysuffix & ":"
tell me to open {myFolder}
end run
on processFilesAndFolders(myfilesorfolders)
if myOutputFolder ≠ "" then
repeat with myitem in myfilesorfolders
tell application "Finder"
if kind of myitem is "folder" then
set myfiles to every file of myitem
repeat with myfile in myfiles
if creator type is "ARTS" then
                doExport(myfile as ¬
alias) of me
                end if
                end repeat
set myfolders to every folder of myitem
tell me to processFilesAndFolders(myfolders)
else
if creator type is "ARTS" then
                doExport(myitem as alias) ¬
of me
                end if
end if
        end tell
    end repeat
    end if
end processFilesAndFolders
on doExport(myexportfile)
set myfilename to name of (info for ¬
myexportfile)
set mynewfile to (myOutputFolder as string) ¬
& myfilename & mysuffix as string
tell application "Adobe Illustrator® 9.0.2"
```

(script continues on next page)

3. `if myOutputFolder = "" then`

You check to see whether the output-folder property has been populated with a folder reference.

4. `set myOutputFolder to choose folder ¬`
`with prompt "Select folder to save " ¬`
`& mysuffix & "'s into:"`
`    end if`

If `myOutputFolder` still has an empty string, you prompt the user to select a folder and store the reference to the folder in `myOutputFolder`.

5. `processFilesAndFolders(myfilesorfolders)`
`end open`

With your output folder set, you can call your handler to process the list of files and folders dropped onto the script.

6. `on run`

You include a run handler so that a user can run the script without dropping items on it.

7. `set myOutputFolder to ""`

When a user runs the script without dropping anything on it, you clear the output-folder reference variable `myOutputFolder` so that the user can change it.

8. `set myFolder to choose folder with ¬`
`prompt "Select folder containing ¬`
`Illustrator files to export as " & ¬`
`mysuffix & ":"`

Because nothing was dropped on the script to process, you prompt the user to select a folder to process.

9. `tell me to open {myFolder}`
`end run`

With the folder reference in `myfolder`, you call the **open** handler, passing it a list containing one item: the folder reference to process.

continues on next page

10. `on processFilesAndFolders¬`
`(myfilesorfolders)`

Your item-processing handler walks through all files and folders, looking for Illustrator files.

11. `if myOutputFolder ≠ "" then`

Before proceeding, you ensure that the myOutputFolder property contains a folder reference.

12. `repeat with myitem in myfilesorfolders`

Your loop traverses all items—files or folders—in your list of items to process.

13. `tell application "Finder"`

You start talking to the Finder to take advantage of its access to file-system properties.

14. `if kind of myitem is "folder" then`

You test the Finder item kind to see whether you have a folder.

15. `set myfiles to every file of myitem`

Now you ask the Finder for a list of files in the current folder.

16. `repeat with myfile in myfiles`

You loop through each file in myfiles.

17. `if kind of myfile is "Adobe ¬`
`Illustrator® document" then`
`  doExport(myfile as alias) of me`
`end if`
`        end repeat`

If the Finder file kind shows that the file is an Illustrator file, you call the doExport handler to output the file from Illustrator.

18. `set myfolders to every folder of ¬`
`myitem`

You ask the Finder for a list of folders in the current folder.

Script 14.2 *continued*

```
                      script
open myexportfile
save document 1 in file mynewfile as eps with ¬
options {compatibility:Illustrator 8, ¬
preview:color Macintosh, embed linked ¬
files:true, include document thumbnails:false, ¬
embed all fonts:true, PostScript:level 2}
close document 1 saving no
    end tell
end doExport
```

EXPORTING FOLDERS OF FILES IN EPS FORMAT

19. `tell me to processFilesAndFolders¬`
`(myfolders)`

With the list of folders, you call the handler you are in, `processFilesAndFolders`, to process the next list of folders.

20. `else`

If the Finder item kind for the current item in your main loop is not a folder, you want to find out about the file kind.

21. `if kind of myitem is "Adobe ¬`
`Illustrator® document" then`
`   doExport(myitem as alias) of me`
`end if`

If the file kind shows that you have an Illustrator file, you call the `doExport` handler to output it.

22. `end if`
`      end tell`
`   end repeat`
`  end if`
`end processFilesAndFolders`

You conclude your conditional tests, `tell` block, and `repeat` loop before ending your handler.

23. `on doExport(myexportfile)`

Your `doExport` handler does all the real work in this script, exporting the file passed to it in `myexportfile` as an EPS file from Illustrator.

24. `set myfilename to name of (info for ¬`
`myexportfile)`

You use the `info for` command from the Scripting Addition to get the name of the file passed to your handler.

25. `set mynewfile to (myOutputFolder as ¬`
`string) & myfilename & mysuffix as ¬`
`string`

You construct a new name for your export file, including the output-folder path, original name, and new file extension.

continues on next page

26. `tell application "Adobe Illustrator® ¬`
`9.0.2"`

You start talking to Illustrator.

27. `open myexportfile`

You must have Illustrator open the file
to export.

28. `save document 1 in file mynewfile ¬`
`as eps with options {compatibility:¬`
`Illustrator 8, preview:color ¬`
`Macintosh, embed linked files:true, ¬`
`include document thumbnails:false, ¬`
`embed all fonts:true, PostScript:¬`
`level 2}`

Next, in one line, you export the file as
an EPS with several optional settings.

29. `close document 1 saving no`
`    end tell`
`end doExport`

You close the document without saving
it before ending your conversation with
Illustrator and your doExport handler.

EXPORTING FOLDERS OF FILES IN EPS FORMAT

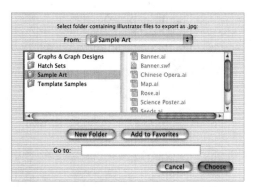

Figure 14.4 The dialog box that the script displays to prompt the user to choose a folder.

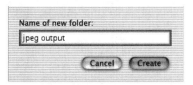

Figure 14.5 The dialog box that the script displays to prompt the user to create a folder.

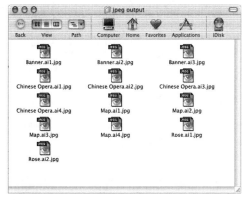

Figure 14.6 A folder of exported JPEG files, each containing a layer of one of the files dropped on the script droplet.

Exporting Individual Layers of a File in JPEG Format

Batch processing has endless applications. In the preceding section, you looked at the most basic of operations: exporting a file in a new format. In this section, you will expand your capabilities to include modifying an image before exporting it to a new format.

Script 14.3 uses the basic shell of the batch-processing script you developed in the preceding section. The only handler you change is the doExport handler at the end. This handler is where you add code to move through each layer in the active document, exporting a separate JPEG file for each layer as the script continues.

Figures 14.4 and **14.5** show the dialog boxes the script displays while it is running. **Figure 14.6** shows a folder of JPEG files, each containing one layer of an Illustrator file processed by the script.

To export all the layers of a set of files as separate JPEG images:

1. Your open, run, and processFilesAndFolders handlers are explained in detail in the preceding section.

2. on doExport(myexportfile)

   Your doExport handler does all the real work in this script, exporting each layer of the file passed to it in myexportfile as an individual JPEG file from Illustrator.

3. set myfilename to name of (info for ¬ myexportfile)

   You use the info for command from Scripting Addition to get the name of the file passed to your handler.

continues on next page

EXPORTING LAYERS IN JPEG FORMAT

4. `tell application "Adobe Illustrator® ¬`
`9.0.2"`

You start talking to Illustrator.

5. `open myexportfile`

You must have Illustrator open the file that you want to change and export.

6. `set the visible of every layer of ¬`
`document 1 to false`

After opening the image, you hide all layers.

7. `repeat with myLayerNum from 1 to ¬`
`number of layers in document 1`

Now you start your loop through each layer in the document.

8. `set the visible of layer myLayerNum ¬`
`of document 1 to true`

You tell Illustrator to show the current layer in your loop.

9. `set mynewfile to (myOutputFolder as ¬`
`string) & myfilename & myLayerNum & ¬`
`mysuffix as string`

You construct a new name for your export file, including the output-folder path, original name, layer number, and new file extension.

10. `export document 1 to file mynewfile ¬`
`as JPEG with options {quality:100, ¬`
`optimization:false, blur:0.0, ¬`
`matte:true, horizontal scaling:200.0, ¬`
`vertical scaling:200.0, anti ¬`
`aliasing:true, artboard clipping:¬`
`false, saving as HTML:false}`

Next, in one line, you export the file as a JPEG image with several optional settings, including scaling to 200 percent.

11. `set the visible of layer myLayerNum ¬`
`of document 1 to false`

Before continuing your loop, you tell Illustrator to hide the layer.

Script 14.3 This script exports individual layers of Illustrator files as JPEG files.

```
                    script
property myOutputFolder : ""
property mysuffix : ".jpg"
on open (myfilesorfolders)
    if myOutputFolder = "" then
        set myOutputFolder to choose folder ¬
with prompt "Select folder to save " & ¬
mysuffix & "'s into:"
    end if
    processFilesAndFolders(myfilesorfolders)
end open
on run
    set myOutputFolder to ""
    set myFolder to choose folder with prompt ¬
"Select folder containing Illustrator files ¬
to export as " & mysuffix & ":"
    tell me to open {myFolder}
end run
on processFilesAndFolders(myfilesorfolders)
    if myOutputFolder ≠ "" then
        repeat with myitem in myfilesorfolders
            tell application "Finder"
                if kind of myitem is "folder" then
                    set myfiles to every file of ¬
myitem
                    repeat with myfile in myfiles
                        if creator type is "ARTS" then
                            doExport(myfile as ¬
alias) of me
                        end if
                    end repeat
                    set myfolders to every folder ¬
of myitem
                    tell me to processFilesAnd¬
Folders(myfolders)
                else
                    if creator type is "ARTS" then
                        doExport(myitem as alias) ¬
of me
                    end if
                end if
            end tell
        end repeat
    end if
end processFilesAndFolders
on doExport(myexportfile)
set myfilename to name of (info for myexportfile
```

(script continues on next page)

Script 14.3 *continued*

```
                    script
tell application "Adobe Illustrator® 9.0.2"
open myexportfile
set the visible of every layer of document 1 ¬
to false
repeat with myLayerNum from 1 to number of ¬
layers in document 1
set the visible of layer myLayerNum of ¬
document 1 to true
set mynewfile to (myOutputFolder as string) & ¬
myfilename & myLayerNum & mysuffix as string
export document 1 to file mynewfile as JPEG ¬
with options {quality:100, optimization:false, ¬
blur:0.0, matte:true, horizontal ¬
scaling:200.0, vertical scaling:200.0, anti ¬
aliasing:true, artboard clipping:false, saving ¬
as HTML:false}
set the visible of layer myLayerNum of ¬
document 1 to false
end repeat
      close document 1 saving no
   end tell
end doExport
```

12. end repeat
```
    close document 1 saving no
      end tell
    end doExport
```

You close the document without saving it before ending your conversation with Illustrator and your doExport handler.

Collecting Linked Art Files

Illustrator is a great application—no question about it. Despite this, you regularly have to deal with some basic aspects of the way the application works. The biggest culprit has got to be dealing with linked art files when you are sharing Illustrator files. Invariably, the linked art files will be missing, misplaced, or hard to find—not a good situation.

AppleScript to the rescue! **Script 14.4** performs much the same function as QuarkXPress's Collect for Output command, gathering all linked art files in the same folder as the Illustrator file itself.

Figure 14.7 shows a folder processed by the script that contains an Illustrator file and all its linked image files, each of which was duplicated into the folder by the script.

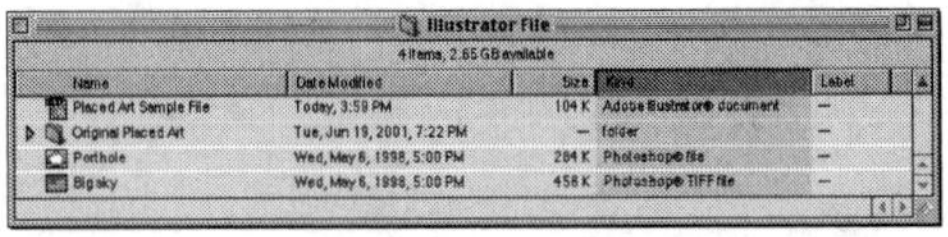

Figure 14.7 The folder processed with the script contained one Illustrator file; now it contains the Illustrator file and both linked image files.

To collect all linked art files into the same folder as the Illustrator file:

1. Your basic batch processing open and run handlers are explained in detail in the preceding section.

2. `on doExport(myexportfile)`

   Your doExport handler does all the real work in this script, opening each file passed to it and duplicating all linked image files into the folder containing the Illustrator file.

3. `try`

   You start with a try statement to catch any errors that come up.

4. `tell application "Adobe Illustrator® ¬`
   `9.0.2"`
   `    open myexportfile`

   Next, you tell Illustrator to open the file.

Script 14.4 This script duplicates all linked art files into the same directory as the Illustrator file.

```
                    script
on run
    set myFolder to choose folder with prompt ¬
"Select folder containing Illustrator files ¬
to collect for output"
    tell me to open {myFolder}
end run
on open (myfilesorfolders)
    repeat with myitem in myfilesorfolders
        tell application "Finder"
            if kind of myitem is "folder" then
                set myfiles to every file of ¬
myitem
                repeat with myfile in myfiles
                    if creator type is "ARTS" then
                        doExport(myfile as alias) ¬
of me
                    end if
                end repeat
                set myfolders to every folder of ¬
myitem
                tell me to open (myfolders)
            else
                if creator type is "ARTS" then
                    doExport(myitem as alias) of ¬
me
                end if
            end if
        end tell
    end repeat
end open
on doExport(myexportfile)
try
tell application "Adobe Illustrator® 9.0.2"
        open myexportfile
set myRasterArtItems to every raster item of ¬
document 1 whose embedded is false
set myPlacedArtItems to every placed item of ¬
document 1
        end tell
collectArt(myRasterArtItems, myexportfile)
collectArt(myPlacedArtItems, myexportfile)
tell application "Adobe Illustrator® 9.0.2" ¬
to close document 1 saving no
on error myerr
        display dialog myerr
    end try
end doExport
```

(script continues on next page)

5. `set myRasterArtItems to every raster ¬`
`item of document 1 whose embedded is ¬`
`false`

In the `myRasterArtItems` variable, you store a list of references to all raster-art items in the document that have external links.

6. `set myPlacedArtItems to every placed ¬`
`item of document 1`
`    end tell`

Before ending your conversation with Illustrator, you store in the `myPlacedArtItems` variable a list of references to all placed art items in the document.

7. `collectArt(myRasterArtItems, ¬`
`myexportfile)`

You call your `collectArt` handler, passing it the list of raster-art items and the reference to the current Illustrator file.

8. `collectArt(myPlacedArtItems, ¬`
`myexportfile)`

You call your `collectArt` handler again, passing it the list of placed art items and the reference to the current Illustrator file.

9. `tell application "Adobe Illustrator® ¬`
`9.0.2" to close document 1 saving no`

You have Illustrator close the document.

10. `on error myerr`
`    display dialog myerr`
`end try`
`end doExport`

Your error-handling code displays the error in a dialog box.

continues on next page

11. on collectArt(myArtItems, myFilePath)

Your collectArt handler does the hard work of finding each linked file and having the Finder duplicate the file into the folder containing your Illustrator file. To perform this task, it needs the list of objects in the file (myArtItems) and the reference to the Illustrator file itself (myFilePath).

12. tell application "Finder" to set ¬ myfilecontainer to container of ¬ myFilePath

You ask the Finder for the folder containing the Illustrator file and store the reference to it in the myfilecontainer variable.

13. repeat with myArtItem in myArtItems

Now you start your loop through every object in the current Illustrator document that was passed to you.

14. tell application "Adobe Illustrator® ¬ 9.0.2" to set myfile to (file path ¬ of myArtItem)

You ask Illustrator for the path to the linked art in the object referred to by myArtItem.

15. tell application "Finder"
   set myItemContainer to container ¬ of myfile

Now you get the Finder involved again, asking it for the folder containing the linked art file.

16. if myItemContainer ≠ myfilecontainer ¬ then

If the two containing folders are not the same, the linked art file is in a different folder from the Illustrator file, so you need to move it.

Script 14.4 *continued*

```
on collectArt(myArtItems, myFilePath)
tell application "Finder" to set ¬
myfilecontainer to container of myFilePath
repeat with myArtItem in myArtItems
tell application "Adobe Illustrator® 9.0.2" ¬
to set myfile to (file path of myArtItem)
tell application "Finder"
        set myItemContainer to container of ¬
myfile
if myItemContainer ≠ myfilecontainer then
set myName to name of myfile
if not (file myName of myfilecontainer exists) ¬
then
duplicate myfile to myfilecontainer
end if
        end if
    end tell
  end repeat
end collectArt
```

17. `set myName to name of myfile`

To get ready to move the file, you first get the name of the linked art file.

18. `if not (file myName of ¬`
`myfilecontainer exists) then`

Next, you check to see whether a file with the name of the linked art file already exists in the folder containing the Illustrator file.

19. `duplicate myfile to myfilecontainer`

If no file with the same name as the linked art file exists, you have the Finder make a copy of the linked art file in the Illustrator file's containing folder.

20. `end if`
`          end if`
`       end tell`
`    end repeat`
`end collectArt`

You end your conditionals, your `tell` block, and your `repeat` loop before concluding your `collectArt` handler.

✔ Tip

■ This script does not work in Mac OS X 10.1, due to problems with Illustrator's capability to return accurate file specifications for the linked objects in a document.

Relating Objects in Illustrator Documents to FileMaker Pro Records

You've waited a long time for Adobe Illustrator to become scriptable. What should you do now that version 9 is fully AppleScriptable? Hook it up to FileMaker Pro, the patriarch of scriptable apps!

Visual information communicates much more than simple numbers or words do. Wouldn't it be wonderful to find a way to use Illustrator as a graphic front end for a database, much the way that the Geographic Information Systems (GIS) maps information on the physical maps of space?

This section shows you how to attach a record in FileMaker to an object in Illustrator and then select and display the database record from Illustrator at the user's request, using three simple scripts and OSA Menu. Install OSA Menu and familiarize yourself with it before you start this section.

You could use **Scripts 14.5, 14.6,** and **14.7** to store data about objects in a floor plan, ads in a paste-up, or buildings in a site plan.

✔ Tip

■ These scripts are meant to be used in conjunction with OSA Menu, which works only with Mac OS 9.

Figure 14.8 shows what the sample Illustrator document looks like. **Figures 14.9** and **14.10** show the sample FileMaker Pro database.

To relate Illustrator objects to FileMaker records:

1. Create the sample database.

   The only required fields are id, which is a numeric field with an auto-enter serial number, and image, which is a container field.

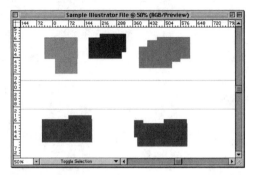

Figure 14.8 The sample Illustrator document contains a few objects that are meant to indicate houses on a street.

Figure 14.9 The Define Fields dialog box of the sample FileMaker Pro database shows all fields required for the script.

Figure 14.10 The sample FileMaker Pro database, shown in layout mode so that you can see the field names.

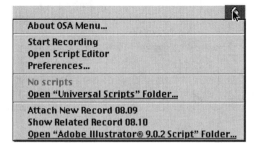

Figure 14.11 OSA Menu shows the two AppleScripts used in Illustrator to relate database records to objects.

2. Create or open an existing Illustrator document like the one shown in Figure 14.8.

3. Enter Script 14.5, and save it in the Adobe Illustrator® 9.0.2 Script folder inside the Scripts folder in your System Folder.

   Now the script will be available from within Illustrator in OSA Menu (**Figure 14.11**).

4. ```
   tell application "Adobe Illustrator® ¬
   9.0.2"
       activate
       set myselection to the selection
   ```
   You start by getting a reference to the selected object in Illustrator.

5. ```
   if myselection ≠ {} and (number of ¬
   items in myselection = 1) then
       set myselection to item 1 of ¬
   myselection
       copy
   ```
   If the selection is not empty, and it is a single object, you set myselection to that object. You also copy the selected object to the Clipboard to get Illustrator to provide a PICT image that you can paste into your container field later.

6. ```
   if name of myselection ≠ "" then
       set myanswer to button returned of ¬
       (display dialog "Replace ¬
   existing relationship with new ¬
   record?")
       if myanswer ≠ "OK" then set ¬
   myselection to {}
   end if
   ```
   You check to see whether the Illustrator object has already been named, because you relate the object to a database record by setting the object's name to the record's unique id field. If the object is already named, you ask the user whether he wants to change the relationship and create a new record name.

continues on next page

Using OSA Menu

All scripts in this section are meant to be used with Script Menu in Mac OS X or OSA Menu in Mac OS 9. The scripts were tested with OSA Menu version 1.2.2.

OSA Menu is developed by Leonard Rosenthal (http://www.lazerware.com/).

RELATING OBJECTS TO FILEMAKER PRO RECORDS
   ```

7. `end if`
`end tell`
`if myselection ≠ {} then`

Before creating a new record and relating it, you make sure that something has been selected in Illustrator.

8. `tell application "FileMaker Pro"`
`    set myrecord to create new record`
`    set myid to cell "id" of myrecord`
`end tell`

Next, you make a new record in your database in FileMaker. You store the unique value from its id field in the myid variable.

9. `tell application "Adobe Illustrator® ¬`
`9.0.2"`
`    set name of myselection to myid`
`end tell`

Now you set the name of the selected object in Illustrator to match the value in the id field from your FileMaker record. This little trick establishes a relationship with the object in Illustrator that you can use later.

10. `tell application "FileMaker Pro"`
`    activate`
`    show myrecord`
`    go to cell "image"`
`    paste`
`    go to cell "address"`
`end tell`
`end if`

Finally, you paste in the PICT image of your selected Illustrator object and place the insertion point in the address field of the new related record before activating FileMaker and leaving the user to complete the record.

Script 14.5 This script is one of three that work together to enable the relating of Illustrator objects to FileMaker records. It works by creating a new record and setting the name of an Illustrator object to that record's unique id field value.

```
tell application "Adobe Illustrator® 9.0.2"
    activate
    set myselection to the selection
if myselection ≠ {} and (number of items in ¬
myselection = 1) then
        set myselection to item 1 of myselection
        copy
if name of myselection ≠ "" then
            set myanswer to button returned of ¬
            (display dialog "Replace existing ¬
relationship with new record?")
            if myanswer ≠ "OK" then set ¬
myselection to {}
        end if
end if
end tell
if myselection ≠ {} then
tell application "FileMaker Pro"
        set myrecord to create new record
        set myid to cell "id" of myrecord
    end tell
tell application "Adobe Illustrator® 9.0.2"
        set name of myselection to myid
    end tell
tell application "FileMaker Pro"
        activate
        show myrecord
        go to cell "image"
        paste
        go to cell "address"
    end tell
end if
```

Script 14.6 The second of three scripts that enable a relationship between Illustrator objects and FileMaker records. This script shows a record with matching id field value based on a selected Illustrator object's name.

```
                        script
tell application "Adobe Illustrator® 9.0.2"
    activate
    set myselection to the selection
if myselection ≠ {} and (number of items in ¬
myselection = 1) then
        set myselection to item 1 of myselection
        set myName to name of myselection
else
        set myName to ""
    end if
end tell
if myName ≠ "" and (myName as integer) > 0 then
tell application "FileMaker Pro"
        show (every record of database 1 whose ¬
cell "id" = myName)
        activate
    end tell
end if
```

To show a record related to the selected object:

1. Enter **Script 14.6,** and save it in the Adobe Illustrator® 9.0.2 Script folder inside the Scripts folder in your System Folder. Now the script will be available from within Illustrator in OSA Menu (refer to **Figure 14.11**).

2. `tell application "Adobe Illustrator® ¬ 9.0.2"`
   `    activate`
   `    set myselection to the selection`

   You start by getting a reference to the selected object in Illustrator.

3. `if myselection ≠ {} and (number of ¬ items in myselection = 1) then`
   `        set myselection to item 1 of ¬ myselection`
   `        set myName to name of myselection`

   If the selection is not empty, and it is a single object, you set myselection to that object. You also store the name of the Illustrator object in a variable, myname.

4. `else`
   `        set myName to ""`
   `    end if`
   `end tell`

   Otherwise, you set myname to an empty string so that your script can detect this state later.

5. `if myName ≠ "" and (myName as ¬ integer) > 0 then`

   You check the name before trying to find a record in FileMaker that matches it.

   continues on next page

6. `tell application "FileMaker Pro"`
   `show (every record of databse 1 ¬`
`whose cell "id"= myName)`
   `activate`
`end tell`
`end if`

Finally, you show the related record and bring FileMaker to the front to display it.

The last script is an easy one. It will be saved inside your database as part of a ScriptMaker script.

To select art from a related FileMaker Pro database:

1. Create a new ScriptMaker script in FileMaker, with a single Perform AppleScript step.

2. Enter **Script 14.7.**

3. `tell application "FileMaker Pro"`
   `set myid to cell "id" of current ¬`
`record of document 1`
   `end tell`

You start by grabbing the value from the id field and storing it in `myid`.

4. `tell application "Adobe Illustrator® ¬`
`9.0.2"`
   `activate`
   `set the selection to {}`
   `set the selected of (every page ¬`
`item of current document whose name ¬`
`= myid) to true`
   `end tell`

You wrap up by activating Illustrator, clearing the selection, and selecting the page item with the name that matches `myid`.

Script 14.7 This is the simplest of the three scripts used to relate Illustrator objects to FileMaker records. This script selects an object in Illustrator whose name matches the unique id value in the current record.

```
script
tell application "FileMaker Pro"
    set myid to cell "id" of current record ¬
of document 1
end tell
tell application "Adobe Illustrator® 9.0.2"
    activate
    set the selection to {}
    set the selected of (every page item of ¬
current document whose name = myid) to true
end tell
```

15

GRAPHICCONVERTER 4

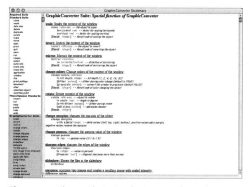

Figure 15.1 The AppleScript dictionary of Graphic-Converter includes its own extensive suite of commands and object classes.

GraphicConverter has been a useful tool to many Mac users for graphic production. Its extensive file-type support and conversion capabilities, combined with its high-level image-analysis and manipulation commands, make it a worthy application. In the program's recent incarnations, including the Carbonized version of GraphicConverter 4, an extensive AppleScript dictionary gives scripters the keys to the powerful graphics engine.

In this chapter, you will explore the batch-processing capabilities of GraphicConverter 4, including the production of JPEGs and optimized GIFs. You'll also take advantage of GraphicConverter's access to the scriptable printing.

Scripting GraphicConverter 4

The scripts in this chapter were tested with both the Carbon and Classic versions of GraphicConverter 4.0.8.

GraphicConverter 4 is shareware. A single user license costs $35.

GraphicConverter 4 is developd by Thorsten Lemke (http://www.lemkesoft.com/).

Batch-Exporting JPEG Files

The power of batch-file conversion is one of GraphicConverter's greatest capabilities. **Script 15.1** demonstrates how to take advantage of the program's support for conversion among a wide array of file types. Save the script as an application to use it as a droplet on which you can drop folders of image files. The script opens each file in GraphicConverter and saves a copy of the file as a JPEG in the same folder as the original.

Figure 15.2 shows a Finder window for a folder containing three original images and three converted JPEG files made by the script.

Figure 15.2 The Finder window for a folder of processed image files shows the new JPEG files created by the script.

To batch-export JPEG files:

1. on run
     tell me to open {(choose folder)}
   end run

The run handler lets us test our open handler within Script Editor.

2. on open (myFolder)
     set myFolder to item 1 of myFolder
     set myfiles to list folder ¬
   myFolder as alias without invisibles

You store the list of items in the folder myFolder in myFiles.

3. repeat with myFile in myfiles

Begin a loop through each item in myFiles, placing the current item in myFile.

4. set mycurrentfile to ((myFolder as ¬
   string) & (myFile as string)) as ¬
   string

Now construct the path to the current file in the loop as a string and store it in the myCurrentFile variable.

Script 15.1 This script droplet batch processes files contained in folders dropped onto it, making a JPEG image file of each file found.

```
                  script
on run
    tell me to open {(choose folder)}
end run
on open (myFolder)
    set myFolder to item 1 of myFolder
    set myfiles to list folder myFolder as ¬
alias without invisibles
repeat with myFile in myfiles
set mycurrentfile to ((myFolder as string) & ¬
(myFile as string)) as string
try
        tell application "Finder" to set mykind ¬
to kind of alias mycurrentfile
if mykind ≠ "folder" then
        doBatchProcess(mycurrentfile)
        else
            tell me to open {mycurrentfile as ¬
alias}
        end if
end try
    end repeat
end open
on doBatchProcess(myFile)
try
tell application "Finder"
        set mynewfile to (duplicate alias ¬
myFile) as alias
        set name of mynewfile to (name of ¬
alias myFile) & ".jpg"
    end tell
tell application "GraphicConverter"
open {mynewfile}
save front window as JPEG
close window 1
        end tell
    end try
end doBatchProcess
```

5. `try`

    `tell application "Finder" to set ¬`
`mykind to kind of alias mycurrentfile`

You have the Finder return in myKind the kind of item at which you are looking.

6. `if mykind ≠ "folder" then`
    `doBatchProcess(mycurrentfile)`
`else`
    `tell me to open {mycurrentfile ¬`
`as alias}`
`end if`

If the item is a folder call the handler doBatchProcess to convert the image.

7. `end try`
`end repeat"`
`end open`

If the item is a folder, call your own open handler with a reference to the folder.

8. `on doBatchProcess(myFile)`

The custom handler starts here, receiving a reference to the file for it to process in myfile.

9. `try`

The try block prevents any errors from stopping the script.

10. `tell application "Finder"`
    `set mynewfile to (duplicate alias ¬`
`myFile) as alias`
    `set name of mynewfile to (name of ¬`
`alias myFile) & ".jpg"`
`end tell`

Construct the new file with file suffix.

11. `tell application "GraphicConverter"`

The script starts talking to GraphicConverter.

12. `open {mynewfile}`

The script asks GraphicConverter to open the file referenced by myfile.

continues on next page

BATCH-EXPORTING JPEG FILES

13. `save front window as JPEG`

Next, the newly opened file, in `window 1`, is saved as a JPEG in the new file with a suffix.

13.
```
close window 1
        end tell
    end try
end doBatchProcess
```

Finally, the window is closed, the `tell` and `try` blocks end before the handler is closed.

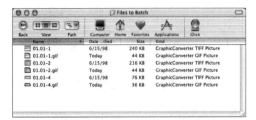

Figure 15.3 The Finder window for a folder of processed image files shows the new GIF files created by the script.

Batch Indexing, Optimizing, and Exporting GIF Files

This section again takes advantage of GraphicConverter's batch-file conversion capabilities. **Script 15.2** demonstrates how to convert image files to the GIF format. Color indexing and color table optimization steps are included in the script's conversion process. Save the script as an application to use it as a droplet on which you can drop folders of image files. Each image file dropped on this script will be opened in GraphicConverter and resaved as a GIF in the same folder as the original.

Figure 15.3 shows a Finder window for a folder containing three original images and three optimized GIF files made by the script.

To batch-index, optimize, and export files as GIF images:

1.
```
on run
    tell me to open {(choose folder)}
end run
on open (myFolder)
    set myfiles to list folder ¬
myFolder as alias without invisibles
    repeat with myFile in myfiles
        set mycurrentfile to ((myFolder ¬
as string) & (myFile as string)) as ¬
string
        tell application "Finder" to set ¬
mykind to kind of alias mycurrentfile
        if mykind ≠ "folder" then
            doBatchProcess(mycurrentfile)
        else
            tell me to open (mycurrentfile ¬
as alias)
        end if
    end repeat
end open
```

The run and open handlers are discussed in detail in Batch exporting JPEG files.

continues on next page

2. `on doBatchProcess(myFile)`

The custom handler starts here, receiving a reference to the file for it to process in `myfile`.

3. `tell application "Finder"`
`   set mynewfile to (duplicate alias ¬`
`myFile) as alias`
`    set name of mynewfile to (name of ¬`
`alias myFile) & ".gif"`
`end tell`

Construct the new file with file suffix.

4. `try`

The `try` block prevents any errors from stopping the script.

5. `tell application "GraphicConverter"`

The script starts talking to GraphicConverter.

6. `open {mynewfile}`

The script asks GraphicConverter to open the file referenced by `myfile`.

7. `set color space of window 1 to indexed`

The newly opened document, in `window 1`, is set to indexed color.

8. `set image bit depth of window 1 to 8`

The color depth of the indexed image is set to 256 colors or 8 bits.

9. `minimize color table of window 1`

The color depth is optimized using GraphicConverter's `minimize color table` command.

10. `save front window as GIF`

Next, the newly opened file, in `window 1`, is saved as a GIF in the new file with a suffix.

11. `close window 1`
`        end tell`
`    end try`
`end doBatchProcess`

Finally, the window is closed, the `tell` and `try` blocks end before the handler is closed.

Script 15.2 This script indexes, optimizes and re-saves image files as GIF files.

```
═══════════════ script ═══════════════
on run
    tell me to open {(choose folder)}
end run
on open (myFolder)
    set myfiles to list folder myFolder as ¬
alias without invisibles
    repeat with myFile in myfiles
        set mycurrentfile to ((myFolder as ¬
string) & (myFile as string)) as string
        tell application "Finder" to set mykind ¬
to kind of alias mycurrentfile
        if mykind ≠ "folder" then
            doBatchProcess(mycurrentfile)
        else
            tell me to open (mycurrentfile as ¬
alias)
        end if
    end repeat
end open
on doBatchProcess(myFile)
tell application "Finder"
        set mynewfile to (duplicate alias ¬
myFile) as alias
        set name of mynewfile to (name of alias ¬
myFile) & ".gif"
    end tell
try
tell application "GraphicConverter"
open {mynewfile}
set color space of window 1 to indexed
set image bit depth of window 1 to 8
minimize color table of window 1
save front window as GIF
close window 1
        end tell
    end try
end doBatchProcess
```

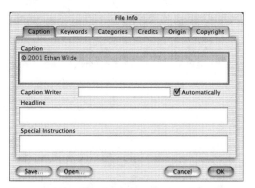

Figure 15.4 The File Info window of a processing image in GraphicConverter shows that the script has set the IPTC image caption text.

Batch-Captioning Files

GraphicConverter provides access to many levels of IPTC file information. This standard for image-file meta information allows you to set many kinds of meta data about each image file. This meta data is stored within the image file and cannot be lost easily. **Script 15.3** sets the IPTC caption text for all image files processed by it.

Figure 15.4 shows the File Info window for a file that has been processed by the script. Notice that the caption text is set to the string defined in the script.

To batch-caption files:

1. property mycaption : "© 2001 Ethan Wilde"

The property mycaption contains the text that will be used to assign a caption to every image processed by this script.

2. on run
    tell me to open {(choose folder)}
end run
on open (myFolder)
    set myfiles to list folder ¬
myFolder as alias without invisibles
    repeat with myFile in myfiles
        set mycurrentfile to ((myFolder ¬
as string) & (myFile as string)) as ¬
string
        tell application "Finder" to set ¬
mykind to kind of alias mycurrentfile
        if mykind ≠ "folder" then
            doBatchProcess(mycurrentfile)
        else
            tell me to open ¬
(mycurrentfile as alias)
        end if
    end repeat
end open

The run and open handlers are discussed in detail in Batch exporting JPEG files.

continues on next page

2. on doBatchProcess(myFile)

The custom handler starts here, receiving a reference to the file for it to process in myfile.

3. try

The try block prevents any errors from stopping the script.

4. tell application "GraphicConverter"

The script starts talking to GraphicConverter.

5. open {alias myFile}

The script asks GraphicConverter to open the file referenced by myfile.

6. set IPTC caption of window 1 to ¬ mycaption

Now the script sets the image's caption text to the property mycaption.

7. close window 1 with saving
          end tell
      end try
end doBatchProcess

Finally, the window is closed, the tell and try blocks end before the handler is closed.

Script 15.3 This script will set the IPTC image caption text for all image files processed to a string defined by a script property.

```
property mycaption : "© 2001 Ethan Wilde"
on run
    tell me to open {(choose folder)}
end run
on open (myFolder)
    set myfiles to list folder myFolder as ¬
alias without invisibles
    repeat with myFile in myfiles
        set mycurrentfile to ((myFolder as ¬
string) & (myFile as string)) as string
        tell application "Finder" to set mykind ¬
to kind of alias mycurrentfile
        if mykind ≠ "folder" then
            doBatchProcess(mycurrentfile)
        else
            tell me to open (mycurrentfile as ¬
alias)
        end if
    end repeat
end open
on doBatchProcess(myFile)
try
tell application "GraphicConverter"
open {alias myFile}
set IPTC caption of window 1 to mycaption
close window 1 with saving
        end tell
    end try
end doBatchProcess
```

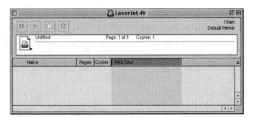

Figure 15.5 This Desktop Printer window shows the printer is processing one of the print jobs sent by the script through GraphicConverter.

Batch-Printing Files

The last arena for this chapter's exploration of GraphicConverter's batch-processing capabilities is printing. The application includes a Print Folder command that allows users to print folders of images. **Script 15.4** takes advantage of this feature by using the printfolder command to let you print, unattended, all the folders dropped on the script droplet.

Figure 15.5 shows the Desktop Printer window for the printer your script sent the output to after the script ran.

To batch-print files:

1. on run
        tell me to open {(choose folder)}
    end run

    The run handler lets us test our open handler within Script Editor.

2. on open (myfolders)
        repeat with myFolder in myfolders

    This loop moves through the list of items dropped onto the script droplet, storing each in myFolder.

3. tell application "Finder" to set ¬
    mykind to kind of myFolder

    The Finder returns the kind of the current item, myFolder, to the variable mykind.

4. if mykind = "Folder" then

    If the current item is a folder, the script will deal further with it.

5. doBatchProcess(myFolder)

    Call the handler to print the folder.

continues on next page

6. `tell application "Finder" to set ¬`
`myfoldersInside to every folder of ¬`
`entire contents of myFolder`

The script asks the Finder to store a list of all folders found inside of the current folder, myFolder.

7. `if class of myfoldersInside is not ¬`
`list then set myfoldersInside to ¬`
`{myfoldersInside}`
`if myfoldersInside ≠ {} then`

If there is a list of folders returned in myfoldersInside, then continue processing.

8. `repeat with myfolderInside in ¬`
`myfoldersInside`

This loop moves through each folder in the current folder.

9. `doBatchProcess(myfolderInside)`

Call the handler to print the folder.

10. `end repeat`
`        end if`
`      end if`
`   end repeat`
`end open`

Close all loops, conditional statements and the on open block.

11. `on doBatchProcess(myFolder)`

The custom handler starts here, receiving a reference to the folder for it to process in myFolder.

12. `try`

The try block prevents any errors from stopping the script.

13. `tell application "GraphicConverter"`

The script starts talking to GraphicConverter.

Script 15.4 This script prints all images in all folders processed without displaying any Print dialog boxes.

```
                     script
on run
    tell me to open {(choose folder)}
end run
on open (myfolders)
    repeat with myFolder in myfolders
tell application "Finder" to set mykind to ¬
kind of myFolder
if mykind = "Folder" then
doBatchProcess(myFolder)
tell application "Finder" to set ¬
myfoldersInside to every folder of entire ¬
contents of myFolder
if class of myfoldersInside is not list then ¬
set myfoldersInside to {myfoldersInside}
        if myfoldersInside ≠ {} then
repeat with myfolderInside in myfoldersInside
doBatchProcess(myfolderInside)
end repeat
        end if
      end if
    end repeat
end open
on doBatchProcess(myFolder)
try
tell application "GraphicConverter"
printfolder myFolder as alias without dialog
end tell
    end try
end doBatchProcess
```

14. `printfolder myFolder as alias ¬`
`without dialog`

The powerful `printfolder` command lets us use GraphicConverter's Print Folder... command from AppleScript.

15 `end tell`
`  end try`
`end doBatchProcess`

Finally, the `tell` and `try` blocks end before the handler is closed.

✔ Tip

- Try to choose the Print Folder command from GraphicConverter's File menu, and a dialog box warns you that Carbon printing is not fully supported by most print drivers. Therefore, automated printing from the `printfolder` or `print` commands in AppleScript may be unable to stop Print dialog boxes or to set printing properties properly. If you have this experience, try using the Classic version of GraphicConverter to take advantage of fully enabled scriptable printing.

BATCH-PRINTING FILES

QuickTime 5

Figure 16.1 The custom suite of QuickTime Player's AppleScript dictionary.

Scripting QuickTime means scripting time and motion. The engineers in Apple's Quick-Time group know about video and video production tasks. They also recognize the usefulness of AppleScript in doing video and sound work.

If you're reading this chapter, you might know a thing or two about video and the time-intensive tasks required to make a good time-based piece of art. Read on if you're looking for some help from AppleScript in your ongoing QuickTime production work.

In this chapter, you'll use the extensive AppleScript support in QuickTime 5 to auto-mate all sorts of useful production tasks. You'll focus on batch-processing files with the QuickTime Player application. QuickTime Player's own large AppleScript dictionary (**Figure 16.1**) provides access to most prop-erties and capabilities of QuickTime movies. Don't worry—you will not need QuickTime Pro for any of the scripts in this chapter except the last one (**Script 16.4**).

Scripting QuickTime Player and QuickTime 5

The scripts in this chapter were tested in QuickTime 5 for Mac OS X and Mac OS 9.1.

QuickTime Pro 5 requires a registration code, available for purchase at Apple's Web site.

QuickTime 5 and QuickTime Player appli-cation are developed by Apple Computer Inc. (http://www.apple.com/).

Enabling Movie Autoplay for Folders of Files

Using QuickTime Player with AppleScript will become a regular activity for you if you deal with any quantity of movie files. Batch-processing files will likely be the most common activity performed by your scripts.

In **Script 16.1,** you will start with a basic batch-processing task: enabling the autoplay feature for existing QuickTime movie files contained in folders. The user can drop folders containing movies on this script when it is saved as a droplet to make all the movies play automatically when opened in the future.

Figure 16.2 shows the conversation between the script and the QuickTime Player application as logged in Script Editor's Event Log window.

Figure 16.2 The conversation between the script and QuickTime Player is shown in Script Editor's Event Log window.

To enable the movie autoplay setting for files contained in one or more folders:

1. `on run`
   `    open {choose folder}`
   `end run`

   The run handler lets you test the rest of the script from within Script Editor. You don't need to run it as a droplet to invoke the open handler.

2. `on open (myfilesorfolders)`

   Your item-processing handler walks through all files and folders, looking for QuickTime files.

3. `repeat with myitem in myfilesorfolders`

   Your loop will traverse all items—files or folders—in your list of items to process.

4. `tell application "Finder"`

   You start talking to the Finder to take advantage of its access to file-system properties.

Script 16.1 This batch-processing script enables the autoplay setting on every movie file it processes.

```
                    script
on run
    open {choose folder}
end run
on open (myfilesorfolders)
    repeat with myitem in myfilesorfolders
        tell application "Finder"
            if kind of myitem is "folder" then
                set myfiles to every file of myitem
                repeat with myFile in myfiles
                    if file type of myFile is ¬
"MooV" or name of myFile ends with ".mov" then
                        makeAutoPlay(myFile) of me
                    end if
                end repeat
                set myfolders to every folder of ¬
myitem
                tell me to open (myfolders)
            else
                if file type of myFile is "MooV" ¬
or name of myFile ends with ".mov" then
                    makeAutoPlay(myitem) of me
                end if
            end if
        end tell
    end repeat
end open
on makeAutoPlay(myFile)
    tell application "QuickTime Player"
        activate
        set ignore auto play to true
        set ignore auto present to true
        stop every movie
        close every movie saving no
        open myFile
        if saveable of movie 1 is true then
            set auto play of movie 1 to true
            rewind movie 1
            save movie 1
        end if
        close movie 1 saving no
        set ignore auto play to false
        set ignore auto present to false
    end tell
end makeAutoPlay
```

5. `if kind of myitem is "folder" then`

You test the Finder item's code style to see whether you have a folder.

6. `set myfiles to every file of myitem`

Now you ask the Finder for a list of files in the current folder.

7. `repeat with myFile in myfiles`

You loop through each file in myfiles.

8. `if file type of myFile is "MooV" or ¬`
`name of myFile ends with ".mov" then`
`  makeAutoPlay(myFile) of me`
`end if`
`        end repeat`

If the Finder file type shows that the file is a QuickTime file, you call your makeAutoPlay handler to change the file.

9. `set myfolders to every folder of ¬`
`myitem`

You ask the Finder for a list of folders in the current folder.

10. `tell me to open (myfolders)`

Now that you have the list of folders, you call the open handler you are in to process the next list of folders.

11. `else`

If the Finder item kind for the current item in your main loop is not a folder, you want to find out about the file type.

12. `if file type of myFile is "MooV" or ¬`
`name of myFile ends with ".mov" then`
`  makeAutoPlay(myitem) of me`
`end if`

If the file type shows that you have a QuickTime file, you call your makeAutoPlay handler to change it.

continues on next page

13. `end if`
     `end tell`
  `end repeat`
`end open`

You conclude your conditional tests, `tell` block, and `repeat` loop before ending your handler.

14. `on makeAutoPlay(myFile)`

You start your `makeAutoPlay` handler, expecting to receive a single file alias value passed to it, which you'll store in `myFile`.

15. `tell application "QuickTime Player"`
  `activate`

Now bring QuickTime Player to the front.

16. `set ignore auto play to true`
`set ignore auto present to true`

You tell the application not to pay any attention to the `autoplay` or `autopresent` settings of any movies subsequently opened.

17. `stop every movie`

All movies running in the player are stopped.

18. `close every movie saving no`

Then all movies are closed without saving any changes in them, in preparation for working with the movie file passed to the handler.

19. `open myFile`

Now you are ready to have the player open the movie stored in `myFile`.

20. `if saveable of movie 1 is true then`

You check to make sure that the movie can be resaved before you try to change its settings.

21. `set auto play of movie 1 to true`

You set the `auto play` property of the movie to `true` to enable automatic playback on opening of the movie.

22. `rewind movie 1`

Just to be sure, you also rewind the movie to the beginning.

23. `save movie 1`
`    end if`

You save the movie with its updated settings.

24. `close movie 1 saving no`

Now you close the movie.

25. `set ignore auto play to false`
`set ignore auto present to false`
`  end tell`

Because you are done, you can restore the application's properties to allow it to pay attention to opened movies' autoplay and autopresent settings before ending the `tell` block.

26. `end makeAutoPlay`

Your handler is over, so you must end it with an `end` statement.

Converting Folders of Files to QuickTime Movies

The QuickTime application takes advantage of QuickTime's capability to open and work with many file types and formats. In this section, you will leverage the broad strengths of QuickTime with your own script to batch-process any number of files contained in folders. The files can be any type that QuickTime Player can open. **Script 16.2** will resave these files as QuickTime movies, using the most recent settings from the player application.

Figure 16.3 shows a folder with original files and new QuickTime movie files created by the script.

To convert folders of files to QuickTime movies:

1. on run
    open {choose folder}
    end run

The run handler lets you test the rest of the script from within Script Editor. You don't need to run it as a droplet to invoke the open handler.

2. on open (myfilesorfolders)

Your item-processing handler walks through all files and folders, looking for QuickTime files.

3. repeat with myitem in myfilesorfolders

Your loop will traverse all items—files or folders— in your list of items to process.

4. tell application "Finder"

You start talking to the Finder to take advantage of its access to file-system properties.

5. if kind of myitem is "folder" then

You test the Finder item kind to see whether you have a folder.

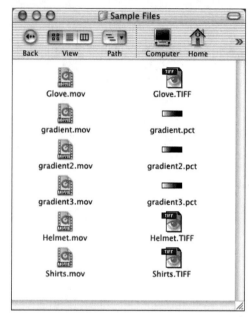

Figure 16.3 A folder processed by the script shows the original files and the new QuickTime versions made by the script.

Script 16.2 This batch-processing script attempts to open every file it processes to convert files to QuickTime format.

```
                     script
on run
    open {choose folder}
end run
on open (myfilesorfolders)
    repeat with myitem in myfilesorfolders
        tell application "Finder"
            if kind of myitem is "folder" then
                set myfiles to every file of myitem
                repeat with myFile in myfiles
                    convertToQuickTime(myFile as ¬
alias) of me
                end repeat
                set myfolders to every folder of ¬
myitem
                tell me to open (myfolders)
            else
                makeAutoPlay(myitem as alias) of me
            end if
        end tell
    end repeat
end open
on convertToQuickTime(myFile)
    with timeout of 1800 seconds
        tell application "QuickTime Player"
            activate
            set ignore auto play to true
            set ignore auto present to true
stop every movie
            close every movie saving no
            --try
            open myFile
            if saveable of movie 1 is true then
                tell application "Finder"
                    set myName to name of myFile
                    set myName to ¬
setFileExtension(myName, "mov") of me
                    set mySourceFolder to the ¬
container of myFile as alias
                    if exists file myName of ¬
mySourceFolder then delete file myName of ¬
mySourceFolder
                end tell
                set myFilePath to ¬
((mySourceFolder as text) & myName)
                export movie 1 to file myFilePath ¬
as QuickTime movie using most recent settings
            end if
            --end try
set ignore auto play to false
```

(script continues on next page)

6. `set myfiles to every file of myitem`

Now you ask the Finder for a list of files in the current folder.

7. `repeat with myFile in myfiles`

You loop through each file in `myfiles`.

8. `convertToQuickTime(myFile as alias) ¬`
`of me`
            `end repeat`

You call your `convertToQuickTime` handler to process the file.

9. `set myfolders to every folder of ¬`
`myitem`

You ask the Finder for a list of folders in the current folder.

10. `tell me to open (myfolders)`

Now that you have the list of folders, you call the `open` handler you are in to process the list.

11. `else`

If the Finder item's kind for the current item in your main loop is not a folder, you use your handler to process it.

12. `makeAutoPlay(myitem as alias) of me`

You call your `convertToQuickTime` handler to process the file.

13. `end if`
        `end tell`
    `end repeat`
`end open`

You conclude your conditional tests, `tell` block, and `repeat` loop before ending your handler.

14. `on convertToQuickTime(myFile)`

Your handler receives a file reference in `myFile`.

continues on next page

15. `with timeout of 1800 seconds`

To allow for big files, you place your code inside a `with timeout` block to give the player 30 minutes to open and resave the file as a QuickTime movie.

16. `tell application "QuickTime Player"`
`   activate`

You start talking to QuickTime Player now.

17. `set ignore auto play to true`
`set ignore auto present to true`

You disable the application's capability to play or present any movies based on the movie settings for this process.

18. `stop every movie`
`close every movie saving no`

You stop any existing open movies and close them without saving.

19. `try`

Now you can attempt to open the file in QuickTime Player.

20. `open myFile`

Here, you ask the player to open `myFile`.

21. `if saveable of movie 1 is true then`

Before doing anything else, you check to make sure that the movie can be saved.

22. `tell application "Finder"`

You start talking to the Finder.

23. `set myName to name of myFile`

You get the name of the file you opened.

24. `set myName to`
`setFileExtension(myName, "mov") of me`

You modify the string to contain a file name for the file you will create soon, adding a file extension with your own handler, `setFileExtension`.

Script 16.2 *continued*

```
                  script

          close movie 1 saving no
      end tell
    end timeout
end convertToQuickTime

on setFileExtension(myFilename, myExtension)
    set myFilename to myFilename as string
    if (offset of "." in myFilename) is not 0 then
        set mycurrentdelimiters to AppleScript's ¬
text item delimiters
        set AppleScript's text item delimiters ¬
to {"."}
        set myFilename to text items 1 thru -2 ¬
of (text items of myFilename) as string
        set AppleScript's text item delimiters ¬
to mycurrentdelimiters
    end if
    if myFilename ends with "." then
        set myFilename to myFilename & ¬
myExtension
    else
        set myFilename to myFilename & "." & ¬
myExtension
    end if
    return myFilename
end setFileExtension
```

25. `set mySourceFolder to the container ¬`
`of myFile as alias`

Now you get a reference to the folder in which `myFile` resides.

26. `if exists file myName of ¬`
`mySourceFolder then delete file ¬`
`myName of mySourceFolder`
`        end tell`

You check to see whether a file with the new name already exists in your folder. If such a file does exist, you delete it.

27. `set myFilePath to ((mySourceFolder ¬`
`as text) & myName)`

Now you construct a full path for the new file.

28. `export movie 1 to file myFilePath ¬`
`as QuickTime movie using most recent ¬`
`settings`
`        end if`

Before ending your `if...then` statement, you ask the player to save the open file as a self-contained movie with your new name.

29. `end try`

You end your `try` block, which was there to keep your script from stopping if the player application had any problems with files.

30. `set ignore auto play to false`
`set ignore auto present to false`

Because you're done, you restore the application's capability to play or present movies automatically.

31. `close movie 1 saving no`
`        end tell`
`    end timeout`
`end convertToQuickTime`

You close the movie before ending your `tell` and `timeout` blocks and your handler.

continues on next page

32. `on setFileExtension(myFilename, ¬`
`myExtension)`

This handler is useful, especially in Mac OS X. Use it to append a file extension to a file-name string. The handler is smart enough to replace any existing extension with the new one. Pass the handler the file name, not the path, and the extension without a leading period.

33. `set myFilename to myFilename as ¬`
`string`

Coerce the file name to make sure that it is a string before you do anything with it.

34. `if (offset of "." in myFilename) is ¬`
`not 0 then`

Check to see whether the file name contains periods. If so, you must perform more steps to ensure that you have only one extension at the end of the string.

35. `set mycurrentdelimiters to ¬`
`AppleScript's text item delimiters`

This line is the first of a cool AppleScript trick that lets you convert between strings and lists by using any character as the separator in the string that indicates the break between list items. AppleScript reserves a special constant called `AppleScript's text item delimiters`, which lets you coerce between strings and lists by using the `text item` property of a string. In any case, this line stores the current settings of this important constant before changing them later. This process is important, because you should restore its normal settings when you're done.

36. `set AppleScript's text item ¬`
`delimiters to {"."}`

Now you change the value of the constant, replacing it with a single-item list that contains the character the script cares about, using a period as the delimiter.

37. `set myFilename to text items 1 thru ¬`
`-2 of (text items of myFilename) as ¬`
`string`

This line does magic; it collects all `text items` of the string from the first through the next to last (-2.). AppleScript uses negative list item values to let you access lists starting from the end, so that -1 is the last item in a list and -2 is the next to last. By eliminating the last item, you lose any existing file extension in the string.

38. `set AppleScript's text item ¬`
`delimiters to mycurrentdelimiters`
`  end if`

Now you restore the constant's original values.

39. `if myFilename ends with "." then`
`   set myFilename to myFilename &`
`myExtension`

You add the extension to the end of the modified file-name string.

40. `else`

If no instance of a period occurs in the string, this `else` clause executes.

41. `set myFilename to myFilename & "." ¬`
`& myExtension`

Because no period exists in the current string, this line adds one at the end and then appends the file-extension string.

42. `end if`

You end the conditional `if` statement.

43. `return myFilename`

Before ending the handler, you must return a value—in this case, the modified file name.

44. `end setFileExtension`

The handler is over, so end it properly.

✔ Tip

■ The handler discussed in steps 32 onward can be used in any script that needs to change or add a file extension to any file name.

Exporting Audio CD Tracks to QuickTime Files

This section gives you a chance to take a break from scripting for productivity's sake alone. When the day is done and you've batch-processed your last movie, wouldn't you like to get AppleScript to do something nice for you? QuickTime Player offers you a chance to do something cool under script control: convert audio CD tracks to any export format the player can handle. **Script 16.3** is a handy script to send to music-loving friends as a gift.

Figure 16.4 shows QuickTime Player processing an audio CD track while the script is running.

To export the audio tracks on an audio CD to files from QuickTime Player:

1. `set myCD to (choose folder with ¬ prompt "Choose audio CD")`

   First, you must get the user to choose the audio CD that he or she wants to convert to QuickTime movie format. Users can choose any folder, but you want them to pick the CD volume mounted that is an audio CD.

2. `tell application "Finder" to set ¬ myKind to kind of myCD`

   Now you ask the Finder for the kind of the item the user selected and store this string value in myKind.

3. `if myKind = "disk" or mykind = ¬ "volume" then`

   This test ensures that you work only with disks in Mac OS 9 and Mac OS X.

4. `set myFolder to (choose folder with ¬ prompt "Folder to save songs") as ¬ string`

   You ask the user for a folder for saving the movie files.

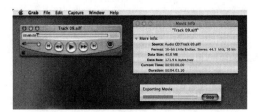

Figure 16.4 The windows of QuickTime Player while the application is processing an audio track under script control.

Script 16.3 This script processes all audio tracks on a mounted audio CD, converting each track to a QuickTime movie.

```
script

set myCD to (choose folder with prompt "Choose ¬
audio CD")
tell application "Finder" to set myKind to ¬
kind of myCD
if myKind = "disk" or mykind = "volume" then
    set myFolder to (choose folder with prompt ¬
"Folder to save songs") as string
    tell application "Finder" to set mySongFiles ¬
to (every file of the myCD whose file type is ¬
"trak" or names ends with ".cdda") as alias list
    repeat with myFile in mySongFiles
        set myNewFile to myFolder & name of ¬
(info for myFile) & ".mov" as string
        try
            tell application "QuickTime Player"
                stop every movie
                close every movie saving no
            end tell
            tell application "Finder"
                activate
                ignoring application responses
                    open myFile using application ¬
file id "TVOD"
                end ignoring
            end tell
            tell application "QuickTime Player"
                activate
                repeat until movie 1 exists
                    delay 1
                end repeat
                with timeout of 1800 seconds
                    export movie 1 to file ¬
myNewFile as QuickTime movie using most ¬
recent settings
                end timeout
                close movie 1 saving no

            end tell
        end try
    end repeat
end if
```

5. `tell application "Finder" to set ¬`
`mySongFiles to (every file of the ¬`
`myCD whose file type is "trak" or ¬`
`names ends with ".cdda") as alias list`

Now you ask the Finder to store in the list variable mySongFiles an alias reference to every file on your CD that is an audio file.

6. `repeat with myFile in mySongFiles`

You loop through the file references, storing the current one in myFile.

7. `set myNewFile to myFolder & name of ¬`
`(info for myFile) & ".mov" as string`

You create a new string variable to hold a path to the file where you'll save the song movie file.

8. `try`

You use a try block to prevent any errors that might occur as you progress through your work.

9. `tell application "QuickTime Player"`
`stop every movie`
`close every movie saving no`
`end tell`

You have the player stop and close any open movies.

10. `tell application "Finder"`
`activate`
`ignoring application responses`
`open myFile using application ¬`
`file id "TVOD"`
`end ignoring`
`end tell`

Now you talk to the Finder. You bring it to the front and ask it to open the current file from the CD, using QuickTime Player. You ask for the player application by its creator code, TVOD, to make sure that the Finder uses the right application to open the file. The ignoring block lets your script proceed without worrying about how the Finder deals with the open command.

continues on next page

EXPORTING AUDIO CD TRACKS

11.
```
tell application "QuickTime Player"
    activate
```
You're ready to bring the player to the front.

12.
```
repeat until movie 1 exists
    delay 1
end repeat
```
This simple loop runs every second, checking to see whether the importation of the audio file is complete.

13.
```
with timeout of 1800 seconds
    export movie 1 to file myNewFile ¬
as QuickTime movie using most recent ¬
settings
end timeout
```
Now you can have the player resave the audio file as a QuickTime movie in the new file location. The timeout block gives the player 30 minutes to save the file.

14.
```
close movie 1 saving no
        end tell
    end try
  end repeat
end if
```
You close the original audio file before ending your conversation with QuickTime Player. You also end your loop and if statement.

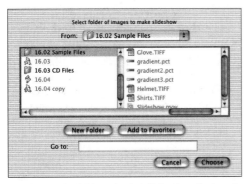

Figure 16.5 The folder-selection dialog box displayed by the script.

Creating a Slide Show from a Folder of Image Files

QuickTime Player can create a QuickTime movie slide show from a folder of image files, but it requires you to name all files using sequential numbers. This function is exposed to AppleScript with the open image sequence command. This script uses the command from AppleScript to make browseable slide shows of all images in a folder, regardless of file names. **Script 16.4** demonstrates how easily you can create slide shows with defined playback characteristics from AppleScript.

Figure 16.5 shows the dialog box the script displays to prompt the user to choose a folder.

To create a slide show from a folder of image files with any file names:

1. set mySlideDuration to 3

   Later in the code, you set the duration of each slide (in seconds) with the mySlideDuration variable.

2. set myFolder to (choose folder with ¬ prompt "Select folder of images to ¬ make slideshow")

   You prompt the user for a folder of images to make into a slide show.

3. set myNewFile to (myFolder as string) ¬ & "Slideshow.mov" as string

   You create a new path, using the path to the source folder for a new file named Slideshow.mov.

4. try

   You use a try block to catch any errors.

   continues on next page

CREATING A SLIDE SHOW

5. `tell application "Finder"`
   `try`
      `set myFirstImageFiles to (every ¬`
`file of myFolder whose file type is ¬`
`"GIFf" or file type is "JPEG" or ¬`
`file type is "PICT" or file type is ¬`
`"TIFF") as alias list`
   `on error`
      `set myFirstImageFiles to ""`
   `end try`
`end tell`

Now you ask the Finder for a list of references to images in the folder that are GIF, JPEG, PICT, or TIFF files. You store this list in the `myFirstImageFiles` variable.

6. `if the myFirstImageFiles is not "" then`

This test makes sure that an image was found in the folder referenced by `myFolder`. If no image was found, the `myFirstImageFile` variable should contain an empty string.

7. `tell application "QuickTime Player"`
   `activate`

You start talking to QuickTime Player and bring it to the front.

8. `stop every movie`
`close every movie saving no`

You stop any movies that are playing and close them without saving any changes.

9. `repeat with myNum from 1 to number ¬`
`of items in myFirstImageFiles`

You start a loop that runs once for each image file found.

10. `set myFirstImageFile to item myNum ¬`
`of myFirstImageFiles`

You assign the file reference for the current file in the loop to the `myFirstImageFile` variable.

Script 16.4 This script uses QuickTime Player's capability to make slide-show movies that have prescribed settings.

```
script

set mySlideDuration to 3
set myFolder to (choose folder with prompt ¬
"Select folder of images to make slideshow")
set myNewFile to (myFolder as string) & ¬
"Slideshow.mov" as string
try
    tell application "Finder"
        try
            set myFirstImageFiles to (every file ¬
of myFolder whose file type is "GIFf" or file ¬
type is "JPEG" or file type is "PICT" or file ¬
type is "TIFF") as alias list
        on error
            set myFirstImageFiles to ""
        end try
    end tell
    if the myFirstImageFiles is not "" then
tell application "QuickTime Player"
        activate
        stop every movie
        close every movie saving no
repeat with myNum from 1 to number of items ¬
in myFirstImageFiles
            set myFirstImageFile to item ¬
myNum of myFirstImageFiles
            open image sequence ¬
myFirstImageFile seconds per frame ¬
mySlideDuration
            if myNum > 1 then
                select movie 1 at 0
                paste movie 1
            end if
            if myNum ≠ number of items in ¬
myFirstImageFiles then
                select all movie 1
                copy movie 1
                close movie 1 saving no
            end if
        end repeat
        delay 30
        tell movie 1
            rewind
            set the full text of annotation ¬
"Full Name" to "My Slideshow"
            set auto present to true
            set auto play to true
            set the presentation mode to
```

(script continues on next page)

Script 16.4 *continued*

```
                     script
            slide show
            set presentation size to ¬
normalset looping to true
            set auto quit when done to false
            set auto close when done to false
        end tell
        save movie 1 in file myNewFile as ¬
self contained
        close movie 1 saving no
      end tell
    end if
end try
```

11. `open image sequence myFirstImageFile ¬`
`seconds per frame mySlideDuration`

Now you use the player's built-in command to open the current image file in the folder. QuickTime usually uses this command to import multiple images with specific numbered file names, but you're using it to open a single file and set a duration on it. You also specify the duration of each frame of the show.

12. `if myNum > 1 then`
`  select movie 1 at 0`
`  paste movie 1`
`end if`

If this movie is the second movie or later, the script pastes all previous slides from the Clipboard into the beginning of this movie.

13. `if myNum ≠ number of items in ¬`
`myFirstImageFiles then`
`  select all movie 1`
`  copy movie 1`
`  close movie 1 saving no`
`end if`

If this file is not the last one to process, you copy its contents to the Clipboard and close it. In this step, you are appending each slide to the Clipboard.

14. `end repeat`

The loop ends when all files are processed.

15. `tell movie 1`

After the loop ends, a single complete movie file is left open in QuickTime Player, ready to be saved.

16. `rewind`

You start talking directly to the open slide show to rewind it and set its properties.

continues on next page

17. `set the full text of annotation ¬`
`"Full Name" to "My Slideshow"`

You set the name of the movie.

18. `set auto present to true`

You set the autopresent mode to true.

19. `set auto play to true`

You turn on the autoplay on open feature.

20. `set the presentation mode to slide show`

You make the whole movie run as a slide show.

21. `set presentation size to normal`

You set the movie to its actual image size.

22. `set looping to true`

You enable endless looping of the slide show during playback.

23. `set auto quit when done to false`

You disable the player's capability to quit when the movie ends.

24. `set auto close when done to false`

You also disable the movie's capability to close itself when it ends.

25. `end tell`

You end your conversation with the movie.

26. `save movie 1 in file myNewFile as ¬`
`self contained`

You ask the application to save a self-contained movie in the new file with its path in `myNewFile`.

27. `close movie 1 saving no`
`        end tell`
`    end if`
`end try`

You close the original window without saving before ending your conversation with QuickTime Player. You also close your `if` and `try` statements.

INTERNET EXPLORER 5 AND NETSCAPE 4.7

17

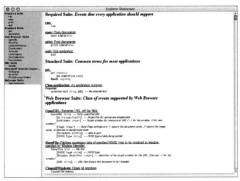

Figure 17.1 The AppleScript dictionary for Internet Explorer 5.1 Preview Edition in Mac OS X.

Figure 17.2 The AppleScript dictionary for Netscape Communicator 4.77.

Netscape Navigator and Microsoft Internet Explorer are revolutionary software applications that support several Internet protocols, including HTTP and FTP. Your focus on these two popular Web browsers will be accessing Web pages via HTTP, whether those pages are stored remotely on servers or locally on your own hard disk or local area network.

Each browser has an AppleScript dictionary with some powerful, rarely used statements—including syntax formed from combinations of nouns and verbs such as OpenURL. Some of the dictionary statements differ subtly between browsers. **Figures 17.1** and **17.2** show the entries in each browser's AppleScript dictionary.

Submitting Form Data from Internet Explorer

One of the most powerful scriptable features of Explorer is its capability to simulate user-entered form data for submission to a Web server. Using the `post data` parameter of OpenURL, you can send form data that a CGI would expect to come from a POST method of submission. In **Script 17.1**, you send POST method data to the Library of Congress's Thomas database of legislation. The principle illustrated by this script can be applied to any Web site that expects to receive form data via the POST method.

Figure 17.3 shows the script's dialog-box prompt for a name.

To submit form POST data via AppleScript:

1. `set mykeywords to text returned of ¬` `(display dialog "Search legislation ¬` `for keywords:" default answer "Internet")`

   You start this script by prompting the user for a domain name, which is what we'll search for on Network Solutions' site. If you're modifying this script to send form data to another site, you'll want to prompt the user for the particular data needed.

2. `set mydefaults to "&docidc107=¬` `&submit=Search"`

   Next you set some constant form field values for the search that Thomas expects to receive. You can find out the variable names that a particular Web site expects to receive by looking through the HTML source code for the form page that you'll emulate with your script.

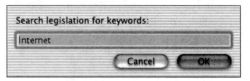

Figure 17.3 The dialog box displayed by the script prompting the user for a domain name to look up.

Script 17.1 This script submits form POST data to the Network Solutions Web site to check the availability of a domain name.

```
set mykeywords to text returned of (display ¬
dialog "Search legislation for keywords:" ¬
default answer "Internet")
set mydefaults to "&docidc107=&submit=Search"
tell application "Internet Explorer"
    Activate
OpenURL "http://thomas.loc.gov/cgi-bin/query" ¬
FormData "queryc107=" & mykeywords & ¬
mydefaults
end tell
```

3. `tell application "Internet Explorer"`
   `Activate`

Now we're ready to talk to Explorer and bring it to the front.

4. `OpenURL "http://thomas.loc.gov/¬`
   `cgi-bin/query" FormData "queryc107=" ¬`
   `& mykeywords & mydefaults`
   `end tell`

Finally, you send the `OpenURL` command with URL and form data. Again, the peculiarities of each Web site will dictate what the URL should look like. You can find out the correct URL to send to the server is by looking at the HTML source code. POST data is formatted `"variable1=value1&variable2=value2..."`

✔ Tips

■ You can construct an URL that contains data for a CGI by using the `GET` method of submission, in which all data is included in the URL (for example, `http://www.yahoo.com/search.cgi?¬p=scripting`), without using the post data parameter of `OpenURL`.

■ You could use **Script 17.1** in a repeat loop to conduct a whole series of searches, or you might use a series of `OpenURL` commands to query a bunch of Web sites with the same search request.

Scripting Internet Explorer

All the Explorer scripts in this chapter were designed and tested for Microsoft Internet Explorer 5.0 and 5.1. Most of these scripts do not work with older versions of Internet Explorer.

Microsoft Internet Explorer is developed by Microsoft Corp. (http://microsoft.com/).

SUBMITTING FORM DATA

Opening a URL quickly

The Internet Suite of commands in Standard Additions includes open location. This magic command uses your preference settings in your Internet preferences to launch the appropriate application based on the kind of URL you specify. open location "http://ww.apple.com", for example, would launch your default browser and send it to Apple's home page. open location "mailto:applescript@mediatrope.com" would launch your default email client and create an outgoing message to applescript@mediatrope.com.

Using GET versus POST

The HTTP protocol defines two ways for Web forms to return form data to the server. The HTML tag <FORM METHOD="POST" ACTION="script.acgi"> determines the method used for a form.

With METHOD="GET", all field data is appended to the end of the URL that the ACTION tag defines. This field data, also known as the *reply string*, is appended to the URL with a question mark indicating its start. Field names and values are paired, with pairs separated by equal signs. Each pair is separated by an ampersand. GET limits the length of form data and lets the user see the form data passed in their browser.

With METHOD="POST", all field data is put into a packet, called the *post data*, by the user's browser and sent along to the URL that the ACTION tag defines. With POST, form data can be much longer and is hidden from the user when submitted.

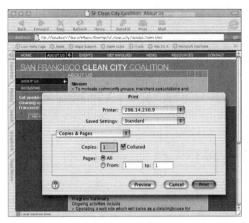

Figure 17.4 The Print dialog box that appears when the script runs in Mac OS X; behind it is the Web page about to be printed.

Script 17.2 This script prints all selected files it processes in Internet Explorer 5.

```
                    script
property myvalidsuffixes : {"htm", "html", "asp"}
on run
   set mybasefolder to choose folder with ¬
prompt "Select the first folder:"
   printHTML(mybasefolder)
end run
on printHTML(myFolder)
myFolderContents to list folder myFolder ¬
without invisibles
   tell application "Internet Explorer" to ¬
Activate
   repeat with myitem in myFolderContents
      set myFilePath to ((myFolder as text) ¬
& myitem)
      tell application "Finder" to set myKind ¬
to kind of alias myFilePath
      if myKind is "folder" then
         printHTML(alias myFilePath)
      else
         tell application "Finder" to set ¬
myName to name of alias myFilePath
         set mysuffix to
getFileExtension(myName)
         if myvalidsuffixes contains ¬
mysuffix then
         tell application "Finder" to set ¬
myOS to (computer "sysv")
            if myOS ≥ 4096 then
```
(script continues on next page)

Printing Web Pages from Internet Explorer

Ever wanted to print out a 100-page Web site for later reference without inducing immediate carpal tunnel syndrome? AppleScript it. (I like the way that sounds, don't you?)

Script 17.2 takes advantage of Explorer's built-in printing support from AppleScript. You'll test for matching file suffixes by using a contains statement to catch files ending with .htm, .html, and .asp.

Figure 17.4 shows the Print dialog box displayed by the Mac OS X version of Internet Explorer when the script runs. The Mac OS 9 version of IE can print without displaying any dialog boxes.

To print local files from Explorer:

1. property myvalidsuffixes : {"htm", ¬
   "html", "asp"}

   You start by defining a property, myvalidsuffixes, to hold a list of all file extensions that you want your browser to open and print.

2. on run
      set mybasefolder to choose folder ¬
   with prompt "Select the first folder:"
      printHTML(mybasefolder)
   end run

   Next, you define a run handler that prompts the user to choose a local folder to search for files to print in your browser.

3. on printHTML(myFolder)

   Next, you define your printHTML function.

   continues on next page

PRINTING WEB PAGES

4. `myFolderContents to list folder ¬`
`myFolder without invisibles`

You copy the list of items contained in
myFolder to the `myFolderContents` variable, ignoring any invisible files such as
icons or the Desktop database.

5. `tell application "Internet Explorer"`
`to Activate`

You want to bring Explorer to the front so
that you can see what is going on before
you start opening and printing files.

Script 17.2 *continued*

```
                    set myurl to "file://localhost/" & findAndReplace(posixPath alias myFilePath, ":", "/")
                else
                    set myurl to "file:///" & findAndReplace(myFilePath, ":", "/")
                end if
                tell application "Internet Explorer" to OpenURL myurl toWindow -1 Flags 7
                delay 10
                tell application "Internet Explorer" to PrintBrowserWindow -1
            end if
        end if
    end repeat
end printHTML
on findAndReplace(mystring, mymatch, myreplace)
    set mynewstring to ""
    repeat with mycharacter in every character of mystring
        if mycharacter as string ≠ mymatch then
            set mynewstring to mynewstring & mycharacter
        else
            set mynewstring to mynewstring & myreplace
        end if
    end repeat
    return mynewstring
end findAndReplace
on getFileExtension(myFilename)
    set myFilename to myFilename as string
    if (offset of "." in myFilename) is not 0 then
        set mycurrentdelimiters to AppleScript's text item delimiters
        set AppleScript's text item delimiters to {"."}
        set myExtension to text item -1 of (text items of myFilename) as string
        set AppleScript's text item delimiters to mycurrentdelimiters
    else
        set myExtension to ""
    end if
    return myExtension
end getFileExtension
```

6. `repeat with myitem in myFolderContents`

Now you're ready to loop through each `myitem` in `myFolderContents`.

7. `set myFilePath to ((myFolder as ¬`
`text) & myitem)`

Next, you store the path to the current file in your loop in a variable, `myfilepath`.

8. `tell application "Finder" to set ¬`
`myKind to kind of alias myFilePath`

Now you can ask the Finder for the kind of item pointed to by `myfilepath`.

9. `if myKind is "folder" then`
`    printHTML(alias myFilePath)`

If `myFile` is a folder, you call the `printHTML` function again to deal with files in the nested folder.

10. `else`
`    tell application "Finder" to set ¬`
`myName to name of alias myFilePath`
`    set mysuffix to ¬`
`getFileExtension(myName)`
`    if myvalidsuffixes contains ¬`
`mysuffix then`

Otherwise, you grab the file extension, which is assumed to be the text following a period. You test `mysuffix` to see if whether is contained in your list of valid extensions, `myvalidsuffixes`. If so, you've found an HTML file that you'll want to open in Explorer. By checking for the existence of the string `mysuffix` in `myvalidsuffixes`, you catch files that have the extension `.htm`, `.html`, and `.asp` with one simple test.

continues on next page

11. `tell application "Finder" to set ¬`
`    myOS to (computer "sysv")`
`    if myOS ≥ 4096 then`
`        set myurl to "file://localhost/" ¬`
`    & findAndReplace(posixPath alias ¬`
`    myFilePath, ":", "/")`

The script checks to see if whether is running on Mac OS X. If so, the script converts the file path to a Unix path to work with IE in Mac OS X. This task requires the freeware System Scripting Addition for the posixPath command.

12. `else`
`        set myurl to "file:///" & ¬`
`    findAndReplace(myFilePath, ":", "/")`

You're ready to construct a valid file URL to your local file. To do so, you need to start the URL with the local file specifier (file:///) and replace any Mac path delimiters (":") with valid URL path delimiters ("/"). You accomplish this task with your findAndReplace handler.

13. `end if`
`    tell application "Internet Explorer" ¬`
`    to OpenURL myurl toWindow -1 Flags 7`

With your URL in myurl, you can tell Explorer to open it in the frontmost window.

14. `delay 10`

Because you can't detect when the page finishes loading from your script, you wait 10 seconds to make sure that all images have resolved.

15. `tell application "Internet Explorer" ¬`
`    to PrintBrowserWindow -1`
`            end if`
`        end if`
`      end repeat`
`    end printHTML`

The wait is over. You can tell Explorer to print your frontmost window before continuing the loop.

16. `on findAndReplace(mystring, mymatch, ¬`
`myreplace)`

Your handy `findAndReplace` handler accepts a string to search, as well as a matching and replacement character, and returns a modified string.

17. `set mynewstring to ""`

Your modified string is built up in `mynewstring`.

18. `repeat with mycharacter in every ¬`
`character of mystring`

To look for the character to replace, you loop through each character in the source string `mystring`.

19. `if mycharacter as string ≠ mymatch then`
`    set mynewstring to mynewstring & ¬`
`mycharacter`

If the current character is not the match, you append it to `mynewstring`.

20. `else`
`    set mynewstring to mynewstring & ¬`
`myreplace`
`end if`

Otherwise, you add the replacement character.

21. `end repeat`
`return mynewstring`
`end findAndReplace`

When you're done with your loop, `mynewstring` will contain an updated string to return.

22. `on getFileExtension(myFilename)`

This handler is useful, especially in Mac OS X. Use it to return a file's extension.

23. `set myFilename to myFilename as string`

Coerce the file name to make sure that it is a string before you do anything with it.

continues on next page

Scripting with the System Scripting Addition

To work in Mac OS X, this script uses the `posixPath` command from the Mac OS X System Scripting Addition.

If you are using Mac OS 9 or Internet Explorer in the Classic environment, you don't need to use the scripting addition.

24. `if (offset of "." in myFilename) is ¬`
`not 0 then`

Check to see whether the file name contains periods. If so, you will perform more steps to ensure that you have only one extension at the end of the string.

25. `set mycurrentdelimiters to ¬`
`AppleScript's text item delimiters`

This line is the first of a cool AppleScript trick that lets you convert between strings and lists by using any character as the separator in the string that indicates the break between list items. AppleScript reserves a special constant called `AppleScript's text item delimiters` to let you coerce between strings and lists by using the `text item` property of a string. In any case, this line stores the current settings of this important constant before changing them later. This process is important, because you should restore its normal settings when you're done.

26. `set AppleScript's text item ¬`
`delimiters to {"."}`

You change the value of the constant, replacing it with a single-item list that contains the character the script cares about with a period as the delimiter.

27. `set myExtension to text item -1 of ¬`
`(text items of myFilename) as string`

This line does magic; it collects the extension, which is after the last period and therefore is the last text item, `-1`. AppleScript uses negative list item values to let you access lists starting from the end, so that `-1` is the last item in a list and `-2` is the next to last. By accessing the last item, you get any existing file extension from the string.

28. `set AppleScript's text item ¬`
`delimiters to mycurrentdelimiters`

You restore the constant's original values.

29. `else`

If the file-name string contains no periods, the `else` clause executes.

30. `set myExtension to ""`
`  end if`

You close the conditional statement.

31. `return myExtension`

Before ending the handler, it is important to return a value—in this case, the modified file name.

32. `end getFileExtension`

The handler is over, so end it properly.

Making Screen Shots of Web Pages from Netscape

Ever wanted to make screen shots of a large Web site instead of printing it? As with printing, you can AppleScript the process.

Script 17.3 takes advantage of Netscape's capability to let your scripts know the status of a loading page—no waiting around needlessly. You'll test for matching file extensions by using a contains statement to catch file names ending with .htm, .html, and .asp.

Figure 17.5 shows a folder of screen-shot JPEGs created from clip2gif by the script.

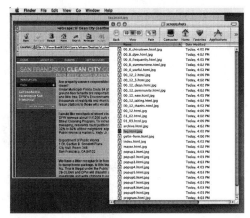

Figure 17.5 The folder of Web-browser screen shots created by clip2Gif under script control.

To make screen shots of local HTML files:

1. `property myvalidsuffixes : {"htm", ¬ "html", "asp"}`

Start by defining a property, myvalidsuffixes, to hold a list of file extensions you want your browser to open and print.

2.
```
on run
    set mybasefolder to choose folder ¬
with prompt "Select the first folder:"
    set myscreenshotsfolder to choose ¬
folder with prompt "Select folder ¬
for screenshots:"
    printHTML(mybasefolder, ¬
myscreenshotsfolder)
end run
```

Next, you define a run handler that prompts the user to choose a local folder to search for files to print.

3. `on printHTML(myFolder, myscreenfolder)`

Next, you define your printHTML function.

4.
```
tell application "Finder" to set ¬
myFolderContents to list folder ¬
myFolder without invisibles
```

You copy the list of items contained in myFolder to the myFolderContents variable, ignoring any invisible files.

Script 17.3 This script makes screen shots of all selected files in Netscape 6 by using the application `clip2gif`.

```
property myvalidsuffixes : {"htm", "html", "asp"}
on run
    set mybasefolder to choose folder with prompt "Select the first folder:"
    set myscreenshotsfolder to choose folder with prompt "Select folder for screenshots:"
    printHTML(mybasefolder, myscreenshotsfolder)
end run
on printHTML(myFolder, myscreenfolder)
    tell application "Finder" to set myFolderContents to list folder myFolder without invisibles
    tell application "Netscape Communicator™" to activate
    repeat with myitem in myFolderContents
        set myFilePath to ((myFolder as text) & myitem)
        tell application "Finder" to set myKind to kind of alias myFilePath
        if myKind is "folder" then
            printHTML(alias myFilePath, myscreenfolder)
        else
            tell application "Finder" to set myName to name of alias myFilePath
            set mysuffix to getFileExtension(myName)
            if myvalidsuffixes contains mysuffix then
                tell application "Netscape Communicator™"
                    open file myFilePath
                    repeat
                        set myWindowStillLoading to the busy of window 1
                        if myWindowStillLoading is 0 then exit repeat
                    end repeat
                end tell
                tell application "clip2gif" to save screen crop {0, 19, 799, 599} as JPEG in file ¬
((myscreenfolder as text) & myName & ".jpg")
            end if
        end if
    end repeat
end printHTML
on getFileExtension(myFilename)
    set myFilename to myFilename as string
    if (offset of "." in myFilename) is not 0 then
        set mycurrentdelimiters to AppleScript's text item delimiters
        set AppleScript's text item delimiters to {"."}
        set myExtension to text item -1 of (text items of myFilename) as string
        set AppleScript's text item delimiters to mycurrentdelimiters
    else
        set myExtension to ""
    end if
    return myExtension
end getFileExtension
```

MAKING SCREEN SHOTS OF WEB PAGES

5. `tell application "Netscape ¬`
`Communicator™" to activate`

You want to bring Netscape to the front so that you can see what is going on before you start opening and printing files.

6. `repeat with myitem in myFolderContents`

Now you're ready to loop through each `myitem` in `myFolderContents`.

7. `set myFilePath to ((myFolder as ¬`
`text) & myitem)`

Next, you store the path to the current file in your loop in a variable, `myfilepath`.

8. `tell application "Finder" to set ¬`
`myKind to kind of alias myFilePath`

Now you can ask the Finder for the kind of item pointed to by `myfilepath`.

9. `if myKind is "folder" then`
`    printHTML(alias myFilePath, ¬`
`myscreenfolder)`

If `myFile` is a folder, you call the `printHTML` function again to deal with files in the nested folder.

10. `else`
`    tell application "Finder" to set ¬`
`myName to name of alias myFilePath`
`    set mysuffix to ¬`
`getFileExtension(myName)`
`    if myvalidsuffixes contains ¬`
`mysuffix then`

Otherwise, you grab the file extension, which is assumed to be the text following a period. You test `mysuffix` to see if whether is contained in your list of valid extensions, `myvalidsuffixes`. If so, you've found an HTML file that you'll want to open in Explorer. By checking for the existence of the string `mysuffix` in `myvalidsuffixes`, you catch files that have the extensions `.htm`, `.html`, and `.asp` with one simple test.

11.

```
tell application "Netscape ¬
Communicator™"
 open file myFilePath
```

You have Netscape open the local file.

12.

```
repeat
 set myWindowStillLoading to the ¬
busy of window 1
  if myWindowStillLoading is 0 then ¬
exit repeat
end repeat
      end tell
```

Netscape lets you check the status of a window to see if whether is still loading images or other assets by looking at the busy property of the window. You use this property in a loop to wait for the page to load before proceeding.

13.

```
tell application "clip2gif" to save ¬
screen crop {0, 19, 799, 599} as ¬
JPEG in file ((myscreenfolder as ¬
text) & myName & ".jpg")
       end if
     end if
   end repeat
end printHTML
```

The wait is over. You can tell clip2gif to capture the current screen below the menu bar by using the rectangle {0,19,799,599}, which defines a rectangle starting at the leftmost pixel of the screen and the 19th pixel down the screen, ending in the bottom-right corner of an 800x600 resolution screen. You may want to change the rectangle.

14. `on getFileExtension(myFilename)`

This handler is useful, especially in Mac OS X. Use it to return a file's extension.

15. `set myFilename to myFilename as string`

Coerce the file name to make sure that it is a string before you do anything with it.

continues on next page

Scripting Netscape Navigator

All the scripts that follow were designed and tested for Netscape Navigator 4.77. Netscape 6, as released at this writing, does not have fully functional AppleScript support.

Navigator is developed by Netscape Communications Corp. (http://www.netscape.com/).

16. `if (offset of "." in myFilename) is ¬`
`not 0 then`

Check to see whether the file name contains any periods. If so, you will perform more steps to ensure that you have only one extension at the end of the string.

17. `set mycurrentdelimiters to ¬`
`AppleScript's text item delimiters`

This line lets you convert between strings and lists by using any character as the separator in the string that indicates the break between list items. AppleScript reserves a special constant called `AppleScript's text item delimiters` to let you coerce between strings and lists by using the `text item` property of a string. In any case, this line stores the current settings of this important constant before changing them later. This process is important, because you should restore its normal settings when you're done.

18. `set AppleScript's text item ¬`
`delimiters to {"."}`

You change the value of the constant, replacing it with a single-item list that contains the character the script cares about, using a period as the delimiter.

19. `set myExtension to text item -1 of ¬`
`(text items of myFilename) as string`

This line collects the extension, which is after the last period and therefore is the last text item, -1. AppleScript uses negative list item values to let you access lists starting from the end, so that -1 is the last item in a list and -2 is the next to last. By accessing the last item, you get any existing file extension from the string.

Scripting clip2Gif

This script uses the highly scriptable freeware application clip2Gif 0.7.2.

clip2Gif is developed by Yves Piguet (http://homepage.mac.com/piguet/).

20. `set AppleScript's text item ¬`
`delimiters to mycurrentdelimiters`

You restore the constant's original values.

21. `else`

If the file-name string contains no periods, the `else` clause executes.

22. `set myExtension to ""`
`  end if`

You close the conditional statement.

23. `return myExtension`

Before ending the handler, it is important to return a value—in this case, the modified file name.

24. `end getFileExtension`

The handler is over, so end it properly.

Putting Netscape in Kiosk Mode

One of the most powerful features of Netscape Navigator can be accessed only through AppleScript: kiosk mode. When Navigator is switched to kiosk mode, most of its menu options and buttons disappear. This state is most useful for presenting Web sites on machines in public settings where you want to restrict the user's options. **Figure 17.6** shows what Navigator's browser window looks like when kiosk mode is invoked.

Script 17.4 is a brief script that switches Navigator to kiosk mode.

To put Netscape Navigator in kiosk mode:

1. `tell application "Netscape ¬ Communicator™"`
   `activate`

   You begin by letting AppleScript know that you want to talk to Netscape and bringing it to the front.

2. `set kiosk mode to 1`
   `end tell`

   Next, you tell Netscape to begin running in kiosk mode. To switch off kiosk mode, you'd use `set kiosk mode to 0`.

✔ Tips

■ Have you ever wanted to demo a Web site on an unmonitored machine in public? Invariably, people will surf off into the outer limits of the Web, leaving your dedicated Mac and browser displaying unwanted Web pages. Kiosk mode will save you. By eliminating most menus and the location bar, kiosk mode makes it much harder for users to take undesirable Web excursions.

Figure 17.6 The Netscape browser window in kiosk mode. Note the lack of controls.

Script 17.4 This script makes Netscape Communicator run in a reduced menu and control mode known as kiosk mode.

```
tell application "Netscape Communicator™"
    activate
    set kiosk mode to 1
end tell
```

■ Kiosk mode is also useful if you want to make a canned presentation to a group from your browser. By invoking kiosk mode, you can guide your audience through a site without any distracting browser controls. Who says a browser-based presentation can't look as slick as something created in a dedicated presentation-software package?

Figure 17.7 The dialog box displayed by the script to allow the user to choose a new file name and location.

Script 17.5 This script saves the source code for the frontmost window in Internet Explorer in a new file named by the user.

```
script
set myFile to choose file name
tell application "Internet Explorer"
    set currentSource to GetSource
end tell
set myFileRef to (open for access myFile with ¬
write permission)
write currentSource to myFileRef
close access myFileRef
```

Retrieving HTML Source Code with Internet Explorer

One of the most useful features of Internet Explorer is its capability to return the source code for a page directly to a script. You can use this feature to create scripts that parse HTML source code intelligently to traverse sites, mine for data, and perform other functions. **Script 17.5** retrieves the current Web page's HTML source code as a string and saves the string in a new text file. Combine this script with an FTP upload routine, and you could process and change pages on a Web server and then upload them again automatically. Hmmm ... quite a thought.

To retrieve HTML source code:

1. `set myFile to choose file name`

   Start by having AppleScript display a New File dialog box and store a reference to the path of the user's new file name in myFile. **Figure 17.7** shows the dialog box displayed by the choose file name command.

2. `tell application "Internet Explorer"`
   `    set currentSource to GetSource`
   `end tell`

   Next, you ask Internet Explorer to return the HTML source code of its frontmost window to the currentSource variable.

3. `set myFileRef to (open for access ¬`
   `myFile with write permission)`
   `write currentSource to myFileRef`
   `close access myFileRef`

   Finally, you write the source-code text in currentSource to myFile.

✔ Tip

■ Try using GetSource to retrieve the HTML source code of the frontmost window in Explorer after querying a server by using Script 17.1. Then parse the code for the search-results data.

Clearing the Browser Cache

As the browser loads files from remote servers, it stores them in a cache to allow quick retrieval for subsequent display. Sometimes, you need to clear the cache. **Script 17.6** uses the Finder to remove the cache file of Internet Explorer or Netscape Navigator.

Figure 17.8 shows the path to a user's Internet Explorer cache file in Mac OS X, as displayed by Sherlock.

To clear your Internet Explorer cache:

1. set myPrefsPath to the path to ¬ preferences folder as text

   The myPrefsPath variable stores the path of your current Preferences folder with AppleScript's preferences folder property.

2. tell application "Finder" to set myOS ¬ to (system attribute "sysv")

   Next, the script gets the system version. Enter the line as system attribute "sysv" in Mac OS X or computer "sysv" in Mac OS 9.

3. if myOS ≥ 4096 then

   You test the system version.

4. tell application "Finder" to set ¬ myLibraryPath to (container of alias ¬ myPrefsPath as alias) as string
   set myCachePath to (myLibraryPath & ¬ "Caches:MS Internet Cache:IE ¬ Cache.waf") as text

   If Mac OS X is the running system, you construct the correct path to the current user's IE cache file.

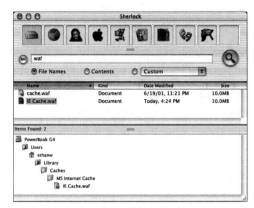

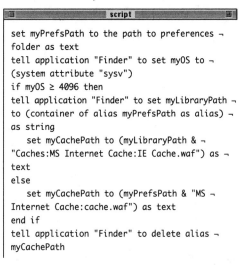

Figure 17.8 The path to a user's Internet Explorer cache file in Mac OS X, as shown by Sherlock.

Script 17.6 This script deletes the Internet Explorer cache file in Mac OS 9 or Mac OS X.

```
set myPrefsPath to the path to preferences ¬
folder as text
tell application "Finder" to set myOS to ¬
(system attribute "sysv")
if myOS ≥ 4096 then
tell application "Finder" to set myLibraryPath ¬
to (container of alias myPrefsPath as alias) ¬
as string
    set myCachePath to (myLibraryPath & ¬
"Caches:MS Internet Cache:IE Cache.waf") as ¬
text
else
    set myCachePath to (myPrefsPath & "MS ¬
Internet Cache:cache.waf") as text
end if
tell application "Finder" to delete alias ¬
myCachePath
```

5. `else`

```
    set myCachePath to (myPrefsPath & ¬
"MS Internet Cache:cache.waf") as text
```

You construct the full path of your Mac OS 9 Internet Explorer cache file and store it in the *myCachePath* variable. To change this script to work with Netscape Navigator, replace the string `"MS Internet Cache:cache.waf"` with `"Netscape Users:<UserName>:Cache ƒ"`. Change `<UserName>` to your user-profile name. You can look inside the Netscape Users folder to figure out your user-profile name, if necessary.

6. `end if`

```
tell application "Finder" to delete ¬
alias myCachePath
```

Finally, you tell the Finder to delete the cache file pointed to by *myCachePath*.

✔ Tip

- See the notes for step 5 to modify this script to work with Netscape Navigator. Instead of deleting Explorer's one huge cache file, the modified script deletes the entire cache folder for a specified Netscape user profile.

Deleting Netscape Cookie Files

Browser *cookies* are variables that Web servers store on your hard disk. These variables can be used to track your site preferences, identity, and other attributes. At times, you want to clear your browser's cookies and start with a clean slate. **Script 17.7** works by using the Finder to remove Netscape's MagicCookies file.

Figure 17.9 shows this file in the Trash after the script has run. This scripting concept will not work in the same fashion with Internet Explorer.

To clear Navigator's cookies file:

1. `set myUserName to "Steve"`

   You begin by defining the user name for your Netscape profile. This user name is created in a separate application called User Profile Manager that resides in the folder with Navigator. Be sure to change the value of the string "Steve" here to your user-profile name. You might also replace this line with a `display dialog` command to prompt users for their profile names every time the script is run.

2. `tell application "Finder"`

   Next, you start speaking to the Finder.

3. `set myPrefsPath to (the startup disk ¬ as string) & ":System Folder:Preferences:"`

   The `myPrefsPath` variable stores the path of your current Preferences folder by using the `preferences folder` property of AppleScript.

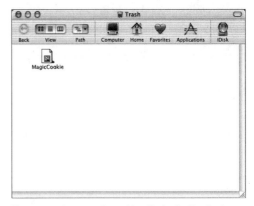

Figure 17.9 Netscape's cookies file in the Trash after the script runs.

Script 17.7 This script deletes the file where Netscape Communicator stores cookie data for a user.

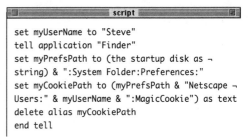

```
set myUserName to "Steve"
tell application "Finder"
set myPrefsPath to (the startup disk as ¬
string) & ":System Folder:Preferences:"
set myCookiePath to (myPrefsPath & "Netscape ¬
Users:" & myUserName & ":MagicCookie") as text
delete alias myCookiePath
end tell
```

4. `set myCookiePath to (myPrefsPath & ¬`
`"Netscape Users:" & myUserName & ¬`
`":MagicCookie") as text`

You construct the full path of your Netscape cookies file in this line and store it in the `myCookiePath` variable.

5. `delete alias myCookiePath`
`end tell`

Now you tell the Finder to delete the cookies file pointed to by `myCookiePath`. You use the word `alias` here to tell the Finder that you're actually talking about a reference to an existing file. Within AppleScript, you always let the Finder know that you are referring to an actual file by referencing it as an `alias` object. To make this concept easier to remember, you might think about `myCookiePath` as though it were itself an alias to the actual file.

OUTLOOK EXPRESS 5

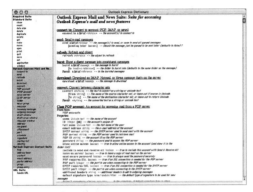

Figure 18.1 Outlook Express' custom suite in its AppleScript dictionary provides access to most mail and news objects and commands.

The original Claris Emailer AppleScript dictionary was so exceptionally well designed that when Microsoft created Outlook Express for the Macintosh, it adopted the vast majority of Emailer's dictionary for Outlook. **Figure 18.1** shows the dictionary entry for the message object in Outlook Express.

Outlook Express is a powerful combination with FileMaker Pro when it is used to create mailing-list databases and mine email for data. Outlook's message object is a perfect analog to FileMaker's record object. When you copy properties from an Outlook message to cells of a FileMaker record, you create a powerful searchable database that you can use to calculate statistics, summarize mail, or send mail, as you'll see in this chapter.

Converting Mail from Eudora or Unix

Script 18.1 converts a Unix or Eudora mail file to Outlook Express format, extracting each message separately into the Inbox. In the Unix world of sendmail, a user's entire mailbox is stored in a single file named after the user. If your file has Unix line feeds in it, set the myFileIsUNIX variable to true. The Macintosh version of Eudora stores each mailbox's messages in a single file. If you're using Eudora files, set myFileIsUNIX to false.

Figure 18.2 shows how Outlook's Inbox looks as the script is running.

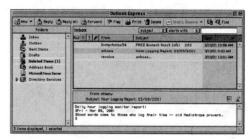

Figure 18.2 The Inbox of Outlook Express shown while the script is running.

To convert mail from Eudora or Unix:

1. on run
        set myFileIsUNIX to true

You begin your on run handler by defining the myFileIsUNIX variable to flag which line-feed type to expect in the mail file. You could set this variable to the results of a display dialog-box command to prompt the user for the file type.

2. if myFileIsUNIX then
        set linefeed to (ASCII character ¬
10) & return

Now you test the variable; if it contains the value true, you set the variable linefeed to ASCII character 10. If you are parsing DOS or PC files, set the linefeed variable to ASCII character 10 & ASCII character 13.

3. else
        set linefeed to return
    end if

If myFileIsUNIX contains the value false, you set the linefeed variable to return, which is a predefined AppleScript constant with a value of ASCII character 13.

Script 18.1 This script converts a Unix or Eudora mail file to Outlook Express format, extracting each message separately into the Inbox.

```
                     script
on run
    set myFileIsUNIX to true
if myFileIsUNIX then
        set linefeed to (ASCII character 10) ¬
& return
else
        set linefeed to return
    end if
set myMailFile to (choose file with prompt ¬
"Mail file to import:")
set myFileRef to (open for access myMailFile)
set myMailDate to (read myFileRef until ¬
linefeed)
    set {mydelimits, AppleScript's text item ¬
delimiters} to {AppleScript's text item ¬
delimiters, " "}
    set mySender to text item 2 of myMailDate
    set AppleScript's text item delimiters to ¬
mydelimits
try
        repeat
set mySubject to ""
set myMailDateFound to false
repeat
set myMail to (read myFileRef until linefeed)
if myMail = linefeed or (count of characters ¬
in myMail) = 1 then exit repeat
set myMail to (characters 1 thru ((length of ¬
myMail) - 1) of myMail as string) & return
if myMail starts with "Subject: " then
                set mySubject to (characters ¬
10 thru (length of myMail) of myMail) as string
            end if
if myMail starts with "Date: " then
set myMailDateFound to true
                set {mydelimits, AppleScript's ¬
text item delimiters} to {AppleScript's text ¬
item delimiters, " "}
                set theDayOfWeek to text item ¬
2 of myMail
set theMonth to text item 4 of myMail
                set theDay to text item 3 of ¬
myMail
                set theTime to text item 6 of ¬
myMail
set theYear to text item 5 of myMail
                set myDateSent to date ¬
```

(script continues on next page)

4. `set myMailFile to (choose file with ¬ prompt "Mail file to import:")`

Next, you prompt the user to select the mail file to import, storing the selection in the myMailFile variable.

5. `set myFileRef to (open for access ¬ myMailFile)`

You open the selected file by using the open for access command.

6. `set myMailDate to (read myFileRef ¬ until linefeed)`
`set {mydelimits, AppleScript's text ¬ item delimiters} to {AppleScript's ¬ text item delimiters, " "}`
`set mySender to text item 2 of ¬ myMailDate`
`set AppleScript's text item ¬ delimiters to mydelimits`

Now you read the first line of the mail file, storing it in a variable named myMailDate. The first line of the mail file often represents a date for the messages it contains.

7. `try`
`    repeat`

Here, you start a repeat loop to capture each mail message contained in the mail file.

8. `set mySubject to ""`

You begin the loop by initializing the mySubject variable, which will end up holding the subject of the current mail message.

9. `set myMailDateFound to false`

Now you initialize the myMailDateFound variable with the value false. You'll use this variable to keep track of whether each individual message you find in the file has its own date.

continues on next page

10. repeat

You begin a nested loop to read sequentially each line of the mail file that composes the header of the current message.

11. set myMail to (read myFileRef until ¬
    linefeed)

You read characters from the mail file until you encounter the end-of-line character that you defined with your linefeed variable in step 2 or 3.

12. if myMail = linefeed or (count of ¬
    characters in myMail) = 1 then ¬
    exit repeat

If the myMail variable contains nothing but the end-of-line character, it's a blank line. A blank line indicates the end of your header, so you exit your loop.

13. set myMail to (characters 1 thru ¬
    ((length of myMail) - 1) of myMail ¬
    as string) & return

You strip the end-of-line character off the myMail variable.

14. if myMail starts with "Subject: " then
      set mySubject to (characters 10 ¬
    thru (length of myMail) of myMail) ¬
    as string
    end if

Then you test to see whether the subject line is in this line. If so, you store that line in the mySubject variable.

15. if myMail starts with "Date: " then

You test to see whether myMail starts with the string "Date:".

16. set myMailDateFound to true
    set {mydelimits, AppleScript's text ¬
    item delimiters} to {AppleScript's ¬
    text item delimiters, " "}
    set theDayOfWeek to text item 2 of ¬
    myMail

Script 18.1 *continued*

```
                                         script
(theDayOfWeek & ", " & theMonth & " " & theDay ¬
& ", " & theYear & " " & theTime as string)
              set AppleScript's text item ¬
delimiters to mydelimits
end if
        end repeat
if not myMailDateFound then
try
              set {mydelimits, AppleScript's ¬
text item delimiters} to {AppleScript's text ¬
item delimiters, " "}
              set mySender to text item 2 ¬
of myMailDate
              set theDayOfWeek to text item ¬
3 of myMailDate
              set theMonth to text item 4 ¬
of myMailDate
              set theDay to text item 5 ¬
of myMailDate
              set theTime to text item 6 ¬
of myMailDate
              set theYear to text item 7 ¬
of myMailDate
              set AppleScript's text item ¬
delimiters to mydelimits
              set myDateSent to date ¬
(theDayOfWeek & ", " & theMonth & " " & theDay ¬
& ", " & theYear & " " & theTime as string)

          end try
        end if
set myBody to ""
        repeat
set myMail to (read myFileRef until linefeed)
considering case
if myMail starts with "From " then exit repeat
          end considering
if length of myMail > 1 then set myMail to ¬
(characters 1 thru ((length of myMail) - 1) ¬
of myMail as string) & return
          set myBody to myBody & myMail
          end repeat
set myMailDate to myMail
makeMessage(mySender, myDateSent, mySubject, ¬
myBody)
```

(script continues on next page)

Script 18.1 *continued*

```
                 script
set mySender to word 2 of myMailDate
      end repeat
   on error
      try
         makeMessage(mySender, myDateSent, ¬
mySubject, myBody)
         end try
      end try
      close access myFileRef
end run
on makeMessage(mySender, myDateSent, ¬
mySubject, myBody)
tell application "Outlook Express"
make new incoming message with properties ¬
{subject:mySubject, content:myBody, ¬
sender:mySender, time sent:myDateSent, read ¬
status:read} at folder "Inbox"
   end tell
end makeMessage
```

If the message header doesn't have its own date, you try to reformat the date string you stored in myMailDate earlier. First, you capture the day of the week in the theDayOfWeek variable.

17. set theMonth to text item 4 of myMail
set theDay to text item 3 of myMail
set theTime to text item 6 of myMail

Because the date will always be in the same format, you can grab the date, time, and day, and store them in your variables.

18. set theYear to text item 5 of myMail
set myDateSent to date (theDayOfWeek ¬
& ", " & theMonth & " " & theDay & ¬
", " & theYear & " " & theTime as ¬
string)
set AppleScript's text item ¬
delimiters to mydelimits

Finally, you capture the year in the theYear variable, which should reside in the seventh word of your date string. This word also contains the end-of-line character, so you strip off the last character of this word before storing it in your new variable.

19. end if
        end repeat

If it does, the message has its own date, so you set your myMailDateFound flag to true to indicate that the date exists in the header stored in myHeader.

20. if not myMailDateFound then

When you've completed the loop to construct your current message's header, you test your myMailDateFound variable to see whether a unique date was found in the header text.

continues on next page

CONVERTING MAIL FROM EUDORA OR UNIX

21.
```
try
    set {mydelimits, AppleScript's text ¬
item delimiters} to {AppleScript's ¬
text item delimiters, " "}
    set mySender to text item 2 of ¬
myMailDate
    set theDayOfWeek to text item 3 ¬
of myMailDate
    set theMonth to text item 4 of ¬
myMailDate
    set theDay to text item 5 of ¬
myMailDate
    set theTime to text item 6 of ¬
myMailDate
    set theYear to text item 7 of ¬
myMailDate
    set AppleScript's text item ¬
delimiters to mydelimits
    set myDateSent to date ¬
(theDayOfWeek & ", " & theMonth & " ¬
" & theDay & ", " & theYear & " " & ¬
theTime as string)
end try
        end if
```

Now you're ready to add a properly formatted date entry to your current message's date, as stored in myDateSent.

22.
```
set myBody to ""
repeat
```

Now you initialize the myBody variable to hold the message body and begin a repeat loop to capture the body of the current message.

23.
```
set myMail to (read myFileRef until ¬
linefeed)
```

Within your loop, you read another line of the mail file; its end is indicated by the character stored in your linefeed variable.

24. `considering case`

You use the `considering case` statement to let AppleScript know that the subsequent comparisons need to be case-sensitive.

25. `if myMail starts with "From " then ¬`
`exit repeat`
            `end considering`

If the current line of your mail file, as stored in `myMail`, begins with `"From "`, you know that a new message is starting, so you exit your loop.

26. `if length of myMail > 1 then set ¬`
`myMail to (characters 1 thru ¬`
`((length of myMail) - 1) of myMail ¬`
`as string) & return`
`set myBody to myBody & myMail`
            `end repeat`

Otherwise, you strip the last character off the current line and add it to the current message's body, which you're storing in the `myBody` variable.

27. `set myMailDate to myMail`

When you finish parsing the body and exit the loop, the current line holds the next date, so you save it in the variable that you'll reformat in steps 18 through 22.

28. `makeMessage(mySender, myDateSent, ¬`
`mySubject, myBody)`

Now that you've found the header and body of a message, you call your `makeMessage` function to create a new message in Outlook's Inbox, passing it the header and body variables.

continues on next page

CONVERTING MAIL FROM EUDORA OR UNIX

29. `set mySender to word 2 of myMailDate`
    `end repeat`
  `on error`
    `try`
`makeMessage(mySender, myDateSent, ¬`
`mySubject, myBody)`
    `end try`
  `end try`
  `close access myFileRef`
`end run`

When you finally encounter the end of the mail file, the end-of-file error triggers this `on error` routine, so you try to create one final message for Outlook by using the current header and body variables. Finally, outside `on error`, you close the mail file with the `close access` command.

30. `on makeMessage(mySender, myDateSent, ¬`
`mySubject, myBody)`

Your `makeMessage` function receives the values for header and body in variables.

31. `tell application "Outlook Express"`

You begin talking to Outlook Express.

32. `make new incoming message with ¬`
    `properties {subject:mySubject, ¬`
    `content:myBody, sender:mySender, ¬`
    `time sent:myDateSent, read ¬`
    `status:read} at folder "Inbox"`
  `end tell`
`end makeMessage`

Now you tell your mail client application to create a new message in the Inbox with read status, indicating that it's already been read.

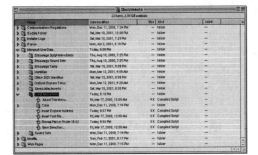

Figure 18.3 The correct location of the folder to place scripts that you want to appear in your Outlook Express Scripts menu.

Revealing Items in the Finder from Email

Script 18.2 shows you how use the Scripts menu of Outlook Express to your advantage. The Scripts menu was created to allow you to create and use scripts that are context-sensitive within an application. In our office, for example, we email file paths to each other for work we need to share. Then we use a Scripts-menu script to select the file in the Finder straight from the email message in Outlook Express.

Figure 18.3 shows the correct location for placing any compiled script files you want to access from Outlook's Scripts menu.

To reveal an item in the Finder from a file path selected in Outlook Express:

1. `tell application "Outlook Express" ¬`
   `to set mySelectedPathText to the ¬`
   `selection as string`

   You begin by asking Outlook Express for the currently selected text. If the user has selected a file path in the body of an open message, you'll get it this way and store it in the `mySelectedPathText` variable.

2. `if mySelectedPathText ≠ "" then`
   `    set mySelectedPathText to ¬`
   `findAndDelete(mySelectedPathText, ¬`
   `return)`

   Next, if you have any text in your selection, you'll strip any return characters introduced by the wrapping of the text in the email message, using your `findAndDelete` handler.

continues on next page

3. `try`

```
    tell application "Finder"
        activate
        reveal item mySelectedPathText
    end tell
end try
end if
```

Finally, you ask the Finder to reveal the item pointed to by the file path mySelectedPathText. You perform this task in a `try` block to prevent any errors if nothing exists at the path location.

4. `on findAndDelete(mystring, mymatch)`

Your handy `findAndDelete` handler accepts a string to search and a deletion character to delete, and then returns a modified string.

5. `set mynewstring to ""`

Your modified string will be built up in `mynewstring`.

6. `repeat with mycharacter in every ¬`
   `character of mystring`

To look for the character to replace, you loop through each character in the source string `mystring`.

7. `if mycharacter as string ≠ mymatch then`
   `set mynewstring to mynewstring & ¬`
   `mycharacter`

If the current character is not the character to delete, you append it to `mynewstring`.

8. `end if`
   `end repeat`
   `return mynewstring`
   `end findAndDelete`

When you're done with your loop, `mynewstring` will contain an updated string to return.

Script 18.2 This script is meant to be run from Outlook's Scripts menu. Run it after selecting the text of a file path. The Finder then reveals the item based on the path.

```
tell application "Outlook Express" to set ¬
mySelectedPathText to the selection as string
if mySelectedPathText ≠ "" then
    set mySelectedPathText to
findAndDelete(mySelectedPathText, return)
try
        tell application "Finder"
            activate
            reveal item mySelectedPathText
        end tell
    end try
end if
on findAndDelete(mystring, mymatch)
set mynewstring to ""
repeat with mycharacter in every character ¬
of mystring
if mycharacter as string ≠ mymatch then
            set mynewstring to mynewstring & ¬
mycharacter
end if
    end repeat
    return mynewstring
end findAndDelete
```

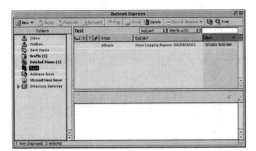

Figure 18.4 The Test mail folder of Outlook Express shown while the script is running.

Filing Mail Based on Keywords

Script 18.3 moves messages that contain certain strings in their subjects or bodies to a specific message folder, which you'll call the Test folder.

Figure 18.4 shows the appearance of this folder as the script is running.

In this script, you'll lay the groundwork for most of the subsequent scripts that deal with email. The main portion of the code contained in the on run handler will be reused in all email scripts that deal with keyword matching. The script can handle sophisticated searches and searching for multiple keywords defined in a list. Both the subject and the body of the email can be searched.

To file mail based on keywords:

1. `global myKeywordMatches`

   You begin by defining the myKeywordMatches variable as global so that both your function and main program can use it.

2. `on run`
   ```
       set myKeywords to {"Raza", ¬
   "Chavez", "Latino"}
       set mySearchType to "or"
       set myIncludeSubject to true
       set myIncludeBody to true
   ```
   Next, you begin your on run handler and define variables to hold your search strings "Raza", "Chavez", and "Latino", the type of search to execute ("or"), and Boolean flags indicating whether to search the subject or body or both. These variables are called myKeywords, mySearchType, myIncludeSubject, and myIncludeBody, respectively.

continues on next page

3. `tell application "Outlook Express"`

Here, you begin talking to Outlook.

4. `set myMessages to every message in ¬`
`folder "Inbox"`

Next, you retrieve a list of all messages in the Inbox.

5. `repeat with myMessage in myMessages`

Then, you start a loop through each message in the list of messages.

6. `set myText to ""`

At the beginning of your loop, you initialize the `myText` variable that you'll search for keyword matches.

7. `set myKeywordMatches to ""`

You also initialize the `myKeywordMatches` variable that you'll use to hold all the matches found in the currently searched message.

8. `if myIncludeBody then set myText to ¬`
`myText & the content of myMessage ¬`
`& return`

If the flag variable `myIncludeBody` is `true`, you'll add the body of the current message to your `myText` variable so that it is searched for matches below.

9. `if myIncludeSubject then set myText ¬`
`to myText & the subject of myMessage`

If the flag variable `myIncludeSubject` is true, you'll add the subject of the current message to your `myText` variable so that it is searched for matches below.

10. `set myFound to false`

Before you start looping through your keywords to test for matches, you need to initialize a variable, `myFound`, that you'll use to indicate whether any matches are found.

Script 18.3 This script moves messages from the Inbox into another mail folder if the message contains any of the keywords.

```
global myKeywordMatches
on run
    set myKeywords to {"Raza", "Chavez", "Latino"}
    set mySearchType to "or"
    set myIncludeSubject to true
    set myIncludeBody to true
    tell application "Outlook Express"
        set myMessages to every message in ¬
folder "Inbox"
        repeat with myMessage in myMessages
            set myText to ""
            set myKeywordMatches to ""
            if myIncludeBody then set myText to ¬
myText & the content of myMessage & return
            if myIncludeSubject then set myText ¬
to myText & the subject of myMessage
            set myFound to false
            considering case
                repeat with myKeyword in myKeywords
                    if myText contains myKeyword then
                        set myFound to true
                        set myKeywordMatches to ¬
myKeywordMatches & myKeyword & " "
                        if mySearchType = "or" ¬
then exit repeat
                    else
                        if mySearchType = "and" ¬
and myKeyword ≠ last item of myKeywords then
                            set myFound to false
                            exit repeat
                        end if
                    end if
                end repeat
            end considering
            if myFound then
                my processMail(myMessage)
            end if
        end repeat
    end tell
end run
on processMail(myMessage)
    tell application "Outlook Express"
        move myMessage to folder "Test"
    end tell
end processMail
```

11. `considering case`

Next, you let AppleScript know that you want it to perform all subsequent string comparisons with case sensitivity.

12. `repeat with myKeyword in myKeywords`

Now you start to loop through your list of keywords.

13. `if myText contains myKeyword then`

You test to see whether your current keyword is found inside myText.

14. `set myFound to true`

If you find a keyword in myText, you set your flag variable myFound to true.

15. `set myKeywordMatches to ¬`
`myKeywordMatches & myKeyword & " "`

You add the found keyword to your myKeywordMatches variable to track which matches are found for the current message.

16. `if mySearchType = "or" then exit repeat`

Next, you check to see whether your search is an "or"-type search. If so, you exit your loop.

17. `else`
`    if mySearchType = "and" and myKeyword`
`  ≠ last item of myKeywords then`
`        set myFound to false`
`        exit repeat`
`  end if`
`end if`
`            end repeat`
`            end considering`

If your search is an "and" search, and you haven't tested the last keyword yet, you clear your flag so that the searching continues, ensuring that all keywords are found. In this case, you set your search to be an "or" search in step 2. You can change mySearchType to "and" to modify this script.

continues on next page

18.
```
if myFound then
   my processMail(myMessage)
end if
     end repeat
   end tell
end run
```

If you have a match, you call your processMail function, passing it the current message.

19.
```
on processMail(myMessage)
    tell application "Outlook Express"
       move myMessage to folder "Test"
    end tell
end processMail
```

Your processMail function receives a message and tells Outlook to move the message to the message folder named Test.

Figure 18.5 The Drafts folder of Outlook Express shown while the script is running.

Script 18.4 This script creates replies to messages from the Inbox if the message contains any of the keywords.

```
global myKeywordMatches
on run
    set myKeywords to {"Raza", "Chavez", ¬
"Latino"}
    set mySearchType to "or"
    set myIncludeSubject to true
    set myIncludeBody to true
    tell application "Outlook Express"
        set myMessages to every message in ¬
folder "Inbox"
        repeat with myMessage in myMessages
            set myText to ""
            set myKeywordMatches to ""
            if myIncludeBody then set myText to ¬
myText & the content of myMessage & return
            if myIncludeSubject then set myText ¬
to myText & the subject of myMessage
            set myFound to false
            considering case
                repeat with myKeyword in myKeywords
                    if myText contains myKeyword then
                        set myFound to true
                        set myKeywordMatches to ¬
myKeywordMatches & myKeyword & " "
                        if mySearchType = "or" ¬
then exit repeat
                    else
                        if mySearchType = "and" ¬
and myKeyword ≠ last item of myKeywords then
                            set myFound to false
                (script continues on next page)
```

Sending Replies Based on Keywords

Script 18.4 sends a reply to the sender of any incoming message that contains certain keywords. You could use this script as a mailbot to send specific information in response to inquiries that have particular phrases in the body or subject of the incoming message.

Figure 18.5 shows what Outlook Express's Drafts folder looks like as the script is running.

To send replies based on keywords:

1. The on run handler of this script is covered in detail in the preceding section.

2. on processMail(myMessage)

   Your processMail function in this script receives a reference to the current message in the myMessage variable.

3. tell application "Outlook Express"

   You begin by letting AppleScript know that you want to speak to Outlook Express.

4. variable set mySubject to "RE: " & ¬ (subject of myMessage)

   Now you define a variable to hold the subject of your new message, basing it on the subject of the message referred to by your myMessage variable.

5. set myAddress to sender of myMessage
   set myRecipName to display name of ¬ myAddress
   set myRecipAddress to address of ¬ myAddress

   Next, you store the address record of the sender of the current message in a variable, myAddress. From this record, you extract the name and email address of the sender and store them in the myRecipName and myRecipAddress variables.

continues on next page

6. `set myBody to "Thanks for inquiring ¬ about " & myKeywordMatches`

You set up the body of your new message in a variable, adding a note about which keywords were matched by including the myKeywordMatches variable, which the preceding code constructed for you.

7. `make new outgoing message with ¬ properties {subject:mySubject, ¬ content:myBody, recipient:{{address:{display ¬ name:myRecipName, address:myRecipAddress}, recipient ¬ type:to recipient, deliverstatus:unsent}}}`
      `end tell`
`end processMail`

You tell Outlook to make a new outgoing message by using the variable you just set up. The reply is ready to be sent.

Script 18.4 *continued*

```
                        exit repeat
                    end if
                end if
            end repeat
        end considering
        if myFound then
            my processMail(myMessage)
        end if
    end repeat
  end tell
end run
on processMail(myMessage)
    tell application "Outlook Express"
        set mySubject to "RE: " & (subject of ¬
myMessage)
        set myAddress to sender of myMessage
        set myRecipName to display name of ¬
myAddress
        set myRecipAddress to address of myAddress
        set myBody to "Thanks for inquiring ¬
about " & myKeywordMatches
        make new outgoing message with ¬
properties {subject:mySubject, content:myBody, ¬
recipient:{{address:{display name:myRecipName, ¬
address:myRecipAddress}, recipient type:to ¬
recipient, deliverstatus:unsent}}}
    end tell
end processMail
```

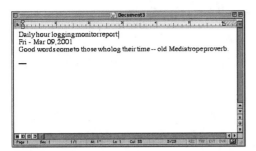

Figure 18.6 A new document created in Microsoft Word, containing the body of an email message that contains a matching keyword.

Importing Mail into Microsoft Word Based on Keywords

Script 18.5 imports into Word the bodies of mail messages that contain keyword matches. Each message is opened into a new window in Word.

Figure 18.6 shows the new document window in Word.

To import mail into Microsoft Word based on keywords:

1. The on run handler of this script is covered in detail in "Filing Mail Based on Keywords" earlier in this chapter.

2. on processMail(myMessage)

   Your processMail function in this script receives a reference to the current message in the myMessage variable.

3. tell application "Outlook Express" to ¬
   set myBody to the content of myMessage

   You begin your function by asking Outlook Express to retrieve the body of the myMessage message passed to the function. You store this string in the myBody variable.

4. tell application "Microsoft Word"
       activate

   Next, you use the activate command to tell Word to come to the front.

5. make new document

   You have Word create a new document.

6. set contents of selection to myBody
       end tell
   end processMail

   Finally, you set the new document's contents to the text taken from the body of the mail message, as stored in the myBody variable.

✔ Tip

■ See Chapter 7 for more information on scripting Microsoft Office 2001.

Script 18.5 This script creates new Word documents that contain the body of email messages with any matching keyword.

```
script
```

```
global myKeywordMatches
on run
    set myKeywords to {"Raza", "Chavez", "Latino"}
    set mySearchType to "or"
    set myIncludeSubject to true
    set myIncludeBody to true
    tell application "Outlook Express"
        set myMessages to every message in folder "Inbox"
        repeat with myMessage in myMessages
            set myText to ""
            set myKeywordMatches to ""
            if myIncludeBody then set myText to myText & the content of myMessage & return
            if myIncludeSubject then set myText to myText & the subject of myMessage
            set myFound to false
            considering case
                repeat with myKeyword in myKeywords
                    if myText contains myKeyword then
                        set myFound to true
                        set myKeywordMatches to myKeywordMatches & myKeyword & " "
                        if mySearchType = "or" then exit repeat
                    else
                        if mySearchType = "and" and myKeyword ≠ last item of myKeywords then
                            set myFound to false
                            exit repeat
                        end if
                    end if
                end repeat
            end considering
            if myFound then
                my processMail(myMessage)
            end if
        end repeat
    end tell
end run
on processMail(myMessage)
tell application "Outlook Express" to set myBody to the content of myMessage
tell application "Microsoft Word"
        activate
make new document
set contents of selection to myBody
    end tell
end processMail
```

Figure 18.7 The sample FileMaker Pro database showing three records imported from Outlook messages.

Creating the Sample Database

1. Choose New from FileMaker's File menu.

2. Name and save the new database.

3. Define the following text fields:

   Sender name

   Subject

   Content

   Sender address

   Time sent

   You database should look like **Figure 18.7** when you are done.

Copying Mail Data to FileMaker Pro

Script 18.6 copies data from any messages in the Inbox that contain the keywords to a new record in a sample FileMaker database. You can use this script to transfer email information to a database by using sophisticated keyword searching of many mail messages.

Figure 18.7 shows what the FileMaker Pro database looks like as the script is running. Refer to Chapter 8 for more information on scripting FileMaker Pro.

To copy mail data to FileMaker Pro:

1. The on run handler of this script is covered in detail in "Filing Mail Based on Keywords" earlier in this chapter.

2. `on processMail(myMessage)`
   `    tell application "Outlook Express"`
   `        move myMessage to folder "Test"`

   You begin your function by telling Outlook Express to move the message to the Test folder so that you don't process it repeatedly.

3. `set mySender to sender of myMessage`
   `set mySenderAddress to address of ¬`
   `mySender`
   `set mySenderName to display name of ¬`
   `mySender`
   `set mySubject to subject of myMessage`
   `set myContent to content of myMessage`
   `set myTimeSent to time sent of myMessage`
   `    end tell`

   Next, you retrieve the sender address and name, subject, body, and send time of the message and store their values in variables. You'll use this data to populate your database.

   continues on next page

4. `tell application "FileMaker Pro"`
   `  tell database "Incoming Mail"`

Now you begin speaking to FileMaker Pro, immediately telling it that you want to speak only to the database Incoming Mail. You'll need to create this database in FileMaker Pro before using this script; the sidebar explains how.

Script 18.6 This script creates a new record in FileMaker with data from each email message in the Inbox that contains any of the matching keywords.

```
                                script
global myKeywordMatches
on run
    set myKeywords to {"Raza", "Chavez", "Latino"}
    set mySearchType to "or"
    set myIncludeSubject to true
    set myIncludeBody to true
    tell application "Outlook Express"
        set myMessages to every message in folder "Inbox"
        repeat with myMessage in myMessages
            set myText to ""
            set myKeywordMatches to ""
            if myIncludeBody then set myText to myText & the content of myMessage & return
            if myIncludeSubject then set myText to myText & the subject of myMessage
            set myFound to false
            considering case
                repeat with myKeyword in myKeywords
                    if myText contains myKeyword then
                        set myFound to true
                        set myKeywordMatches to myKeywordMatches & myKeyword & " "
                        if mySearchType = "or" then exit repeat
                    else
                        if mySearchType = "and" and myKeyword ≠ last item of myKeywords then
                            set myFound to false
                            exit repeat
                        end if
                    end if
                end repeat
            end considering
            if myFound then
                my processMail(myMessage)
            end if
        end repeat
    end tell
end run
```

(script continues on next page)

Script 18.6 *continued*

```
===================== script =====================

on processMail(myMessage)
    tell application "Outlook Express"
        move myMessage to folder "Test"
set mySender to sender of myMessage
        set mySenderAddress to address of mySender
        set mySenderName to display name of ¬
mySender
        set mySubject to subject of myMessage
        set myContent to content of myMessage
        set myTimeSent to time sent of myMessage
    end tell
tell application "FileMaker Pro"
        tell database "Incoming Mail"
set myNewRecord to (make new record)
set cell"sender name" of myNewRecord to ¬
mySenderName
        set cell"sender address" of ¬
myNewRecord to mySenderAddress
        set cell"subject" of myNewRecord ¬
to mySubject
        set cell"content" of myNewRecord ¬
to myContent
        set cell"time sent" of myNewRecord ¬
to myTimeSent as text
end tell
    end tell
end processMail
```

5. `set myNewRecord to (make new record)`

Next, you create a new record and store a reference to the new record in the myNewRecord variable.

6. `set cell "sender name" of myNewRecord ¬`
`to mySenderName`
`set cell "sender address" of ¬`
`myNewRecord to mySenderAddress`
`set cell "subject" of myNewRecord ¬`
`to mySubject`
`set cell "content" of myNewRecord ¬`
`to myContent`
`set cell "time sent" of myNewRecord ¬`
`to myTimeSent as text`

You have FileMaker Pro fill the fields of the new record with the data you captured from the mail message.

7. `end tell`
`end tell`
`end processMail`

You end your conversation with the database and FileMaker, and end your handler.

✔ Tips

■ If you know that you created the fields in your database as listed in the sidebar, you can replace step 6 with this code to make your script faster:

`set myNewRecord to (create new record`
`with data {mySenderName,`
`mySenderAddress, mySubject,`
`myContent, myTimeSent})`

■ FileMaker Pro processes the single event of creating a new record and populating that record's sequential fields with data much faster than processing the creation of a record and then a series of separate set commands.

COPYING MAIL DATA TO FILEMAKER PRO

Creating a Mailing List with FileMaker Pro

Script 18.7 loops through the currently found set of records in a database of mail messages, generating a new outgoing email message with a subject and body defined by variables in your `processMail` function.

This script can be used to run a broadcast-only mailing list from Outlook Express. This capability would be useful if you had a contact database in FileMaker filled with many kinds of people (vendors, friends, clients, and so on), and you had a message specifically tailored for one of these groups. With this script, you could find only the recipients you want in FileMaker and then run this script to send them all a message.

Figure 18.8 shows the Outlook Express Drafts folder while the script is running.

To create a mailing list with FileMaker Pro:

1. `on run`
> `tell application "FileMaker Pro"`
>> `tell document "Incoming Mail"`

Here, you begin talking to FileMaker Pro. You immediately let FileMaker know that you want to speak directly to the open database named Incoming Mail. By referencing the database as `document` "Incoming Mail", you let FileMaker know that you want to deal only with the currently found set of records in the database. If you referenced the database as `database` "Incoming Mail", FileMaker would give you access to all records in the database.

The sidebar "Creating the Sample Database" explains how to create this database.

Figure 18.8 The Drafts folder of Outlook Express shown while the script is running.

2. `repeat with i from 1 to number of ¬`
`every record`
   `set mySenderName to cell "sender ¬`
`name" of record i`
   `set mySenderAddress to cell "sender ¬`
`address" of record i`

You begin a loop through each database record in the current found set, capturing the values of the fields for the name and email address to which to send your message.

3. `my processMail(mySenderName, ¬`
`mySenderAddress)`
            `end repeat`
         `end tell`
      `end tell`
`end run`

You call your `processMail` function, passing it the name and address of your message recipient.

continued on next page

Script 18.7 This script creates an email message for each record in the current found set of a FileMaker database.

```
on run
    tell application "FileMaker Pro"
        tell document "Incoming Mail"
repeat with i from 1 to number of every record
            set mySenderName to cell "sender name" of record i
            set mySenderAddress to cell "sender address" of record i
my processMail(mySenderName, mySenderAddress)
         end repeat
      end tell
    end tell
end run
on processMail(mySenderName, mySenderAddress)
    tell application "Outlook Express"
set mySubject to "Mailing List Announcement"
      set myBody to "The new message text goes here!"
make new outgoing message with properties ¬
        {subject:mySubject, content:myBody, recipient:{{address:{display name:mySenderName, ¬
address:mySenderAddress}, recipient type:to recipient, delivery status:unsent}}}
    end tell
end processMail
```

CREATING A MAILING LIST WITH FILEMAKER PRO

4. `on processMail(mySenderName, ¬`
`mySenderAddress)`
   `tell application "Outlook Express"`

Your `processMail` function in this script is passed the values for name and email address in the `mySenderName` and `mySenderAddress` variables. Then you let AppleScript know that you want to speak to Outlook Express.

5. `set mySubject to "Mailing List ¬`
`Announcement"`
`set myBody to "The new message text ¬`
`goes here!"`

You define variables to hold the subject and message body for your outgoing message.

6. `make new outgoing message with ¬`
`properties ¬`
   `{subject:mySubject, content:myBody,`
`recipient:{{address:{display ¬`
`name:mySenderName,`
`address:mySenderAddress}, recipient ¬`
`type:to recipient, delivery ¬`
`status:unsent}}}`
   `end tell`
`end processMail`

You tell Outlook Express to make a new outgoing message, ready to be sent.

✔ Tip

- See Chapter 8 for more information on scripting FileMaker Pro.

FETCH 4 AND INTERARCHY 5

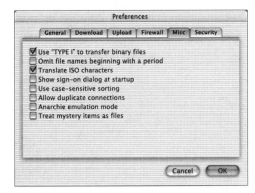

Figure 19.1 Fetch's Preferences dialog with the Misc tab showing. Notice that the Show Sign-On Dialog at Startup checkbox is unchecked to enable unattended script control of Fetch.

Fetch is a fully recordable and scriptable FTP client application. You can use it to get and send files, list directories, and do such things as synchronize remote directories with local folders.

Interarchy does everything Fetch does and more. With Interarchy 5.0.1, you can even retrieve files and whole sites from HTTP servers (Web servers).

Both Fetch and Interarchy offer complete AppleScript dictionaries. Fetch includes partial support for Interarchy's AppleScript dictionary along with its own commands and is fully recordable. To see fully formed object-model code appear before your eyes, try recording some of your own actions in Fetch. Before you start scripting, make sure to review your application preferences. To enable scripts to launch Fetch without your intervention, be sure to disable the automatic sign-on dialog box. Look in Fetch's Miscellaneous Preferences window to disable this default option. **Figure 19.1** shows the Misc tab of Fetch's Preferences dialog box with this option disabled.

Sending a File via FTP with Fetch

Script 19.1 uploads files to a remote server. To send a file from your local file system to a remote server via FTP, simply set the variables inside the on open handler and drop files on the script application's icon.

Figure 19.2 shows a transfer window in Fetch immediately after a user has dropped the file Default.html on your saved script application. Note that the file has been uploaded and appears in the remote FTP server's directory.

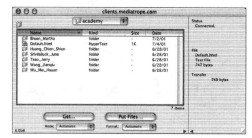

Figure 19.2 Transfer window in Fetch after the script has run, uploading a file to the remote FTP site.

To send a file via FTP from Fetch:

1. on run
    open {choose file}
end run

The run handler lets you test this script in Script Editor.

2. on open myUploadItems
    set myUser to ""
    set myPassword to ""
    set myHost to ""
    set myDirectory to ""

You begin by storing in myUploadItems the files passed by the drag-and-drop method and then setting variables for user name, password, host name, and directory. You could have used dialog boxes to set these variables, so that the script would be able to log onto any server, but to simplify matters, you are going to hard-code them into your script.

3. set myurl to "ftp://" & myUser & ":" ¬
    & myPassword & "@" & myHost & "/" & ¬
    myDirectory

Next, you assemble an FTP URL out of the variables you just defined.

Script 19.1 This script uploads items via FTP, using Fetch, when they are dropped on the script droplet.

```
                    script
on run
    open {choose file}
end run
on open myUploadItems
    set myUser to ""
    set myPassword to ""
    set myHost to ""
    set myDirectory to ""
set myurl to "ftp://" & myUser & ":" & ¬
myPassword & "@" & myHost & "/" & myDirectory
with timeout of 300 seconds
        repeat with myUploadItem in myUploadItems
            tell application "Finder" to set ¬
myFilename to name of myUploadItem as string
            set myUploadPath to myDirectory & ¬
"/" & myFilename as string
            tell application "Fetch 4.0.1"
set myBinPref to the add I suffix
                set the add I suffix to false
put into url myurl item myUploadItem text ¬
format Raw Data binary format Raw Data
                set the add I suffix to myBinPref
            end tell
    end repeat
        tell application "Fetch 4.0" to quit
    end timeout
end open
```

4. with timeout of 300 seconds
    repeat with myUploadItem in ¬
myUploadItems
        tell application "Finder" to set ¬
myFilename to name of myUploadItem ¬
as string
        set myUploadPath to myDirectory ¬
& "/" & myFilename as string
        tell application "Fetch 4.0.1"

Now you begin speaking to Fetch inside a with timeout statement. This statement instructs AppleScript to wait 300 seconds for the code in it to execute before continuing. You use this instruction in case Fetch fails to make a connection to the server. If Fetch cannot make a connection after five minutes, the script will fail.

5. set myBinPref to the add I suffix
set the add I suffix to false

Now you save the current preference setting for adding a MacBinary file extension (.bin) to uploaded files and then set the preference to false. You change this setting to ensure that your file is uploaded as raw data without any MacBinary II encoding. You should change this setting to true only if you are uploading Mac files that another Mac user will need to download via FTP. The MacBinary II format preserves the data and resource forks of a Mac file, as well as its creator and file-type information.

continues on next page

6. `put into url myurl item myUploadItem ¬`
`text format Raw Data binary format ¬`
`Raw Data`
`set the add I suffix to myBinPref`
`        end tell`

Then you send the file via FTP to the server as a raw-data file. If this file is for a Mac that has a resource fork, you can use MacBinaryII format.

7. `end repeat`
`tell application "Fetch 4.0.1" to`
`quit`
`    end timeout`
`end open`

You quit Fetch and end the script.

✔ Tip

■ You can modify this script to upload multiple folders of files or even test file names for matches to decide whether to upload them.

Scripting Fetch

All the Fetch scripts in this chapter were designed and tested for Fetch 4.0.1.

Fetch, written by Jim Matthews and developed by Fetch Softworks, can be reached at http://www.fetchsoftworks.com/).

Figure 19.3 Connection window in Interarchy while script is running, uploading a file to the remote FTP site.

Sending a File via FTP with Interarchy

Script 19.2 uploads files to a remote server. To send a file from your local file system to a remote server via FTP, simply set the variables inside the on open handler and drop files on the script application's icon.

Figure 19.3 shows a transfer window in Interarchy immediately after a user has dropped the file default.html on your saved script application. Note that the file has been uploaded and appears in the remote FTP server's directory.

To send a file via FTP from Interarchy:

1. on run
    open {choose file}
end run

The run handler lets you test this script in Script Editor.

2. on open myUploadItems
    set myUser to ""
    set myPassword to ""
    set myHost to ""
    set myDirectory to ""

You begin by storing in myUploadItems the files passed by the drag-and-drop method and then setting variables for user name, password, host name, and directory. You could have also used dialog boxes to set these variables, so that the script would be able to log onto any server.

continues on next page

3. `with timeout of 300 seconds`
  `    tell application "Interarchy 5.0.1"`
  `        activate`

Now you begin speaking to Interarchy inside a `with timeout` statement. This statement instructs AppleScript to wait 300 seconds for the code in it to execute before continuing. You use this instruction in case Interarchy fails to make a connection to the server. If Interarchy cannot make a connection after five minutes, the script will fail.

4. `repeat with myUploadItem in ¬`
  `myUploadItems`
  `    store myUploadItem host myHost path ¬`
  `myDirectory user myUser password ¬`
  `myPassword with binary`

Then you send the file via FTP to the server as a raw-data file. If this file is for a Mac that has a resource fork, you can use MacBinaryII format.

5. `end repeat`
  `quit`
  `        end tell`
  `    end timeout`
  `end open`

You end the script.

✔ Tip

■ You can modify this script to upload multiple folders of files or even test file names for matches to decide whether to upload them.

Script 19.2 This script uploads items via FTP, using Interarchy, when they are dropped on the script droplet.

```
on run
    open {choose file}
end run
on open myUploadItems
    set myUser to ""
    set myPassword to ""
    set myHost to ""
    set myDirectory to ""
with timeout of 300 seconds
        tell application "Interarchy 5.0.1"
            activate
repeat with myUploadItem in myUploadItems
                store myUploadItem host myHost ¬
path myDirectory user myUser password ¬
myPassword with binary
end repeat
            quit
        end tell
    end timeout
end open
```

Scripting Interarchy

All the Interarchy scripts in this chapter were designed and tested for Interarchy 5.0.1.

Interarchy is shareware. A single copy costs $35.

Interarchy 4.0 was written by Peter N. Lewis and is developed by Stairways Software (http://www.stairways.com/).

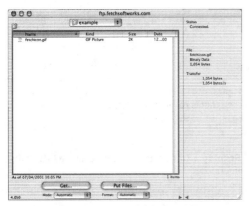

Figure 19.4 Transfer window in Fetch while the script is running, downloading a file from a remote FTP site.

Script 19.3 This script downloads a file via FTP, using Fetch.

```
set myUser to "anonymous"
set myPassword to "name@domain.com"
set myHost to "ftp.fetchsoftworks.com"
set myDirectory to "example"
set myFile to "fetchicon.gif"
set myurl to "ftp://" & myUser & ":" &
myPassword & "@" & myHost & "/" & myDirectory
set myFolder to (choose folder)
tell application "Fetch 4.0.1"
    activate
open url myurl
set download folder to myFolder
download remote file myFile
close transfer window 1
end tell
```

Retrieving a File via FTP with Fetch

Script 19.3 uses Fetch to retrieve a file from a remote server to your local file system.

Figure 19.4 shows the transfer window that the script creates in Fetch.

To retrieve a file via FTP from Fetch:

1. `set myUser to "anonymous"`
   `set myPassword to "name@domain.com"`
   `set myHost to "ftp.fetchsoftworks.com"`
   `set myDirectory to "example"`
   `set myFile to "fetchicon.gif"`

   You begin by hard-coding the variables you will need for user name, password, host name, directory, and the file to get.

2. `set myurl to "ftp://" & myUser & ":" ¬`
   `& myPassword & "@" & myHost & "/" & ¬`
   `myDirectory`

   As you did earlier in this chapter, you assemble an FTP URL based on your newly defined variables.

3. `set myFolder to (choose folder)`

   Now you prompt the user to choose a folder in which to save the retrieved file.

4. `tell application "Fetch 4.0.1"`
   `    activate`

   You are ready to bring Fetch to the front.

5. `open url myurl`

   You open an FTP connection to the appropriate host and directory.

6. `set download folder to myFolder`
   `download remote file myFile`

   Then you get the specified file, saving it in myFolder.

7. `close transfer window 1`
   `end tell`

   You close the open transfer window in Fetch and end the script.

Retrieving a File via FTP with Interarchy

Script 19.4 retrieves a file—specifically, a sample file from the Fetch Softworks public FTP site—from a remote server to your local file system via FTP, using Interarchy.

Figure 19.5 shows the Interarchy connection window while the script is running.

To retrieve a file via FTP from Interarchy:

1. `set myUser to "anonymous"`
   `set myPassword to "name@domain.com"`
   `set myHost to "ftp.fetchsoftworks.com"`
   `set myDirectory to "example"`
   `set myFile to "fetchicon.gif"`

   You begin by hard-coding the variables you will need for user name, password, host name, directory, and the file to get.

2. `set myFolder to (choose folder) as ¬`
   `string`

   Now you prompt the user to choose a folder in which to save the retrieved file.

3. `tell application "Interarchy 5.0.1"`
   `   activate`

   Now you are ready to bring Interarchy to the front.

4. `fetch alias (myFolder & myFile) host ¬`
   `myHost path (myDirectory & "/" & ¬`
   `myFile) user myUser password ¬`
   `myPassword with binary`
   `end tell`

   You retrieve the file with a single line command, specifying where to save the download locally, the host, the remote path, the user name, and the password.

Figure 19.5 Connection window in Interarchy while the script is running, downloading a file from a remote FTP site.

Script 19.4 This script downloads a file via FTP, using Interarchy.

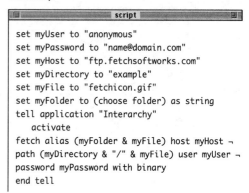

```
set myUser to "anonymous"
set myPassword to "name@domain.com"
set myHost to "ftp.fetchsoftworks.com"
set myDirectory to "example"
set myFile to "fetchicon.gif"
set myFolder to (choose folder) as string
tell application "Interarchy"
    activate
fetch alias (myFolder & myFile) host myHost ¬
path (myDirectory & "/" & myFile) user myUser ¬
password myPassword with binary
end tell
```

Figure 19.6 Transfer window in Fetch while the script is running, retrieving the directory listing from the remote FTP site.

Retrieving a Directory Listing via FTP

Why would you want a directory listing? Suppose that you want to check a specific server periodically to see whether a certain file, such as a new beta version of software, is available. Using **Script 19.5** as a basis, you could write a script to get the directory listing and then test for the existence of a specific file name. If the file exists, you could use the code from the preceding section to retrieve it.

Figure 19.6 shows a new transfer window in Fetch with the directory listing displayed as the script is running.

To retrieve a directory listing via FTP:

1. `set myDirectory to`
`"ftp://ftp.apple.com/"`

You begin by setting the directory name for which you'll return the listing. You can set this URL to anything you like.

2. `set {myItemNames, myItemTypes} to ¬`
`listDirectory(myDirectory)`

Next, you call the `listDirectory` function, passing it the directory name you want to get a listing for in the `myDirectory` variable. You should receive two lists back. `myItemNames` contains names of items in the directory, and `myItemTypes` contains types of items

3. `choose from list myItemNames`

Just to prove that you have the directory, you ask the user to choose an entry in the directory list.

continues on next page

4. `on listDirectory(myDirectory)`
  `tell application "Fetch 4.0.1"`

Here, you define your `listDirectory` function to list the FTP directory passed in the `myDirectory` variable.

5. `open url myDirectory`
  `set view order of transfer window 1 ¬`
  `to byName`
  `set itemCount to count transfer ¬`
  `window 1 each remote item`

Now you open the directory in Fetch, view it by name, and get the count of items in the directory.

6. `set myItemNames to {}`
  `set myItemTypes to {}`

Next, you initialize two list variables: one to hold item names, and one to hold the item types.

7. `repeat with itemIndex from 1 to ¬`
  `itemCount`

Now you begin a loop to go through each item.

8. `set curItemName to (name of remote ¬`
  `item itemIndex)`

You set `curItemName` to the file name of the current item in your loop.

9. `set myItemNames to myItemNames & ¬`
  `curItemName`

You append the file name stored in `curItemName` to the end of your list of file names, `myItemNames`.

10. `set curItemType to (item type of ¬`
  `remote item itemIndex)`

You set `curItemType` to the file type of the current item in your loop.

Script 19.5 This script returns the names and types of all entries in a remote FTP directory, using Fetch, and displays the list of names.

```
set myDirectory to "ftp://ftp.apple.com/"
set {myItemNames, myItemTypes} to ¬
listDirectory(myDirectory)
choose from list myItemNames
on listDirectory(myDirectory)
    tell application "Fetch 4.0.1"
open url myDirectory
        set view order of transfer window 1 to ¬
byName
        set itemCount to count transfer window ¬
1 each remote item
set myItemNames to {}
        set myItemTypes to {}
repeat with itemIndex from 1 to itemCount
set curItemName to (name of remote item ¬
itemIndex)
set myItemNames to myItemNames & curItemName
set curItemType to (item type of remote item ¬
itemIndex)
set myItemTypes to myItemTypes & curItemType
        end repeat
    end tell
return {myItemNames, myItemTypes}
end listDirectory
```

11. `set myItemTypes to myItemTypes & ¬`
`curItemType`
    `end repeat`

You append the file type stored in `curItemType` to the end of your list of file types, `myItemTypes`.

12. `return {myItemNames, myItemTypes}`
`end listDirectory`

Finally, your function returns the list of item names and list of item types to the line of the script that called the function in the first place.

Making the Script Work with Interarchy

Interarchy can get an FTP server's directory listing in a single command, but the results must be saved in a text file for later use. This code will save your directory listing in a file named by the user:

```
set myFile to new file
tell application "Interarchy 5.0.1"
  list myFile host "ftp.apple.com" ¬
path "/" user "anonymous" password ¬
"name@domain.com"
end tell
```

Updating a Remote Directory via FTP with Fetch

Script 19.6 compares the contents of a local folder with a remote directory via FTP. Any new or updated files in the local directory will be copied to the remote server.

Figure 19.7 shows a new transfer window in Fetch with a file being uploaded as this script is running.

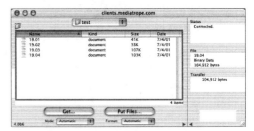

Figure 19.7 Transfer window in Fetch while the script is running, uploading files that don't exist or are new to the remote FTP site.

To update a remote directory via FTP from Fetch:

1. `set myurl to "ftp://user:password¬`
   `@host.domain.com/test/"`
   `set myFolder to (choose folder) as ¬`
   `string`

   You begin by setting the FTP URL for the remote directory and prompting the user for the name of the local folder with which to compare it.

2. `tell application "Fetch 4.0.1"`
   `   with timeout of 300 seconds`
   `      open url myurl`
   `   end timeout`

   Now you have Fetch open the directory within a 300-second timeout. If the procedure takes more than 300 seconds, the script will fail.

3. `end tell`
   `tell application "Finder"`
   `   set myFolderItems to list folder ¬`
   `alias myFolder without invisibles`
   `      repeat with myitem in myFolderItems`

   When the directory is opened in Fetch, you talk to the Finder, storing the list of items in your local folder in the myFolderItems variable. By adding the qualifier without invisibles, you omit any hidden files from your list. You begin a loop through each item.

UPDATING A REMOTE DIRECTORY WITH FETCH

Script 19.6 This script compares the contents of a local folder with the contents of a remote FTP directory, copying files to the remote directory if they don't exist or are older.

```
                    script
set myurl to ¬
"ftp://user:password@host.domain.com/test/"
set myFolder to (choose folder) as string
tell application "Fetch 4.0"
    with timeout of 300 seconds
        open url myurl
    end timeout
end tell
tell application "Finder"
    set myFolderItems to list folder alias ¬
myFolder without invisibles
    repeat with myitem in myFolderItems
try
        tell application "Fetch 4.0.1" to set ¬
myRemoteDate to modification date of remote ¬
item myitem
            set myExistFlag to true
        on error
            set myExistFlag to false
        end try
if kind of alias (myFolder & myitem) is not ¬
"folder" then
if myExistFlag then
tell application "Finder" to set myLocalDate ¬
to modification date of alias (sourceFolder ¬
& myitem)
set myUploadFlag to (myRemoteDate < myLocalDate)
        else
            set myUploadFlag to true
        end if
if myUploadFlag then
            with timeout of 300 seconds
                tell application "Fetch 4.0.1" ¬
to put into transfer window 1 item alias ¬
(myFolder & myitem)
            end timeout
        end if
    end if
    end repeat
end tell
```

4. try
    tell application "Fetch 4.0.1" to set ¬
myRemoteDate to modification date of ¬
remote item myitem
        set myExistFlag to true
on error
    set myExistFlag to false
end try

Now you have Fetch try to get the file date of an item in the remote directory with the same name as the current local item in the loop. If you get an error, the item doesn't exist in the remote directory. If the item exists, you set the flag variable myExistFlag to true; otherwise, you set myExistFlag to false.

5. if kind of alias (myFolder & myitem) ¬
is not "folder" then

Now you check to make sure that your local item isn't a folder.

6. if myExistFlag then

If the local item isn't a folder, you check your myExistFlag variable to see whether an item with the same name exists in the remote directory.

7. tell application "Finder" to set ¬
myLocalDate to modification date of ¬
alias (sourceFolder & myitem)

Now you set the myLocalDate variable to the date of your local file.

continues on next page

8. `set myUploadFlag to (myRemoteDate < ¬`
`myLocalDate)`
`        else`
`set myUploadFlag to true`
`        end if`

You're ready to compare the local file date with the remote file date and store the results (`true` or `false`) in the flag variable `myUploadFlag` to indicate whether you'll upload the file later. If no remote item with that name exists, you set the flag variable `myUploadFlag` to true as well.

9. `if myUploadFlag then`
`    with timeout of 300 seconds`
`        tell application "Fetch 4.0.1" to ¬`
`put into transfer window 1 item ¬`
`alias (myFolder & myitem)`
`    end timeout`
`end if`
`        end if`
`    end repeat`
`end tell`

If the upload flag `myUploadFlag` is `true`, you tell Fetch to copy the local file to the remote directory (which is still open in the frontmost transfer window, `transfer window 1`) within a 300-second timeout before continuing the repeat loop.

Figure 19.8 A sample downloaded source file shown in TextEdit after being retrieved via the script.

Script 19.7 This script retrieves the source code for a specific file via the HTTP protocol, using Interarchy.

```
set myFile to (path to desktop as string) & ¬
"Temp File.html"
tell application "Interarchy 5.0.1" to webfetch ¬
alias myFile url "http://www.apple.com/"
set myFileRef to (open for access alias ¬
myFile)
set myHTML to (read myFileRef)
close access myFileRef
```

Retrieving a File via HTTP with Interarchy

Interarchy speaks more than just FTP (the File Transfer Protocol); it can also talk to Web servers in their native HTTP (Hypertext Transfer Protocol). **Script 19.7** retrieves the source code file for Apple's home page (at www.apple.com) and stores it on your local hard disk.

Figure 19.8 shows the source file saved by the script open in TextEdit.

To retrieve a Web file via http from Interarchy:

1. `set myFile to (path to desktop as ¬ string) & "Temp File.html"`

   You start by storing a path to a new temporary file that you'll have Interarchy create. This file, named Temp File will be saved in the Desktop folder.

2. `tell application "Interarchy 5.0.1" ¬ to webfetch alias myFile url ¬ "http://www.apple.com/"`

   Now you have Interarchy retrieve the file from the server defined by the URL http://www.apple.com/ and store it in a new file defined by myFile.

3. `set myFileRef to (open for access ¬ alias myFile)`

   Next, you open the text file saved by Interarchy in myFile and store the reference to your open file in the myFileRef variable.

4. `set myHTML to (read myFileRef)`

   Then you get all the text in the file and store it in the myHTML variable.

5. `close access myFileRef`

   You close the file.

Retrieving an Entire Site's Files via HTTP with Interarchy

With Interarchy's getwebsite command, it is possible to gather an entire Web site's collections of files and directories systematically for local use. **Script 19.8** retrieves an entire site's files and directory structure. You might use this script in conjunction with the browser-based Web-page printing scripts in Chapter 6 to print an entire site's Web pages on a regular basis for archival purposes.

Figure 19.9 shows the powerful getwebsite command definition from Interarchy AppleScript dictionary.

To retrieve an entire Web site from Interarchy:

1. set myFolder to (choose folder with ¬ prompt "Folder to save web files:")

   You start by prompting the user for a folder in which to save the Web site's files and directories You store this reference in the myFolder variable.

2. tell application "Interarchy 5.0.1" ¬ to getwebsite myFolder url ¬ "http://www.apple.com/"

   Next, you have Interarchy retrieve the files and directories at the desired URL by using its getwebsite command. In this example, you are retrieving Apple's Web site. To adapt this script for your own use, substitute the appropriate URL for http://www.apple.com/.

Figure 19.9 The dictionary entry for Interarchy's getwebsite command.

Script 19.8 This script retrieves all linked files from a remote HTTP URL, using Interarchy.

```
set myFolder to (choose folder with prompt ¬
"Folder to save web files:")
tell application "Interarchy 5.0.1" to getwebsite ¬
myFolder url "http://www.apple.com/"
```

BBEdit
Pro 6.1

BBEdit was a relatively unknown application used primarily by serious programmers working in CodeWarrior and other C++ compilers until the World Wide Web arrived on the scene. With HTML files being merely glorified text files, a great many people suddenly needed a powerful, complete text-based editor for the Mac. BBEdit was there waiting all along.

In its latest incarnation, BBEdit includes a complete suite of tools for HTML, XML, Perl, and other script editing. BBEdit's extensive AppleScript support extends to these tools, making BBEdit a powerhouse for creating and modifying scripted text documents.

Scripting BBEdit Pro

For all the scripts in this chapter that use BBEdit, you will need at least a couple of text files. You can find some old SimpleText-based Read Me files on your hard disk, or you can follow the steps in this section to create some sample files. In either case, place your text files in a folder named Text Files and store the folder in a readily accessible place, such as the Desktop.

To get ready for the following AppleScripts for BBEdit:

1. Launch BBEdit.

2. Create a new file.

3. Type the sample text "The quick brown fox jumps over the lazy dog."

4. Save the file as 1 (**Figure 20.1**).

5. Create another new file, type slightly different sample text, and save it as 2 (**Figure 20.2**).

Now you're ready to move on to the scripts.

✔ Tip

■ BBEdit Pro 6.1 is attachable, which means that it has a Script menu. You can put scripts in this menu, so you can perform actions right in BBEdit on your current text selection.

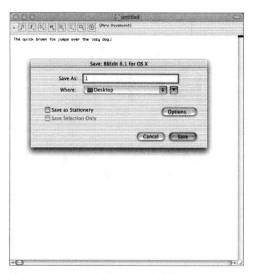

Figure 20.1 Saving the first sample BBEdit document after entering some text.

Figure 20.2 Saving the second sample BBEdit document after entering some text.

Scripting BBEdit

All the scripts in this chapter were designed and tested for BBEdit Pro 6.1 and BBEdit Pro 6.1 for Mac OS X.

BBEdit is developed by Bare Bones Software (http://www.barebones.com/).

Figure 20.3 The dialog box displayed by the script and, behind it, the sample file in BBEdit as changed by the script.

Using Pattern Matching to Search and Replace

One of BBEdit's most powerful features is its capability to search for patterns of text and then replace them with new text. This pattern-searching feature, derived from capabilities of Unix systems, is known by the Unix term *grep*. The power of this feature is simply too great to describe in a few words, but perhaps an example will serve to illustrate the potential of grep searches.

Script 20.1 finds every instance in a file of the word *the* followed by a space and another word and replaces it with the words *the crazy*. You won't need to open any file in BBEdit manually; your script will handle this task for you. You can run this script from Script Editor.

To use grep pattern matching to search for and replace text in a file:

1. `set myfile to (choose file)`

   First, you prompt the user to select the file to open and store the reference to that file (as an alias) in the myFile variable.

2. `tell application "BBEdit 6.1 for OS X"`

   Now you let AppleScript know that you want to send commands to BBEdit.

3. `open myfile`

   Then you have BBEdit open the file referred to by myFile.

continues on next page

4. `set myNumReplaces to replace "The ¬`
`[a-z]+" using "the crazy" searching ¬`
`in window 1 options {search ¬`
`mode:grep, starting at top:true}`
`end tell`

This simple line does something fairly incredible, thanks to grep pattern matching. This code finds every instance of the literal text *the* followed by a space and another word (which is defined in grep as one or more characters between a and z). When it finds an instance, BBEdit replaces the characters with the literal text *the crazy*.

5. `display dialog myNumReplaces & ¬`
`replacements made." as string`

Finally, you display how many changes were made.

Script 20.1 Using a grep search and replace in BBEdit to match patterns and replace them.

```
set myfile to (choose file)
tell application "BBEdit 6.1 for OS X"
open myfile
set myNumReplaces to replace "The [a-z]+" ¬
using "the crazy" searching in window 1 ¬
options {search mode:grep, starting at top:true}
end tell
display dialog myNumReplaces & " replacements ¬
made." as string
```

A Guide to grep Patterns

.	matches any character.
#	matches any digit.
^	matches the beginning of a line.
$	matches the end of a line.
[abc]	matches any character a, b, or c.
[^abc]	matches any character except a, b, or c.
[a-e]	matches any character from a to e.
\t	matches a tab.
\r	matches a return.
A*	matches zero or more As.
A+	matches one or more As.
A?	matches zero or one A.
(A)	creates a group match that can be referred to in the replace string by \n, in which n refers to the nth instance of (), as in \1, \2.

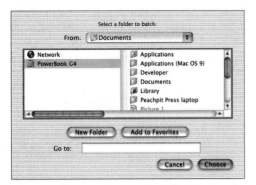

Figure 20.4 The Choose Folder dialog box displayed by the script.

Batch Searching and Replacing Many Files

For your next BBEdit trick, you'll create a script that will become a drag-and-drop application to batch-process any number of text files in any number of nested folders (**Script 20.2**). The heart of your routine will be the same replace command you used in Script 20.1

Keep in mind that after you've opened the file in BBEdit, you can issue replace commands to modify the open file before your script saves the changed file and moves on.

After you've entered this script in Script Editor, save it as an application on your Desktop, checking the Never Show Startup Screen checkbox. This will make the script execute immediately when a user double-clicks its icon or drops files on it. Then drop the Text Files folder you created earlier on the script or double-click it to be prompted to find a folder to process.

Figure 20.4 shows what happens if you double-click the script application instead of dropping a folder on it.

To batch-search and replace text in many files:

1. on run

   To start, you define an on run handler to deal with occasions when the user double-clicks the script application instead of dropping a folder on it.

2. set myfolder to choose folder with ¬ prompt "Select a folder to batch:"

   If the script was run by double-clicking, you prompt the user to select a folder to batch-process and store the reference to that folder in the myFolder variable.

continues on next page

3. `batchProcess(myfolder) of me`
   `end run`

Then you call the main function, `batchProcess`, passing to it the reference to the folder contained in `myFolder`.

4. `on open myfolder`
   `    batchProcess(myfolder) of me`
   `end open`

If the user drops a folder on the script application, the Finder will pass a reference to the folder to your script in the `myFolder` variable. Then you call the main function as above, passing the reference to the folder.

5. `on batchProcess(myCurrentFolder)`

Here, you begin your function, `batchProcess`, and tell AppleScript to store any value passed to it in the `myCurrentFolder` variable.

6. `tell application "Finder"`

Next, you let AppleScript know that you want to talk to the Finder.

7. `set myFolderContents to list folder ¬`
   `myCurrentFolder without invisibles`

You ask the Finder to return a list of items contained in the folder referred to by `myCurrentFolder` and store it in `myFolderContents`.

8. `repeat with myfile in myFolderContents`

Now you begin a `repeat` loop, placing one item from the `myFolderContents` list in the `myFile` variable for each loop until you reach the end of the list.

9. `if kind of alias (myCurrentFolder & ¬`
   `myfile as text) is "folder" then`

You ask the Finder for the type of item `myFile` in the folder referred to by `myCurrentFolder`. If the item is a folder, your script executes the next line.

Script 20.2 This elaborate script allows the user to drag and drop or select folders to batch search and replace within BBEdit, saving the changes.

```
                          script
on run
set myfolder to choose folder with prompt ¬
"Select a folder to batch:"
batchProcess(myfolder) of me
end run
on open myfolder
    batchProcess(myfolder) of me
end open
on batchProcess(myCurrentFolder)
tell application "Finder"
set myFolderContents to list folder ¬
myCurrentFolder without invisibles
repeat with myfile in myFolderContents
if kind of alias (myCurrentFolder & myfile ¬
as text) is "folder" then
batchProcess(myCurrentFolder & myfile as text) ¬
of me
else
            tell application "BBEdit 6.1 for ¬
OS X"
open alias (myCurrentFolder & myfile as text)
set myNumReplaces to replace "The [a-z]+" ¬
using "the crazy" searching in window 1 ¬
options {search mode:grep, starting at ¬
top:true}
close front window saving in (myCurrentFolder ¬
& myfile as text) saving yes
            end tell
        end if
    end repeat
  end tell
end batchProcess
```

10. `batchProcess(myCurrentFolder & ¬`
`myfile as text) of me`

If your function encounters another
folder, it calls itself, passing a reference
to the enclosed folder so that your script
processes all folders nested inside the
original.

11. `else`
`    tell application "BBEdit 6.1 for OS X"`

If the `myFile` item in the folder isn't a
folder, you begin talking to BBEdit.

12. `open alias (myCurrentFolder & myfile ¬`
`as text)`

You ask BBEdit to open the `myFile` item
inside `myCurrentFolder`. You have to
coerce the values to text to make sure
that AppleScript doesn't evaluate them
as a list, which would generate an error.

13. `set myNumReplaces to replace "The ¬`
`[a-z]+" using "the crazy" searching ¬`
`in window 1 options {search ¬`
`mode:grep, starting at top:true}`

Now BBEdit replaces your search string
with the replace text, using grep pattern
matching and starting at the beginning
of the document, returning the number
of replacements in your `myNumReplaces`
variable.

14. `close front window saving in ¬`
`(myCurrentFolder & myfile as text) ¬`
`saving yes`
`            end tell`
`        end if`
`    end repeat`
`  end tell`
`end batchProcess`

Finally, you have BBEdit save the
changed file over itself and conclude
your conversation, your `if` statement,
your `repeat` loop, and your function.

Finding Differences Between Two Files

Often, you'd like to compare two files to see whether they are different. BBEdit makes this process very easy with its `find differences` statement.

Script 20.3 compares two files specified by the user and reports whether they are the same or different. You can run this script from Script Editor.

Figure 20.5 shows the result of a comparison of your two sample text files, 1 and 2.

To find differences between two files:

1. `set myFile1 to (choose file with ¬ prompt "Select first file for ¬ comparison:")`

   You begin this script by prompting the user to select the first file for comparison and saving the reference to the file in the `myFile1` variable.

2. `set myFile2 to (choose file with ¬ prompt "Select second file:")`

   Then you prompt for the second file and save its reference in `myFile2`.

3. `tell application "BBEdit 6.1 for OS X"`
   `    set areDifferent to differences ¬`
   `found of (compare myFile1 against ¬`
   `myFile2)`

   Here, you ask BBEdit to compare the two files and return the result of the comparison as a Boolean (true or false) value in the `areDifferent` variable.

4. `close every window`
   `end tell`

   Next, you have BBEdit close the Find Differences windows that it may have opened in the last command.

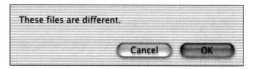

Figure 20.5 The script displays this dialog box when the two compared files are different.

Script 20.3 Comparing text files with BBEdit.

```
                    script
set myFile1 to (choose file with prompt ¬
"Select first file for comparison:")
set myFile2 to (choose file with prompt ¬
"Select second file:")
tell application "BBEdit 6.1 for OS X"
    set areDifferent to differences found of ¬
(compare myFile1 against myFile2)
close every window
end tell
if areDifferent then
    display dialog "These files are different."
else
    display dialog "These files are the same."
end if
```

5. if areDifferent then
    display dialog "These files are ¬
different."
else
    display dialog "These files are ¬
the same."
end if

Finally, you evaluate the value of
areDifferent and display one of two
dialog boxes based on its value.

Labeling Changed Files in the Finder

So now that you can slice, dice, and puree your text files with BBEdit and AppleScript, wouldn't it be nice to keep track of what's changed in a simple, clear manner? And what could be easier than labeling any changes in the Finder so that you can see what's happened at a glance?

Script 20.4 replaces any instances of *dog* that it finds in a text file with *cat*, labeling the file in the Finder if any changes were made. Try running this script from Script Editor and selecting one of your sample text files.

Figure 20.6 shows the result of this script.

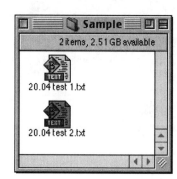

Figure 20.6
The Finder window containing the processed file. Notice that the script has labeled the file.

✔ Tip

■ See Chapter 6 for more information on scripting the Finder.

To label changed files in the Finder:

1. `set myFile to (choose file)`

   First, you prompt the user to select the file to open and store the reference to that file (as an alias) in the `myFile` variable.

2. `tell application "BBEdit 6.1"`

   Now you let AppleScript know that you want to send commands to BBEdit.

3. ```
   set myFound to found of (replace ¬
   "dog" using "cat" searching in myFile ¬
   options {search mode:literal, ¬
   starting at top:true, returning ¬
   results:false, showing results:false} ¬
   saving yes)
   end tell
   ```

   Next, you try to replace the search string *dog* with *cat* in the file referred to by `myFile`. You store the Boolean flag returned from the batch find in the `myFound` variable.
   ```

Script 20.4 This script replaces any instances of *dog* it finds in a text file with *cat*, labeling changed files in the Finder.

```
script

set myFile to (choose file)
tell application "BBEdit 6.1"
set myFound to found of (replace "dog" using ¬
"cat" searching in myFile options {search ¬
mode:literal, starting at top:true, returning ¬
results:false, showing results:false} saving ¬
yes)
end tell
if myFound then
tell application "Finder" to set the label ¬
index of myFile to 2
end if
```

4. `if myFound then`

    You test myFound to see whether any replacements were made.

5. `tell application "Finder" to set the ¬`
    `label index of myFile to 2`

    You tell the Finder to set the label of the file to indicate that it's been changed.

✔ Tip

■ This script does not work in the Finder of Mac OS X version 10.1, because the Finder does not yet support labels.

Deleting Matching Lines of Text

Script 20.5 traverses every line of text in a file sequentially, searching for lines below the current line that match it. All matching lines are replaced with a null string, eliminating them. This script is useful for stripping duplicate entries from flat text-file databases.

Figure 20.7 shows the active window in BBEdit as it appears while the script is running.

To delete matching lines of text:

1. `tell application "BBEdit 6.1 for OS X" activate`

    You begin by telling BBEdit to come to the front.

2. `repeat with i from 1 to ((number of ¬ lines in window 1) - 1)`

    Then you start looping through each line of the frontmost open window in BBEdit.

3. `set myLine to contents of (line i of ¬ window 1) & return`

    Next, you set myLine to the contents of the current line in your loop. You append a carriage return to include the whole line, break and all.

4. `select (line (i + 1) of window 1)`

    Then you tell BBEdit to move the selection to the line just after the current line.

5. `replace myLine using "" searching in ¬ window 1 options {search mode:literal, ¬ starting at top:false}`

    Now you have BBEdit search from the line below the current line to the end of the document without using grep pattern matching, replacing any duplicate lines it finds with null strings.

Figure 20.7 The active BBEdit window while the script is running.

Script 20.5 This script traverses every line of text in a file sequentially, searching for lines below the current line that match it.

```
script

tell application "BBEdit 6.1 for OS X"
    activate
repeat with i from 1 to ((number of lines in ¬
window 1) - 1)
set myLine to contents of (line i of window 1) ¬
& return
select (line (i + 1) of window 1)
replace myLine using "" searching in window 1 ¬
options {search mode:literal, starting at ¬
top:false}
if i > (number of lines in window 1) then exit ¬
repeat
end repeat
end tell
```

6. `if i > (number of lines in window 1) ¬`
   `then exit repeat`

Before repeating the loop, you check to see whether the document now contains fewer lines than the line number toward which you are looping. If you have exceeded the line count, you exit the loop.

7. `end repeat`
   `end tell`

Your loop ends, and you conclude your conversation with BBEdit.

✔ Tip

- Save this script as a compiled script in BBEdit's Scripts folder to include the script in BBEdit's Scripts menu the next time you launch it.

Cleaning Visual Editors' HTML Code

Script 20.6 is a variation on the batch-replace script you created earlier in this chapter (**Script 20.2**). This script is a drag-and-drop application that can batch-process any number of text files in any number of nested folders. The script removes all tabs and multiple spaces in the files, saving disk space by eliminating the unneeded code indentation added by most visual editors.

Figures 20.8 and **20.9** display the BBEdit windows for a file before and after processing, showing the differences.

To clean visual editors' HTML code:

1. `on run`

   To start, define an on run handler to deal with occasions when the user double-clicks the script application instead of dropping a folder on it.

2. `set myfolder to choose folder with ¬`
   `prompt "Select a folder to clean:"`

   If the script was run by double-clicking, you prompt the user to select a folder to batch-process and store the reference to that folder in the `myfolder` variable.

3. `batchProcess(myfolder) of me`
   `end run`

   Then you call the main function, `batchProcess`, passing to it the reference to the folder contained in `myfolder`.

4. `on open myfolder`
   `   batchProcess(myfolder) of me`
   `end open`

   If the user drops a folder on the script application, the Finder will pass a reference to the folder to your script in the `myfolder` variable. Then you call the main function as above, passing the reference to the folder.

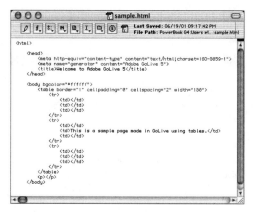

Figure 20.8 The BBEdit window before the script runs. Notice the white space in the file.

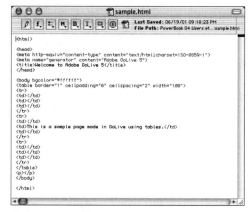

Figure 20.9 The BBEdit window after running the script. Notice that the white space has been deleted.

Script 20.6 This script removes all tabs and multiple spaces in a file, eliminating the unneeded code indentation added by most visual editors.

```
                   script
on run
set myfolder to choose folder with prompt ¬
"Select a folder to clean:"
batchProcess(myfolder) of me
end run
on open myfolder
    batchProcess(myfolder) of me
end open
on batchProcess(myCurrentFolder)
tell application "Finder"
set myFolderContents to list folder ¬
myCurrentFolder without invisibles
repeat with myfile in myFolderContents
if kind of alias (myCurrentFolder & myfile as ¬
text) is "folder" then
batchProcess(myCurrentFolder & myfile as text) ¬
of me
else
            tell application "BBEdit 6.1 for ¬
OS X"
open alias (myCurrentFolder & myfile as text)
set myNumReplaces to replace (tab & "+") using ¬
"" searching in window 1 options {search ¬
mode:grep, starting at top:true}
            set myNumReplaces to replace ¬
" +" using " " searching in window 1 options ¬
{search mode:grep, starting at top:true}
set the line breaks of text document 1 to DOS
close front window saving in (myCurrentFolder ¬
& myfile as text) saving yes
            end tell
        end if
    end repeat
  end tell
end batchProcess
```

5. `on batchProcess(myCurrentFolder)`

Here, you begin your function, `batchProcess`, and tell AppleScript to store any value passed to it in the `myCurrentFolder` variable.

6. `tell application "Finder"`

Next, you let AppleScript know that you want to talk to the Finder.

7. `set myFolderContents to list folder ¬`
`myCurrentFolder without invisibles`

You ask the Finder to return a list of items contained in the folder referred to by `myCurrentFolder` and store it in `myFolderContents`.

8. `repeat with myfile in myFolderContents`

Now you begin a `repeat` loop, placing one item from the `myFolderContents` list in the `myfile` variable for each loop until you reach the end of the list.

9. `if kind of alias (myCurrentFolder ¬`
`& myfile as text) is "folder" then`

You ask the Finder for the type of item `myfile` in the folder referred to by `myCurrentFolder`. If the item is a folder, your script executes the next line.

10. `batchProcess(myCurrentFolder & ¬`
`myfile as text) of me`

If your function encounters another folder, it calls itself, passing a reference to the enclosed folder, so that your script processes all folders nested inside the original.

11. `else`
`   tell application "BBEdit 6.1 for OS X"`

If the `myfile` item in the folder isn't itself a folder, you begin talking to BBEdit.

continues on next page

12. `open alias (myCurrentFolder & myfile ¬`
`as text)`

You ask BBEdit to open the `myfile` item inside `myCurrentFolder`. You have to coerce the values to text to make sure that AppleScript doesn't evaluate them as a list, which would generate an error.

13. `set myNumReplaces to replace (tab & ¬`
`"+") using "" searching in window 1 ¬`
`options {search mode:grep, starting ¬`
`at top:true}`
`set myNumReplaces to replace " +" ¬`
`using " " searching in window 1 ¬`
`options {search mode:grep, starting ¬`
`at top:true}`

Now BBEdit replaces all tabs with a null string and all multiple space characters with a single space, eliminating the file-bloating code indentation that many visual editors add to HTML files.

14. `set the line breaks of text document ¬`
`1 to DOS`

Next you have BBEdit set the line-break style of the text document to DOS line breaks, so that Windows users opening the text file will see it displayed properly.

15. `close front window saving in ¬`
`(myCurrentFolder & myfile as text) ¬`
`saving yes`
`            end tell`
`        end if`
`    end repeat`
`  end tell`
`end batchProcess`

Finally, you have BBEdit save the changed file over itself and conclude your conversation, your `if` statement, your `repeat` loop, and your function.

CLEANING VISUAL EDITORS' HTML CODE

BUILDING APPLESCRIPT CGIS

CGI ... ICG ... GCI ... GIC. Do you care where this strange acronym came from? You do.

The mysteries of the parent words are the key to understanding how these Web-enabled scripts work. *Common Gateway Interface* is the phrase that was coined to describe the manner in which local scripts on a server receive data from an Internet client and return results at the end of their execution. A group of standards describes the way CGIs communicate on each platform. In Unix, script and server sometimes share data via environment variables. On the Mac, the natural avenue for CGIs is Apple Events, which makes AppleScript a good choice for handling the passing of data.

CGIs in Mac OS 9 are often AppleScript script applications or FaceSpan applications. Most Mac Web servers, including WebSTAR and Apple's Mac OS 9 Personal Web Sharing, are set up out of the box to support the .acgi and .cgi file extensions to run AppleScript applications that support the standard CGI event handler you're about to meet.

AppleScript CGIs, Mac OS X, and Mac OS X Server

Are you dedicated to running Mac OS X and using AppleScript CGIs? As of version 10.1, the built-in Apache Web server of Mac OS X has no support for AppleScript CGIs. But Mac OS X Server has an Apache module for ACGI use.

Using CGIs in Mac OS 9

A standard event to allow AppleScripts to communicate with Web servers has existed for some time. This event was known as «event WWWΩsdoc» before the advent of Mac OS 8.5. The event becomes known as on handle CGI request in Mac OS 8.5 and later. AppleScript automatically returns Web server information to a script's on handle CGI request handler.

Understanding FIFO: First In, First Out

Programmers often use FaceSpan for creating AppleScript CGIs to take advantage of its built-in *FIFO* (first in, first out) capabilities. When multiple CGI calls are sent to a normal script application, the last person to call the application gets the results first—a process called *LIFO* last in, first out). This order of execution isn't desirable in a CGI environment, so it's often worthwhile to save your CGI script applications as FaceSpan standalone applications to get FIFO performance. See Chapter 23 for more information on FaceSpan.

Saving your CGI script

After writing your CGI script, save your script as a stay-open application that never shows the startup dialog box.

When you're choosing among file suffixes, .acgi is most often the right choice instead of .cgi. Why? The *a* in .acgi stands for *asynchronous*, meaning that the Web server will continue to work on other tasks while waiting for the CGI to return results. If you use the .cgi suffix for your CGI, the Web server will wait for your CGI to get back to it before doing anything else—usually not a good thing.

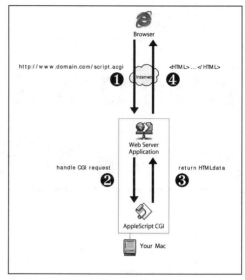

Figure 21.1 This diagram shows the AppleScript-based exchange of information that takes place between a Web-server application and an AppleScript CGI. When a user requests a URL for your server (step 1), the Web-server software calls your AppleScript's handle CGI request handler (step 2). At the end of your handler, return the HTML you want to send to the user (step 3). The Web-server software will send the HTML text back to the user's browser (step 4).

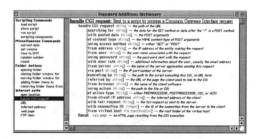

Figure 21.2 The dictionary entry for the handle CGI request handler from the Standard Additions Scripting Addition.

Using Encode URL and Decode URL

After you write a CGI, you'll discover quickly that you need to convert encoded text from the Web. You probably have seen strings such as %20 in the location bar of your browser before. This encoding, %20, stands for a space character, which otherwise would not transmit properly. Other %xx codes exist for all nonalphanumeric ASCII characters.

The Encode URL Scripting Addition adds the AppleScript command encode URL, which takes a standard string as an argument and returns the string encoded in the URL %x scheme so that extended ASCII characters are transmitted over the Web properly. As you might suspect, the decode URL command does the opposite.

Mac OS 9.2.1 and CGIs

All the scripts in this chapter were designed and tested for Mac OS 9.2.1. The on handle CGI request handler has been available since AppleScript 1.3.1 in Mac OS 8.5.

Most of these scripts do not work with older versions of the Mac OS or with the built-in Apache Web server in OS X 10.1.

Understanding GET Data

All data that goes to your AppleScript CGI application for processing comes from a Web client and is submitted to the server via the GET or POST method. Forms submitted with the GET method generate their name-value pairs and add them to the end of the submitted URL. When you submit an HTML form with the user-entered data John Doe in the field named "name", the URL sent to the server will have the values of the form field encoded this way: http://www.domain .com/script.acgi?name=John%20Doe.

Figure 21.3 shows the results returned for **Script 21.1** as a CGI.

Figure 21.3 The browser displays the result of the CGI. The user entered John Doe in the form field in the preceding screen to get to this screen. Because the GET method is used to submit the form, the URL contains the form-field data.

To parse GET data from the URL reply string:

1. on handle CGI request myurl searching ¬ for mySearchArgs

You begin your CGI handler by putting the searching for property into your mySearchArgs variable. searching for contains the reply string from the URL. The reply-string value is all the text that follows the question mark in the URL.

2. set myArgList to (tokenize ¬ mySearchArgs with delimiters {"&", "="})

Acme Script Widgets adds the statement tokenize, which returns a list from a string with list-item delimiters—in this case, the ampersand (&) and the equal sign (=). You convert the string mySearchArgs to a series of items in a list, following the format {name, value}.

Scripting with Acme Script Widgets

This script requires the Scripting Addition Acme Script Widgets. You must have Acme Script Widgets installed in your Scripting Additions folder for this script to work.

Acme Script Widgets is shareware. It costs $29 for a single-user license.

Acme Script Widgets is developed by Acme Technologies (http://www.acmetech.com/).

Script 21.1 This script is designed to be used as an AppleScript CGI application. It parses a form field submitted to it in the URL string and returns HTML that includes the value found for the form field. This script uses Scripting Additions to perform string-manipulation tasks.

```
                      script

on handle CGI request myurl searching for ¬
mySearchArgs
set myArgList to (tokenize mySearchArgs with ¬
delimiters {"&", "="})
set mySearchValue to (offset in list myArgList ¬
of "name" with returning next item)
set crlf to (ASCII character 13) & (ASCII ¬
character 10)
set myHTML to "HTTP/1.0 200 OK" & crlf & ¬
"Server: MacHTTP/2.0" & crlf & "MIME-Version: ¬
1.0" & crlf & "Content-type: text/html" & crlf ¬
& crlf
set myHTML to myHTML & "<HTML><BODY><P>Your ¬
name is " & mySearchValue & "</BODY></HTML>"
return myHTML
end handle CGI request
```

Scripting with Encode URL and Decode URL

The Scripting Additions Encode URL and Decode URL are freeware. You can find them at http://www2.starnine.com/ extendingwebstar/osax/.

Both Scripting Additions were written by Chuck Shotton and developed by BIAP Systems Inc, (http://www.biap.com/).

3.
```
set mySearchValue to (offset in list ¬
myArgList of "name" with returning ¬
next item)
```
Acme Script Widgets also adds the `offset in list` statement. Now you retrieve the value for the "name" field, using `offset in list` with the `returning next item` modifier to give you the item in the list right after "name", which is where the item's value is stored.

4.
```
set crlf to (ASCII character 13) & ¬
(ASCII character 10)
```
For convenience and prettier code, you store the line-break character sequence needed for your HTML data header in a variable, `crlf`. These two characters, a return (13) and a line break (10), make up the standard HTML line-break string.

5.
```
set myHTML to "HTTP/1.0 200 OK" & ¬
crlf & "Server: MacHTTP/2.0" & crlf ¬
& "MIME-Version: 1.0" & crlf & ¬
"Content-type: text/html" & crlf & crlf
```
You initialize a variable for your returned data with the CGI header to let the server know you're returning text as HTML.

6.
```
set myHTML to myHTML & "<HTML><BODY>¬
<P>Your name is " & mySearchValue & ¬
"</BODY></HTML>"
```
Next, you add your results string to your variable by adding the value of the form field "name" to the user.

7.
```
return myHTML
end handle CGI request
```
Finally, you return the text to your Web server in the myHTML variable.

To prepare your script as a CGI:

1. To make your AppleScript work as a CGI, save the script as an application.

   It is best to save your AppleScript CGI application so that it stays open. By staying open, your CGI script application will run faster, because it won't have to be launched every time it's called.

2. Name your application `script.acgi`, and move it into the same folder as WebSTAR (or whichever folder is the designated CGI folder for your Web-server software).

3. Try sending your Web server the URL `http://www.domain.com/script.acgi?name=John%20Doe`, substituting your server's host name for `www.domain.com` to test your new AppleScript CGI.

✔ Tip

- "Parsing Form POST Data" later in this chapter shows you how to tokenize data and get offsets in lists by using functions instead of a Scripting Addition.

GET versus POST

The HTTP protocol defines two ways for Web forms to return form data to the server. The HTML tag `<FORM METHOD="GET" ACTION="script.acgi">` determines the method used for a form.

With `METHOD="GET"`, all field data is appended to the end of the URL that the `ACTION` tag defines. This field data, also known as the *reply string,* is appended to the URL with a question mark indicating its start. Field names and values are paired and separated by an equal sign. Each pair is separated by an ampersand. `GET` limits the length of form data and lets the user see the form data passed in his or her browser.

With `METHOD="POST"`, all field data is put in a packet, called the *post data,* by the user's browser and sent along to the URL defined by the `ACTION` tag. With `POST`, form data can be much longer and is hidden from the user when submitted.

Figure 21.4 The browser displays the results of the CGI. The user entered John Doe in the form field in the preceding screen to get to this screen. Because the POST method is used to submit the form, the URL doesn't contain the form-field data.

Parsing Form POST Data

Any forms submitted via the POST method generate their name-value pairs as part of the post data of the reply. The post data is the data entered by the user in a form that has its METHOD tag set to "POST".

The post data sent back to the URL contains name=John%20Doe when the user entered John Doe in the "name" field of the form. **Figure 21.4** shows the result returned for **Script 21.2** as a CGI, with the user's entered form data (John Doe) embedded in the returned HTML by your CGI.

This time, you will create your own functions to handle the tasks of *tokenizing* (separating the string into a list of items) the returned post data and finding the offset in a list of items of a specific string. As a result, you don't need the Acme Script Widgets Scripting Addition for this script.

To parse form data:

1. on handle CGI request myurl with ¬
   posted data mySearchArgs

   You begin your CGI handler by capturing the post-data value using posted data and storing the value in mySearchArgs. AppleScript automatically returns many server variables to any on handle CGI request handler. Here, you're concerned only with posted data, because it holds the form's post data.

2. set myArgList to goTokenize¬
   (mySearchArgs, {"&", "="})

   As before, you convert the string to a series of items in a list, following the format {name, value}. This time, you use your own function, goTokenize, to do what Acme Script Widgets did in **Script 21.1.**

   continues on next page

3. `set mySearchValue to goOffsetInList¬`
`(myArgList, "name")`

Now you retrieve the value for the field "name", using your own function, `goOffsetInList`, to give you the item following "name", where its value is stored.

4. `set crlf to (ASCII character 13) & ¬`
`(ASCII character 10)`

For convenience, you store the line-break character sequence needed for your HTML data header in a variable, `crlf`. These two characters, a return (13) and a line break (10), compose the standard HTML line-break string.

5. `set myHTML to "HTTP/1.0 200 OK" & ¬`
`crlf & "Server: MacHTTP/2.0" & crlf ¬`
`& "MIME-Version: 1.0" & crlf & ¬`
`"Content-type: text/html" & crlf & crlf`

You initialize a variable, `myHTML`, for your returned data with the CGI header to let the server know you're returning text as HTML.

Script 21.2 This script is designed to be used as an AppleScript CGI application. It parses a form field submitted to it as POST data and returns HTML that includes the value found for the form field. This script uses handlers instead of Scripting Additions to perform string-manipulation tasks.

```
                                            script
on handle CGI request myurl with posted data mySearchArgs
set myArgList to goTokenize(mySearchArgs, {"&", "="})
set mySearchValue to goOffsetInList(myArgList, "name")
set crlf to (ASCII character 13) & (ASCII character 10)
set myHTML to "HTTP/1.0 200 OK" & crlf & "Server: MacHTTP/2.0" & crlf & "MIME-Version: 1.0" & crlf &
"Content-type: text/html" & crlf & crlf
set myHTML to myHTML & "<HTML><BODY><P>Your name is " & mySearchValue & "</BODY></HTML>"
return myHTML
end handle CGI request
on goTokenize(incomingData, incomingDelimits)
set incomingDataitems to characters of incomingData as list
set outgoingList to {}
    set currentData to ""
repeat with incomingItem in incomingDataitems
set myflag to false
        repeat with incomingDelimit in incomingDelimits
if contents of incomingItem = contents of incomingDelimit then
```

(script continues on next page)

Script 21.2 *continued*

```
           set myflag to true
           exit repeat
       end if
   end repeat
if myflag then
       set outgoingList to outgoingList & ¬
currentData
       set currentData to ""
   else
       set currentData to currentData & ¬
incomingItem
       end if
   end repeat
   set outgoingList to outgoingList & currentData
return outgoingList
end goTokenize
on goOffsetInList(incomingList, incomingItem)
set outgoingPosition to 0
   set outgoingItem to ""
repeat with i from 1 to number of items in ¬
incomingList
       set incomingListItem to item i of ¬
incomingList
       if incomingItem = incomingListItem then
           set outgoingPosition to i
           exit repeat
       end if
   end repeat
try
       if outgoingPosition > 0 then set
outgoingItem to item (outgoingPosition + 1) ¬
of incomingList
   end try
   return outgoingItem
end goOffsetInList
```

6. `set myHTML to myHTML &`
`"<HTML><BODY>¬`
`<P>Your name is " & mySearchValue & ¬`
`"</BODY></HTML>"`

Next, you add to myHTML your mySearchValue variable, which holds the "name" field's value.

7. `return myHTML`
`end handle CGI request`

You return the text to your Web server in the myHTML variable.

8. `on goTokenize(incomingData, ¬`
`incomingDelimits)`

Your goTokenize function receives two values when called: incomingData, to hold the string to be tokenized, and incomingDelimits, to hold the characters where the string should be broken into separate items. This function replaces the tokenize command of Acme Script Widgets.

9. `set incomingDataitems to characters ¬`
`of incomingData as list`

You first convert the string incomingData to a list, incomingDataitems, in which each item equals a single character.

10. `set outgoingList to {}`
`set currentData to ""`

Then you initialize two variables. You will use outgoingList to build the final list to return at the end of the function. currentData will hold the string of each item as it is assembled in the loops later in the script.

11. `repeat with incomingItem in ¬`
`incomingDataitems`

You start to loop through each character in the incoming string.

continues on next page

12.
```
set myflag to false
repeat with incomingDelimit in ¬
incomingDelimits
```

Here, you clear the flag variable myFlag, which you'll use to indicate when a delimiter is found in the loop that cycles through each delimiter in incomingDelimits.

13.
```
if contents of incomingItem = ¬
contents of incomingDelimit then
  set myflag to true
  exit repeat
end if
    end repeat
```

While looping through each delimiter, you test the current character in incomingItem to see whether it matches the delimiter. If so, you set the flag myFlag to true and exit the loop.

14.
```
if myflag then
    set outgoingList to outgoingList ¬
& currentData
  set currentData to ""
else
  set currentData to currentData & ¬
incomingItem
end if
  end repeat
  set outgoingList to outgoingList ¬
& currentData
```

After you've tested the current character in incomingItem against all the delimiters, you check to see whether it matched any of them by looking at myFlag. If a match exists, you add the string built up in currentData to outgoingList. Otherwise, you simply append the current character in incomingItem to the end of currentData. When the loop is over, you add the remaining characters to your list.

15.
```
return outgoingList
end goTokenize
```

With the loop complete, you're ready to return the list of tokenized items.

16.
```
on goOffsetInList(incomingList, ¬
incomingItem)
```

Your goOffsetInList function receives two values when called. incomingList holds the list to be searched for the matching item incomingItem. This function replaces the offset in list command of Acme Script Widgets.

17.
```
set outgoingPosition to 0
set outgoingItem to ""
```

You clear the variables that you'll use to hold the position for an item that matches incomingItem and the value of the item right after the match.

18.
```
repeat with i from 1 to number of ¬
items in incomingList
  set incomingListItem to item i of ¬
incomingList
  if incomingItem = incomingListItem ¬
then
    set outgoingPosition to i
    exit repeat
  end if
end repeat
```

Now you loop through each item in incomingList, checking its contents for a match with the contents of incomingItem. If a match is found, you set outgoingPosition to the matching item's position and exit the loop.

continues on next page

19.
```
try
    if outgoingPosition > 0 then set ¬
outgoingItem to item ¬
(outgoingPosition + 1) of incomingList
    end try
    return outgoingItem
end goOffsetInList
```

Finally, you see whether a match was found by checking the value of outgoingPosition. If a match was found, you copy the value of the item right after the matching one to outgoingItem. Then you return the value.

To prepare your script as a CGI:

◆ Move your CGI application into the same folder as WebSTAR (or whichever folder is the designated CGI folder for your Web-server software).

The URL for your CGI, when it is in your server's root folder should be http://www.domain.com/script.acgi, in which www.domain.com is your server's host name and script.acgi is the name of your script application. The actual URL depends on how your Web server is configured.

✔ Tip

■ To make your AppleScript work as a CGI, you must save the script as an application. It is best to save your AppleScript CGI application so that it stays open. By staying open, your CGI script application will run faster, because it won't have to be launched every time it's called.

Making an HTML Page to Call Your New CGI

Make a new document in a text editor such as BBEdit or SimpleText, and type the following:

```
<HTML>
    <HEAD>
    </HEAD>
    <BODY>
        <FORM METHOD="POST"
ACTION="script.acgi">
        <INPUT TYPE=TEXT NAME="name" ¬
SIZE=10>
        <INPUT TYPE=SUBMIT>
    </BODY>
</HTML>
```

Now save the file with the name form.html in the same Web-server directory as your CGI. Then point your Web browser to http://www.domain.com/form.html, in which www.domain.com is your server's host name.

Figure 21.5 The browser displays the HTML returned by the CGI, which includes the user's browser type and referrer URL.

Parsing Server Variables

Server variables offer untold power for customizing CGI results. Information such as user name, password, referrer URL, browser type, and client address is delivered to the script by the server when you use the `handle CGI request` handler. **Script 21.3** shows you how to get those values from the server and put them into variables that you can use throughout a script.

Figure 21.5 shows the result of this script run as a CGI.

To parse server variables:

1. `on handle CGI request myurl of ¬`
`    content type myContentType using ¬`
`    access method myAccessMethod from ¬`
`    user myUser using password myPassword ¬`
`    referred by myReferrer from browser ¬`
`    myBrowser from client IP address ¬`
`    myAddress`

You begin your CGI handler by storing the content type of the data returned from a submitted form in `myContentType`, the access method of the form (`GET` or `POST`) in `myAccessMethod`, the user name of the client who sent the form in `myUser`, the user's password in `myPassword`, the referrer URL (or URL of the submitted form) in `myReferrer`, the client's browser type in `myBrowser`, and the client address in `myAddress`.

2. `set crlf to (ASCII character 13) & ¬`
`    (ASCII character 10)`

To make life easier, you store the line-break character sequence needed in your HTML data header in a variable, `crlf`. These two characters, a return (`13`) and a line break (`10`), make up the standard HTML line-break string.

continues on next page

PARSING SERVER VARIABLES

3. `set myHTML to "HTTP/1.0 200 OK" & ¬`
`crlf & "Server: MacHTTP/2.0" & crlf ¬`
`& "MIME-Version: 1.0" & crlf &`
`"Content-type: text/html" & crlf & ¬`
`crlf`

You initialize a variable, myHTML, for your returned data with the CGI header to let the server know you're returning text as HTML.

4. `set myHTML to myHTML & "<HTML><BODY>¬`
`<P>Your browser is " & myBrowser`
`set myHTML to myHTML & "<P>Referred ¬`
`to by " & myReferrer & "</BODY></HTML>"`
`return myHTML`
`end handle CGI request`

The remainder of the script simply prints back to the client the myBrowser and myReferrer variables. You probably will want to make more elaborate scripts that do more stuff with these values.

To prepare your script as a CGI:

◆ Move your CGI application into the same folder as WebSTAR (or whichever folder is the designated CGI folder for your Web-server software).

The URL for your CGI, when it is in your server's root folder, should be `http://www.domain.com/script.acgi`, in which `www.domain.com` is your server's host name and `script.acgi` is the name of your script application. The actual URL depends on how your Web server is configured.

Script 21.3 This script is designed to be used as an AppleScript CGI application. It parses particular Web-server variables, such as browser type, and returns HTML that includes some server-variable values.

```
                            script
on handle CGI request myurl of content type ¬
myContentType using access method ¬
myAccessMethod from user myUser using password ¬
myPassword referred by myReferrer from browser ¬
myBrowser from client IP address ¬
myAddress
set crlf to (ASCII character 13) & (ASCII ¬
character 10)
set myHTML to "HTTP/1.0 200 OK" & crlf & ¬
"Server: MacHTTP/2.0" & crlf & "MIME-Version: ¬
1.0" & crlf & "Content-type: text/html" & ¬
crlf & crlf
set myHTML to myHTML & "<HTML><BODY><P>Your ¬
browser is " & myBrowser
    set myHTML to myHTML & "<P>Referred to by ¬
" & myReferrer & "</BODY></HTML>"
    return myHTML
end handle CGI request
```

Scripting with Acme Script Widgets

This script requires the Scripting Addition Acme Script Widgets.

Figure 21.6 The browser is redirected to the URL http://www.apple.com by the CGI.

Returning Content via Redirection

Sometimes, rather than creating a large block of data to return from a CGI, the most efficient thing to do is send the user to another URL as the result of the CGI.

To accomplish this task, you use URL redirection. You can perform the task in the CGI header, but in **Script 21.4**, you'll do it simply by using an HTML META tag.

Figure 21.6 shows the browser result of this script run as a CGI, with the form field "url" containing the value www.apple.com.

To return content via redirection:

1. on handle CGI request myurl searching ¬ for mySearchArgs

   You begin your CGI handler by putting the searching for property in your mySearchArgs variable. searching for contains the reply string from the URL. The reply-string value is all the text that follows the question mark in the URL.

2. set myArgList to (tokenize ¬ mySearchArgs with delimiters {"&", "="})

   Acme Script Widgets adds the tokenize statement, which returns a list from a string with list-item delimiters—in this case, the ampersand (&) and the equal sign (=). You convert the mySearchArgs string to a series of items in a list, following the format {name, value}.

   continues on next page

3. `set mySearchValue to (offset in list ¬`
`myArgList of "url" with returning ¬`
`next item)`

Acme Script Widgets also adds the offset in list statement. Now you retrieve the value for the "name" field, using offset in list with the modifier returning next item to give you the item in the list right after "name", which should be where its value is stored.

4. `set crlf to (ASCII character 13) & ¬`
`(ASCII character 10)`

You store the line-break character sequence needed in your HTML data header in a variable, crlf. These two characters, a return (13) and a line break (10), are the standard HTML line-break string.

5. `set quote to ASCII character 34`

Again, to make your code easy on the eyes, you set aside a quote mark in a quote variable for later use.

6. `set myHTML to "HTTP/1.0 200 OK" & ¬`
`crlf & "Server: MacHTTP/2.0" & crlf ¬`
`& "MIME-Version: 1.0" & crlf & ¬`
`"Content-type: text/html" & crlf & crlf`

You initialize a variable for your returned data with the CGI header to let the server know you're returning text as HTML.

7. `set myHTML to myHTML & "<HTML><HEAD>¬`
`<META HTTP-EQUIV=REFRESH CONTENT=" ¬`
`& quote & "0; URL=http://" & ¬`
`mySearchValue & quote & ">"`

Next, you add an HTML META tag to force the browser to redirect to the URL passed by the form field "url" in the post data and stored in the mySearchValue variable.

8. `set myHTML to myHTML & "</HEAD><BODY>¬`
`</BODY></HTML>"`

You add closing tags to the HTML.

Script 21.4 This script is designed to be used as an AppleScript CGI application. It redirects a user to a URL value passed to it in the URL reply string.

```
┌─────────────────── script ───────────────────┐
on handle CGI request myurl searching for ¬
mySearchArgs
set myArgList to (tokenize mySearchArgs with ¬
delimiters {"&", "="})
set mySearchValue to (offset in list myArgList ¬
of "url" with returning next item)
set crlf to (ASCII character 13) & (ASCII ¬
character 10)
set quote to ASCII character 34
set myHTML to "HTTP/1.0 200 OK" & crlf & ¬
"Server: MacHTTP/2.0" & crlf & "MIME-Version: ¬
1.0" & crlf & "Content-type: text/html" & ¬
crlf & crlf
set myHTML to myHTML & "<HTML><HEAD><META
HTTP-EQUIV=REFRESH CONTENT=" & quote & "0;
URL=http://" & mySearchValue & quote & ">"
set myHTML to myHTML &
"</HEAD><BODY></BODY></HTML>"
return myHTML
end handle CGI request
```

Scripting with Acme Script Widgets

This script requires the Scripting Addition Acme Script Widgets.

9. `return myHTML`
`end handle CGI request`

Finally, you return the text to your Web server in the myHTML variable.

To prepare your script as a CGI:

◆ Move your CGI application into the same folder as WebSTAR (or whichever folder is the designated CGI folder for your Web-server software).

The URL for your CGI, when it is in your server's root folder, should be `http://www.domain.com/script.acgi`, in which `www.domain.com` is your server's host name and `script.acgi` is the name of your script application. The actual URL depends on how your Web server is configured.

✔ Tip

■ **Script 21.2** earlier in this chapter shows you how to tokenize data and get offsets in lists by using functions instead of a Scripting Addition.

Making an HTML Page to Call Your New CGI

Make a new document in a text editor such as BBEdit or SimpleText, and type the following:

```
<HTML>
  <HEAD>
  </HEAD>
  <BODY>
    <FORM METHOD="GET"
ACTION="script.acgi">
    <INPUT TYPE=TEXT NAME="url" ¬
SIZE=10>
    <INPUT TYPE=SUBMIT>
  </BODY>
</HTML>
```

Now save the file with the name form.html in the same Web-server directory as your CGI. Then point your Web browser to `http://www.domain.com/form.html`, in which `www.domain.com` is your server's host name.

RETURNING CONTENT VIA REDIRECTION

Returning Content from Other Scriptable Applications

Script 21.5 uses Finger to do a whois query on the InterNIC's domain-name database to check on the status of a domain name passed by the calling form's field named "domain". The InterNIC holds the registry of domain names worldwide. This script lets you check on the availability of any domain name quickly.

The script illustrates the principle of integrating the features and capabilities of high-level AppleScriptable applications with CGIs.

Figure 21.7 shows the browser result for the domain name apple.com. You can use this script to Finger any Unix system.

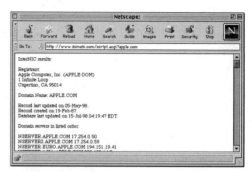

Figure 21.7 The screen returned by the CGI script if www.apple.com is the domain name entered in the form field submitted to the script.

To return whois query results from the InterNIC with Finger 1.5:

1. on handle CGI request myurl searching ¬ for mySearchArgs

You begin your CGI handler by capturing the reply-string value with searching for and storing the value in mySearchArgs.

2. set myArgList to (tokenize ¬ mySearchArgs with delimiters {"&", "="})

Next, you convert the string to a series of items in a list, following the format {name, value}.

3. set myDomainName to (offset in list ¬ myArgList of "domain" with returning ¬ next item)

Now you retrieve the value for the field "domain", using offset in list to give you the item following "domain", where its value is stored.

continues on next page

Scripting Finger

This script was designed and tested for Finger 1.5.

Finger is shareware. It costs $10.

Finger is written by Peter N. Lewis and is developed by Stairways Software (http://www.stairways.com/).

RETURNING CONTENT FROM OTHER APPS

Scripting with Acme Script Widgets

This script requires the Scripting Addition Acme Script Widgets.

4.
```
tell application "Finger"
    set myResults to fetchurl ¬
("whois://rs.internic.net/" & ¬
myDomainName as string)
end tell
```
Next, you get Finger to retrieve the result of a whois query to the InterNIC for the domain name passed in the myDomainName variable.

5.
```
set crlf to (ASCII character 13) & ¬
(ASCII character 10)
```
You store the line-break character sequence needed in your HTML data header in a variable, crlf. These two characters, a return (13) and a line break (10), make up the standard HTML line-break string.

6.
```
set myHTML to "HTTP/1.0 200 OK" & ¬
crlf & "Server: MacHTTP/2.0" & crlf ¬
& "MIME-Version: 1.0" & crlf & ¬
"Content-type: text/html" & crlf & crlf
```
You initialize a variable for your returned data with the CGI header to let the server know you're returning text as HTML.

continues on next page

Script 21.5 This script is designed to be used as an AppleScript CGI application. It uses Finger to perform a whois lookup on a domain name. The domain name to look up is passed to the CGI in a form field.

```
                                    script
on handle CGI request myurl searching for mySearchArgs
set myArgList to (tokenize mySearchArgs with delimiters {"&", "="})
set myDomainName to (offset in list myArgList of "domain" with returning next item)
tell application "Finger"
        set myResults to fetchurl ("whois://rs.internic.net/" & myDomainName as string)
    end tell
set crlf to (ASCII character 13) & (ASCII character 10)
set myHTML to "HTTP/1.0 200 OK" & crlf & "Server: MacHTTP/2.0" & crlf & "MIME-Version: 1.0" & crlf & ¬
"Content-type: text/html" & crlf & crlf
set myHTML to myHTML & "<HTML><BODY><P>InterNIC results: "
    set myHTML to myHTML & (ACME replace return with "<BR>" & return in myResults) & "</BODY></HTML>"
return myHTML
end handle CGI request
```

7. `set myHTML to myHTML & "<HTML><BODY>¬`
`<P>InterNIC results: "`
`set myHTML to myHTML & (ACME replace ¬`
`return with "<BR>" & return in ¬`
`myResults) & "</BODY></HTML>"`

You add the InterNIC result to your myHTML variable, using Acme Script Widgets' `ACME replace` statement to substitute HTML breaks for return characters. This technique preserves paragraph breaks in the HTML so that it looks the same as the text received from the InterNIC server.

8. `return myHTML`
`end handle CGI request`

Finally, you return the text to your Web server in the myHTML variable.

Making an HTML Page to Call Your New CGI

Make a new document in a text editor such as BBEdit or SimpleText, and type the following:

```
<HTML>
   <HEAD>
   </HEAD>
   <BODY>
      <FORM METHOD="GET"
ACTION="script.acgi">
      <INPUT TYPE=TEXT NAME="domain"
SIZE=10>
      <INPUT TYPE=SUBMIT>
   </BODY>
</HTML>
```

Now save the file with the name `form.html` in the same Web-server directory as your CGI. Then point your Web browser to `http://www.domain.com/form.html`, in which `www.domain.com` is your server's host name.

Figure 21.8 Using a partial reply, the CGI script has sent back some HTML for the browser to display before the remainder of the reply.

Sending Partial Replies with WebSTAR

WebSTAR supports extended communication between CGIs and itself with partial replies. With a partial reply, a CGI can begin returning data to the user before completing its operations. This technique, demonstrated in **Script 21.6,** offers users a sense of improved performance and keeps the user occupied while you do some more work.

Figure 21.8 shows the browser result before the final data has been returned.

To send partial CGI replies with WebSTAR:

1. `on handle CGI request myurl searching ¬ for mySearchArgs with connection ID ¬ myConnection`

    You begin your CGI handler by capturing the reply-string value with `searching for` and storing the value in `mySearchArgs`. You also store the unique ID for this connection with the server in `myConnection`. This unique ID is generated by the Web-server software. You'll use this data later to let WebSTAR know which connection to associate with the parts of your reply you'll send back.

2. `set myArgList to (tokenize ¬ mySearchArgs with delimiters {"&", "="})`

    Next, you convert the string to a series of items in a list, following the format `{name, value}`.

3. `set myDomainName to (offset in list ¬ myArgList of "domain" with returning ¬ next item)`

    Now you retrieve the value for the field `"domain"`, using `offset in list` to give you the item following `"domain"`, where its value is stored.

continues on next page

Scripting WebSTAR

These scripts were designed and tested for WebSTAR Server Suite 4.0.

WebSTAR is developed by ACI US (http://www.acius.com/).

4. `set crlf to (ASCII character 13) & ¬`
`(ASCII character 10)`

Store the line-break character sequence needed in your HTML data header in a variable, crlf.

5. `set myHTML to "HTTP/1.0 200 OK" & ¬`
`crlf & "Server: MacHTTP/2.0" & crlf ¬`
`& "MIME-Version: 1.0" & crlf & ¬`
`"Content-type: text/html" & crlf & crlf`

You initialize a variable for your returned data with the CGI header to let the server know you're returning text as HTML.

6. `set myHTML to myHTML & "<HTML><BODY>¬`
`<P>InterNIC search in progress... <BR>"`

Once you have parsed the form data, you then put some HTML together to let the user know things are happening.

Scripting with Acme Script Widgets

This script requires the Scripting Addition Acme Script Widgets.

Script 21.6 This script is designed to be used as an AppleScript CGI application. It demonstrates the use of partial replies to return portions of HTML information over time.

```
script
on handle CGI request myurl searching for mySearchArgs with connection ID myConnection
set myArgList to (tokenize mySearchArgs with delimiters {"&", "="})
set myDomainName to (offset in list myArgList of "domain" with returning next item)
set crlf to (ASCII character 13) & (ASCII character 10)
set myHTML to "HTTP/1.0 200 OK" & crlf & "Server: MacHTTP/2.0" & crlf & "MIME-Version: 1.0" & crlf & ¬
"Content-type: text/html" & crlf & crlf
set myHTML to myHTML & "<HTML><BODY><P>InterNIC search in progress... <BR>"
tell application "WebSTAR 4.0" to «event WWWΩSPar» myHTML with «class Kmor» given «class ¬
Kcid»:(myConnection as integer)
tell application "Finger" to set myResults to fetchurl ("whois://rs.internic.net/" & myDomainName as string)
set myHTML to myHTML & (ACME replace return with "<BR>" & return in myResults) & "</BODY></HTML>"
return myHTML
end handle CGI request
```

7. `tell application "WebSTAR 4.0" to ¬`
`«event WWWΩSPar» myHTML with «class ¬`
`Kmor» given «class ¬`
`Kcid»:(myConnection as integer)`

Here, you do a send partial to WebSTAR, returning HTML with the connection ID of your connection so that WebSTAR knows the connection with which to associate the data. You include the with more modifier to let WebSTAR know that more data is coming and that the connection shouldn't be closed.

8. `tell application "Finger" to ¬`
`set myResults to fetchurl ¬`
`("whois://rs.internic.net/" & ¬`
`myDomainName as string)`

Next, you use Finger to retrieve the result of a whois query to the InterNIC for the domain name passed in the myDomainName variable.

9. `set myHTML to myHTML & (ACME replace ¬`
`return with "<BR>" & return in ¬`
`myResults) & "</BODY></HTML>"`

You add the InterNIC result to your myHTML variable, using Acme Script Widgets' ACME replace statement to substitute HTML breaks for return characters. This technique preserves paragraph breaks in the HTML so that it looks the same as the text received from the InterNIC server.

10. `return myHTML`
`end handle CGI request`

Finally, you return the text to your Web server in the myHTML variable.

Creating Protected Realms in WebSTAR

The final script in this chapter, **Script 21.7,** shows you how to create and add password-protected directories, or *realms,* for WebSTAR. These settings will generate HTTP authentication prompts on the user's end when the user accesses URLs that contain the realm's match string.

Figure 21.9 shows WebSTAR's password dialog box with your new realm and user added.

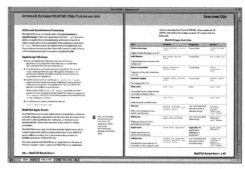

Figure 21.9 WebSTAR includes detailed documentation on the application's entire AppleScript dictionary, including commands, objects, and properties.

To add a protected realm and user to WebSTAR:

1. `set myRealm to "ADMINAREA"`
    `set myMatchString to "CLIENT-ADMIN"`
    `set myUser to "john"`
    `set myPassword to "test"`

    You begin by setting some variables for your new realm, myRealm; its match string, myMatchString; and your user and password, myUser and myPassword.

2. `tell application "WebSTAR 4.0"`

    Now you're ready to talk to WebSTAR.

3. `set myExistingRealms to realms`

    You retrieve WebSTAR's current realm list, using the application's realms property, and store it in the myExistingRealms variable.

4. `if myExistingRealms does not contain ¬`
    `(myRealm & return) then`
    `    set realms to realms & "REALM " ¬`
    `& myMatchString & " " & myRealm & ¬`
    `return as string`
    `end if`

    Now you check to make sure that the new realm myRealm doesn't already exist.

Script 21.7 This script adds a protected realm in WebStar 4.0. The script also adds a new user, with password, to this realm.

```
script
set myRealm to "ADMINAREA"
set myMatchString to "CLIENT-ADMIN"
set myUser to "john"
set myPassword to "test"
tell application "WebSTAR 4.0"
set myExistingRealms to realms
if myExistingRealms does not contain (myRealm ¬
& return) then
        set realms to realms & "REALM " & ¬
myMatchString & " " & myRealm & return as string
    end if
set myExistingUsers to validate user myUser ¬
password myPassword realm myRealm
if myExistingUsers is false then
        add user myUser password myPassword ¬
realm myRealm
    end if
end tell
```

5. `set myExistingUsers to validate user ¬`
`myUser password myPassword realm ¬`
`myRealm`

Then you check to see whether the user and password already exist in the realm.

6. `if myExistingUsers is false then`
`    add user myUser password myPassword ¬`
`realm myRealm`
`end if`
`end tell`

If the user is not already defined, you add the user with a password and realm association.

NETWORK ADMINISTRATION SCRIPTING

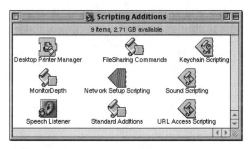

Figure 22.1 The recommended installation for Mac OS 9 includes the Network Setup Scripting application in the Scripting Additions folder.

One of the greatest things about AppleScript is that you can administer multiple Macs from your desktop.

To really take advantage of what scripting can offer an administrator, you need to get control of the networking software Mac OS 9 and earlier, Open Transport. In this chapter, you'll look at the capabilities of Mac OS 9.2.1 as you script the Open Transport networking database, which users ordinarily access through the TCP/IP and Remote Access control panels. Thanks to the faceless Network Setup Scripting application that comes with Mac OS 9.2.1, you'll create and manage networking configurations without opening any control panels. **Figure 22.1** shows the Network Setup Scripting application in the Scripting Additions folder while the application is running.

You'll also investigate scripting control of file-sharing states, as well as users and groups, thanks to the scriptable File Sharing control panel.

Creating a TCP/IP Configuration

Since the introduction of Mac OS 8.5, Apple-Script has had a complete set of AppleScript statements to control every aspect of Open Transport, including the creation of new configurations. In this section, you'll create a new TCP/IP configuration by calling the Network Setup Scripting application. **Script 22.1** shows the complete script.

Figure 22.2 shows the TCP/IP control panel with the new configuration active.

To create a new TCP/IP configuration:

1. `tell application "Network Setup ¬ Scripting"`

   You begin by letting AppleScript know that you want to talk to the Network Setup Scripting application.

2. `open database`

   Next, you tell the application to open the Open Transport configurations database.

3. `begin transaction`

   With this line, you create an exclusive transaction with the application (in this case, the Network Setup Scripting application). This code ensures that the database won't change while you work with it.

4. `if not (TCPIP v4 configuration "New ¬ Config" exists) then`

   Here, you make sure that no configuration already exists with the name of your new configuration, `"New Config"`.

5. `make new TCPIP v4 configuration "New ¬ Config" with properties {connecting ¬ via:Ethernet, configuration method:¬ manual, IP address:"206.14.230.16", ¬ subnet mask:"255.255.255.0", implicit ¬ search start:"", implicit search ¬ end:"", user mode:basic}`

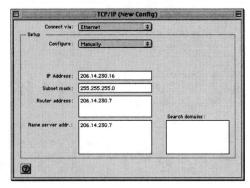

Figure 22.2 The new TCP/IP configuration created by the script, shown in the TCP/IP control panel.

You create your new configuration, in this case connecting via an Ethernet connection, using manual settings for IP address and subnet mask. Be sure to use your own IP address in this line.

6. `tell TCPIP v4 configuration "New Config"`
`    make new name server address 1 with ¬`
`data "206.14.230.7"`
`    make new router address 1 with ¬`
`data "206.14.230.7"`
`end tell`
`    end if`

Next, you create a name-server address and router address for your new Ethernet TCP/IP configuration. You can get this information from your ISP or system administrator.

7. `end transaction`
`close database`
`end tell`

Finally, you end your exclusive transaction, close the database, and conclude your conversation with the application.

✔ Tips

■ If you want to create a new TCP/IP configuration that uses Point-to-Point Protocol (PPP) instead of Ethernet, simply substitute PPP for `Ethernet` in step 5.

■ You can also create and delete configurations for the AppleTalk, Modem, and Remote Access control panels by modifying **Script 22.1.**

Script 22.1 This script creates a new TCP/IP configuration with the Network Setup Scripting application.

```
                              script
tell application "Network Setup Scripting"
open database
begin transaction
if not (TCPIP v4 configuration "New Config" exists) then
make new TCPIP v4 configuration "New Config" with properties {connecting via:Ethernet, configuration ¬
method:manual, IP address:"206.14.230.16", subnet mask:"255.255.255.0", implicit search start:"", ¬
implicit search end:"", user mode:basic}
tell TCPIP v4 configuration "New Config"
        make new name server address 1 with data "206.14.230.7"
        make new router address 1 with data "206.14.230.7"
    end tell
  end if
end transaction
  close database
end tell
```

Enabling Multihoming with TCP/IP

With *multihoming*, your single Mac can respond to multiple IP addresses on a single TCP/IP connection. This configuration enables you to run multiple Web sites or other Internet servers with their own dedicated IP addresses.

Open Transport versions 1.3 and later support multihoming for manually configured TCP/IP. (Any version of Mac OS 8.1 or later should have at least version 1.3 of Open Transport.) **Figure 22.3** shows the text file required to define secondary IP addresses for Open Transport.

To enable multihoming in Open Transport, you need to create a specially formatted text file named IP Secondary Addresses and save it in the Preferences folder inside your System Folder. **Script 22.2** makes this process easy. Just set the three list variables at the beginning of the script to include each IP address, its subnet mask, and its router address.

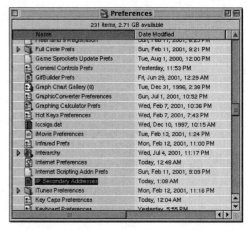

Figure 22.3 The script creates the text file in the Preferences folder that Open Transport requires to enable multiple IP addresses.

Script 22.2 This script creates the text file Open Transport needs to enable your computer to respond to multiple IP addresses.

```
set myIPs to {"192.0.0.1", "192.0.0.2", "192.0.0.3"}
set mySubnets to {"255.255.255.0", "255.255.255.0", "255.255.255.0"}
set myRouters to {"192.0.0.10", "192.0.0.12", ""}
set myIPConfig to ""
repeat with i from 1 to number of items in myIPs
set myIPConfig to myIPConfig & "ip=" & (item i of myIPs) & space
    set myIPConfig to myIPConfig & "sm=" & (item i of mySubnets) & space
    set myIPConfig to myIPConfig & "rt=" & (item i of myRouters) & return
end repeat
tell application "Finder"
    set myPrefs to the path to preferences folder
    set myIPFile to myPrefs & "IP Secondary Addresses" as text
if alias myIPFile exists then delete file myIPFile
set myFileRef to (open for access file myIPFile with write permission)
    write myIPConfig to myFileRef
    close access myFileRef
end tell
```

To enable multihoming with TCP/IP:

1. `set myIPs to {"192.0.0.1", ¬`
`"192.0.0.2", "192.0.0.3"}`
`set mySubnets to {"255.255.255.0", ¬`
`"255.255.255.0", "255.255.255.0"}`
`set myRouters to {"192.0.0.10", ¬`
`"192.0.0.12", ""}`

You begin by defining three lists to hold your secondary IP addresses, as well as subnet masks and router addresses for each. In this case, you define three additional IP addresses.

2. `set myIPConfig to ""`

Next, you initialize an empty string variable to hold the constructed text for the special text file you'll create later in this script.

3. `repeat with i from 1 to number of ¬`
`items in myIPs`

You begin a **repeat** loop to cycle through all the IP addresses in your list of addresses.

4. `set myIPConfig to myIPConfig & "ip=" ¬`
`& (item i of myIPs) & space`
`set myIPConfig to myIPConfig & "sm=" ¬`
`& (item i of mySubnets) & space`
`set myIPConfig to myIPConfig & "rt=" ¬`
`& (item i of myRouters) & return`
`end repeat`

Now you append properly formatted text to your string to define your new IP address and its subnet and router. Here, you use AppleScript's built-in string concatenation symbol, the ampersand (&), to join all your strings and store them in the myIPConfig variable.

continues on next page

ENABLING MULTIHOMING WITH TCP/IP

5. `tell application "Finder"`
   `set myPrefs to the path to ¬`
`preferences folder`
   `set myIPFile to myPrefs & "IP ¬`
`Secondary Addresses" as text`

You construct a path to the final location of your secondary IP address file, starting with the path to your current Preferences folder from the Finder.

6. `if alias myIPFile exists then delete ¬`
`file myIPFile`

You check with the Finder to see whether the file already exists and delete it if it does exist.

7. `set myFileRef to (open for access ¬`
`file myIPFile with write permission)`
`write myIPConfig to myFileRef`
`close access myFileRef`
`end tell`

Now you create the text file with write access, write the string defining your new IPs to it, and close the file.

✔ Tip

- If you omit the subnet or router values, the primary configuration's settings will apply.

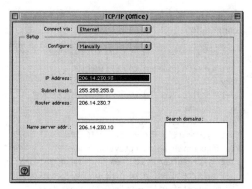

Figure 22.4 The TCP/IP configuration made active by the script, shown in the TCP/IP control panel.

Switching TCP/IP Configurations

The capability to switch TCP/IP configurations easily can be useful if you have different networking environments for your computer. A PowerBook, for example, might use a TCP/IP-enabled Ethernet network during the day and a PPP dial-up account at night. Each mode of accessing the Internet requires a different TCP/IP configuration with its own name server, router, and IP information. In **Script 22.3**, you'll change the active TCP/IP configurations.

Figure 22.4 shows the TCP/IP control panel with the new active configuration set by the script.

To set the active TCP/IP configuration:

1. `set myNewConfigName to "Office"`

   You begin by defining the name of the TCP/IP configuration you want to try to activate.

2. `try`

   Next, you start a `try` block to handle any errors during your work with the Network Setup Scripting application.

3. `tell application "Network Setup ¬ Scripting"`

   You begin your conversation with Network Setup Scripting.

4. `open database`

   You open the network configurations database managed by Network Setup Scripting.

5. `set mytransaction to begin transaction`

   To perform changes in the database, you need to start a transaction so that your changes can't be affected by anyone else who is using the database at the same time.

continues on next page

6. set myCurrentConfig to every TCPIP ¬
v4 configuration whose active is true

You get the list of current TCP/IP configurations that are active (only one, of course).

7. set myCurrentConfig to item 1 of ¬
myCurrentConfig

Because you get a list with only one item in it, you get that item.

8. set myCurrentConfig to name of ¬
myCurrentConfig

Now you can get the name of the active configuration and store it in myCurrentConfig.

9. if myCurrentConfig ≠ myNewConfigName ¬
then

set myNewConfig to every TCPIP v4 ¬
configuration whose name is ¬
myNewConfigName

You check to see whether the desired configuration is already active. If not, you get a list of references to configurations that have a matching name, which should be only one.

10. set myNewConfig to item 1 of ¬
myNewConfig
set active of myNewConfig to true
end if

You get the first item from the list of matching configurations and make it active.

11. end transaction
close database
end tell

You end the transaction and close the database before ending your conversation with Network Setup Scripting.

Script 22.3 This script changes the active TCP/IP configuration.

```
set myNewConfigName to "Office"
try
tell application "Network Setup Scripting"
open database
set mytransaction to begin transaction
set myCurrentConfig to every TCPIP v4 ¬
configuration whose active is true
set myCurrentConfig to item 1 of myCurrentConfig
set myCurrentConfig to name of myCurrentConfig
if myCurrentConfig ≠ myNewConfigName then
        set myNewConfig to every TCPIP v4 ¬
configuration whose name is myNewConfigName
set myNewConfig to item 1 of myNewConfig
        set active of myNewConfig to true
    end if
end transaction
    close database
  end tell
display dialog "Old TCP/IP configuration:" & ¬
myCurrentConfig buttons {"OK"}
on error
    try
        tell application "Network Setup Scripting"
            end transaction
            close database
        end tell
    end try
end try
```

12.
```
display dialog "Old TCP/IP ¬
configuration:" & myCurrentConfig ¬
buttons {"OK"}
```

To inform the user, you display the name of the old configuration.

13.
```
on error
  try
      tell application "Network Setup ¬
Scripting"
          end transaction
          close database
      end tell
  end try
end try
```

In case an error happens during your work on the network configuration database, you want to do your best to close everything properly, so you end your transaction and close the database in your error handler.

Changing Your File-Sharing Status

The capability to change your file-sharing status via AppleScript can be helpful. If you use **Script 22.4** as the basis for a CGI, you could toggle the file-sharing and program-linking state of a Web server remotely over the Internet.

Figure 22.5 shows the file-sharing settings in Script Editor's Event Log window after this script has run.

To toggle your file-sharing and program-linking status:

1. `tell application "File Sharing"`

   You begin by letting AppleScript know that you want to talk to the File Sharing control panel.

2. `set mySharing to file sharing`
   `set file sharing to not mySharing`

   Next, you store the current state of file sharing in a variable called `mySharing`, and you set the file-sharing state to the opposite of the variable's Boolean value, toggling it. (A Boolean value can be either true or false, as you saw in Chapter 3.)

3. `set myLinking to program linking`
   `set program linking to not myLinking`

   You do the same thing with program linking, storing the current state of program linking in a variable and then setting the program-linking state to the opposite of the variable's Boolean value, toggling it.

4. `quit`
   `end tell`

   Finally, you tell the File Sharing control panel to quit and end your conversation with it.

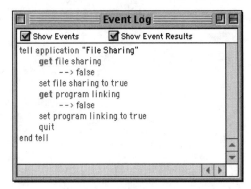

Figure 22.5 The file-sharing settings are shown in the Script Editor's Event Log window after the script has run.

Script 22.4 This script toggles the file-sharing and program-linking states of your computer.

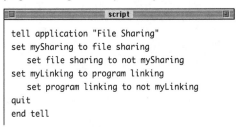

```
tell application "File Sharing"
set mySharing to file sharing
    set file sharing to not mySharing
set myLinking to program linking
    set program linking to not myLinking
quit
end tell
```

Figure 22.6 The File Sharing control panel shows the user created by the script.

Script 22.5 This script creates a new user with the File Sharing control panel.

```
tell application "File Sharing"
set myNewUser to make new user
set the can connect of myNewUser to false
set the can change password of myNewUser to false
set the can do program linking of myNewUser to true
set name of myNewUser to "Steven"
quit
end tell
```

Scripting File Sharing for Users and Groups

The AppleScripts discussed in this section show how you can create new users and add users to groups automatically. You can use such scripts to manage local user and group settings for multiple machines on a local network or even across the Internet by using Program Linking over TCP/IP.

Figure 22.6 shows a new user window in Users & Groups created by **Script 22.5**.

To make a new user in the File Sharing control panel:

1. `tell application "File Sharing"`
   You begin by letting AppleScript know that you want to talk to the File Sharing control panel.

2. `set myNewUser to make new user`
   Next, you have the control panel create a new user and store a reference to that user in a variable called myNewUser.

3. `set the can connect of myNewUser to false`
   You set the can connect property of the new user to false.

4. `set the can change password of ¬ myNewUser to false`
   You also set the can change password property of the new user to false.

5. `set the can do program linking of ¬ myNewUser to true`
   You set the can do program linking property of the new user to true.

6. `set name of myNewUser to "Steven"`
   You set the name of the new user.

7. `quit`
   `end tell`
   Then you ask the control panel to quit and end your conversation.

✔ Tip

■ The File Sharing control panel will not let a script set a user's password. If you need to script new users complete with passwords, try creating a template user with a password and duplicating that user in your script with the `duplicate` command. Or use the third-party Scripting Addition Users and Groups, which lets you change users' passwords from AppleScript. Check `http://www.macscripter.net/` for this OSAX.

Figure 22.7 shows a group containing all defined users created by **Script 22.6**.

To add all existing users to a group:

1. `set myGroupName to "Everybody"`

You begin by setting the name of your group in a variable called `myGroupName`.

2. `tell application "File Sharing"`

Next, you let AppleScript know that you want to talk to the File Sharing control panel.

3. `set myNewGroup to make new group`

Then you have the control panel create a new group.

4. `try`
    `set name of myNewGroup to myGroupName`

Now you try to set the name of the group to your desired name inside an error-handling routine, so that you won't get an error if the name already exists.

5. `on error`
    `delete myNewGroup`
`end try`

If you get an error, you delete the new group that you just created with the `make new group` command so that you can use the existing group with the proper name.

Figure 22.7 The File Sharing control panel's group window shows the group and all users included in it as created by the script.

Script 22.6 This script creates a new group and adds all existing users to that group.

```
set myGroupName to "Everybody"
tell application "File Sharing"
set myNewGroup to make new group
try
        set name of myNewGroup to myGroupName
on error
        delete myNewGroup
    end try
set myUsers to users
repeat with myUser in myUsers
if name of myUser ≠ "Guest" then add myUser ¬
to group myGroupName
    end repeat
quit
end tell
```

Using the Users and Groups Scripting Addition

The Users and Groups OSAX lets you create users for Mac OS 9 with passwords.

The scripting Additon is freeware and was written by Quinn. It can be found at www.osaxen.com.

6. `set myUsers to users`

Now you get a list of all defined users from the control panel and store them in the myUsers variable.

7. `repeat with myUser in myUsers`

You're ready to add each user to the group in a loop.

8. `if name of myUser ≠ "Guest" then add ¬`
`myUser to group myGroupName`
   `end repeat`

"Guest" can't be in any groups, so you add a conditional statement to add users to the group so long as they are not "Guest". Notice the use of the ≠ operator, which you should read as "does not equal."

9. `quit`
`end tell`

At the end of your script, you quit the control panel and end your conversation with it.

GIVE YOUR SCRIPTS A FACE

Figure 23.1 The FaceSpan Project window.

■ Apple's AppleScript Studio offers a development environment that makes Mac OS X Cocoa applications.

■ FaceSpan 3.5.2 is designed to work with Mac OS 9.1. It has been tested successfully in the Classic environment of Mac OS X in a limited fashion.

FaceSpan is a cutting-edge tool for interface design and rapid application development. It gives you the power to build and customize Macintosh applications quickly and easily by using AppleScript as the underlying programming language for the entire application. Using FaceSpan, you can create simple interfaces such as floating tool palettes that give you quick access to your favorite scripts. Or you can create more sophisticated applications that integrate the features of other applications that you control via AppleScript from your FaceSpan project.

Bringing one of your scripts into FaceSpan to give it a complete interface is one of the easiest, most rewarding AppleScripting experiences available.

In this chapter, you'll move your user-creation script from Chapter 22 into FaceSpan.

Figure 23.1 shows FaceSpan's Project window. You'll see this window after you've created a new project.

✔ Tips

■ The news is spreading. To keep up with the times, Digital Technology International is rewriting FaceSpan to bring it to Mac OS X.

Creating a Window with Controls

You'll begin your new project by creating a window and some controls to hold the user-configurable values of your script. First, you'll need to create a new window in the Project window. After you have your new window, you'll create a table and a button.

Make your window look like the one in **Figure 23.2**, naming the text boxes and buttons as shown there. The code was written with references to these object names and won't work if it doesn't find them.

To create a window with controls:

1. Create a new window in the Project window.

2. Name the window main, and set its title property to "User Manager".

3. Open the window.

4. Create a table with two columns and 20 rows, and name the table users.

5. Hide the row names.

6. Create a button and name it Add Users, using the same text for its title.

✔ Tip

■ FaceSpan's object-editing palette gives you complete control of the selected object's properties. **Figure 23.3** shows a user about to edit a button's title property by choosing it from a pop-up menu of properties.

Figure 23.2 The window you create with all the controls you need.

Figure 23.3 Changing a button's title by choosing the title property from the editing palette's pop-up menu.

Scripting FaceSpan

All the scripts in this chapter were designed and tested for FaceSpan 3.5.2.

FaceSpan is developed by Digital Technology International (http://www.facespan.com/).

Figure 23.4 The Project script window is open, with your script added to the default script.

Script 23.1 The main run handler for your project goes in the project script.

```
on run
    open window "main"
tell application "File Sharing"
        set file sharing to false
        quit
    end tell
end run
```

Entering the Project Script

The project script is the main code for your FaceSpan script application. Click the Project Script button to open the project script, and paste the script you'll create in this section into the run handler in the default project script. The following exercise covers every line of **Script 23.1**.

Figure 23.4 shows the Project Script button in the Project window.

To enter your project script:

1. on run
    open window "main"

Inside your FaceSpan project script, use your main run handler to open your window.

2. tell application "File Sharing"
        set file sharing to false
        quit
    end tell
end run

You also take this chance to turn file sharing off, because your Scripting Addition Users and Groups can't make new users when file sharing is running.

Adding Scripts to Your Window and Controls

Now you're ready to add scripts to your window and the window's buttons. **Script 23.2** is a simple window script that preserves the settings of your window whenever it is closed.

Figure 23.5 shows you how to open a script for the selected object in FaceSpan.

To add a script to your window:

1. Select the window, and choose Object Script from the Object menu.

2. `on close`

    Your window, main, has only one script attached to it. This script runs when the window is closed.

3. `save window "main"`
    `end close`

    The script saves the states of all objects in the window before closing it, preserving all data entered in the table.

Script 23.3 Creates new file sharing users.

To add a script to the window's button:

1. Click the Add Users button.

2. Choose Object Script from the Object menu.

3. `on click`

    Your Add Users button has only one script attached to it. This script runs when the user clicks the button.

4. `display dialog "Add all users?"`
    `if the button returned of the result ¬`
    `= "OK" then`

    You prompt the user to make sure that he or she really wants to add users to this computer.

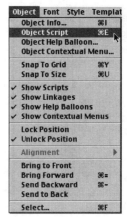

Figure 23.5 Opening the object script from the Object menu in FaceSpan.

Script 23.2 The window's close handler uses the save command to preserve the settings of the window when it is reopened later.

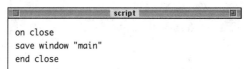

```
on close
save window "main"
end close
```

5. `set myContents to contents of table "users"`

Next, you store the nested lists that make up the data of your two-column table in a variable, myContents.

6. `repeat with myRow in myContents`

Now you are ready to loop through all rows in the table.

7. `set myNewUser to item 1 of myRow as string`
`set myNewPassword to item 2 of myRow as string`

You retrieve the values for the user and password from the current row in your loop.

8. `if myNewUser ≠ "" and myNewPassword ≠ "" then`

Next, you make sure that the user and password entries do not contain blank strings.

continues on next page

Script 23.3 This script is attached to the Add Users button in the window to provide functionality when a user clicks the button.

```
on click
display dialog "Add all users?"
    if the button returned of the result = "OK" then
set myContents to contents of table "users"
repeat with myRow in myContents
set myNewUser to item 1 of myRow as string
        set myNewPassword to item 2 of myRow as string
if myNewUser ≠ "" and myNewPassword ≠ "" then
try
                get user info myNewUser
on error
                create user name myNewUser password myNewPassword with linking, login and change password
            end try
        end if
end repeat
    end if
end click
```

9. `try`

    `get user info myNewUser`

You try to get information about the new user. If this operation succeeds, the user already exists, so you don't want to do anything.

10. `on error`

  `create user name myNewUser password myNewPassword with linking, login and change password`
`end try`
      `end if`

If the attempt to get information fails, you can assume that no user of the new name exists, so you use your Scripting Addition's `create user` command to create a new user with a password and program linking, password changing, and login access.

11. `end repeat`

  `end if`
`end click`

You continue your loop through all rows in the table before ending.

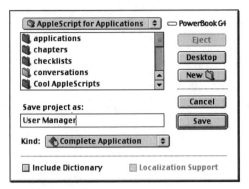

Figure 23.6 FaceSpan's Save dialog box, set to save your project as a complete application.

Figure 23.7 Your FaceSpan project running as a stand-alone application.

Saving the Project As an Application

Finally, you can save your FaceSpan project. **Figure 23.6** shows FaceSpan's Save dialog box configured to save the current project as a stand-alone application. **Figure 23.7** shows your project running as a stand-alone application.

To save a project as an application:

◆ When you're ready to save your project as a stand-alone application, choose Save As from the File menu.

DEBUGGING
APPLESCRIPT

AppleScripts can be easy to write. AppleScript looks like simple written English in its most elegant object-model form. With the myriad applications that support AppleScript, however, unique commands and unusual implementations have left many scripters struggling to get the syntax exactly right.

In this chapter, you'll look at the debugging tools of Apple's free Script Editor, as well as three commercial AppleScript editors: Scripter, Script Debugger, and FaceSpan.

The functioning of your AppleScripts can also be affected by how your system software is configured. This chapter concludes with a look at the System components that AppleScript requires to work properly in System 7.x; Mac OS 8, 8.5, 9.x; and Mac OS X.

The hottest news for Mac OS X is the arrival of AppleScript Studio for Mac OS X 10.1. This development environment lets scripters build Cocoa application using AppleScript. See Chapter 4 for more information on AppleScript Studio.

✔ Tip

■ Other script editors are available, including the popular editor Smile.

Debugging with Script Editor

Apple's Script Editor has two basic debugging tools available for your use. The Event Log window allows you to watch the Apple Events sent to other applications and the results those applications return. The Result window shows the most recent evaluated result of an expression. These windows are invaluable tools for debugging scripts in Script Editor. **Figure 24.1** shows the Event Log window, and **Figure 24.2** shows the Result window.

To use Script Editor to debug your scripts:

◆ Always test your scripts in Script Editor before saving them. When an error occurs during execution, Script Editor conveniently highlights the offending line of code in your script.

◆ Leave the Event Log window open at all times when you run scripts from within Script Editor.

◆ Open the Result window to see the result of running a single line of code in Script Editor.

◆ Use AppleScript's special `stop log` and `start log` commands in your script to hide and show selected portions of your code's activity in the Event Log, instead of having to look at all the results of your entire script.

Figure 24.1 The Event Log window displays all events sent by your script and any results returned.

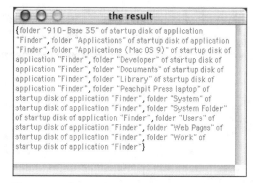

Figure 24.2 The Result window of Script Editor displays the most recent result returned from any executed script.

◆ Insert temporary `display dialog` commands into your script to display the contents of variables during your script's execution. When your script is debugged, you can delete any of these commands easily.

◆ In Mac OS 8.5 and later, you can insert temporary `say` commands into your script to have AppleScript speak the contents of variables during execution instead of using `display dialog`.

◆ For the best error handling, add to your scripts complete `try` statements that deal intelligently with errors. See Chapter 3 for more information.

Using Script Editor

Script Editor is installed as part of the recommended installation for Mac OS 9 and Mac OS X.

Script Editor 1.6 and 1.7 is developed by Apple Computer Inc. (http://www.apple.com/).

Debugging with Scripter 2.5

Scripter 2.5, from Main Event Software, offers a unique suite of AppleScript debugging tools available. The application palette lets you put the dictionaries of the programs you script just a click away. **Figure 24.3** shows the application toolbar in Scripter.

Scripter's Build a Command window (**Figure 24.4**) uses AppleScript dictionaries to help you construct legal command syntax based on a program's own dictionary definitions.

To use Scripter to debug your scripts:

◆ For quick access to dictionaries, assign space on the application palette for your most frequently scripted programs.

◆ Use the Build a Command window to understand command syntax when scripting.

◆ Test your CGI handlers inside Scripter by calling them from Scripter's Call Box.

All the debugging techniques recommended for Script Editor also work in Scripter.

✔ Tips

■ Scripter does not compile on run handlers, which are optional anyway in AppleScript. If you use Scripter, be sure to omit any on. . . run. . . end. . . run lines you might have.

■ Scripter is designed for Mac OS 9 and earlier.

Figure 24.3 Scripter's application palette allows quick access to specific applications' AppleScript dictionaries.

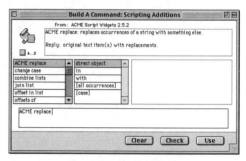

Figure 24.4 The Build a Command window walks you through the construction of proper AppleScript syntax.

Using Scripter

Scripter 2.5 is developed by Main Event Software (http://www.mainevent.com/).

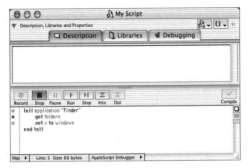

Figure 24.5 Script Debugger's Script window with a single debugging breakpoint set.

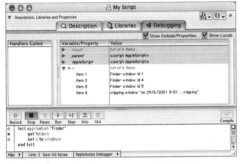

Figure 24.6 The Debugging pane of the Script window shows the values of all objects, variables and properties of a script.

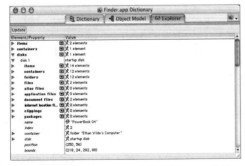

Figure 24.7 The Explorer pane of the Dictionary window shows real-time data for all of an application's objects and properties.

Debugging with Script Debugger 3

Script Debugger 3.0, from Late Night Software, is the only AppleScript editor that is itself scriptable. It is also the only commercial script editor that is Mac OS X-native.

Script Debugger includes an amazing assortment of debugging tools, including its own AppleScript Debugger OSA language, which lets you step through your scripts one line at a time anywhere your script runs. No other tool offers this level of debugging support.

The Script window includes breakpoints, which let you indicate a point in code at which you want execution to be halted (**Figure 24.5**). The Data window (**Figure 24.6**) lets you track the current value of any variable or property you type.

Script Debugger's dictionary includes an amazing Explorer pane that displays live results of all AppleScript objects and properties in any object-model-compliant application. **Figure 24.7** shows the Dictionary window's Explorer pane for the Finder.

DEBUGGING WITH SCRIPT DEBUGGER 3

To use Script Debugger to debug your scripts:

◆ Use breakpoints to interrupt script execution or pause so that you can step through your code line by line as it runs, checking values and monitoring for errors.

◆ Add important variable and property names to the Data window to track your script's activities more closely.

◆ Beyond the typical techniques, Script Debugger's AppleScript Debugger OSA component lets you add breakpoints and step through your code one line at a time.

◆ Script Debugger's AppleScript Debugger OSA component can also be used from FaceSpan, compiled CGI applets, and other scripting environments. When a breakpoint is hit, Script Debugger comes to the front and displays the running script.

All the debugging techniques recommended for Script Editor also work in Script Debugger.

Using Script Debugger

Script Debugger 3.0 is native in both Mac OS 9 and Mac OS X.

Script Debugger 3.0 is developed by Late Night Software (http://www.latenightsw.com/).

Figure 24.8 FaceSpan's Dictionary window displays an application's objects as text that can be dragged into a script.

Figure 24.9 The Script window of FaceSpan has pull-down menus to help you construct code for event handlers and object properties.

Debugging with FaceSpan 3.5

FaceSpan is not just a complete application development environment for AppleScript; it also includes script-editing and debugging capabilities. FaceSpan's Dictionary window (**Figure 24.8**) shows all events and objects as text that can be dragged into the Script window.

The dictionary also remembers the dictionaries of applications you use. FaceSpan's Script window (**Figure 24.9**) offers pull-down menus for objects and events, enabling you to insert script code quickly and easily.

To use FaceSpan to debug your scripts:

◆ Keep the Dictionary window open for quick syntax reference and drag-and-drop script construction.

◆ Use the Script window's pull-down menus to insert FaceSpan events and objects.

◆ Open FaceSpan's Message window all the way to see the Event Log.

All the debugging techniques recommended for Script Editor also work in FaceSpan.

Using FaceSpan

FaceSpan 3.5.2 is developed by Digital Technology International (http://www.facespan.com/).

DEBUGGING WITH FACESPAN 3.5

Configuring Your System Software Properly for AppleScript

As AppleScript has matured, its System Folder components and their placement have changed slightly from System 7.x to Mac OS 8 and again in Mac OS 8.5 and 9.x.

Finally, in Mac OS X, everything changed entirely. In this domain-based environment, scripting additions and scripts can have multiple homes.

The four figures to the right show the minimum required System Folder components and their proper placement for each version of Mac OS. **Figure 24.10** shows the components for System versions 7.x. **Figure 24.11** shows the components for Mac OS 8.0 through 8.1. **Figure 24.12** shows the components for Mac OS 8.5 through 9.x. **Figure 24.13** shows the components for Mac OS 9.1.

To use the ScriptingAdditions folder in Mac OS X:

◆ All System Scripting Additions reside in the ScriptingAdditions folder inside the System Folder's Library folder.

◆ Scripting Additions to be made available to every user on the machine go in the ScriptingAdditions folder in the root-level Library folder.

◆ Each user can keep Scripting Additions just for his own use in the ScriptingAdditions folder inside the Library folder in the user's home folder.

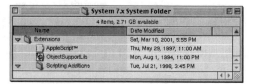

Figure 24.10 Proper System software configuration for System 7.x.

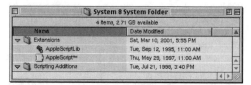

Figure 24.11 Proper System software configuration for Mac OS 8.0 and 8.1.

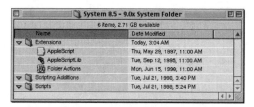

Figure 24.12 Proper System software configuration for Mac OS 8.5 through 9.x.

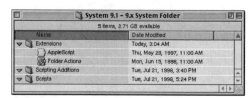

Figure 24.13 Proper System software configuration for Mac OS 9.1.

CONFIGURING YOUR SYSTEM SOFTWARE

Table 24.1

AppleScript Components and Mac OS Versions

MAC OS	APPLESCRIPT	EXTENSIONS FOLDER ITEMS
7.1.1	1.0	AppleScript, ObjectSupportLib, ScriptingAdditions folder
7.5x-7.6x	1.1	AppleScript, AppleScriptLib, ObjectSupportLib, ScriptingAdditions folder
8.0–8.1	1.1.2	AppleScript, AppleScriptLib
8.5–9.0x	1.3.4-1.4.0	AppleScript, AppleScriptLib, Folder Actions
9.1	1.5.5	AppleScript, Folder Actions
9.2.1	1.6	AppleScript, Folder Actions
X 10.0.0-10.0.4	1.6.0	Not applicable
X.10.1	1.7.0	Not applicable

To use the ScriptingAdditions folder in Mac OS 8.x and 9.x

◆ Beginning with version 8.0 of the Mac OS, the ScriptingAdditions folder migrated to live inside the System Folder. Earlier versions of the system software expected the ScriptingAdditions folder to be inside the Extensions folder.

◆ If you can't seem to use commands from scripting additions, or if scripts won't run or compile properly, check the location of the ScriptingAdditions folder. Some software installers add a ScriptingAdditions folder to the Extensions folder, confusing AppleScript. You can solve this problem by moving any Scripting Additions or dialects to the real ScriptingAdditions folder right inside the System Folder. Be sure to delete the extra Scripting-Additions folder.

To use ObjectSupportLib:

◆ The ObjectSupportLib file is required in System 7.x versions of AppleScript. Some versions of this file are faulty, however, and prevent AppleScript scripts from running properly. ObjectSupportLib versions 1.0.4 and 1.1.1 break some applications' Apple Events handling.

◆ Delete any copy of ObjectSupportLib from your System Folder if you're running Mac OS 8.0 or later.

◆ Go to the Technical Information Library at http://til.info.apple.com/ and search for *objectsupportlib* to find more details.

✔ Tip

■ Mac OS X marks a new era of change and improvement for AppleScript. Using Sherlock, search the Apple Technical Information Library (TIL) for *applescript*.

LEARNING MORE ABOUT APPLESCRIPT

In this appendix, you'll find out where to learn more about AppleScript on the World Wide Web, through mailing lists, and in print.

Many wonderful scripting additions and scriptable applications could not be covered in this book. Wander the Web and check out some of the online AppleScript resources to continue your discovery of the powers of AppleScript.

AppleScript Resources on the World Wide Web

Check out these Web sites to further your AppleScript education.

◆ http://www.apple.com/applescript

Apple's official AppleScript Web site (**Figure A.1**) is not to be missed for official news on AppleScript.

◆ http://www.macscripter.net/

"Your best source for all things AppleScript" is this site's tag line. Visit, and you will find a complete site with regular updates. Links to most AppleScript resources online are available.

◆ http://www.applescriptsourcebook.com/

The AppleScript Sourcebook is the best place to find detailed explanations, analyses, and observations on the AppleScript language. The site is maintained by Bill Cheeseman.

◆ http://listserv.dartmouth.¬ edu/archives/macscrpt.html

This site hosts the Macscrpt mailing list's Web archives (**Figure A.2**). This searchable archive of the Macintosh Scripting Systems mailing list is an invaluable resource for up-to-the-minute AppleScript discussions, news, and scripter-to-scripter help.

◆ http://www.scriptweb.com/

This site is a long-running reference to Mac scripting, with a database of Scripting Additions (OSAX) www.osaxen.com.

◆ http://www.maccentral.com/

This site features Bill Briggs' regular series on AppleScript, including sample scripts and detailed explanations.

Figure A.1 Apple's official AppleScript Web site at http://www.apple.com/applescript.

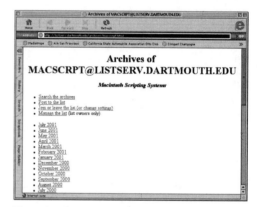

Figure A.2 The Macscrpt mailing-list archives at http://listserv.dartmouth.edu/archives/ macscrpt.html.

◆ `ftp://mirror.apple.com/mirrors¬`
`/gaea.scriptweb.com/`

This site is Apple's archived mirror site for the GAEA scriptweb archive of AppleScript files. It includes many older Scripting Additions, shareware, and utilities.

◆ `http://justapplescript.weblogs.com/`

Ed Stockly's very personal diary of AppleScript observations offers interesting observations and links to AppleScript resources.

◆ `http://www.latenightsw.com/`

This site is the Web site of Late Night Software, creator of Script Debugger.

◆ `http://www.mainevent.com/`

This site is the Web site of Main Event Software, creator of Scripter and PhotoScripter.

◆ `http://www.facespan.com/`

This site is the official FaceSpan Web site.

AppleScript Resources

AppleScript Mailing Lists

Check out these mailing lists for the latest AppleScript info.

◆ **Macscrpt mailing list.** To subscribe, visit `http://listserv.dartmouth.edu/archives/macscrpt.html`, or send e-mail to `listserv@dartmouth.edu`. Put SUB MACSCRPT and your name in the body of the message.

◆ **Apple's AppleScript user mailing list.** Visit `http://www.lists.apple.com/mailman/listinfo/applescript-users` to find out how to subscribe.

APPLESCRIPT MAILING LISTS

APPLESCRIPT
REFERENCE

This appendix covers just about every one of AppleScript's standard commands, control statements, handlers, references, operators, variable and property assignments, and constants.

For information on other commands, statements, and objects, see the dictionary for the specific application or Scripting Addition.

Visit http://www.apple.com/applescript to find Adobe Acrobat versions of the official AppleScript Language Guide and other useful documentation for downloading and printing.

Commands

Optional terms are shown in brackets: [optional].

Italicized placeholder terms (such as *reference*) are meant to be replaced with appropriate information. See "Placeholder Definitions" later in this appendix for detailed definitions of placeholder terms.

Each command definition includes an example code snippet with description.

activate

- ◆ `activate`
- ◆ `tell application "FreeHand 8.0" to ¬`
  `activate`

  You tell FreeHand to become the frontmost application.

close

- ◆ `close reference`
- ◆ `close reference saving in reference`
- ◆ `tell application "Fetch" to close ¬`
  `transfer window 1`

  You tell Fetch to close the current transfer window.

copy

- ◆ `copy expression to variable`
- ◆ `copy 4*2 to x`

  You copy the results of the calculation 4 x 2 into the variable x, which will contain 8 after this line is executed.

- ◆ `tell application "Photoshop 5.0" ¬`
  `to copy`

  The standard AppleScript copy command has nothing to do with the Clipboard. Some applications may implement their own copy command used within a `tell` statement. In this case, using PhotoScripter and Photoshop's copy command copies the current selection in Photoshop to the Clipboard.

- ◆ `set myList to {1,2,3}`
  `copy myList to mySecondList`
  `set myThirdList to myList`
  `set item 2 of myList to 4`
  `get item 2 of myThirdList`

  AppleScript's copy and set commands are similar, but they differ in one unique way: the copy command simply copies data from one container to another. In this example, the list in `myList` is replicated into `mySecondList`. The set command, however, tries to share data between containers. Therefore, this example yields the result 4, because when you change item 2 of `myList`, you're also changing item 2 of `myThirdList`, because you used a set command to share the data between the two variables. The value in item 2 of `mySecondList` will remain the original 2, because you used copy to duplicate the data from `myList` into `mySecondList`.

count

- ◆ `number of objectClass in reference`
- ◆ `count every objectClass in reference`
- ◆ `set x to {1,2,3}`
  `get number of items in x`

  You put the list {1,2,3}into the variable x. Then you retrieve the count of items in the list contained by x. The result is 3.

delete

- ◆ `delete reference`
- ◆ `tell application "Finder" to delete ¬`
  `file "Temp" of folder "Files" of ¬`
  `startup disk`

  You tell the Finder to delete the file named Temp located in the Files folder on your startup disk.

duplicate

- ◆ duplicate *reference*
- ◆ duplicate *reference* to *reference*
- ◆ tell application "Photoshop 5.0" ¬
  to duplicate layer 1 of document 1

  You tell Photoshop to duplicate the first layer of your current document.

exists

- ◆ exists *reference*
- ◆ *reference* exists
- ◆ tell application "Finder"
     if disk "HD" exists then beep
  end tell

  You tell the Finder to have your computer beep if a volume named HD is mounted on your Desktop.

get

- ◆ get *expression*
- ◆ get *expression* as *objectClass*
- ◆ get "My name "&return&"is Mac. " ¬
  as string

  Returns this string to the result:

- ◆ My name
  is Mac

launch

- ◆ launch
- ◆ tell application "Netscape ¬
  Navigator 4.07" to launch

  Tells Netscape to behave as though it were double-clicked in the Finder. This command is redundant unless all you want to do is launch the program, because any command sent to an application will cause it to launch automatically if it is not running.

make

- ◆ make [new] *objectClass* at *reference*
- ◆ make [new] *objectClass* at *reference* ¬
  with properties { *propertyName*: ¬
  propertyValue [,*propertyName*: ¬
  propertyValue]...}
- ◆ make [new] *objectClass* at *reference* ¬
  with data *value*
- ◆ tell application "Finder" to make ¬
  new folder at startup disk with ¬
  properties {name: "New"}

  You tell the Finder to create a folder named New on the startup disk.

move

- ◆ move *reference* to *reference*
- ◆ tell application "Photoshop 5.0" to ¬
  move selection to {10 as pixels,10 ¬
  as pixels}

  You tell Photoshop to move the current selection to the coordinates 10 pixels in the x plane and 10 pixels in the y plane.

open

- ◆ open *reference*
- ◆ open *listOfReferences*
- ◆ tell application "Quark Xpress" ¬
  to open alias "HD:Quark Doc"

  You tell Quark to open a file named Quark Doc on the volume named HD.

print

- ◆ print *reference*
- ◆ tell application "Claris Emailer ¬
  2.0" to print window 1

  You tell Emailer to print the frontmost window on the default printer.

quit

- ◆ quit
- ◆ tell application "Microsoft Word" to quit

  You tell the Word application to quit.

run

- run

- run *reference*

- tell application "FileMaker Pro 4.0" ¬
  to run

  You tell the FileMaker application to run. This command is redundant unless all you want to do is run the application, because sending any command to an application will cause it to run if it is not running. Sending this event to a stay-open script application or FaceSpan application will cause that script to execute its on run handler.

save

- save *reference* in *reference*

- tell application "FreeHand 8.0" to ¬
  save in file "HD:image.jpg" as JPEG

  You tell FreeHand to save the current document as a JPEG with the file name image.jpg on the volume HD.

set

- set *variable* to *expression*

- set *reference* to *expression*

- tell application "Finder" to set ¬
  the name of file "Test" of startup ¬
  disk to "New Test"

  You tell the Finder to rename the file named Test on your startup drive to New Test by having the Finder set the name property of the file.

- set myList to {1,2,3}
  copy myList to mySecondList
  set myThirdList to myList
  set item 2 of myList to 4
  get item 2 of myThirdList

AppleScript's copy and set commands are similar, but they differ in one unique way: the copy command simply copies data from one container to another.
In this example, the list in myList is replicated into mySecondList. The set command, however, tries to share data between containers. Therefore, this example yields the result 4, because when you change item 2 of myList, you're also changing item 2 of myThirdList because you used a set command to share the data between the two variables. The value in item 2 of mySecondList will remain the original 2, because you used copy to duplicate the data from myList into mySecondList.

start log

- start log

- start log

  This command is relevant only when you're running your script within Script Editor with the Event Log window open. When AppleScript encounters this command during the execution of a script, it begins displaying event execution and results information normally in the Event Log window.

stop log

- stop log

- stop log

  This command is relevant only when you're running your script within Script Editor with the Event Log window open. When AppleScript encounters this command during the execution of a script, it stops displaying information in the Event Log window until a start log command is encountered.

Control Statements

if

◆ if *boolean* then *statement*

◆ if *boolean* [then]
   [*statement*]...
  [else if *boolean* [then]
   [*statement*]...]...
  [else
   [*statement*]...]
  end [if]

◆ if 2>3 then beep

This statement will not result in a beep being generated, because the Boolean test 2>3 results in false. See "Comparisons and Control Statements" in this appendix and Chapter 3 for more information on if.

repeat

◆ repeat
   [*statement*]...
   [exit repeat]...
  end [repeat]

◆ repeat *integer* [times]
   [*statement*]...
  end [repeat]

◆ repeat while *boolean*
   [*statement*]...
  end [repeat]

◆ repeat until *boolean*
   [*statement*]...
  end [repeat]

◆ repeat with *variable* from *integer* ¬
  to *integer* [by *integer*]
   [*statement*]...
  end [repeat]

◆ repeat with *variable* in *list*
   [*statement*]...
  end [repeat]

◆ repeat with x from 1 to 10
    display dialog x
  end repeat

This code will generate a loop that runs for 10 cycles, incrementing the value in the variable x from 1 to 10. In each cycle, a dialog box displays the current value of x. See "Repeat Loops" in Chapter 3 for more information.

tell

◆ tell reference to statement

◆ tell *reference*
   [*statement*]...
  end [tell]

◆ tell application "Sherlock" to quit

Sends the quit command to the Sherlock application.

try

◆ try
   [*statement*]...
  on error ¬
  [*variable*]¬
  [number *variable*]¬
  [from *variable*]¬
  [partial result *variable*]¬
  [to *variable*]
   [*statement*]...
  end [try]

◆ try
   quit
  on error myErr
   display dialog myErr
  end try

This try statement will execute the error handler if the quit command fails, displaying a dialog box that shows the error-message string. See "Error Handling" in Chapter 3 for more information.

with timeout

◆ with timeout [of] *integer* seconds
   [*statement*]...
end [timeout]

◆ with timeout of 50 seconds
   tell application "Netscape
Navigator 4.0"
    OpenURL
"http://www.apple.com/"
  end tell
end timeout

You tell Netscape to open the URL
http://www.apple.com/, allowing as
much as 50 seconds for the operation to
be completed. See "Waiting with Timeout"
in Chapter 3 for more information.

considering

◆ considering *attribute*
[,*attribute*... and *attribute*] [but
ignoring *attribute* [,*attribute*...
and *attribute*]]
   [*statement*]...
end considering

◆ considering case
   if "Help" starts with "H" then
beep
end considering

This code will generate a beep, because
your string does start with a capital H
and you are conducting the comparison
with case sensitivity turned on.

ignoring

◆ ignoring *attribute* [,*attribute*...
and *attribute*] [but considering
attribute [,*attribute*... and
attribute]]
   [*statement*]...
end ignoring

◆ ignoring application responses
   tell application "Finder" to
duplicate alias "HD:My Folder"
   tell application "Finder" to
duplicate alias "HD:My Other Folder"
end ignoring

By ignoring application responses, you
have the Finder duplicate two folders
simultaneously. Your script does not wait
for a response from each of the duplicate
commands.

Attributes for Considering and Ignoring

◆ application responses

If ignored, AppleScript won't wait for responses from applications before proceeding to the next statement in a script. Any results or errors returned are ignored.

◆ case

If considered, AppleScript makes string comparisons with case sensitivity.

◆ diacriticals

If ignored, AppleScript ignores diacritical marks in string comparisons.

◆ expansion

If ignored, AppleScript sees æ, Æ, œ, and Œ as single characters and not equal to the character pairs ae, AE, oe, and OE.

◆ hyphens

If ignored, AppleScript ignores hyphens in string comparisons.

◆ punctuation

If ignored, AppleScript ignores punctuation marks in string comparisons.

◆ white space

If ignored, AppleScript ignores spaces, tab characters, and return characters in string comparisons.

Handlers

Handlers are covered in depth in Chapter 3.

on

◆ on *subroutineName* ([*variable1* ¬
[,*variable2*]...])
 [*statement*]...
 [return *expression*]...
end [subroutineName]

◆ on showScore(score)
display dialog score
end showScore

You can create your own functions, or *subroutines,* within your scripts. These custom handlers can receive values and return resulting values. This example shows a dialog box that displays the value passed to it. See "Handlers" in Chapter 3 for more information on creating your own handlers.

on idle

◆ on idle
 [*statement*]...
end [idle]

◆ on idle
 set x to x+1
end idle

This built-in handler will execute every 30 seconds by default while your script application is running.

on open

♦ on open (*reference*)
   [*statement*]...
  end [open]

♦ on open (*listOfReferences*)
   [*statement*]...
  end [open]

♦ on open (myfiles)
   tell application "Finder" to ¬
  reveal myfiles
  end open

This built-in handler is executed when your script is saved as an application and items are dropped on the application's icon in the Finder. References to the items dropped on the application are passed to the handler. This example has the Finder show all items dropped on the script application. See "Making Drag-and-Drop Applications with on open" in Chapter 3 for more information.

on quit

♦ on quit
   [*statement*]...
   [continue quit]
  end [quit]

♦ on quit
   close access myfile
   continue quit
  end quit

This built-in handler is executed when your script application receives the quit Apple Event before your script application does its own quit routine. Include a continue quit statement at the end of your handler to be sure that AppleScript gets a chance to quit your stay-open script application properly. This example closes the file referenced by myfile before quitting.

on run

♦ on run
   [*statement*]...
  end

♦ on run
   display dialog "Hello World"
  end

This built-in handler executes whenever your script is run, from Script Editor, as a compiled script or as a stand-alone script application. If you have loose code in your script, AppleScript assumes that the code is your implied on run handler. You can't have both loose code and an explicit on run handler in a script. See "Using on run and Saving Scripts As Applications" in Chapter 3 for more information.

References

AppleScript lets you refer to objects in applications and in the operating system by using references. A *reference* identifies an object by describing something unique about the object, such as its index location, its name, or a particular property.

ID

objectClass ID *IDvalue*

◆ tell application "FileMaker Pro 4.0" ¬
  to get cell "Name" of record ID ¬
  myID

  You tell FileMaker Pro to return the value in the field "Name" for the record with the ID value stored in the variable myID.

  Not all applications support IDs.

Index

first *objectClass*

second *objectClass*

third *objectClass*

fourth *objectClass*

fifth *objectClass*

sixth *objectClass*

seventh *objectClass*

eighth *objectClass*

ninth *objectClass*

tenth *objectClass*

integer st *objectClass*

integer nd *objectClass*

integer rd *objectClass*

integer th *objectClass*

last *objectClass*

front *objectClass*

back *objectClass*

middle *objectClass*

some *objectClass*

every *objectClass*

every *objectClass* from *reference* to *reference*

objectClass from *reference* to *reference*

objectClass *integer* through *integer*

objectClass *integer* through *integer*

objectClass *integer* through *integer*

objectClass *integer* through *integer*

set x to {1,2,3,5}

  get the third item of x

  This code generates the result 3.

Name

objectClass named *string*

◆ tell application "Finder" to get
  label index of file named "My File"
  of startup disk

  You tell the Finder to return the label
  index property for a file looked up by
  name.

Property matching

reference whose

reference where

◆ tell application "Finder" to get
  name of every item of startup disk
  where kind is "folder"

  The result of this code is a list of every
  item in your startup disk's top directory
  that is a folder.

Relative

objectClass before *reference*

objectClass front of *reference*

objectClass in front of *reference*

objectClass after *reference*

objectClass back of *reference*

objectClass in back of *reference*

in *reference* in *reference*

of *reference* of *reference*

◆ set x to character 2 of word 3 of
  "Hey you there"

  This code generates the result h.

Operators

Operators are covered in detail in Chapter 3.

Table B.1

Arithmetic Operators			
OPERATOR	MEANING	EXAMPLE	VALID VALUE TYPES
^	Raise to the power of	2^4=16	number
*	Multiply	1*3=3	number
+	Add	2+7=9	date, number
-	Subtract	5-2=3	date, number
/	Divide	8/2=4	number
div	Divide without remainder	11 div 2=5	number
mode	Divide returning remainder	11 mod 2=1	number

Table B.2

Logical Operators
OPERATOR MEANING EXAMPLE
and returns true is both tests are true
x and y returns true only if x is true and y is true.
or returns true is either test is true
x or y returns true as long as either x or y is true.
not returns true if test is false; returns false if test is true
not x returns false if x is true.
not x returns false if x is true.

Containment operators

contains

- *list* contains *list*
- *record* contains *record*
- *string* contains *string*

does not contain

- *list* does not contain *list*
- *record* does not contain *record*
- *string* does not contain *string*

ends with

- *list* ends with *list*
- *string* ends with *string*

is in

- *list* is in *list*
- *record* is in *record*
- *string* is in *string*

is not in

- *list* is not in *list*
- *record* is not in *record*
- *string* is not in *string*

starts with

- *list* starts with *list*
- *string* starts with *string*

Comparison operators

=

- equal
- equals
- equal to
- is
- is equal to

  expression = *expression*

≠

- does not equal
- doesn't equal
- is not
- is not equal to
- isn't
- isn't equal to

  expression ≠ *expression*

<

- comes before
- is less than
- is not greater than or equal to
- isn't greater than or equal to
- less than

  date < *date*

  integer < *integer*

  real < *real*

  string < *string*

>

- comes after
- greater than
- is greater than
- is not less than or equal to
- isn't less than or equal to

  date > *date*

  integer > *integer*

  real > *real*

  string > *string*

≤

<=

- ◆ does not come after
- ◆ doesn't come after
- ◆ is less than or equal to
- ◆ is not greater than
- ◆ isn't greater than
- ◆ less than or equal to

  date ≤ date

  integer ≤ integer

  real ≤ real

  string ≤ string

≥

>=

- ◆ does not come before
- ◆ doesn't come before
- ◆ greater than or equal to
- ◆ is greater than or equal to
- ◆ is not less than
- ◆ isn't less than

  date ≥ date

  integer ≥ integer

  real ≥ real

  string ≥ string

Concatenation operator

&

string & string

list & list

Value type/class coercion operator

as

- ◆ `set x to 1 as string`

  When you `set` a variable or retrieve a value from an application, using *as* tells AppleScript to try coerce the value to become the class or type you're requesting. If you don't use *as* when getting data from an application, values will be returned as the types that are defined in the application's dictionary. When you set a variable, as in this example, using *as* makes AppleScript coerce the conversion of the value to the type you want. In most cases, AppleScript will convert values to the type required by a command automatically.

- ◆ `set x to number as string`

  Any number can be coerced into a string.

- ◆ `set x to date as string`

  Any date can be coerced into a string. You can also use the date constant to create date values: `set x to date "8/2/67"`.

- ◆ `set x to string as number`

  Any string that is a valid number, such as "200", can be coerced to a number.

- ◆ `set x to reference as string`

  Any alias reference or file specification can be coerced to a string. Aliases must refer to an existing file; file specifications can refer to files that haven't been created yet.

OPERATORS

Variable and Property Assignments

Variable assignment

- ◆ copy *expression* to *variable*
- ◆ copy *reference* to *variable*
- ◆ set *variable* to *expression*
- ◆ set *variable* to *reference*
- ◆ set x to 10

  This code stores the value 10 in the variable x.

Global-variable declaration

- ◆ global *variable* [, *variable*]...
- ◆ global k

  This code establishes the variable k as a global variable whose value will be directly accessible from all handlers in your script.

Local-variable declaration

- ◆ local *variable* [, *variable*]...
- ◆ local z

  This code establishes the variable z as a local variable. You never need to define local variables explicitly, because they are declared automatically when a value is assigned to them.

Script property assignment

- ◆ property *propertyName* : *expression*
- ◆ property myname: "John Doe"

  This code establishes the property myname and assigns the string value "John Doe" to the property. Property values survive across separate executions of a script and are handy places to store preference settings for a script's behavior.

Constants and Predefined Variables

current application

◆ *reference*

The default target application.

false

◆ *boolean*

The Boolean false value.

it

◆ *reference*

The default target.

me

◆ *reference*

The current script; used in tell me to call handlers of the current script.

pi

◆ *real*

The value π (approximately 3.14159).

◆ **result**

◆ *any value type or class*

The result returned by the most recently executed command or expression.

return

◆ *string*

A return character: ASCII character 13.

space

◆ *string*

A space character: ASCII character 32.

tab

◆ *string*

A tab character: ASCII character 9.

text item delimiters

◆ AppleScript's text item delimiters

◆ text item delimiters of AppleScript

◆ *list*

The text item delimiters property is a list of the delimiters AppleScript uses to coerce lists to strings and to get text items from strings.

true

◆ *boolean*

The Boolean true value.

Placeholder Definitions

attribute

A characteristic that can be considered or ignored by invoking the `considering` and `ignoring` statements.

Example: `considering case`

```
set myflag to "help" contains "E"
end considering
```

boolean

A logical value of either `true` or `false`. Boolean is a value type or class. The results of comparisons are always Boolean values.

Example:

```
set x to true
```

date

The AppleScript value type, or class, that specifies a time, day, month, and year.

expression

Any series of words or terms that have a value.

Examples:

```
"s" & "mith"
(2^3)+9.5-myVariable
```

integer

A positive or negative number without any decimal component. `integer` is a value type or class.

Example:

```
set z to 2 as integer
```

list

An ordered collection of values. Lists are enclosed by curly braces, and pairs of items are separated by a comma. `list` is a value type or class.

Example:

```
{1,4,5, "e",1}
```

objectClass

A category of objects that have similar properties and elements and respond to similar commands.

Examples:

```
characters, words, lines, paragraphs
windows, documents, files
```

propertyName

For a user-defined script property, the name of the property container. User-defined script properties are like variables, but their values are persistent and are saved when a script is run. Objects also have properties that can be set and read.

Example:

```
get the label index of alias ¬
"HD:My File"
```

propertyValue

For a user-defined script property, the value stored in the property container. User-defined script properties are like variables, but their values are persistent and are saved when a script is run. Objects also have properties that can be set and read.

Example:

```
make new folder with properties
{name: "Hey"
```

real

A number that can include a decimal component. `real` is a value type or class.

Example:

```
set q to 2.475 as real
```

record

An unordered collection of properties. Properties are referenced by a name and stored as a name-value pair. record is a value type or class.

Example:
```
set b to {name: "Me", address: "100 Main Street"} as record
```

reference

A phrase that specifies one or more objects, using standard reference forms. Applications, documents, windows, and all other objects can be referenced by variables. reference is a value type or class.

Example:
```
set x to the current location
```

statement

A series of words or terms in your script that contain a request for an action or evaluate an expression.

Example:
```
put 2*4 into x
```

string

An ordered series of characters. string is a value type or class.

Example:
```
set r to "hello" as string
```

subroutine

A combination of statements that is executed in response to a user-defined handler.

Example:
```
on showscore(score)
     display dialog score
end showscore
```

value

Data that can be manipulated and stored in scripts. value types, or classes, include: boolean, constant, data, date, integer, list, real, record, reference, and string.

Examples:
```
"me"
set y to 1
```

variable

A named container used to store a value.

Examples:
```
set x to "me" as string
set y to 1
```

INDEX

A

Acme Script Widgets, 61, 144, 372
activate command, 140, 432
administering networks. *See* network
    administration scripting
Adobe Illustrator 9, 239–258
    AppleScript dictionary, 239
    collecting linked art files, 250–253
    exporting
        file layers as JPEG images, 247–249
        folders of files in EPS format, 242–246
    Layers palette, 240
    moving every object to its own layer,
        240–241
    relating objects to FileMaker records,
        254–258
        selecting art from a related FileMaker
            Pro database, 258
        showing records related to selected
            objects, 257–258
    scripting, 239
Adobe InDesign 1.5, 177–186
    AppleScript dictionary, 177
    counting words in a selection, 186
    creating an index page of styled words,
        180–183
    modifying graphic shapes and text,
        178–179
    modifying matching words, 184–185
    scripting, 177
Adobe Photoshop 5, 187–206

animations
    creating, 202
    exporting with GifBuilder, 205–206
    previewing, 203–204
AppleScript dictionary, 187
creating graphics and text, 188–192
document layers
    exporting as separate files, 193–194
    importing a folder of files as, 195–197
PhotoScripter plug-in, 187
transparency of grayscale images,
    198–201
alpha channels, 198
animations
    Photoshop
        creating, 202
        exporting with GifBuilder, 205–206
        previewing, 203–204
    Stone Create
        creating for export, 236–237
        sample animation script, 237
Appearance control panel, 90–91
AppendSuffix function, 107–108
Apple Events, 3
Apple Menu Options control panel, 117
AppleScript
    architecture, 5
    debugging, 417–425
    dictionaries, 10
    file extensions, 52
    how it works, 3

INDEX